IRELAND: A SOCIOLOGICAL PROFILE

IRELAND:
A SOCIOLOGICAL PROFILE

EDITED BY:
Patrick Clancy
Sheelagh Drudy
Kathleen Lynch
Liam O'Dowd

Institute of Public Administration
in association with
The Sociological Association of Ireland

First published 1986
by the Institute of Public Administration,
57–61 Lansdowne Road,
Dublin, Ireland.

Designed by Della Varilly
Cover design and diagrams
by Ailbhe Phelan

ISBN 0 906980 48 8 hbk
ISBN 0 906980 58 5 pbk

Typeset by Computertype Limited
and printed by Mount Salus Press

CONTENTS

CONTRIBUTORS

Patrick Clancy
Department of Sociology, University College Dublin

Patrick Commins
Economic and Rural Welfare Research Centre, Agricultural Institute, Dublin

Damien A. Courtney
Department of Business and General Studies, Cork Regional Technical College

John Coward
Department of Environmental Studies, University of Ulster, Coleraine

Chris Curtin
Department of Political Science and Sociology, University College, Galway.

Hastings Donnan
Department of Social Anthropology, Queen's University, Belfast

Sheelagh Drudy
Dublin Institute of Technology, College of Commerce, Rathmines, Dublin 6.

Ellen Hazelkorn
Dublin Institute of Technology, College of Commerce, Rathmines

John Hickey
(formerly) Department of Sociology and Anthropology, University of Ulster, Coleraine

vii

Pauline Jackson	Department of Social Administration, University College Dublin
Mary Kelly	Department of Sociology, University College, Dublin
Kathleen Lynch	Education Department, University College, Dublin
Ciaran McCullagh	Department of Social Theory and Institutions, University College, Cork.
Michael McCullagh	College of Business Studies, Belfast
Graham McFarlane	Department of Social Anthropology, Queen's University, Belfast
Kieran McKeown	Department of Sociology, University College, Dublin
Robert Miller	Department of Social Studies, Queen's University, Belfast
Dominic Murray	Education Department, University College, Cork.
Máire Nic Ghiolla Phádraig	Department of Sociology, University College, Dublin
Liam O'Dowd	Department of Social Studies, Queen's University, Belfast
Michel Peillon	Department of Social Studies, St. Patrick's College, Maynooth
James Wickham	Department of Sociology, Trinity College, Dublin

1
Introducing Sociology

PATRICK CLANCY, SHEELAGH DRUDY,
KATHLEEN LYNCH AND LIAM O'DOWD

Sociology in its modern form is a relatively new discipline in Ireland. In the 1960s the subject expanded rapidly in western Europe attracting a growing number of teachers, researchers and students. Its expansion in Ireland was, in part, a recognition of international developments and in part a response to accelerating social change, modernisation and conflict in the Republic of Ireland and Northern Ireland.

Yet, a number of factors have served to limit the public impact of the discipline. Firstly, as a latecomer on the Irish intellectual scene, some confusion remains about the nature and scope of the discipline. Secondly, social commentary and analysis in Ireland has been dominated by long-established disciplines such as history, literature, social philosophy and ethics, and economics. Thirdly, there has been a tendency within many educational institutions to limit the teaching of sociology to students contemplating careers in social work or social welfare administration. Finally, the funding of the discipline has been extremely poor by international standards. This is particularly the case in the Republic of Ireland, within the universities, other third level institutions and research agencies. The situation is somewhat better in Northern Ireland with its greater research

1

funding and bigger teaching staffs. Whereas sociology is not yet
on the secondary school curriculum in the Republic of Ireland,
it is well-established as an O- and A-level subject in Northern
Ireland's schools and colleges.

What is sociology?

Sociology is the systematic study of human societies. Such a bald
definition does not take us very far, however. Societies are rather
abstract and intangible entities; we cannot see and touch them
as we can individuals and groups. Furthermore, sociologists use
the term 'society' in many different ways. While they commonly
use it to refer to national societies or nation-states, they also use it
with respect to sub-groups or communities within nation-states.
It is important, therefore, to be aware of the context in which the
term society is used.[1]

The fundamental assumption of sociology is that men and
women are relational beings, that is, that human beings are
formed by their relationships with others. Needless to say
sociologists recognise, for example, that the genetic make-up of
parents and ancestors does result in individual differences. They
do not specifically and methodically explore these differences
from the standpoint of genetics, however. Instead they tend to
examine how individual and group differences may be pat-
terned or shaped by the way a society is organised.

Sociology, of course, shares the study of society with several
other disciplines such as economics, politics, history, psychology, and human geography. In fact, much debate within
sociology concerns the scope and boundaries of the discipline.
This is scarcely surprising, given the history of the subject. It was
not until the nineteenth century that the various social science
specialisms began to emerge in modern form. Prior to that,
theology, philosophy and political economy provided rather
more undifferentiated social analyses, while containing within
them the seeds of the modern social sciences.

Origins of the sociological tradition

Modern sociology has its origins in nineteenth century western

Europe. These origins were twofold: on the one hand, the tradition of social and statistical surveys including governmental enquiries; on the other, the writings of the major social theorists. The former tradition, sometimes associated with political economy, was committed to fact-gathering on a wide range of issues, such as industrial conditions, crime, suicide, health and poverty. It was generally part of the social reform movement developed by government and voluntary agencies alike. The social theorists, on the other hand, were concerned with explaining the broad patterns of social change, and in this they were heavily influenced by the example of the physical and biological sciences, which were developing general scientific laws. They included Max Weber, Ferdinand Tonnies and Georg Simmel in Germany; Henri St. Simon, Auguste Comte and Emile Durkheim in France; Herbert Spencer in England; and Karl Marx who lived in all three countries at various times.

The influence of Marx, Weber and Durkheim has been particularly important in shaping modern sociology. While they did not always provide an adequate account of their own societies, they nevertheless identified trends and processes which are only now coming to full fruition nearly one hundred years later. Marx's analysis of the development of capitalist production and class retains a relevance for analysing advanced and developing countries alike. Weber's emphasis on the growth of bureaucracy, the importance of market relationships and the nature of political power still informs much sociological research. The same is true of Durkheim's work on religion, shared moral values and the growing complexity of the division of labour.

Nevertheless, the writings of the major social theorists have not provided a homogeneous and unified basis for social science. They contain widely divergent views on politics and social analysis. For Marx it was the mode of production which distinguished one type of society from another. He sought to explain how capitalism had overthrown feudalism and how the former would ultimately give way to socialism. He saw class struggle as the engine of social change. Each mode of production, prior to socialism, was defined by two antagonistic classes locked together in struggle over the means of production. While actual capitalist societies contained several classes, the capitalist mode of production was defined by the struggle between the capitalist class and the proletariat or working-class. The former owned and controlled the means of production — land, capital, including banks, factories and machinery. The latter had nothing to sell but their labour power, having been forced off the land into cities and factories. Yet, it was the proletariat which Marx saw as the key to the ultimate overthrow of capitalism and the setting up of the future classless socialist society (1976 ed.).

Unlike Marx, Weber stopped short of developing a general explanatory theory of social change, but he too examined the reasons for the rise of capitalism in western Europe. In one of his most famous and controversial works he stressed the crucial role played by the Reformation and Protestant ideas in the process (1930). For Weber, capitalism was not so much defined by its mode of production as by the spread of market and money relationships. Weber also critically evaluated the growth of bureaucracy — a phenomenon that was to prove of even greater importance in the twentieth century.

Durkheim (1933) put forward a basic two-stage model of social change. He argued that European society was moving from a society based on 'mechanical solidarity' to one based on 'organic solidarity'. The former was characterised by shared moral values, especially religion, and by a simple division of labour. Organic solidarity was based on the growing interdependency engendered by an ever more complex division of labour. Like Marx and Weber, he argued that religion was losing its force in urban industrial society.

While the nineteenth century social theorists differed in many of their assumptions about society, science and social change, in retrospect what they shared seems just as important as their differences. They all felt that they belonged to the most advanced society in human history, a view which seemed to be confirmed by the imperial power of the western European states and their economic, scientific and technological pre-eminence.

They all felt that they were living at a crucial period of transition from a traditional, feudal and largely agricultural society to one which was increasingly industrial, urban and scientific. Their response to the prevalent ideas of evolutionary progress was sometimes tinged with racist assumptions about the superiority of the white races. More generally, they all shared a commitment to comparative and historical analysis and to addressing the large issues of social change and development. Along with their similarities, their limitations can be seen more clearly in retrospect, especially the bias engendered by seeing the rest of the world from the standpoint of late nineteenth century western Europe.

There is a sense, of course, in which sociology has moved far beyond its nineteenth century originators. In the twentieth century it developed enormously in the USA. Here it became heavily empirical, and specialised into sub-disciplines dealing with areas such as rural and urban life, class and stratification, deviance, religion and education. Considerable advances have been made in statistical and survey techniques and sociology has become established as a major university discipline in North America, Europe and indeed further afield. Interestingly, even state socialist systems have developed their own specialised empirical sociologies.

The emergence of newly independent Third World states, since 1945, with their problems of socio-economic development, has led sociologists to re-evaluate the general theories of social change advanced by the nineteenth century writers. This has been stimulated by the accelerated pace of scientific and technical changes in the developed countries, and their attendant problems. The spread of multi-national corporations; the rise of a global economy; the development of new patterns of work, politics and urbanisation; the revitalisation of fundamentalist religions; the widely divergent experiences of social change in Latin America, Asia and Africa; and the emergence of the USA, the USSR, China, Japan, and the EEC in a new world order, all have had a major influence on sociology. One result has been to greatly increase the richness and diversity of the discipline. It now draws on an ever-increasing range of societies and social experience, and on a large number of theoretical perspectives, methodologies and techniques of investigation.

Sociology in Ireland: origins and development

Even though sociology in its modern sense is of recent vintage in Ireland, it too has been affected by many of the international influences described above. In particular, two broad intellectual traditions have shaped the emergence of the discipline. One was associated with the British administration in Ireland under the Union, the other with the Catholic Church. The former, of course, is part of a broader British tradition and was developed in Ireland by colonial administrators, lawyers and political economists. It comprised various strands, some of which were influenced by the statistical and social inquiry tradition in Britain. This tradition still finds an echo in the Statistical and Social Inquiry Society of Ireland which originated in 1847. Others sought to apply the theories of the political economists and the social evolutionists to Irish conditions. Indeed major figures such as J. S. Mill, Marx and Engels wrote extensively on Irish questions.

Underlying much of the British tradition was an attempt to understand why nineteenth century Ireland appeared to be a land of 'strange anomalies'; anomalous, that is, with respect to England, in terms of economic conditions, religion, politics, demography and land tenure. Political independence and partition greatly weakened this tradition. Social reform based on detailed and systematic empirical analysis had little place within official nationalist and unionist thinking. The empirical tradition that survived was represented by a small number of statisticians employed by government; by some medico-social research, especially in Belfast; and by occasional small-scale poverty and housing studies carried out by academics and others.

The second major tradition influencing Irish sociology derived from 'Catholic sociology'. This had its origins in continental western Europe in the social encyclicals of successive popes, and the Catholic social movement of the late nineteenth and early twentieth century. It was meant to counteract the rise of socialism and secularism in Europe and the social theories advanced by Marx, Durkheim and other contemporary non-christian social theorists. It contained within it an explicit social ideal — a society which would be a via media between Capitalism and Socialism, founded on Catholic social principles. This was advocated strongly in the Republic of Ireland after partition by a large number of Catholic, especially clerical, writers. It advanced a series of prescriptions for a vocationalist or corporate order. It advocated a rural way of life, strong family units, and the widest possible diffusion of private property. It was also suspicious of growing state involvement in welfare services.

By the 1920s Cronin's *Primer of the Principles of Social Science* (1927) was in circulation in Catholic schools. By the 1930s, there were professors of Social Science and Catholic Action in Dublin's Jesuit seminary and Maynooth College respectively. In 1937, a lectureship in sociology was established in University College Cork and sociology was first offered as a degree course at University College Dublin in 1953.

By the 1950s, however, the limitations of this type of sociology were becoming very apparent. The social ideal which it contained seemed farther than ever from realisation in the wake of economic stagnation, large scale emigration and the continued disintegration of Irish rural society. Even sympathetic commentators began to be critical of the lack of empirical analysis in this tradition. Newman (1955, p. 9) wrote that 'in Ireland there had been practically no attention at all given to factual studies; what are called sociological studies are usually expositions of social principles'. In a similar vein, Roseingrave (1963, p. 217) identified the imbalance between 'the social ethical and the empirical', suggesting that too often what was passed off as sociology was really moral philosophy. In Northern Ireland at this time there was even less interest in empirical social research.

The economic and social crises of the 1950s in the Republic of

Ireland generated a new interest in the empirical analysis of social change and marked the beginnings of a marriage between international secular sociology and its Catholic counterpart. The Catholic Church dropped its previous opposition to welfare state measures and developed an ideology of 'social concern' which encouraged research on rural communities, social provision, poverty and inequality. The influence of Dutch rural sociology and Arensberg and Kimball's classic anthropological study of County Clare (1940) began to register in local analyses of rural problems.

By the early 1970s, chairs were held by academic sociologists in the colleges of the National University of Ireland, Trinity College and Maynooth College. Sociological research began to be undertaken in a number of research institutes such as the Economic and Social Research Institute and the Agricultural Institute (Foras Taluntais). In Northern Ireland, the setting up of modern sociology departments coincided with the outbreak of the 'troubles' and the arrival of many visiting social scientists to study the conflict. The Sociological Association of Ireland, the sponsor of this introductory text, was formed in 1973, and began to act as a forum for research and a sponsor for published work[2]. Sociology in Ireland now became more integrated into the international mainstream of the discipline, and began to struggle with its theoretical diversity and with the problem of applying sociological perspectives to Irish society. The contributions to this book reflect the way in which theoretical perspectives are used to inform empirical research on some central aspects of Irish social structure. The various perspectives adopted are shaped by somewhat different conceptions of the scientific status of sociology foreshadowed by the nineteenth century founders of the discipline.

Sociology as a science

The nineteenth century social theorists were deeply impressed by the development of the natural sciences and by technological advances in the Europe of their time. Marx and Durkheim argued that social science could develop general theories and laws in the manner of the natural sciences. Weber, on the other hand, doubted this, and sought to develop a more interpretive model for social science which would allow for the distinctiveness of its subject matter. These different approaches to sociology as a science inform two major theoretical perspectives which are discussed below. The structuralist perspective is closer to the natural science model, while the interpretive perspective owes more to Weber and his followers.

Durkheim made the most explicit attempt to model sociology on the natural sciences. He sought to establish 'social facts' as the specific subject matter of sociology. Such facts included, for example, language and religion. He saw them as the product of social groups, not of individuals; as 'external' to individuals and shaping their behaviour. Sociology is then, for Durkheim, a study of objective social facts:

> A social fact (being) every way of acting, fixed or not, capable of exercising on the individual an external constraint; or again, every way of acting which is general throughout a given society, while at the same time existing in its own right independent of its individual manifestations. (1938, p. 13).

Durkheim sought to model sociology on the natural sciences of the time by emphasising its objective nature, its reliance on quantitative data, and its capacity to formulate general laws of behaviour. His famous study of suicide (1951) found that suicide rates varied inversely with the degree of social integration or cohesion in society. Broadly speaking, therefore, we can see that Durkheim sought to apply the scientific method to what he saw as the central problem of sociology — social order or how societal cohesion was maintained.

While Weber held that like 'all scientific observation' sociology 'strives for clarity and verifiable accuracy of insight and comprehension' (1947, p. 90), he argued that social science could not be modelled on the natural sciences. Social science was set apart by its subject matter — human beings or social actors. It must therefore allow for the meanings that people attach to their actions, and take full advantage of the social scientists' capacity to understand and interpret human intentions and meanings. Sociology was therefore not inferior to natural science; rather it was a different type of science:

> a science which attempts the interpretive understanding of social action in order thereby to arrive at a causal explanation of its course and effects. In 'action' is included all human behaviour when and in so far as the acting individual attaches a subjective meaning to it. (Weber 1947, p. 88).

It must be remembered, however, that the definition of scientific method has continued to change even in the natural sciences, and the gap between objective and subjective approaches is not as clearcut nowadays as it once seemed. Instead, the assumptions, perspective and instruments used by natural scientists are now seen to have a direct influence on how they analyse the natural world. Social scientists are not alone, therefore, in struggling with the problem of subjectivity and objectivity.

In the following sections we outline briefly how the contributions to this book fit into two major perpectives in contemporary sociology: the structuralist and interpretive approaches.

The structuralist perspective: consensus and conflict

The structuralist perspective has two dimensions: one seeks to address the question of social order, that is, how societies persist, cohere and remain stable and generally integrated units. The assumption here is that societies strive always to maintain cohesion around shared values. This is the consensus approach advanced by major theorists such as Durkheim and more recently by Talcott Parsons (1951). The conflict approach traces its origins to Karl Marx. It assumes that societies are built not around consensus or shared values but around conflicting interests and considerable coercion. The main focus here is on change as generated by conflict and struggle. Both the conflict and consensus approaches share the view that the organisation and structure of society strongly influences the attitudes, values, institutions and relationships we develop. Similarly, both approaches tend to give quantitative, statistically aggregated data a priority over non-quantitative evidence.

Two types of quantitative evidence are used by sociologists: information collected by means of social surveys, and official statistics. The procedures used in social surveys follow a natural science or positivistic model of sociology. Use is made of scientific sampling, structured interviews and/or questionnaires, and statistical analysis. Data are frequently presented in the form of correlations and tabulations. Generalisations or 'law-like' statements may be made, although these will be couched in terms of probability or tendencies. Miller's paper, for example, generalises from the findings of a survey on social mobility, in order to make statements about the importance of class origin for the class position people ultimately attain.

Official statistics, usually collated by state agencies, also provide a most valuable source of information for sociologists. Many papers in this volume draw on official statistics. Courtney and Coward, for example, rely heavily on census data for their demographic analysis. These statistics, however, must be interpreted with caution. Michael McCullagh's paper emphasises the point that even apparently factual statistics on unemployment have to be critically assessed in the light of the changing definitions of the term used by successive political and administrative élites.

To judge by the contributions to this book, Irish sociological research has been heavily influenced by the structuralist tradition. Firstly, the primary source of evidence in a majority of cases is statistical rather than ethnographic; secondly, the emphasis in a number of papers is on how social structures in Irish society influence and control social behaviour. Commins, for example, highlights the changes which have occurred in rural life in the Republic by presenting quantitative evidence on structural factors such as population distribution, farm size, output and income.

It is no surprise, perhaps, to find a strong emphasis on structures. As an introduction to modern Ireland, the book is primarily concerned with institutional changes, processes and conflicts, and the structuralist perspective lends itself to an analysis of these. Few chapters can be easily classified as being either consensus or conflict-oriented in their analysis, however. This is due, in part, to an attempt to provide an overview of various perspectives as in McCullagh's chapter on crime and deviance. Clancy also draws on both dimensions to highlight the role schools play in reproducing social inequality. He combines the consensus theorists' concept of socialisation with the marxist notion of social reproduction to explain how this occurs.

In a sense, it is by their omissions rather than their choices that we can identify the theoretical leanings of our authors. For example, neither Nic Ghiolla Phádraig's nor Hickey's paper on religion assume that religion plays a role in reproducing class inequalities. Similarly, while Curtin's review of research on marriage and the family makes us aware of the different ways of organising heterosexual relationships, it does not attempt to address the relationship between familial organisation and the capitalist mode of production, as marxists would. These chapters, therefore, lean towards the consensus perspective, by default if not by design.

The conflict perspective is emphasised in a number of chapters — most explicitly perhaps in Kelly's discussions of how media images of the Maze escape were tied to the ideologies and interests of political and military élites. O'Dowd's and Wickham's analyses of industrialisation and employment in Northern Ireland and the Republic of Ireland respectively, argue that the persistence of uneven economic development, among and within countries, lends credence to conflict theories of socio-economic development. Peillon, McKeown, Jackson and Hazelkorn also use conflict perspectives to analyse conflicts over urban land use; class and stratification; male-female relations; and the Republic of Ireland's party system. While much use is made of quantitative evidence in these chapters, qualitative evidence is also utilised. For example, Curtin draws on ethnographic accounts of family life, and Kelly takes media reports as her main object of analysis. More typically, however, non-quantitative evidence is associated with the interpretive perspective.

The interpretive perspective

This approach, which owes much to Weber's influence, is concerned with subjective meanings and human intentions. Data are more likely to be drawn from informal, unstructured and open-ended interviewing. When the whole way of life of a social group is the object of inquiry, ethnography is a method which is frequently used. Originating in anthropology, it involves 'participant observation' on the part of the researcher, who for a time becomes a member of the group. The keeping of detailed notebooks, tape-recordings, and more formal interviews are also part of the method. Data are often presented in narrative style rather than in the form of statistics and tables.

The interpretive tradition has been developed considerably in the USA in the work of Mead (1964), Goffman (1962) and others. Often termed 'symbolic interactionism' this approach seeks to illuminate how individuals interpret and define their own situations and roles. Studies are geneally small in scale, focussing on particular places such as hospitals and prisons and on small group interaction.

Ethnomethodologists such as Cicourel (1964) and Garfinkel (1967) are also within the interpretive tradition. Like symbolic interactionists, they study inter-personal interaction using qualitative research methods. They are primarily concerned, however, with studying the methods whereby social actors produce meaning. For ethnomethodologists the common social world is constructed from the 'sense-making' work of individuals. They differ from symbolic interactionists insofar as they focus on the methods of constructing meaning, rather than on the subjective meaning itself.

To the extent that this book is representative of Irish social research, it is clear that the interpretive approach is a minority interest and has a limited influence on the methods and concepts employed in sociological research. In fact there is a substantial tradition of social anthropological studies undertaken by non-Irish social scientists. The paper by Donnan and McFarlane, two Northern Irish social anthropologists, is the main recognition of this tradition represented in the book. They rely principally on participant observation techniques to illuminate the fabric of rural life in Northern Ireland. Similarly, Murray employs participant observation techniques to develop an understanding of segregated education in Northern Ireland.

Scope of the book

While the book may not be representative of all current sociological research in Ireland, it does address key aspects of institutions and structures in both parts of Ireland. In dealing with both the Republic of Ireland and Northern Ireland, the book incorporates one of the integral features of the sociological perspective — the comparative method. This comparison has been pursued as far as is practicable, given the current interests and activities of sociologists working in Ireland. The first two parts of the book examine the social structures and institutions of the Republic of Ireland and Northern Ireland respectively. There are twin chapters on demography, education, social stratification and religion. The chapters on rural change and industrialisation in the Republic of Ireland are complemented by a chapter on post-industrial society in Northern Ireland. The latter chapter illustrates the parallels in the socio-economic development of both parts of the island, notwithstanding the different starting points and separate political structures. Parallel processes are identified and examined in other chapters too: the significance of migration; reductions in fertility; high levels of religious belief and practice; low rates of social mobility; high levels of unemployment; and acute dependency on foreign investment and multi-national corporations.

Important North-South differences are also revealed. The salience of political division and conflict in Northern Ireland is seen to pervade all aspects of social structures. It is inextricably linked to the religious divide, and adds a distinct dimension to the analysis of segregated education, the distribution of employment opportunities, and even to the seemingly neutral process of demographic projections.

If an awareness of conflict pervades the Northern Ireland chapters in Part 2, a preoccupation with the causes and consequences of rapid social change is the dominant theme of the chapters on the Republic of Ireland in Part 1. The transition from a predominantly agricultural society to an urban, and in some respects at least, advanced industrial structure, has been extremely rapid. The economic and demographic changes may be the most apparent, although the cultural transformations may be ultimately more pervasive in their impact. Growing secularisation, changes in sexual mores, destabilisation of family and the reorientation of education towards utilitarianism are some of the changes which have occurred in unison with the new emphasis on economic growth and rationality. As these chapters make clear, however, change has been uneven. For example, the strong commitment to economic growth in recent decades has not been matched by a similar commitment to equity in the distribution of wealth. Thus, notwithstanding impressive aggregate economic growth, existing inequalities have not been reduced, while several social groups, such as the poor and the unemployed, have been marginalised.

The seven chapters in Part 3 address important issues and processes in Irish society in a more eclectic way. With the exception of Kelly's case study on media reporting of the Northern Ireland conflict, the authors have limited their analysis to either the Republic of Ireland or Northern Ireland. Thus, for example, McKeown's discussion of urbanisation is confined to the Republic of Ireland, while M. McCullagh's chapter on the social construction of unemployment deals with Northern Ireland. However, the reader will quickly realise that neither analysis is geographically bounded. McKeown's analysis of urbanisation in terms of production and consumption might as easily be applied to Belfast as to Dublin. Similarly,

McCullagh's analysis of the social construction of unemployment statistics has an obvious relevance to the Republic of Ireland, where scepticism about the true level of unemployment has not been confined to sociologists.

Taken together, the nineteen chapters amount to a distinctive, if not complete, portrait of Irish society. There are omissions engendered by gaps in the current development of Irish sociology, or by lack of space due to the attempt to deal with two separate political units in the one volume. There are, for example, no separate chapters on the state, ideology, popular culture, or the legal and penal systems. While our coverage is not comprehensive, neither is it unduly idiosyncratic. Each of the chapters attempts to accomplish two objectives. It presents information on Irish society, and it seeks to illustrate the sociological perspective by showing how sociologists analyse society. Beyond this, the aim of the book is to stimulate more systematic and critical reflection on the nature of our society, as well as on the 'alternative futures' which are open to us.

Notes

1. Several good introductions to sociology as a discipline are available: *See,* for example, T. Bilton *et al. Introductory Sociology,* London, Macmillan, 1981 and M. Haralambos and R. M. Heald, *Sociology: Themes and Perspectives,* Slough, University Tutorial Press, 1985.

2. Recent examples of work sponsored by the Sociological Association of Ireland may be found in the following books:
   M. Kelly, L. O'Dowd and J. Wickham (eds.) *Power, Conflict and Inequality,* Dublin, Turoe Press, 1982
   C. Curtin, M. Kelly and L. O'Dowd (eds.) *Culture and Ideology in Ireland,* Galway University Press, 1984
   C. Curtin, P. Jackson and B. O'Conner (eds.) *Gender in Irish Society,* Galway University Press, 1986 (forthcoming).

References

ARENSBERG, C. M. and S. T. KIMBALL 1940. *Family and Community in Ireland,* Cambridge, Harvard University Press.

CICOUREL, A. 1964. *Method and Measurement in Sociology,* New York, Free Press.

CRONIN, M. 1927. *Primer of the Principles of Social Science,* Dublin, M. H. Gill and Son Ltd.

DURKHEIM, E. 1933. *The Division of Labour in Society,* trans. by G. Simpson, New York, The Free Press.

DURKHEIM, E. 1938. *The Rules of Sociological Method,* Chicago, University of Chicago.

DURKHEIM, E. 1951. *Suicide,* New York, The Free Press.

GARFINKEL, H. 1967. *Studies in Ethnomethodology,* New York, Prentice Hall.

GOFFMAN, E. 1962. *Asylums: Essays on the Social Situation of Mental Patients and Other Inmates,* Chicago, Aldine.

MARX, K. 1976. *Das Capital Volume 1,* intro. E. Mandel, trans. B. Fowkes, Middlesex, Penguin.

MEAD, G. H. 1964. *On Social Psychology: Selected Papers,* A. Strauss (ed.) Chicago, University of Chicago Press.

NEWMAN, J. 1955. 'Towards a Catholic Sociology', *University Review,* Vol. 1, No. 4, pp. 3-12.

PARSONS, T. 1951. *The Social System,* London, Routledge and Kegan Paul.

ROSEINGRAVE, T. 1963. 'Sociology in Ireland', *Administration,* Vol. 11, pp. 207-223.

WEBER, M. 1930. *The Protestant Ethic and The Spirit of Capitalism,* trans. by T. Parsons, London, Allen and Unwin.

WEBER, M. 1947. *The Theory of Social and Economic Organisation,* T. Parsons (ed.), Glencoe, Ill, The Free Press.

Part I
Social Structure and Institutions: Republic of Ireland

Introduction

The analysis of the social structure and institutions of the Republic of Ireland commences with an examination of its demographic structure. Damien Courtney contends that the nature of human society cannot be fully understood without a clear comprehension of population processes. While the author begins with a brief overview of the approach, methods and sources used in demography, the prime focus of the paper is on the dramatic demographic transformation in the Republic of Ireland over the past three decades. The recent rapid population growth, after more than a century of decline, mainly reflects changes in migration patterns. Other demographic processes examined by Courtney include the rise in nuptiality, the decline in fertility and the decline in mortality. The implications of the unique age structure of the population in the Republic of Ireland are also discussed.

Demographic change in rural areas, with its social implications, is one of the themes explored in Patrick Commins's paper on rural social change. Value changes are also examined here: the author identifies a decline in rural fundamentalism and a growing emphasis on rationalism and economic efficiency. The value shift is complemented by institutional changes both in the agricultural economy and in community life: Commins examines changing income and resource differentials, both within the farming community itself and between urban and rural dwellers. Subsequent to this he presents a brief analysis of a number of approaches that have been adopted to bring about planned change at local community level. Most of the studies on rural social change cited by Commins are informed by modernisation theory, which developed within the structural functionalist perspective. However, as the final section of the paper suggests, this is not the only perspective available; the assumptions behind an alternative structural thesis, which is marxist in orientation, are also briefly described.

The choice which exists between alternative theoretical models in sociology is also made explicit by James Wickham in his paper on industrialisation, work and unemployment. Modernisation theory and dependency theory (the latter more favoured by Wickham) offer alternative explanations of the process of industrialisation in the Republic of Ireland. From a discussion of theoretical perspectives, the paper proceeds to examine conflict and control at work, arguing that there are fundamental conflicts of interest between employers and employees in a capitalist society like the Republic of Ireland. Some of the reasons why industrial conflict occurs disproportionately in the public sectors are also examined. In the final section of the paper Wickham turns his attention to labour markets, suggesting that it is misleading to think that there is just one labour market. He examines 'who gets what jobs?' and 'who stays unemployed?'. The latter question has a particular significance in a society with an unemployment rate of more than seventeen per cent.

The fourth paper in this section presents an analysis of stratification and class, a topic which has never been far from centre stage in sociological analysis. The first part of Michel Peillon's paper examines three dimensions of social stratification based on material, prestige and power inequalities respectively. The second part of the paper is devoted to a review of various approaches to class analysis, a level of inquiry which Peillon regards as distinct from that involving the study of stratification. He first presents the major features of an orthodox marxist model, followed by a discussion of the class structuration approach, which is derived ultimately from the work of Weber. Peillon concludes with a summary of his own approach, which seeks to identify the class structure in the Republic of Ireland through the observed patterns of social differentiation.

Patrick Clancy's paper on socialisation, selection and reproduction in education naturally follows on from the analysis of stratification and class. This paper starts with an overview of the main theoretical perspectives in the sociology of education. Here the author examines the functionalist and marxist perspectives, the main theoretical traditions in structuralism. These different structuralist models are used in the remainder of the paper to analyse the role of the educational system in the Republic of Ireland. It is suggested that education involves two key processes. The first comprises socialisation and the moulding of consciousness, evidenced by the role schools play in fostering religious, nationalist and economic interests and values within society. The second process involves selection and social reproduction as demonstrated by the role of the school in perpetuating the prevailing system of class relations.

A high level of religious belief and practice has long been a hallmark of society in the Republic of Ireland and this provides the focus of Máire Nic Ghiolla Phádraig's paper. The paper starts with a brief review of some of the sociological approaches to the study of religion. The second section of the paper examines the social significance of religion in society in the Republic of Ireland. It assesses, in particular, the power and influence of the churches. The final section of the paper is devoted to a discussion of secularisation, a process which is linked with modernisation, urbanisation and industrialisation. Nic Ghiolla Phádraig presents survey data showing that indicators of modernisation are negatively related to measures of religiosity, thus suggesting that a process of secularisation is evident in the Republic of Ireland.

The final paper in this section deals with marriage and the

family. Chris Curtin's analysis has a historical and comparative dimension; he argues that we need to view the family 'not so much as a universal natural institution but as a socially conditioned product'. His analysis of marriage centres on the way in which a variety of norms, restrictions and controls define the shape of the institution in any particular society. In his discussion of the family, Curtin examines marital roles and authority, child-rearing, old age and wider kinship. The final section of the paper includes a short review of changes in the family in the Republic of Ireland.

2
Demographic Structure and Change

DAMIEN A. COURTNEY

Demography provides a statistical description of human populations. The nature of human society cannot be fully understood without a clear comprehension of the integral role played by population processes in the dynamics of social life. The two basic processes in every population system — entering and leaving — determine changes in population size. The pre-occupation of sociologists with social change has led them to the study of demography, because social change involves population change. Demographic structures and events are also of particular interest to sociologists. They may utilise them in other analytical frameworks and thus enhance their understanding and explanations. Demography was included by Durkheim as one of seven sections in *L'Année Sociologique*, the first sociological journal.

In spite of some explanatory limitations, modernisation theory, which is functionalist inspired, is of considerable descriptive value and has been the key theoretical perspective used in social demography. The central analytical issue concerns the interaction between demographic processes of population change, i.e. fertility, mortality and migration on the one hand, and socio-economic processes of modernisation on the other. In addition, an examination of the social differentials of fertility, mortality and migration is complementary and crucial in understanding social groups and communities within societies (Goldscheider 1971). In sociology comprehensive data are essential for the construction of theories and whilst demographic material has been of considerable administrative and bio- graphical value, both to civil and religious authorities, its over- emphasis on empirical analysis has generally been to the detri- ment of its theoretical development. In fact, interactionist, phenomenological and other micro approaches consider demo- graphy more an administrative method than a sociological one. Nevertheless we will consider at the outset the essential features of two separate frameworks which attempt to explain demo- graphic change.

Malthus was the first to provide a consistent theory of popula- tion in his *Essay on the Principles of Population*. Most attention centres around his global argument that population, when un- checked, doubles every generation i.e. increases in a geometrical progression (1, 2, 4, 8 ...) whereas, in the most favourable cir- cumstances, the food supply increases in an arithmetical pro- gression (1, 2, 3, 4 ...). A positive check, however, is achieved through 'misery' from increasing mortality due to disease, famine, warfare and excesses. Preventive checks cause decreas- ing fertility and are achieved by 'moral restraint' through late marriages and with no extra-marital sex, or alternatively, by 'vice' resulting from birth control. He was correct in anticipat- ing population growth but he greatly underestimated the sub- sequent advances in technology and communications. Malt- hus's more specific argument concerning families and social groups in particular cultures stated that the balance between population and subsistence depends on a range of economic, social and political factors.

The second analytical framework grew out of the demo- graphic and socio-economic development of advanced societies during the nineteenth and early twentieth centuries. These changes gave rise to the theory of demographic transition which distinguished five phases: (1) a stationary phase in which mortality and fertility are high, (2) an early expanding one when mortality begins to decline and fertility remains unchanged at a high level, (3) a late expanding one, when the decline in fertility follows the decline of mortality, (4) a low stationary one, when mortality and fertility are both at a similar level, (5) a diminishing one, when fertility declines below the level of mortality, which ceases to decline, and so the population begins to diminish (Blacker 1947). What happens between the 'transitional' and 'modern' societies is only vaguely explained by the theory. Like modernisation theory it is unidirectional and underestimates the importance of regional variations in the developmental process.

In western Europe there were two fundamental demographic transitions. Firstly, there was the Malthusian transition (or Hajnal's (western) European pattern of late marriage and high rates of celibacy that occurred after the sixteenth century). Secondly, there was the neo-Malthusian transition of the nineteenth century characterised by a decline in marital fertility (Coale 1969). The role of migration in demographic transition theory may be conceptualised in two ways. The first position argues that migration provides a short-term safety valve relieving population pressure and delaying fertility decline. The second is a modified Malthusian argument of multiphase response, i.e. migration, along with mortality and fertility, is one of various responses to the pressures of population growth and relative socio-economic deprivation (Goldscheider 1981).

Demographic sources

Generally the sociologist personally observes the phenomenon to be studied. However, in Ireland population statistics are collected, compiled, analysed and published by the Central Statistics Office which has statutory powers and the necessary resources to undertake such diverse and complex operations.

The *Census of Population* consists of demographic, economic, social and political data, gathered at a given time, relating to all persons and households in a country. It provides information about the population's structure such as age, sex, conjugal condition, industrial and occupational status, housing and house-hold composition, Irish language, religion, fertility, migration and education. Apart from 1821 and 1831 all the Census years and populations are indicated in Table 1. The most recent one was taken in April 1981. A special 5 per cent sample of those re-turns offers useful analytical and methodological possibilities (Garvey 1983). The HBS was carried out on a national basis for the first time in 1973 and was repeated in 1980. As in other EEC states there has been a *Labour Force Survey* undertaken biennially between 1975 and 1983 and in the Republic of Ireland annually since then. The compulsory registration of births, deaths and marriages since 1864 provides continuous and complementary data which are available in quarterly reports and later in the annual *Report on Vital Statistics*. Further demographic material is available in the *Statistical Abstract of Ireland* and the *Irish Statistical Bulletin*, whilst unpublished cross-tabulated Census data are also obtainable.

Information is collected primarily in response to the needs of government departments and agencies. Sociologists under-taking research may have to rely on data collected for other pur-poses, e.g. most measurements of class structure in the Republic of Ireland are based on classifications which are not sociologically informed (see Chapter 15). This highlights the need for a preliminary critique of the questions used and the manner in which the information is collected. Improvements are desirable in reducing the delay in publication and providing more accurate details of migration. The importance of such ob-servation, or more specifically data collection, cannot be over-emphasised. Though it is often difficult to accomplish, it must precede analysis and explanation. Analysis of population move-ment is essentially concerned with its primary components, i.e. fertility, mortality and migration (see Pressat 1978 for a short and eminently clear introduction to basic statistical techniques in demography).

Population change

In Ireland, the late eighteenth and early nineteenth centuries were times of rampant population growth for which the economic system proved inadequate. After the famine of the 1840s Malthus's ideal was achieved when population declined dramatically for the remainder of the nineteenth century and thereafter stayed relatively stable until the 1960s (Table 1). This had the most profound and devastating effect on values, attitudes and behaviour patterns. Assuming the absence of economic development, the Commission on Emigration and Other Population Problems (1954) projected in one of its estimates, a population of little more than two and a half million in the Republic of Ireland today. The presence of over three and a half million despite a recent resurgence in emigration demonstrates the transformation that has occurred in the past quarter of a century. The growth in the 1960s was confined generally to urban areas. During the 1970s a growth rate of 1.55 per cent per annum — over four times the EEC average — encompassed most parts of the country. In 1981 56 per cent of the population lived in towns of 1,500 persons or more compared with 32 per cent in 1926. The medium-sized towns have been the major beneficiaries of the recent growth (see Chapter 3). Yet, within the EEC, the Republic of Ireland has the lowest population density and apart from Luxembourg is numerically the smallest.

Demographic change is explained by means of the following population components equation:

$$P_1 = P_0 + (B - D) + (I - E)$$

where P_0 and P_1 represent a population at the beginning and end of a year, where persons enter the population through births (B) and immigration (I) and leave it through deaths (D) and emigration (E). The combination of births and deaths constitutes the natural increase while the addition of net migrants indicates total change. The corresponding rates used in Table 1 are ratios (per 1,000) of the different components of population change to the mean population.

$$\text{Rate of natural increase} = \frac{\text{Natural increase}}{\text{Mean population}} \ (\times \ 1,000).$$

Table 1: **Population and average annual rates (per 1,000) of population change in Ireland, 1871–1984**

Intercensal period	Population (000s)[1]	Marriage rate[2]	Birth rate	Death rate	Rate of natural increase	Migration rate	Rate of increase
1871–81	3,870	4.5	26.2	18.1	8.0	-12.7	-4.6
1881–91	3,469	4.0	22.8	17.4	5.3	-16.3	-10.9
1891–01	3,222	4.5	22.1	17.6	4.5	-11.9	-7.4
1901–11	3,140	4.8	22.4	16.8	5.6	-8.2	-2.6
1911–26	2,972	5.0	21.1	16.0	5.2	-8.8	-3.7
1926–36	2,968	4.6	19.6	14.2	5.5	-5.6	-0.1
1936–46	2,955	5.4	20.3	14.5	5.9	-6.3	-0.4
1946–51	2,961	5.5	22.2	13.6	8.6	-8.2	+0.4
1951–56	2,898	5.4	21.3	12.2	9.2	-13.4	-4.3
1956–61	2,818	5.4	21.2	11.9	9.2	-14.8	-5.6
1961–66	2,884	5.7	21.9	11.7	10.3	-5.7	+4.6
1966–71	2,978	6.5	21.3	11.2	10.1	-3.7	+6.4
1971–79	3,368	6.8	21.6	10.5	11.1	+4.3	+15.4
1979–81	3,443	6.3	21.5	9.7	11.8	-0.7	+11.0
1981–84 (est)	3,535	5.8	20.1	9.5	10.6	-5.2	+5.4

[1]Population at end of intercensal period.

Population (000s) in 1841:6,529; 1851:5,112; 1861:4,402; 1871:4,053; 1984 is an estimate.

[2]The marriage rates, 1871–1926 are averaged around end of year rather than April, e.g. 1871–80.

Source: *Censuses of Population* and *Reports on Vital Statistics*.

This crude rate of natural increase is of course the difference between the (crude) birth and death rates. In the Republic of Ireland, while the birth rate has remained (until the early 1980s) quite constant at high levels, the decline in the death rate has resulted, since the 1940s, in a steady rise in the rate of natural increase. Stability in the birth rate was achieved ironically as a result of a rising marriage rate and a declining fertility rate. In most countries population change is largely determined by natural increase yet in spite of its generally high level in Ireland it has been less important than migration (Table 1, Fig. 1). The net immigration, between 1971 and 1979 — the first since the seventeenth century plantations — contributed to the overall growth then, in contrast with the traditionally mitigating effect of net emigration.

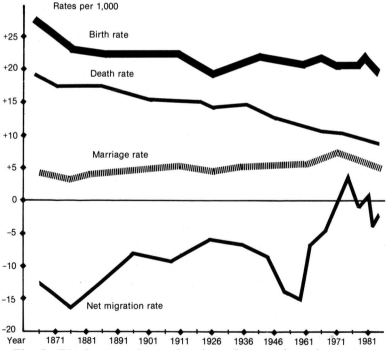

Fig. 1. **Birth, marriage, death and net migration rates (per 1,000 population), 1871-1984.**

Fertility and nuptiality

Natality is used to describe the number of births which has occurred *in toto* in a population and is expressed by the birth rate whereas fertility is not used as an absolute value in itself but as a phenomenon relating to individuals directly concerned with it, namely women in their childbearing years. As the propensity to marry is so important it is necessary to consider nuptiality in conjunction with fertility. The two are interwoven, one having a behavioural influence on the other.

The number who marry and the age at marriage are matters of immense social significance especially in Ireland where relatively high permanent celibacy and late age at marriage provided the classic example of the Malthusian preventive check. Such marriage characteristics have been attributed to the large proportion of the population engaged in agriculture, the family system of inheritance, the lack of urbanisation, the poor economic conditions and the indirect effects of emigration (Coward 1978). Not until the late 1950s were patterns reversed. Between 1961 and 1971 there was an almost 50 per cent increase in the age-specific marriage rate though it declined by 15 per cent between 1971 and 1979 (see Clancy 1984). A significant decline over twenty years in the median age of brides and grooms ended in 1977. This has risen slightly since then along with a fall in the number of marriages. In fact, western European countries generally have experienced a greater decline in marriages with an increasing incidence of cohabitation. In the Republic of Ireland the predominant influence in recent years may be the protracted economic recession and the effects of rising unemployment. The greater decline in the age of grooms reflects a greater degree of similarity in the spouses' ages compared with earlier times whilst the proportion of single has fallen to a level more in line with developed countries.

The traditional marriage pattern was counterbalanced by high levels of fertility. By 1946 Irish families were twice as large on average as those in Europe's low fertility countries in spite of the prevalence of late marriage (Walsh 1980). Table 2 indicates

Table 2: **Percentage distribution of completed families by number of children for women aged 25–29 years at marriage and married for 25 to 29 years, 1911, 1946, 1961, 1971**

Census year	0 %	1–3 %	4–6 %	7–9 %	10 and over %	Total %
			Completed family size			
1911	7	12	31	36	14	100
1946	9	27	38	21	5	100
1961	8	34	40	15	3	100
1971	7	34	41	15	3	100

Source: *Clancy (1984, p. 21)*

a decline in completed family size since 1911 due particularly to a fall in the number of very large families. In 1911 the modal completed family size was seven to nine children whereas at the later Censuses it was four to six children. Cohort analysis underlines the prevalence of the four-child family in the Republic of Ireland today and illustrates a broad similarity in the distribution of families by number of children between 1961 and 1971. The largest families are found among those of long marriage duration and young age of the wife at marriage. The 1971 data provide evidence of younger brides having achieved a reduction in fertility for all marriage durations in contrast with the situation for over a century up to 1961 (Clancy 1984).

The standard of living and 'stem family' (see Chapter 8) theses fail to explain the traditionally high level of marital fertility. This is paradoxical as they were frequently advanced, until the 1950s, as explanations of other Irish demographic peculiarities: postponed marriage, permanent celibacy and high emigration (Kennedy 1973). An extensive analysis of economic records, ethnographic studies and Census data from 1926 to 1971 along with an intensive sample survey of farm families in 1970–1 illuminate the relationship between fertility patterns and value systems in both the peasant and modern type societies (Hannan 1979). The value system in the peasant economy provided an incentive to family formation which was relatively independent of economic factors whereas in a market economic system such is not the case.

Though it provides an essential longitudinal perspective, cohort analysis is limited by data availability. In contrast, period analysis for a calendar year involves different cohorts each with their own fertility histories. The difficulty in correctly interpreting the relative effects of variations either in completed fertility or in the length of interval between births is a serious drawback. For that reason it is difficult to establish whether the recent fertility decline is merely a temporary phenomenon or an indication of a fundamental long-term diminution. Table 3 suggests such a fall in marital fertility rates especially among older women. Marital fertility declined by 12 per cent for 1961–71 and a further 27 per cent for 1971–81 (by 36 per cent for 1961–81). In the earlier decade the fertility level was generally higher and the rate of decline slower in the western counties of the country. By the 1970s this was much less pronounced. The influence of social status and religion on fertility throughout the country in 1971 is indicated in Table 4. Of particular significance is a decline in marital fertility of 10.7 per cent for 1981–3,

Table 3: **Marital fertility rates, 1961–81 (per 1,000)**

Age group	1961	1971	1981	% Change 1961–81
15–19	612.6	681.6	549.5	−10.3
20–24	478.0	459.3	326.5	−31.7
25–29	392.4	350.5	262.5	−33.1
30–34	298.6	249.1	188.2	−37.0
35–39	202.4	160.7	105.7	−47.8
40–44	77.1	58.7	30.7	−60.2
45–49	5.8	4.3	2.9	−50.0

Source: *Censuses of Population* and *Reports on Vital Statistics*

Table 4: **Total fertility per 100 families by socio-economic group and religion, 1971**[1]

Socio-economic group	All durations
Farmers, farmers' relatives and farm managers	387
Other agricultural occupations and fishermen	367
Higher professional	299
Lower professional	323
Employers and managers	304
Salaried employees	305
Intermediate non-manual workers	315
Other non-manual workers	339
Skilled manual workers	347
Semi-skilled manual workers	340
Unskilled manual workers	380
Unknown	288
Total	345

Religious denomination	All durations
Catholic	352
Church of Ireland	229
Other stated religions	233
Others	315
Total	345

[1]Data standardised for age of wife at marriage.
Source: Sexton and Dillon (1984, p. 39).

i.e. an average annual decline of 5.5 per cent compared with 3.1 per cent and 1.2 per cent for 1971–81 and 1961–71, respectively (Sexton and Dillon 1984).

While we lack a clear understanding of the processes involved in establishing new family size goals, it has been suggested that the breakdown of kinship dominance, improvements in living standards and mobility aspirations are of crucial importance (Goldscheider 1971). Specifically, Irish fertility changes are attributed to varying patterns of nuptiality and migration, occupational changes from agriculture into production and service industries, increasing regional development and urbanisation, EEC membership with greater general receptivity to new ideas and increasing numbers of married women in the labour force (Coward 1982). A growing proportion of the younger generation is planning its families with profound effects on the life-cycle of the average married woman. The labour force participation rate for married women has increased from 8 per cent in 1971 to 17.4 per cent in 1981 (Conniffe and Kennedy 1984). This trend is likely to intensify in coming decades when a substantial number of Irish women, at a much younger age than hitherto, will have reared their families. The reduction in fertility has been facilitated by a number of legislative changes. The Health (Family Planning) (Amendment) Act, 1985 makes available non-medical contraceptives of all kinds without prescription to anyone of eighteen years and over. It amended the 1979 Act — an Irish solution to an Irish problem — which had legalised the sale of contraceptives for 'bona fide family planning' purposes in response to the 1973 Supreme Court decision in the McGee case.

A steady rise in the proportion of marriages in which a first birth is recorded in the year of marriage suggests a significant increase in the number involving pre-nuptial conceptions. This is most common among teenage brides and younger women generally. Two related matters are those of extra marital fertility and abortion. The proportion of extra marital births registered in the Republic of Ireland has risen dramatically from 1.6 per cent in 1960 to 7.8 per cent in 1984. There has been a dramatic increase in the number of legal abortions carried out in England and Wales on women, mostly single, who gave the Republic of Ireland as their place of residence: 3,946 in 1984 compared with 2,183 in 1977, i.e. 6.1 per cent and 3.2 per cent of live births in those years respectively. As for extra marital births most abortions are carried out on women in their early twenties. When added to the extra marital rate they represent 13.9 per cent of all births in the Republic of Ireland in 1984[1].

In conclusion, Ireland's fertility is still relatively high compared with other EEC states which are now significantly below the replacement level. Ireland is in the third phase of demographic transition in contrast with many other western European countries which are in phase five. Nevertheless, the overall transformation that has occurred in recent nuptiality and fertility trends is neo-Malthusian in essence and reflects a significant shift in the culture, behaviour and value system of our society.

Mortality

Mortality has decreased very significantly in the last half of the nineteenth century. This decrease, though less dramatic, has continued throughout the twentieth century. The level of mortality in the Republic of Ireland compares most favourably with other countries and it is now the least volatile of its demographic components. Though variations according to age and sex are indicated by age(-sex)-specific mortality rates in the same way as marriage and fertility rates, the most complete statistical profile is provided by life tables. They reveal the significance of the decline in infant mortality (deaths of under one year) and the impact which the latter has had on overall mortality. After surviving the first year of life the probability of death decreases significantly and is not as high again until about the age of 60. Table 5 provides details of life expectancy at different ages for males and females. Increased longevity has been accompanied by a widening gap between males and females and the disappearance of Ireland's traditionally relatively high female mortality. International data suggest that lower socio-economic

Table 5: **Expectation of life at various ages, 1841–1979**

Period		Males age (years)					Females age (years)				
		0	1	15	35	55	0	1	15	35	55
1841	CD	24.0	30.7	30.3	20.6	12.7	24.2	30.3	31.3	22.3	13.8
	RD	29.6	37.8	36.2	26.4	14.8	28.9	36.1	35.1	25.6	14.4
1890–92	IRL	49.1	NA	45.8	30.6	16.5	49.2	NA	45.5	30.5	16.2
1925–27	IRL	57.4	61.2	50.7	34.4	19.1	57.9	60.8	50.5	34.7	19.6
1960–62	IRL	68.1	69.3	56.0	37.0	19.5	71.9	72.7	59.2	39.9	22.1
1970–72	IRL	68.8	69.2	55.7	36.8	19.3	73.5	73.8	60.2	40.8	22.7
1978–80	UD	68.1	68.2	54.6	35.7	18.3	74.3	74.3	60.7	41.2	23.1
	IRL	69.5	69.5	55.9	36.9	19.3	75.0	74.8	61.1	41.6	23.3

NA, not available; IRL, Irish Life table; CD, Civic District, population of towns containing 2,000 inhabitants and upwards; RD, Rural District, population of all towns containing less than 2,000; UD, Urban Districts, population residing within the boundaries of county and municipal boroughs and urban districts.
Source: *Report of Census Commissioners 1841* (Appendix, pp. lxxx–i), *Commission on Emigration and other Population Problems* (p. 106) and *Irish Life Tables*.

groups are prone to higher mortality risks and this is especially true in cases of perinatal (stillbirths plus deaths during the first four weeks) and infant mortality. Other important factors are birthweight and the mothers' biological attributes (Kirke 1981). Changing patterns of mortality also reflect changes in the cause of death. The historic killer, tuberculosis, is now insignificant by comparison with the 1940s, especially among younger age groups. Heart disease continues to be the single biggest cause of death though its rate has declined recently compared with cancer which increased by 29 per cent between 1960-2 and 1975-7. Finally, marginally higher levels of mortality in urban areas reflect differing life styles and environmental conditions. The differential is miniscule, however, by comparison with that which prevailed in the last century (Table 5).

Migration

Migration is the most difficult component of population change to define and measure. It is generally defined in terms of the area to be studied and can be either international or internal. The absence of compulsory registration in the Republic of Ireland, such as exists in some other western European countries, and more particularly, the absence of border controls makes migration estimation for intercensal periods a hazardous business. The population estimate for 1979 made in advance of the Census was about 100,000 or 3 per cent too low because the turnaround in the traditional pattern of net emigration could not be measured. However, alternatives such as the use of electoral registers (Whelan and Keogh 1980) and social security records here and abroad (Durkan 1979) would have given very poor results for periods since 1979.

The human tragedy of emigration from Ireland reached catastrophic proportions after the famine and again during the 1950s with Britain replacing the United States as the major destination. In recent years there has been increasing emigration to other EEC states and the Middle East. In the 1950s the pattern was one of heavy emigration of single persons who married and had their children abroad. A proportion of those took advantage of the opportunities to return to the Republic of Ireland with their families during the 1970s. Industrial developments, new industrial incentives and accessibility to EEC markets provided highly skilled jobs for many of those migrants of whom 19,000 were born in Northern Ireland, 69,000 in Great Britain and 21,000 elsewhere (Garvey, 1985). In 1980-1 the largest occupational group of immigrants consisted of professional and technical workers. In contrast, many others in the labour force, especially farmers on marginal holdings and unskilled labourers remain in residual classes and are particularly vulnerable to emigration (Rottman *et al.*, 1982). Net emigration is estimated at 5,000 for 1979-81 and at 20,000 for 1982-4 after net immigration of 2,000 for 1981-2. Such estimates are derived by the Central Statistics Office using the population components equation. The recurrence of net emigration, though relatively small compared with the net loss of 40,000 per annum (1.4 per cent of the population), during the 1950s, is highly significant. In addition, the unprecedented average number of 214,000 persons on the Live Register of unemployed during 1984 (16.2 per cent of the labour force) reflects to a large extent the failure of successive governments to balance the supply of and demand for labour.

In contrast, internal migration has traditionally been much less prominent. The decline in emigration and the demographic growth of the 1960s increased its importance. Nevertheless, it remains very low by international standards (Hughes and Walsh 1980). It is highest among teenagers, especially the unmarried and the economically active and declines with advancing years. Shorter mobility in urban areas reflects changes in residence and marital status, with movement of longer distances due to labour force considerations. Industrial development provided considerably greater opportunities for skilled manual and junior white collar workers. The most important destination is the eastern region comprising Meath, Kildare, Wicklow and especially Dublin. The latter now has over 29 per cent of the state's population by comparison with just 17 per cent in 1926 but like the Republic of Ireland's other cities has been experiencing inner decline with substantial growth occurring in the suburbs and satellite towns. This has been recognised to some extent by the re-organisation of local authorities in 1985.

Finally, Walsh (1984) found that 48 per cent of school leavers throughout the country definitely intended to migrate from home owing to a perceived lack of occupations there, compared with 47 per cent who were undecided and a mere 5 per cent who definitely intended to remain in their home localities. This involuntary migration is predominant among females and broadly similar to Hannan's (1970) findings in Cavan almost twenty years earlier in spite of greater participation in post-primary education, more career guidance and training centres and further restructuring of employment opportunities in the manufacturing sector in the interim.

Age, sex and dependency

The two most important demographic variables used in sociological surveys to understand and explain the structure of society are those of age and sex. Further characteristics of population composition such as stratification and class, education, occupation and unemployment, place of residence and religious affiliation are discussed in other chapters. The composition of a population by age and sex affects the entire social, cultural, economic and political fabric of a society. Its effect on marriage patterns, fertility, mortality and migration determines population size and specifically influences dependency levels, (wo)manpower availability and employment opportunities.

The population pyramid provides the best graphical representation of such variables. Figure 2 indicates changes in population structure from the traditional triangular pyramid through to the present time. The 1841 pyramid, for that part of Ireland which now constitutes the Republic, just prior to the famine is that of a population characterised by high fertility and low life expectancy. The broad based pyramid narrows quickly

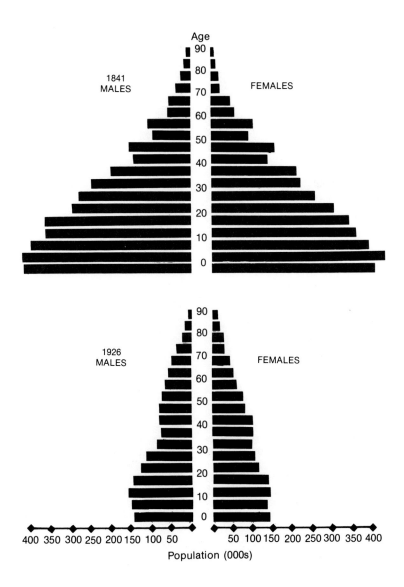

Fig. 2a **Population pyramids, 1841–1926.**

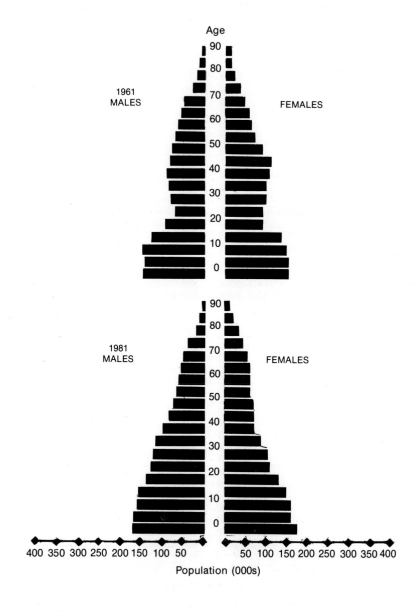

Fig. 2b. **Population pyramids, 1961-1981.**

and is indicative of a pre-transition demographic régime. The pyramid of 1926 provides dramatic evidence of the effects of the famine, eighty years after the event. The population size has contracted fundamentally owing to unprecedented levels of mortality and emigration. The effect on family formation has resulted in an ageing process (Table 6). The year 1961 marks a watershed in the Republic's recent demographic history and the extremely irregular pyramid for that year is due to previously heavy emigration especially during the 1950s. Though the young population has proportionately increased, this is over-shadowed by further ageing and increased longevity. By 1981 a

Table 6: **Age distribution of population, 1841–1981**

	Age group (%)				
Year	0–14	15–44	45–64	64+	All ages
1841	38.1	45.9	12.9	3.1	100
1926	29.2	42.8	18.9	9.1	100
1961	31.1	36.4	21.3	11.2	100
1981	30.3	41.8	17.2	10.7	100

Source: *Censuses of Population*

more regular structure reflects the growth in the interim incorporating a reversal in traditional patterns of emigration. Whilst the proportion of elderly persons is consistent with other European countries the relative number of young people remains somewhat aberrant. The Republic of Ireland's best known cliché is that 'half the population is under the age of 25' (the actual percentage under 25 years is 48 per cent). Its sex ratio (that is, ratio of males to females) is also exceptional. The Republic has almost 16,000 more males than females. The higher number of male births is usually reversed by the greater longevity of females. The smaller life expectancy differential together with broadly similar numbers emigrating is the cause. There are, however, considerably more females than males over

65 years. Sex imbalances have had social and psychological repercussions with a depressing impact on marriage patterns
especially in rural areas. The farming population has about 25
per cent over 65 years whereas in farms of 50 acres, or less, the
proportion of males over 55 years and unmarried has more than
doubled between 1926 and 1971 (Raftery, 1983). The
urban/rural divergence — though decreasing — remains,
owing to the increasing importance of internal migration. A
younger urban population at each Census also reflects
urban/rural differences in family patterns and occupational
structures.

Dependency is crucial in understanding the relationship
between population and policy. The *dependency ratio* is the ratio of
persons in dependent ages i.e. under 15 years together with those
65 years and over to persons in economically productive age
groups. Between 1926 and 1961 the dependency level, both
young and old, increased at almost every Census (Table 6). The
greater increase in the 1950s was due to the effect of emigration
on the young active population. Dependency levels have since
decreased and the sustained fall in fertility indicates a continua-
tion of this trend though increasing unemployment represents
additional real dependants. Nevertheless, age dependency in
1981 of 69 for every 100 in the active category compares very unfavourably with the EEC average of 53. This is an indication of
the difficulty in maintaining or improving the standard of
living. While the Republic of Ireland's exceptionally young
population is better educated than ever before, those under 25
years represent about 30 per cent of the Live Register of
unemployed at the end of May 1985. Although the young constitute the largest component of dependency, a fall in the size of
the young population no longer necessarily implies an easing of
the economic burden of dependency (Blackwell 1983a). An increase in those of working age may require a continued high
level of social security transfers unless employment increases. In
addition, the resource costs of health and personal social services
for the elderly, especially those over 75 years, are far greater
than for the young. This has serious implications for public

expenditure and the taxpayer. Notwithstanding the heavy expenditure by the state in health and social welfare old age is often associated with poverty and loneliness. In 1971 42 per cent of one-person household heads were aged 65 and over, of whom many lacked basic sanitary facilities (Blackwell, 1983b).

In general, the age structure, the sex ratio and the extent of dependency can affect the degree of either vitality or conservatism in a society and ultimately through voting behaviour influence policy priorities including the type and level of social service provision.

Conclusion

This chapter provides a necessarily limited account of demography in the Republic of Ireland with particular reference to the post-war period. Following the depressing 1950s there has been extraordinary population growth which during the 1970s affected almost every corner of the country. While patterns of fertility and nuptiality are now closer to those in other western European countries than before, they continue nevertheless to be quite distinctive. Reproduction rates remain high despite a significant fall in the number of births since 1980. Mortality is relatively low by comparison with elsewhere. The impact of emigration is becoming significant again though there was net immigration, 1971-9. The peculiar age structure is the Republic's best-known demographic feature and accentuates the need for sustained employment creation. The latter would benefit the young especially, reduce emigration and ultimately ensure a balanced age profile which should prevent the problems of an ageing population generally found in developed countries today.

In the Republic of Ireland, as in other countries, demography benefits from the state's regularly furnishing essential statistics. Demography provides an essential basis for much sociological analysis. There is a need to integrate the two in the development of new research methods. Furthermore, sociological studies on the various components of population movement and structure are essential. Finally, population and labour force projections for 1986 and 1991 were published by the Central Statistics Office in April 1985 and will be modified and updated periodically. The projected average annual change in population varies between +0.6% and +0.8% for 1981-6 and between zero and +0.4% for 1986-91. Earlier projections undertaken by the National Economic and Social Council (Blackwell and McGregor 1982) were followed by studies (Blackwell 1983b, Courtney and McCashin 1984, Murphy 1984, Raftery 1984) of the effects of such population change on housing, social welfare, education and the health services. Though they fall outside the ambit of this chapter they deserve serious consideration.

Notes

1   Data provided by the Office of Population Censuses and Surveys, London, suggest that an annual number of about 1,200 single women who were born in the Republic of Ireland had extra marital births in England and Wales in the early 1980s. It is impossible, however, to discern how many of those were usually resident there or in the Republic.

References

BLACKER, C. P. 1947. 'Stages in population growth', *Eugenics Review*, Vol. 39, pp. 81-101.

BLACKWELL, JOHN 1983a. 'Economic Aspects of Changing Population Trends and the Implications of Social Policy', read at 12th Regional Symposium of the International Council on Social Welfare, Dublin, 18 July.

BLACKWELL, JOHN 1983b. *Housing Requirements and Population Change, 1981-1991*, Dublin, National Economic and Social Council, Report No. 69.

BLACKWELL, JOHN and JOHN McGREGOR 1982. *Population and Labour Force Projections by County and Region, 1979-1991*, Dublin, National Economic and Social Council, Report No. 63.

CLANCY, PATRICK 1984. 'Demographic Changes and the Irish Family', *The Changing Family*, Dublin, University College, pp. 1-38.

COALE, A. J. 1969. 'The decline of fertility in Europe from the French Revolution to World War II', in S. J. Behrman, L. Corsa Jr. and R.

Freedman (eds.), *Fertility and Family Planning: A World View*, Ann Arbor, University of Michigan Press.

COMMISSION ON EMIGRATION AND OTHER POPULATION PROBLEMS, 1948–54. *Reports*, Dublin, Stationery Office.

CONNIFFE, DENIS and KIERAN A. KENNEDY (eds.) 1984. *Employment and Unemployment Policy for Ireland*, Dublin: Economic and Social Research Institute.

COURTNEY, DAMIEN and ANTHONY McCASHIN 1984. *Social Welfare: The Implications of Demographic Change*, Dublin, National Economic and Social Council, Report No. 72.

COWARD, JOHN 1978. 'Changes in the Pattern of Fertility in the Republic of Ireland', *Tijdschrift voor Economische en Sociale Geografie*, Vol. 69, No. 6, pp. 353–361.

COWARD, John 1982. 'Fertility Changes in the Republic of Ire-land during the 1970s', *Area*, Vol. 14, No. 2, pp. 109–117.

DURKAN, J. 1979. 'The Census: Coming or Going?', *Magill*, Vol. 3, No. 2, pp. 65–67.

GARVEY, DONAL 1983. 'A Profile of the Demographic and Labour Force Characteristics of the Population — Sample Analysis of the 1981 Census of Population', *Journal of the Statistical and Social Inquiry Society of Ireland*, Vol. XXIV, Part V, pp. 104–139.

GARVEY, DONAL 1985. 'The History of Migration Flows in the Republic of Ireland', *Population Trends*, No. 39, (Spring), pp. 22–30.

GOLDSCHEIDER, CALVIN 1971.

Population, Modernization, and Social Structure, Boston, Little, Brown and Company.

GOLDSCHEIDER, CALVIN 1981. 'Societal Change and Demographic Transitions: Selected Theoretical Issues and Research Strategies', read at the *Chaire Quetelet (Population et Structures Sociales)*, Louvain, 6–8 May.

HANNAN, DAMIAN F. 1970. *Rural Exodus*, London, Geoffrey Chapman.

HANNAN, DAMIAN F. 1979. *Displacement and Development: Class, Kinship and Social Change in Irish Rural Communities*, Dublin, The Economic and Social Research Institute, Paper No. 96.

HUGHES, J. G. and B. M. WALSH 1980. *Internal Migration Flows in Ireland and their Determinants*, Dublin, The Economic and Social Research Institute, Paper No. 98.

KENNEDY, ROBERT E. JR 1973. *The Irish: Emigration, Marriage and Fertility*, Berkeley, University of California Press.

KIRKE, PEADAR 1981. 'Perinatal and Infant Mortality in Ireland and Selected Countries: Variations in Underlying Factors', *Irish Medical Journal*, Vol. 74, No. 8.

MURPHY, DENIS 1984. *Education: The Implications of Demographic Change*, Dublin, National Economic and Social Council, Report No. 71.

PRESSAT, ROLAND 1978. *Statistical Demography*, London, Methuen. (Translated and adapted by Damien A. Courtney from *Démographie Statistique*, 1972, Paris, Presses Universitaires de France).

RAFTERY, JAMES 1984. *Health Services: The Implications of Demographic Change*, Dublin, National Economic and Social Council, Report No. 73.

RAFTERY, T. F. 1983. 'Employment — Prospects in Agriculture' address to *An Foras Forbartha Open Forum*, Dublin, 4 October.

ROTTMAN, DAVID B., DAMIAN F. HANNAN, NIAMH HARDIMAN and MIRIAM M. WILEY 1982. *The Distribution of Income in the Republic of Ireland: A Study in Social Class and Family-Cycle Inequalities*, Dublin, The Economic and Social Research Institute, Paper No. 109.

SEXTON, J. J. and MICHELE DILLON 1984. 'Some Recent Changes in Irish Fertility', *Quarterly Economic Commentary*, May, pp. 21-40.

WALSH, BRENDAN 1980. 'Recent Demographic Changes in the Republic of Ireland', *Population Trends*, Vol. 21 (Autumn), pp. 3-9.

WALSH, JAMES A. 1984. *To Go Or Not To Go - The Migration Intentions of Leaving Certificate Students*, Dublin, Carysfort College.

WHELAN, BRENDAN J. and GARY KEOGH 1980. 'The Use of the Irish Electoral Register for Population Estimates', *The Economic and Social Review*, Vol. 11, No. 4, p. 301-318.

3
Rural Social Change

PATRICK COMMINS

Ireland entered an era of major social transformation in the late 1950s. The essential features of this change have been described elsewhere (see, for example, Litton 1982) and many of its characteristics will also be examined by the contributors to the present volume. The purpose of this chapter is to discuss specifically rural social change in the Republic. In doing so we adopt a general classificatory scheme, corresponding to several levels or types of change. Within this framework we select a limited numbers of issues or themes and explore these to illustrate the concepts and perspectives of sociology. Accordingly, the presentation is divided into a number of sections, as follows:

(i)   Demographic change
(ii) Chages in values
(iii) Institutional change
(iv) Change in the distribution of possessions, rewards and life-chances
(v)   Planned change — or rural development
(vi) Main theoretical orientations in understanding social change.

At the outset, however, it is necessary to enter a caution about the term 'rural'.

What is 'rural'?

There has been a futile search in rural sociology for an accept-able *sociological* definition of rural (Newby and Buttel 1980, p. 4). While dichotomous classifications such as rural and urban were convenient, most scholars recognised that these were crude attempts at differentiating types of society. In the 1950s and 1960s it was argued that there existed a rural-urban continuum. In other words, 'rural' and 'urban' are two ideal types at polar extremes. As human communities are arrayed along the spec-trum from one to the other, consistent variations occur in social structure and patterns of behaviour (e.g. in family size, crime rates). However, research gradually questioned the validity of this idea. For example, similar types of social relationships (e.g. in kinship) could be found at each end of the continuum and social change did not always spread from urban to rural settings. Thus, the English sociologist Pahl (1966, p. 322) concluded: 'Any attempt to tie patterns of social relationships to specific geographical milieux is a singularly fruitless exercise'.

Pahl went on to imply that, whether in metropolitan areas or remote villages, the important categorisations and interrelationships were the 'local' and the 'national', and the 'small-scale' and 'large-scale'. We could add that perhaps social class and not place of residence is the important — as distinct from the spurious — determinant of social behaviour. In any case, from a sociological perspective, rural society should not be considered a separate entity except in limited circumstances. It should be studied as an integral element of the structures and processes of the larger society.

Here, therefore, we are simply following convention and con-venience by using spatial or geograpical criteria to delineate the 'rural' in Irish society. Moreover, in practice the dividing point between the rural and the urban is made with reference to the population size of places (towns and villages) as determined by the Census of Population. Places with 1,500 persons or upwards are regarded as 'urban', the remainder being classified as 'rural'. Changes within these categories are examined below.

Demographic change

A full treatment of demographic change would cover not only
changes in population *size* and distribution but also shifts in
population *structure* (e.g. occupational composition) and *demographic processes* (e.g. migration, marriage rates). However, the
analysis here is confined to the salient changes in population
size.

Despite the rapid pace of urbanisation in recent years Ireland
still has a strong rural-based population. Furthermore, in sharp
contrast to earlier decades of depopulation, the late 1960s and
1970s have brought a re-population of rural areas.

Population distribution

In 1981, 44 per cent of the Republic's 3.44 million inhabitants
were living in places having less than 1,500 persons (Table 1). In
fact most of these (or 37 per cent of the national population)
lived in the open countryside. The open countryside and the
larger urban areas combined account for the majority (75 per
cent) of the Irish population. The lack of a medium-sized urban
system is related to the historical pattern of rural migration to
overseas urban areas rather than to provincial urban centres at
home. Dublin city and its satellite areas account for about half of
the Republic's urban residents.

Making a broad distinction between the eastern and western
counties, we find the degree of rurality quite pronounced in the
west, where three out of every four people live in rural areas.
Nevertheless, the spatial distribution of population continues to
shift in favour of the urban centres. Throughout the 1970s the
medium and large urban areas increased their share of the
national total from 45 per cent to 50 per cent, while in open
country areas the proportion dropped from 41 per cent to 37 per
cent.

Population renewal in rural areas

This distribution shift has occurred despite the general renewal
of rural population (Table 1). This is because the rate of
population growth has been faster in urban areas — 22 per cent

Table 1: **Population distribution 1981, and population change 1981–1981**

Size of place (persons)	% distribution 1981			% change 1971–1981		
	West[a]	Rest of state	Total state	West[a]	Rest of state	Total state
URBAN						
Large (20,000+)	4.7	49.3	37.7	+42.5	+19.3	+19.9
Medium (5,000–20,000)	13.4	12.1	12.4	+59.7	+60.1	+60.0
Small (1.5–5,000)	6.4	5.2	5.5	-6.9	-8.7	-8.2
RURAL						
Towns and villages (<1,500)	11.5	5.6	7.2	+23.0	+26.1	+24.8
Open country	64.0	27.8	37.2	+1.7	+7.2	+4.7
TOTAL	100.0	100.0	100.0	+10.1	+17.7	+15.6

[a]Eleven western counties (Connacht, Ulster and Counties Kerry, Clare and Longford). Size of place figures are those for respective census years.
Source: Derived from *Census of Population*.

as against 9 per cent during 1971-1981.

In the case of rural areas, however, the more appropriate comparison is with the rural trends of earlier decades, and these show a long history of depopulation. During the 1950s rural population decline was particularly heavy. In areas of extremely high losses out-migration during those years accounted for over 60 per cent of the young adult age groups, resulting in the decimation of many of the remote rural communities. However, during 1971-1981 the reversal of this long-term decline was quite widespread across the country, though not universal. Of the one hundred and sixty Rural Districts[1] in the state, 80 per cent recorded population increases in the 1970s.

Did the population turn-around occur among the traditionally migrating young adult age groups? Reference to the trends in the age-group aged 15-29 years shows that their numbers in the aggregate rural areas of the state increased by 18 per cent between 1971 and 1981. Even in the 11 western counties the corresponding increase was 15 per cent. In these predominantly rural counties there are now more young people than there were in 1951, i.e., before the decade of mass out-migration.

Continuous decline in farm population
Within the shadow of the demographic recovery in rural areas generally, the farming population continues to decline rapidly. Up to date information is not available for the 'farming population' as such, but the data from the farm *labour force* show a steady 2.5 to 3.5 per cent annual decline over the past three decades. The 190,000 people currently working on farms represent about half the corresponding number in the 1960s.

Social implications
Population growth in rural areas can be traced mainly to state-sponsored policies of rural industrialisation, while agricultural population decline is related to major structural change in the farming economy. This latter issue will be taken up in a later section. Here it is sufficient to note that population changes — especially from severe decline to steady growth — pose

challenges for social planning. Will employment be available to those age-groups who no longer have recourse to emigration? Population growth, together with rising marriage rates, means a greater demand for housing, educational and recreation facilities.

Increases in industrial employment bring other social changes, including greater physical mobility, the erosion of social and cultural isolation in rural communities, and heterogeneity of social values for life-styles in rural areas (O'Connor and Daly 1983, p. 104). In particular, the presence of a consumer-oriented young adult population and the emergence of a 'youth culture' contrast with the migration trends of the past.

Changes in values

Before turning to aspects of institutional change we need to advert to a more basic change in rural society, namely, a shift of emphasis in social values. Values are the criteria (often implicit) by which judgments are made about what is desirable or undesirable in human affairs. They help shape institutional structures and provide a 'guiding image' to policy-makers in selecting policy goals. The value change we wish to refer to here may be termed 'the decline of rural fundamentalism'.

Rural fundamentalism
Rural fundamentalism may be thought of as a set of values and beliefs by which a positive view was taken of
— the family-owned farm as the basic unit of agricultural pro-
   duction
— having a numerous class of landowners
— farming as an occupation
— agriculture as the basis of national prosperity.
— farm or small-town living.

Irish rural fundamentalism shared the beliefs of a similar ideology found in other countries which 'regarded family farming and rural life as the well-spring of political stability, democracy and equality' (Fite 1962, pp. 1203-1211). This tradition informed De Valera's philosophy. Support for the family farm ideal, as well as for having as many as possible working on the land, is enshrined in the Constitution (Bunreacht na h-Eireann 1937, Art. 45). The land reforms of the 1920s and 1930s were based on socially re-distributive criteria rather than on economic or technical considerations.

The Irish strain of rural fundamentalism also found some of its basis in Catholic ethico-social thought, which advocated the wide diffusion of property and emphasised the intrinsic value of agricultural work, together with the desirability of owner-operated family farms (CTS 1961, pp. 30-49). Perhaps the most forceful expression of fundamentalist values was that contained in Bishop Lucey's Minority Report to the Commission on Emigration in the early 1950s (*Commission on Emigration and other Population Problems, 1948-54,* 1955, pp. 335-363). He argued that:
— ownership of land should be more widely diffused
— holdings should be small (15-20 acres)
— the rural home always has been, and is still, the best place to raise a family
— control of agricultural education and advisory services should be transferred from central government to farmers' organisations
— the growth of Dublin should be halted.
By then, however, rural fundamentalism had largely given way to other sets of values more in line with the requirements of the modern era of economic development.

Rationalism and economic efficiency
In the late 1950s central government began to play a more direc-tive role in economic and social affairs. By 1969 official policy had accepted the inevitability of a fall in agricultural employ-ment (*Third Programme: Economic and Social Development 1969-72,* 1969, pp. 44-45). What was then regarded as desirable was the maintenance of the country's rural (if not farm) population. Rural prosperity was to be sought not only in agriculture but in

the comprehensive development of industry, tourism and other enterprises. In this way a better balance between agricultural and non-agricultural activities would enable population to be maintained in rural areas.

Agriculture in particular became increasingly organised according to criteria of technical and economic rationality. In 1962 the standard of viability for holdings created by the Irish Land Commission (the state land restructuring agency), was raised from 33 acres to 40–45 acres. More recently, emphasis has shifted somewhat from the desirability of land ownership to the need for productive land use. Indeed the owner-occupancy tenure system is now seen to have many disadvantages from a land-use standpoint. Science and technology, promoted through state-sponsored agencies (as well as by private and farmers' organisations), have increasingly influenced production methods. Prices and incomes, the extrinsic rewards from farming activity, have become more salient among the farm population than the intrinsic benefits formerly presumed to be inherent in the 'farming way of life'. State social welfare schemes have tended to provide the security formerly considered to be found in property ownership. Trends in the economic organisation of agriculture are considered in more detail below.

Institutional change

Under this heading we confine the discussion to change in the agricultural economy and in the rural community. Some reference to change in the rural family will be found in a later chapter.

The agricultural economy
The transformation of rural society is best illustrated by the changes occurring within the agricultural economy. Several interrelated processes may be observed resulting in two dominant but contrasting trends — commercialisation and marginalisation (Commins et al. 1978; Commins 1983).

Machines and biochemical technology have altered production conditions on the farm. Capital technology comes in increasingly 'heavy' forms so fixed costs increase. At the same time the retail demand for food is unresponsive to changes in price and in incomes, while an increasing share of retail food expenditure goes to processing and marketing enterprises. This results in a cost-price squeeze for the producer. The producer's response is to try and increase the scale of the individual farm business so the size-threshold of farm viability continues to rise. Besides this enlargement of scale, modern commercial farming also calls for greater specialisation through the reduction of the number of enterprises per farm and the concentration of production in a narrowing span of farm sizes. The most remarkable shift of this kind in recent years has been in the structure of dairy farming. Over the last decade or so milk production has shifted to the larger farms. The average size of herd has doubled. Output per producer has increased considerably, and the number of milk producers has been halved.

Technology replaces labour, but the labour decline in agriculture is a most selective process. In the western counties, for example, the male agricultural labour force has been halved since 1926 while the numbers of older, unmarried farmers have doubled. Thus, the numbers of farm households at the terminal stage of the family life-cycle have increased. In this regard studies show that poor farming performance is associated with 'weak' household demographic structure. The general outcome of this process is a growing social differentiation between a commercial farming category, i.e. those adapting to a high technology, high cost, high output and high income agriculture and the remainder — the marginalised or displaced category. This widening differentiation is based on the initial farm size (Table 2).

There is a clear contrast between larger and smaller farms in the rates of increase in output, expenses and incomes. These differences are also related to the farm enterprise. The strong shift of dairying to the larger farms means that the less intensive, less lucrative cattle enterprises have come to characterise much of small-scale farming. Size of farm is not the complete explana-

Table 2: **Index of changes in gross output, net expenses and family farm income per farm, 1955–58 to 1980–83**[a]

Period	Farm size (acs)					
	5–15	15–30	30–50	50–100	100–200	200+
Gross output: 1955–58 = 100						
1972–75	157	188	252	290	324	329
1980–83	501	574	812	1149	1152	1290
Net expenses: 1955–58 = 100						
1972–75	173	205	258	290	301	313
1980–83	723	777	1119	1500	1409	1526
Family farm income: 1955–58 = 100						
1972–75	147	178	248	289	356	354
1980–83	371	457	604	836	840	902
Per cent of farm work force 1981	3.6[b]	15.9	25.6	34.1	15.5	5.3

[a]For all farms in the Republic   [b]10–15 acres
Source: Derived from *National Farm Survey* (CSO 1961). *Farm Management Survey* (An Foras Taluntais, various years). *Census of Population 1981*, Volume 4.

tion of socio-economic differentiation, however. Neither are the demographic or other variations between big and small farms. Differentiation trends are reinforced by various policies. Price policy favours the large producer and thus strengthens his or her position in obtaining credit or buying more land. EEC development schemes are biased in favour of those who already have good land resources, and research and advisory services focus on a limited clientele which actively seeks information and has the means to implement new technology.

Many small farmers succeed in getting a non-farm job[2] but others on low incomes have to rely on state income maintenance schemes. In 1980 state transfers accounted for 37 per cent of gross household income on under-30 acre farms and 18 per cent of such incomes on 30–50 acre farms (CSO 1982). Nevertheless, in the same year gross incomes in farming households below 50 acres were less than those in homes headed by semi-skilled or un-skilled manual workers. We return to this point later.

Community change
In turning to social change at community level, we enter a realm of several classic studies. It has also been an area of scholarly debate both as regards the accuracy of the descriptions of com-munity and the validity of the theories or assumptions which guided the studies.

The basic reference point is the work of two American anthro-pologists, Arensberg and Kimball, in a small-farm community in Clare in the 1930s (Arensberg and Kimball 1940). They came to Clare with a definite mental image or model of society as an organic or 'integrated system of mutually interrelated parts'. Hence they were not so much interested in the particular locality itself but rather in a study which would verify the con-cept they had about the structure and functioning of society in general. Guided by this integrationist thinking they painted a picture of rural Ireland as a stable, cohesive, harmonious entity organised around two central institutions: the family and the community. The roles of men and women were separate but complementary, both necessary (functional) for the survival of the family. Emotional forces were balanced, the mother a counterpoise to the father's stern paternality. The countryman was part of an extended family — the community — where slender resources were pooled in systems of mutual aid and re-ciprocal obligation. Even exchange relationships in the local economy were part of the interwoven pattern of complemen-tarities, the small farmer selling his surplus to his larger neigh-bour. Central to the maintenance of this web of social organisation was the arranged marriage — the 'match'.

In subsequent studies change was portrayed as alterations in this idyllic and optimistic picture. A study in county Limerick during the late 1950s (Newman 1964) drew attention to the high emigration rates among unmarried women and farm labourers, indicating the rejection of rural life by these groups. In a vivid description of social atrophy and demoralisation in *Inishkillane* — a composite of the west of Ireland rural communities — during the 1960s, Hugh Brody contrasted the community disintegration which he found with the harmonious and self-maintaining system seen by Arensberg and Kimball (Brody 1973). The people of Inishkillane had lost any belief in the social advantage or moral worth of their own small society. The divergence between people's needs and the possibilities offered by their society was due to a change in the people themselves as well as in their social milieu. Their consciousness was being changed by the intrusion of an urban culture of personal freedom, the coming of the 'cash economy', new concepts of 'success', and new possibilities for comparison and evaluation. According to Brody, this transformation from past cohesion to current demoralisation was relatively sudden, but Arensberg and Kimball could not have foreseen it because, he argued, they were hampered by their commitment to a rigid harmonious model of society.

Subsequently Brody himself was severely criticised for assuming Arensberg and Kimball's analysis to be accurate while at the same time claiming to reject their organic-functionalist perspective. Gibbon (1973) maintained that the changes described by Brody were neither novel nor recent. Disintegration could be traced back to post-famine times. By seeking to explain a relatively sudden collapse, Brody 'set himself a false problem'.

More recent studies by Hannan (1979; 1982) suggest that criticism of Arensberg and Kimball is justified when it refers to the extent to which their model led them to overstate the degree of integration, harmony and stability in their Clare community. However, Hannan maintains that this criticism should not extend to denying that a quite distinctive economic and social structure existed among the smaller farmers in the west of Ireland in the early part of this century (Hannan 1982, pp. 161–162). This may be understood in terms of a 'peasant model' having the following characteristic features:

— a familial economy (e.g. family farms not employing labour)

— subsistence production (rather than commercial production)
— definite arrangements for inheritance, marriage and property transfer (e.g. 'settling' of heirs)
— a locally-bound communal system in which mutual aid arrangements between neighbours and kinship groups mitigate class differentiation tendencies.

Rapid change in this context has had uneven effects. Reporting on their recent study of west Limerick, O'Connor and Daly (1983, p. 106) conclude that traditional behaviour patterns and values co-exist with modern, urbanised lifestyles and values. Any general picture masks variation occurring among subgroups. Some, because of their reduced resources for coping with change, become alienated and marginalised.

We have already noted this as an outcome of capitalist commercialisation in the farm economy. The former land and resource differences — subdued in the peasant economy — are accentuated in the growing differentiation in output and incomes. Cumulative economic differentiation is reinforced by social differences as reflected, for example, in the contrasting opportunities for marriage between small and large farmers (Commins *et al.* 1978, pp. 22–41). The peasant farming community of the 1930s is thus reduced to a residual post-peasant class, economically and socially isolated (Kelleher and O'Hara, 1978; Hannan 1982, p. 162).

Possessions, rewards and life-chances

While the basic institutional structure of society may remain substantially unaltered (e.g. in its form of government, economic system, etc.), social change can occur rapidly within this basic framework and can have significant impact on the distribution of possessions, rewards and life chances among different categories of the population. Differentiation occurs between farm and non-farm sectors and, as we have seen, within the farm sector itself. Where this differentiation accentuates past distributions, class structures become solidified. Selected aspects of change under this heading are discussed later.

In the nineteenth century it was anticipated by some scholars that capitalist agriculture would result in the concentration of land among few landowners (Banaji 1980, pp. 39–82; also see Tovey 1982, pp. 75–77). This has not happened in Ireland. Average farm size has not risen dramatically in the context of the changes in the structure of agricultural production, and the numbers of landholders (now at 241,000 over 5 acres) have remained relatively static compared to the numbers of farmers (now about 150,000). However, where the size of farm units is increased temporarily by short-term rentings, most of such land is now taken by the larger farmers. This is in complete contrast to the situation in the 1950s (Commins 1983, pp. 182–183). Various policy measures, such as farmer retirement schemes, have been implemented to encourage elderly farmers to surrender the ownership or usage rights of their holdings to more active farmers, but these have not met with much success.

One reason is that, where smallholders possess marketable skills, they can obtain an off-farm job and still retain ownership of their holdings. Therefore, all farmers displaced from commercial agriculture are not impoverished. Low output landholders or marginal farmers who obtain non-farm employment have levels-of-living comparable to full-time farmers (Kelleher and O'Mahony 1983).

Household Budget Surveys for 1973 and 1980 show increases in the percentages of rural and farming households having various types of modern domestic facilities and appliances (CSO 1977; 1984). While farm households in general have reduced the gap between themselves and urban households for the possession of such items as washing machines, refrigerators and central heating (Higgins 1983b) the differences remain between the larger and smaller farmer categories.

'Rewards' consist of tangibles like income but also include prestige, status or reputation. We have already noted the widening income gaps within the farming population (Table 2). In terms of absolute differences, family farm incomes on the over-200 acre farms are still about four times higher than those earned on the 30–50 acre holdings. When total household income is taken into account, households on farms over 100 acres have incomes greater than those of most social groups in urban areas. The relativities for both direct and disposable incomes are expressed in Table 3, as percentages of the respective national averages. In regard to disposable income there is as much variation between the different farm size groups as between the different occupational groups in urban areas.

As already noted, policy measures such as agricultural price supports affect the distribution of possessions and rewards. The state system of taxation and of cash transfers helps to correct inequities. It re-distributes income from urban to rural — and especially to farming — households. Thus in 1980 the disposable income of urban households fell below their direct income while the opposite was true for farming households (Table 3). However, although there was little difference between the direct income of farming and that of other rural households, farmers paid less tax and therefore had more disposable income than their non-farming neighbours. Despite the general redistribution of income from urban to rural areas there is still a relatively high incidence of poverty in small-farming and other rural households (Kelleher and O'Mahony 1984).

'Life-chances' refer to opportunities people have to gain access to, and share in, the social and 'cultural' goods of their society. These opportunities may include access to public services, access to decision-making, opportunities for employment or marriage. Life-chances are obviously closely dependent on possessions and rewards. In the case of services, there has been a tendency towards universal provision (e.g. free education, medical services etc.) but low population density in rural areas creates special problems of access, especially where the trend is to centralise facilities (schools, hospitals, farmer training centres, etc.). For example, in relation to medical services, western counties are less well catered for than those in the rest of the country (O'Mahony 1982).

Where inequities persist in the distribution of possessions, rewards and life-chances across rural areas or regions, we are faced with problems of 'structured underdevelopment'

Table 3: **Types of household income expressed as a percentage of respective national averages; disposable income expressed as a percentage of direct income for each social group, 1980**

Social groups (category of worker)	*Income*		*Disposable income as % of direct income*
	Direct[a]	*Disposable*[b]	
URBAN[c]			
1. Professional, managerial, etc	177	149	80.7
2. Salaried non-manual	123	112	87.0
3. Other non-manual	96	96	96.0
4. Skilled manual	119	111	89.5
5. Semi-skilled or unskilled	75	86	108.9
All urban households	113	107	90.7
RURAL NON-FARM	82	88	102.8
RURAL FARM			
Under 30 acres	42	66	151.4
30–50 acres	70	83	113.3
50–100 acres	94	104	105.6
100 acres +	129	133	99.4
All rural-farm households	81	94	111.1
STATE	100	100	95.8

[a] Income of a recurring nature, before deduction of taxes or addition of state cash benefits.
[b] Direct income plus state cash benefits but less direct taxes.
[c] Defined here as those in towns of 1000 or more persons.
Sources: Derived from *Household Budget Survey* (CSO 1982; 1984).

(Conway and O'Hara 1983, p. 29). Rural policies and programmes attempt to counter underdevelopment and to modify the forces of 'spontaneous' change.

Planned change — rural development

From the various efforts to bring about development in rural areas we may identify four basic models, or approaches, that differ as regards their underlying assumptions, their strategies and methods. As these have been discussed elsewhere (Commins 1979; Ó Cearbhaill and Ó Cinnéide 1983) they are dealt with briefly here.

Public planning

Under this heading are included the activities of central government, state-sponsored bodies and local authorities. Basically, this approach assumes that rural development is best conducted by public bureaucratic organisations employing experts/professionals who can use specialist knowledge, technical skills and rational planning procedures. Although frequently criticised for being too centralised and not allowing for public participation in their decision-making, Irish statutory agencies have a considerable degree of success in developing agriculture, industry, tourism and social services in rural areas.

Co-operativism

Co-operativism is a philosophy based on the idea of self-reliance and on a particular organisational structure — the co-operative — as a means for people to provide services for themselves. Rural co-operatives in the Republic of Ireland are typically agricultural marketing or processing organisations. Until the 1960s farmer co-operatives were generally locally-based small organisations. Over the past two decades, however, in response to the technical and economic demands of the wider commercial environment, these have amalgamated into large multi-purpose trading organisations run by professional management. This trend has reduced the differences between co-operatives and other commercial organisations. In recent years there has also been the emergence of community development co-operatives especially in the western counties (Commins 1982).

Community development (CD)

CD emphasises the ideal of a unified effort by a local community to identify its own needs and to set up local democratic structures to deal with these. It stresses not alone the attainment of specific development objectives but also the educational process of building up a community's capacity to act effectively.

Apart from the community co-operatives mentioned above, local community councils (non-statutory) may be considered to follow this model. Such community councils have done much to improve local infra-structural facilities and services (e.g. piped water schemes) in rural areas.

Social action

The social action model presupposes a disadvantaged section of a community or population that needs to be organised (perhaps in alliance with other disadvantaged groups) to make demands on the larger society for increased resources or better treatment, according to criteria of equity or social justice. The basic strategy of change is one of raising people's consciousness about their situation, especially about the way economic and social institutions impinge on their lives.

This rather radical approach has not been adopted generally in rural areas. However, it could be said to be reflected in the 'action-education' methods employed in the Combat Poverty projects of the 1970s among small fishermen, marginalised farmers and other disadvantaged groups in the west of Ireland (*National Committee on Pilot Schemes to Combat Poverty 1981*, pp. 190–207).

General comment

In general, official policy in the Republic with regard to rural development is based on the assumption that centralised government is the best-equipped to deal with rural problems. On the other hand, non-statutory organisations perform important functions, complementing statutory agencies and even pioneering novel approaches to meeting needs. One of the contemporary concerns in rural development is that of finding an appropriate integration of public planning and other endeavours.

Theoretical orientations in understanding rural change

What are the causes of persistent underdevelopment in rural regions like the west of Ireland? To answer questions like this we need to establish a 'theoretical perspective', that is, we need to formulate ideas, assumptions and basic propositions that will guide the search for an answer. Two broad theoretical orientations have been used in examining underdevelopment and social change in rural areas. These are the modernisation approach and the structural thesis[3].

The modernisation approach

Modernisation refers to the evolutionary process by which traditional (underdeveloped) societies are transformed into the types of societies that characterise the economically advanced (developed) countries of the modern western world. It is assumed that it is possible to identify the distinctive features of both underdeveloped and developed societies. Development, then, is a matter of changing from one type to the other. Within a single society the 'modern' regions or areas have the kinds of technology and forms of socio-economic organisation typical of developed economies. The underdeveloped areas are seen as 'traditional', with archaic structures (e.g. subsistence farms) and conservative attitudes. The basic obstacles to development are assumed to be 'the human factors', i.e. the traditional values, ways of thinking, lack of initiative and slothful habits of the people.

In modernisation theory, development strategy basically consists of policies of economic development. However, it is accepted that various prerequisites facilitate such development. These include political stability, good communications, commercial institutions such as credit agencies, educational systems, and a minimum of state regulation. Economic development here means the introduction of modern technologies, the commercialisation of agriculture, the promotion of industrialisation and the utilisation of rational economic procedures. Great emphasis is placed on changing individual behaviour. Modern entrepreneurial attitudes are cultivated. People are motivated by various incentives and grants, and it is expected that they will respond rationally to economic opportunity. Those not able to cope with the demands of modernisation can benefit from state social security or other income maintenance systems.

The structural thesis

According to this view the causes of underdevelopment are not to be sought in factors that can be located inside the boundaries of underdeveloped regions. The problem has to be examined in the context of the structures of the society as a whole.

Rural underdevelopment is a matter of structured inequalities between regions and societies. Moreover, the structural thesis holds that continuing inequalities are inherent in the modern capitalist socio-economic system. Rural or regional poverty, therefore, is not an anachronism in the modern world but is in fact created — however unintentionally — by policies of modern economic development. Thus, the basic causes of underdevelopment are not the cultural characteristics of people but the character of the main structures and institutions — the economy, government, the law, etc. These institutions are seen to be maintained because they serve the ideologies and class interests of those who control power and economic resources.

The strategy of change, therefore, involves firstly an examination of the way institutions have developed historically and of how they operate to perpetuate underdevelopment. Development means more radical and longer-term change than that envisaged in the modernisation perspective. It calls for policies in the economic, fiscal and social fields to achieve a greater degree of regulation of market forces, and a re-distribution of political power, wealth and income.

Although the structural thesis does not emphasise change in individual behaviour as a primary mechanism of development, it recognises the need for 'conscientisation', that is, for people in underdeveloped areas to be made aware of the structural causes of underdevelopment.

Conclusion

The modernisation and structural perspectives are clearly contrasting views about the causes of rural underdevelopment. It follows that there is no simple answer to the question posed at the beginning of the previous section. The discussion even begs the further question: what do we mean by development?

The modernisation approach has been the dominant model implicitly followed in the various policies in Irish rural development. Industrialisation has brought demographic renewal, a more heterogeneous rural population and a revitalisation of many decimated rural communities. Yet commercialisation in agriculture has left behind in those same communities a disadvantaged segment of the farming population. Regional disparities, in economic and social indicators, still exist between the west of Ireland and the rest of the state.

These remarks serve to make the concluding point that there is no single approach in sociology itself. Any piece of social data is capable of differential interpretation for purposes of understanding the causes and consequences of social change or for planning social change. Students or practitioners, therefore, have to make judgments and interpretations about various facts and propositions. For this reason they must constantly develop their own theoretical perspectives by relating different approaches to different problems and systematically evaluating them (see Coulson and Riddell 1970, p. 6).

Notes

1　Rural Districts (RDs) are census enumeration units and do not coincide exactly with 'rural areas' as defined by size of place in that RDs may sometimes include towns with more than 1,500 persons.

2　About one-quarter of farm operators now have another occupation besides running the farm (Higgins 1983a).

3　A more extended summary is available in Kelleher (1983). See also Long (1977) and Havens (1972).

References

ARENSBERG C., and S. KIM-BALL 1940. *Family and Community in Ireland*, Harvard, Harvard Press.

BANAJI, J. 1980. 'Summary of Selected Parts of Kautsky's *The Agrarian Question*', in F. H. Buttel and H. Newby, *The Rural Sociology of the Advanced Societies*, New York, Croom Helm, pp. 39–82.

BRODY, H. 1973. *Inishkillane*, London, Penguin.

Bunreacht na h-Eireann 1937.

COMMINS, P. 1979. 'Co-operation and Community Development in the West of Ireland', paper to Fifth International Seminar on Marginal Regions, Trinity College Dublin, August.

COMMINS, P. 1982. 'State, Co-operatives and Language in the Gaeltacht,' paper to Conference, Comhdhail na Gaeltachta, Galway, June.

COMMINS, P. 1983. 'The Land Question: Is Leasing the Answer', Proceedings of Conference, Agricultural Institute, Dublin, November, pp. 156–196.

COMMINS, P., et al. 1978. *Rural Areas: Change and Development*, National Economic and Social Council, Report No. 41, Dublin.

COMMISSION ON EMIGRATION AND OTHER POPULATION PROBLEMS 1948–54, 1955. *Reports*, Dublin, Stationery Office.

CONWAY, A. G. and P. O'HARA 1983. 'Integrated Rural Development in the West of Ireland: Theoretical and Methodological Issues', Dublin, Agricultural Institute.

CSO, *National Farm Survey 1955–56, 1957–58*, 1961. Dublin, Stationery Office.

CSO, *Household Budget Survey 1973*, 1977, Vol. 4, Dublin, Stationery Office.

CSO, *Household Budget Survey 1980*, 1982. Dublin, Stationery Office.

CSO, *Household Budget Survey 1980*, 1984. Vol. 4, Dublin, Stationery Office.

CTS (Catholic Truth Society), 1961. *New Light on Social Problems*, London.

COULSON, M. and D. S. RIDDELL 1970. *Approaching Sociology*, London, Routledge and Kegan Paul.

FARM MANAGEMENT SURVEY, Dublin, An Foras Taluntais.

FITE, G. G. 1962. 'Historical Development of Agricultural Fundamentalism in the Nineteenth Century', *Journal of Farm Economics*, Vol. 44, pp. 1203–1211.

GIBBON, P. 1973. 'Arensberg and Kimball Revisited', *Economy and Society*, Vol. 4, pp. 479–498.

HANNAN, D. F. 1979. *Displacement and Development: Class, Kinship and Social Change in Irish Rural Communities*, ESRI, Paper No. 96, Dublin.

HANNAN, D. F. 1982. 'Peasant Models and the Understanding of Social and Cultural Change in Rural Ireland', in P. J. Drudy (ed.), *Ireland: Land, Politics and People*, Cambridge, Cambridge University Press.

HAVENS, A. E. 1972. 'Methodological Issues in the Study of Development', *Sociologia Ruralis*, Vol. 12, pp. 252–272.

HIGGINS, J. 1983a. 'Part-time Farming — Its Incidence and Performance', Proceedings of Conference, Dublin, Agricultural Institute, November.

HIGGINS, J. 1983b. 'Comparing the Spending Power of Farm and Non-Farm Households', *Farm and Food Research*, Dublin, An Foras Taluntais. April, pp. 55–56.

KELLEHER, C. 1983. 'Implications of Different Theoretical Approaches for Policy and Interventions', *Irish Journal of Agricultural Economics and Rural Sociology*, Vol. 9, pp. 133–160.

KELLEHER, C. and P. O'HARA 1978. *Adjustment Problems of Low-Income Farmers*, Dublin, Agricultural Institute.

KELLEHER, C. and ANN O'MAHONY 1983. 'Marginalisation in Irish Agriculture: A Study of Low Output Farmers,' paper to Agricultural Economics Society of Ireland, Dublin. November.

KELLEHER, C. and ANN O'MAHONY 1984. *Marginalisation in Irish Agriculture*. Dublin, An Foras Talántais.

LITTON, FRANK, (ed.) 1982. *Unequal Achievement*, Dublin, Institute of Public Administration.

LONG, NORMAN 1977. *An Introduction to the Sociology of Rural Development*, London, Tavistock Publications.

NATIONAL COMMITTEE ON PILOT SCHEMES TO COMBAT POVERTY, 1981. *Final Report*, Dublin.

NEWBY, H., and F. H. BUTTEL 1980. 'Toward a Critical Rural Sociology' in F. H. Buttel and H. Newby, (eds.), *The Rural Sociology of the Advanced Societies*, New York, Croom Helm, pp. 1–35.

NEWMAN, J. (ed.) 1964. *Limerick Rural Survey*, Tipperary, Muintir na Tire.

Ó CEARBHAILL, D. and M. S. Ó CINNÉIDE 1983. *Community Developement in the Killala Area*, Social Sciences Research Centre, Galway University College.

O'CONNOR, J. and M. DALY 1983. *The West Limerick Study*, Limerick, Social Research Centre.

O'MAHONY, ANN 1982. 'Social Service Provision in Low-Income Farming Communities', paper to International Association of Schools of Social Work Research Seminar, University of Sussex, August.

PAHL, R. E. 1966. 'The Rural-Urban Continuum', *Sociologia Ruralis*, Vol. 6, pp. 299–329.

Third Programme: Economic and Social Development, 1969. Dublin, Stationery Office.

TOVEY, HILARY 1982. 'Milking the Farmer? Modernisation and Marginalisation in Irish Dairy Farming' in M. Kelly *et al.* (eds.), *Power, Conflict and Inequality*, Dublin, Turoe Press.

4
Industrialisation, Work and Unemployment

JAMES WICKHAM

This paper introduces some themes from the broad area of industrial sociology. Sociology as a distinct discipline began in the nineteenth century when European social theorists attempted to analyse what they saw as the new industrial society taking shape around them (Kumar 1978). For them this new society was shaped by modern industry, and it was the existence of modern industry that for them distinguished the society in which they were living from all previous societies.

One feature of the new industrial society was the way in which 'work' became separated from other areas of social life. Today most people 'go out to work', and work is something that one does away from home in an office, factory or other 'workplace' during 'working hours'. This rigid division in terms of time and space between work and leisure, work and home, is historically novel. In addition, if work only means an activity done for payment outside the home, then the *economic* importance of domestic work is ignored. Cleaning the house, cooking meals, looking after children are all hardly leisure activities and without them economic life as a whole would be impossible. Although it is increasingly realised that the nature of this domestic work affects work outside the home, industrial sociology usually does not focus on it, just as it also usually excludes agricultural work.

The empirical study of the different situations in which people work really only began in the 1920s, in particular in the USA, where some employers hoped that they could use sociologists and psychologists to suggest ways in which employees could be made to feel more satisfied with their situation. For some time afterwards, industrial sociology remained committed to such a 'consensus' view of society, implicitly assuming that employers and employees shared common interests, so that conflict, including conflict in industry and at work (such as between unions and employers) was seen as an aberration; as a deviation from what normally should occur.

Much recent industrial sociology rejects this approach. It attempts to relate how work is organised, and how people behave 'at work', to social inequality and the conflicts that this tends to produce. Accordingly, the first part of the chapter places work in the Republic of Ireland in the context of inequality between societies. We shall be examining in particular the theory of *dependency*. The second part of the chapter looks at how people are controlled, and this involves discussing the theory of *class conflict*. Discussing people 'at work' makes us consider how they 'got work' — the crucial question of employment in relation to unemployment. The final part of the chapter therefore places work in the context of the *labour market*, and we shall see that the labour market too is shaped by social inequality both between societies and between social classes.

Industrial development

It is common to talk of the Republic of Ireland today as an 'industrialising' society: it is, for example, well known that manufactured goods now comprise a larger share of all exports than do agricultural products, and that industry's share of total GNP has risen in the last 20 years. At a broader level, the Republic of Ireland is also commonly described as a 'modernising' society: our values, our life-styles, our political concerns, are assumed to be becoming more similar to those of the richer and more 'developed' European countries. Such broad changes provide the context within which work occurs and hence they are fundamental to the concerns of industrial sociology. However, within sociology there are several very different ways in which these changes are understood, whether they occur in Ireland or in other societies (McCullagh 1978).

Until recently, sociologists tended to understand changes such as those that have been occurring in the Republic of Ireland in terms of *modernisation theory*. For example, the influential study by the American sociologist Clark Kerr, *Industrialism and Industrial Man* (1973) focusses on the role of industry within the broader process of social modernisation. According to Kerr, once a society begins to industrialise, then what he terms 'the dictates of industrial technology' necessitate that *whatever its initial starting point*, the society becomes more and more similar to other industrial societies. Thus, as societies industrialise their occupational structures become more similar: the types of jobs become more alike, and particular occupations have the same relative importance within each society. All industrial societies have to have managers, white-collar workers and skilled manual workers, and these occupations become more important the more industrialised the society is. Equally, as societies industrialise, people begin to accept this basic division of labour as the only possible one. Social conflict is no longer about the nature of society itself: bureaucratic bargaining replaces ideological struggle.

Such an argument relies on three assumptions which many people (both sociologists and non-sociologists) would consider self-evident. (1) The theory rests on technological determinism, that is, it assumes that technology by itself causes particular social changes. (2) It assumes convergence, claiming that as societies industrialise they necessarily become more similar. (3) It assumes consensus, i.e. that all the major groups in a society share common interests.

However, these assumptions are in fact challenged by another approach within sociology, that of dependency theory. Whereas modernisation theory began in the 'developed' USA, dependency theory emerged in 'underdeveloped' Latin America. Writers such as Frank (1972) argued that the underdevelopment of Latin American societies had to be understood in their international context. Rather than underdevelopment being a stage in the development of all societies towards industrialisation, it was a situation that the developed societies (termed 'core' or 'metropolitan' societies) imposed on the underdeveloped societies (termed 'peripheral' or 'satellite' societies). The pattern of trade between peripheral and core societies, in which the former exported raw materials and agricultural products to the latter, did not derive simply from comparative advantages as conventional economic theory claimed, but from a division of labour which the dominant core societies had imposed on the dominated peripheral societies to their own advantage. Hence, whereas modernisation theory considers societies as isolated units, dependency theory stresses that a peripheral society is shaped by its relationships to other societies — relationships which involve unequal power.

Dependency theory initially assumed that no economic development was possible in a peripheral society so long as it remained dominated by core societies. Subsequent versions of the theory recognised that, especially because of manufacturing investment by foreign multi-national corporations (MNCs), some development was occurring in the 1960s in some dependent societies. Writers such as Cardoso (1972) termed this form of industrialisation 'dependent industrialisation', for the industrialisation was of a different form to that which the developed core societies (such as the USA) had already undergone. The MNCs ensured that only the least skilled and lowest paid manufacturing activities were located in the peripheral society and that much economic control remained outside the national boundaries. Instead of societies 'converging' as they industrialised, dependent industrialisation meant that metropolitan and satellite societies would remain different in structure. Furthermore, far from these developments being caused by technology, most dependency theorists see the sort of technology that is adopted in a peripheral society as the result of the society's relationships to other more powerful and dominant societies. Finally, all versions of dependency theory also stress the existence of different and conflicting interests both between core and peripheral societies and within peripheral societies.

In many ways each of the two versions of dependency theory appear to describe different periods of the Republic's experience (Wickham 1984). From the 1920s until the 1950s, despite the achievement of political independence from Britain and the subsequent (and not entirely unsuccessful) attempts at industrialisation of the early Fianna Fáil governments, the Republic of Ireland remained an almost classic example of a dependent society in the sense outlined by Frank. Exports were mostly of unprocessed agricultural produce (in particular cattle exported 'on the hoof') to the British market. Since the ending of protectionism in 1958, however, manufactured exports have become more important (Table 1) and export markets have diversified (Table 2). Yet this industrialisation seems in turn to be a clear example of dependent industrialisation.

As is well known, over a third of the entire workforce in manufacturing industry today is employed by foreign-owned firms. The first firms that set up plants in the Republic of Ireland were largely from European countries and were attracted above all by cheap labour. US firms followed, attempting to gain access to

Table 1: **Composition of exports: Republic of Ireland 1958–1984**

	1958 %	1984 %
Live Animals	37.3	2.9
Other Food	30.7	20.3
Manufactured Goods	17.1	63.2
Others	14.8	13.6
Total[1]	99.9	100.0

Source: Central Statistics Office, *Trade Statistics of Ireland*

Table 2: **Destination of exports: Republic of Ireland 1959-1984**

	1959 %	1984 %
Great Britain	60.4	27.8
Northern Ireland	14.6	6.6
Rest of EEC 9	6.0	33.7
USA	7.8	9.7
Rest	11.2	22.2
Total	100.0	100.0

Source: Central Statistics Office, *Trade Statistics of Ireland*
[1]Total percentage figures in the Tables do not always add up to 100 per cent because of rounding decimal points.

the EEC market by locating the final stage of their manufacturing processes within the Republic. For both groups the tax concessions and government grants on offer were of course also important. Although these foreign firms are concentrated in the 'high technology' industries such as chemicals and electronics, this hardly means that all employees are skilled. More than ten years ago the paradox of industrial development in the Republic of Ireland was pointed out: expansion was concentrated in science-based industries, but these used little research and development within the country (Cooper and Whelan 1973).

Industrialisation has undoubtedly increased the importance of skilled occupations in the Republic's industry as a whole. However, the occupational structure of much of this industry clearly results from the particular role of the Irish factory in an international division of labour within the MNC: only the less skilled operations are moved to Ireland, leaving the more skilled activities in the 'home' country.

This pattern is clearly shown in the case of the electronics industry in the Republic of Ireland. Here most workers are employed by companies which have their Research and Development activities located in their home country, usually the USA:

very little research and development is carried out within the Republic of Ireland (Cogan and O'Brien 1983). Comparing columns (2) and (3) of Table 3 shows that the Republic's electronics industry has proportionately more employees with professional or technical qualifications (the categories 'Profes-

Table 3: **Occupational structure of US electronics industry, Irish electronics industry, all Irish industry (various years) (Irish Republic)**

	US Electronics (1980) (1) %	Irish Electronics (1981) (2) %	All Irish Industry (1976) (3) %
Managers	11	6.4	6.5
Professionals	17	5.3	1.3
Administrators	na	3.9	5.2
Technicians	11	7.8	1.6
Supervisors	na	5.1	4.7
Sales	1	na	na
Clerical	12	7.5	7.7
Craft Workers	10	3.1	12.6
Apprentices	na	—	4.2
Operatives etc[1]	32	57.4	56.3
Labourers etc[2]	4	3.2	na
Service Workers	2	na	na
Total	100	99.7	100.1
N	1,572,800	11,338	220,500

[1]'Operatives' (USA); 'Non-Craft Production Workers' (Irish Electronics); 'Other Workers' (All Irish Industry).
[2]'Labourers' (USA); 'Others' (Irish Electronics).
Source: US Electronics: *Global Electronics Information Newsletter*, September 1982; Irish Electronics: Postal Survey, 1981: All Irish Industry: AnCO, Research and Planning Division, *Manpower Survey 1976*.

sionals' and 'Technicians' in the Table) than does Irish industry as a whole. However, comparing columns (2) and (3) of the same Table also shows that there are proportionately fewer employees in these categories in Irish electronics than in the electronics industry in the USA. Equally, over half of those working in the Irish electronics industry are semi-skilled assemblers and operatives, as against only 32 per cent of those in the US industry. This is hardly surprising, because US companies locate plants in the Republic of Ireland to carry out the final (and less skilled) stages of production here in order that their products can then be sold on the European market. The growth of an industry like electronics does not necessarily mean that the Republic of Ireland is 'catching up' with more developed countries.

Dependent industrialisation has involved other changes in the structure of Irish industry. Firstly, it has involved a restructuring of ownership. Many home-owned manufacturing firms started in the 1930s, when government policy attempted to develop industry by building up the domestic market behind tariff barriers. Today most of such protectionism has ended, particularly because of membership of the EEC, and indigenous firms have to compete on the home market with foreign firms which have often larger resources and better and cheaper products. Many are unable to compete. Despite popular belief in 'fly by night multi-nationals', over the last decade it has probably been people working for indigenous firms who have been more likely to lose their jobs.

Secondly, dependent industrialisation has restructured the location of industry. One inadvertent result of protectionism was to concentrate industry even more in Dublin and the East Coast, since firms needed to be near to Britain from where they were importing their supplies. From the 1960s, however, manufacturing industry has become more dispersed around the country, partly because government grants have been more favourable in the less developed areas, while transport costs have become less important. Probably another reason for the growth of industry away from the traditional centres has been that firms have wished to avoid Dublin with its historic tradition of trade union organisation. Such changes have meant that, although overall (until the beginning of the current recession) more jobs have been gained than have been lost in industry, different groups of people have been involved.

'Dependent industrialisation' focusses our attention on the structure of industry, but the occupational structure of a society involves far more than just people working in industry. For example, in the Republic of Ireland today about 260,000 people are employed in the state sector, as opposed to 210,000 in manufacturing industry. Over the last fifty years the most fundamental change in the occupational structure as a whole has been the falling number of people who gain their livelihood from their own (small) property, working for themselves or for their family on a farm, shop or small business (Rottman and Hannan 1982, p. 48). Thus while in 1926 such people comprised just under a half of the workforce, in 1979 they amounted to less than a quarter. Equally, the fastest growing occupations over the same period have been skilled manual workers, white-collar and professional employees.

These changes *are* common to all industrial societies, and so they might appear to confirm an argument such as that of Kerr with which this section began: in this sense at any rate, as societies industrialise they become more similar. Nonetheless, Table 4 shows that in terms of social structure, Ireland remains most similar not to the more developed societies such as Britain or Germany, but to those countries such as Greece, Spain and Portugal which have also been described as part of the 'periphery' of Europe (Seers 1979). Furthermore, there is some evidence that white-collar employment has been growing more slowly in Ireland than in more advanced countries such as the USA (Bannon 1982). In these terms, far from 'catching-up', the Republic is falling further behind. In conclusion, therefore, even when we broaden our perspective from industry to the wider occupational structure, some of the fundamental assumptions of modernisation theory do not appear to hold: industrialisation in Ireland does not involve convergence.

Table 4: **Occupational structure: selected EEC countries (1981)**

	Employers and Self-Employed as % of Total Workforce	Agricultural Workforce as % of Total Workforce
Republic of Ireland	21.8	17.2
UK	9.4	2.6
West Germany	8.6	4.8
Italy	23.3	11.0
Greece	38.0	30.1
EEC 10	13.8	7.2

Note: 'Total Workforce' here refers to women and men with *full-time* occupations.
Source: Eurostat, *Labour Force Sample Survey 1981*.

Conflict and control at work

When there is a strike or a work-to-rule in industry, it is often blamed on a 'failure of communications'. Such an explanation is a practical example of sociological consensus theory, for it implies that underneath the conflict there lies a basic consensus of interests and values. If both sides were reasonable and listened to each other, so the argument goes, then they would be able to come to some sensible agreement.

There are two problems with this view. Firstly, in any given situation the interests of employers and employees conflict. While both sides certainly have an interest in the survival of the enterprise, how its profits are distributed and how work within it is organised (to name only the most obvious issues) are matters on which both sides have differing interests. Hence, if employers and employees rationally pursue their own interests, then there will be conflict between them. To blame conflict on a failure of communications is therefore as absurd as to say that if only each of the two competing teams at a football match could see the other's point of view, they would stop playing against each other!

Secondly, as an individual, an employee is almost powerless in relation to his or her employer. This *individual* powerlessness is of course the reason why employees combine together in trade unions. Yet although trade unions can restrict the power of employers, ultimately within a private enterprise system the final decision-making power must remain with the employer. The two sides are not equal.

Much modern industrial sociology therefore starts from the assumption that 'Employees and employers are enmeshed in economic relations which by their very nature contain powerful oppositional elements.' (Hill 1981, p. 2). This is not to deny that both sides also have interests in common, but it is to deny that there can ever be a complete and voluntary consensus between them.

Once this 'conflict' perspective is adopted, one has then to ask how it is that these conflicts of interest do not in fact usually lead to actual overt conflict. The answer is usually seen in terms of management's success in enforcing control. Much discussion of this topic derives from the work of Braverman (1974), who argued that the key method of managerial control in a capitalist society is what he termed 'deskilling.' According to Braverman, employers in a capitalist society try to organise the 'labour process' (roughly the total activity of work) so that work becomes as simple and as routine as possible. If only a relatively small number of employees are skilled, then wage costs will be lower. Less obviously, but more fundamentally, concentrating all skill and knowledge in the hands of management means that workers become interchangeable, easily replaceable, and above all, have little basis on which to resist management.

Braverman's argument challenges the idea that technology is neutral. The type of technology that is introduced, like the organisation of work in general, is shaped by this basic need to control the workforce: capitalist technology de-skills workers.

According to Braverman, some groups of workers have skills which enable them to control the labour process. He sees technological innovation as a way in which managers impose their control in these situations. For example, the introduction of computerised typesetting in the newspaper industry can be seen as a way in which employers are attempting to weaken the powerful print workers and their unions (Cockburn 1983). Whereas technologies such as numerically controlled machine tools could have been designed in such a way that they would have enhanced workers' skills, the logic of capitalist industry has ensured that they replaced skilled workers with semi-skilled operatives (Noble 1979).

While Braverman's work has been very influential, it has also been widely criticised (Wood and Kelly 1982). Firstly, it concentrates solely on changes in the manufacture of existing products, ignoring the fact that the production of new products (or the development of totally new ways of making existing ones) may well require new skills (Gershuny 1978, p. 124). It is only when this is realised that one can explain how, despite Braverman's claim that capitalist technology produces more semi-skilled workers and fewer skilled workers and technical employees, it is the latter groups that have been increasing the fastest, as we have already seen is the case in the Republic of Ireland.

Secondly, the same technology can be used in different ways and with differing mixes of skilled and unskilled workers. Thus, Hartmann *et al.* (1983) have shown that in West German engineering factories craft workers are trained to program computerised machine tools, whereas in Britain, because managers trust their workers less, programming and operating are more likely to be completely separated jobs. In other words, the German workers are being 'reskilled', the British ones 'de-skilled', but by the same technology.

Thirdly, control can involve much more than merely the immediate organisation of work. One concern of management is often to ensure that employees identify with the firm enough to act 'responsibly' on their own initiative without direct supervision: something that may be required in many jobs which are in a technical sense almost completely unskilled. Thus in many electronics factories in the Republic of Ireland assembly work requires little technical training, but nonetheless the firms prefer employees to have good educational qualifications and to have undergone relatively extensive training. Such selection procedures, although not technically necessary, ensure that these firms acquire 'responsible' workers (Murray and Wickham 1983).

Fourthly, Braverman fails to consider the way in which workers resist managerial control. Such resistance can delay the introduction of new technology and work organisation; it can force management to change its strategy of control. This resistance is almost inherent in the employment relationship. Many of the informal practices of shopfloor workers which to management often appear as 'laziness' or 'bloody-mindedness' appear quite rational once the fundamental conflict of interest between employers and employees is recognised (Roy 1952). In terms of this informal resistance there is an important difference between male and female workers. For men the culture of resistance of the shopfloor is often the basis for their more formal trade union organisation (Willis 1979). However, as Harris (1982) has shown for women workers in a North Mayo factory, given both the way they see their employment and the fact that trade unions remain largely run by men for men, this informal resistance rarely translates into organised trade union activity. The discussion of control suggests that industrial conflict occurs where management control over employees is relatively weak. The absence of such conflict does not mean that employers and employees share common values, let alone common interests, but merely that management is able (in various ways) to *successfully enforce its control*. For example, in the Republic most strikes occur not within the foreign-owned sector of manufacturing industry, but in the public sector and in Irish-owned enterprises.

As we have seen, much foreign-owned industry in the Republic of Ireland is located away from the centres of traditional trade union activity, so that workers have little trade union experience. Even when the plants (like most electronics ones) are in urban areas, the workers themselves tend to be young and never to have been trade union members. In addition, in many of these companies the trade union organisation is set up in agreement with the firm before the factory opens, so workers have little active involvement in the union. At the same time, many of the more recently arrived foreign firms have a company policy to actively oppose trade union organisation (Murray and Wickham 1982).

By contrast, it is politically difficult for state employees to be openly prevented from joining a trade union. In the state sector, as in those indigenous firms that still have a protected market, many jobs are effectively permanent or at least shielded from the direct effects of competition. Here strikes will cost workers money, but not jeopardise their jobs.

There are two other less obvious reasons why industrial conflict is likely in the state sector. Firstly, for several decades the governments in the Republic of Ireland have had a more or less explicit wages policy, laying down the level of wage increases that they consider desirable in a particular year (Roche 1982). While individual private employers may conclude higher wage settlements with their own employees, the state as an employer usually enforces its own wage policy inflexibly, thus stimulating conflict.

Secondly, the fact that state employment is sheltered from the market also means that management is under less pressure to settle disputes. Bargaining both over wages and issues such as discipline can drag on indefinitely and so frustration mounts (Sweeney 1980). By contrast, in private firms which are explicitly opposed to trade union organisation, personnel managers in particular have to be receptive to the complaints of individual workers, so that they can ensure that grievances do not build up (Wallace 1982). An anti-union management in the private sector is therefore often much less remote from its employees than a pro-union management in the state sector.

The importance of state employment in the Republic of Ireland is one reason why proportionately more employees are organised in trade unions here than in most other European countries. In turn, the expansion of state employment can in part be explained by trade union pressure. Governments have attempted to restrain wages by involving the leaderships of the trade unions firstly in the institutions of economic decision-making, and then, during the 1970s, in the determination of wages policy itself (Roche 1982). As a compensation for accepting wage restraint, the trade unions sought an expansion of state expenditure and employment. They justified this expansion through the benefits provided to trade unionists by state services such as health, education and social welfare. However, much state expenditure in these areas disproportionately benefits the better off groups in society rather than those trade unionists who will have to pay for it through PAYE. Indeed, a fundamental reason for trade union support of increased state expenditure is the simple fact that the trade union movement is heavily influenced by state employees, who now comprise about half of all trade union members (Raftery 1982).

This section began by arguing that there are fundamental conflicts of interest between employers and employees. To a certain extent these conflicts of interest can be seen as conflicts of interest between different social classes. However, we have also seen that whether these conflicts of interest actually 'surface' as overt conflicts depends on the effectiveness of managerial control. The importance and form of state employment in Ireland means that, paradoxically, the conflict between employers and employees which is inherent in a capitalist society does not occur primarily within private employment.

The labour market and unemployment

Today in the Republic of Ireland more people are officially registered as unemployed (231,026 in July 1985; 17.4 per cent of the labour force) than are employed in all of manufacturing industry. This reminds us that work occurs in the context of the labour market. In the labour market there is a 'demand' for labour from employers (they look for people for particular jobs) and a 'supply' of labour from potential employees (they offer themselves for particular jobs). This part of the chapter will see how different sorts of people are recruited for different sorts of jobs (the demand side of the labour market); how different groups of people become available for work (the supply side of the labour market); how women and men are segregated into different jobs; and how some people get no jobs at all.

Terms like 'labour market', 'demand for labour' or 'supply of labour' sound more appropriate to economics than sociology. However, industrial sociologists (like many economists) have been interested in the way in which the labour market is not, and indeed cannot be, a pure market. This is clear if we look at how people are recruited into jobs. Talk of 'skill' and 'qualifications' assumes that what employers are looking for is what is explicitly taught in educational and training processes — namely manual dexterity, technical skills and technological knowledge. Yet this is clearly not all that is involved.

The previous part of the chapter showed that because employers have to control employees, they necessarily seek to recruit what they term 'responsible' employees. As writers such as Offe (1976) have argued, employers look not so much for the skills or even knowledge that people have, but for the sort of person that people are. Yet it would be difficult for an employer to explicitly advertise: 'Obedient Workers Wanted!' Hence, so the argument goes, firms look for qualifications because they consider them to be signs of an individual's personality ('if you can stick school long enough to get the Leaving, then you must be a reliable sort of person').

In much the same way, educational qualifications are also often used to screen applicants for jobs. When there is widespread unemployment, people 'trade down' and accept jobs for which they would have been previously over-qualified, thus ensuring that those with few or no educational qualifications have even less chance of getting a job at all. This process can be clearly seen in Table 5. As unemployment rose from 1981 onwards those with the Leaving Certificate were more and more likely to end up in manual jobs.

Perhaps the most important way in which talking of 'the labour market' is misleading is that there is not one labour mar-

Table 5: **School leavers with leaving certificate in full-time employment, 1981 and 1984**

	Females		Males	
	1981 %	1984 %	1981 %	1984 %
Occupations:				
Managerial/ Professional	17.8	15.0	17.7	6.7
Clerical	64.2	34.2	28.5	11.8
Service Occupations	13.1	34.4	14.4	23.5
Agricultural	0.1	0.8	7.0	7.0
Skilled and Semi- skilled Manual	4.4	14.4	29.7	48.9
Other Manual	—	1.3	2.8	2.0
Total	99.6	100.1	100.1	99.9
N	12,600	8,500	7,800	5,200

Note: The figures show the jobs in May/June of each year for those who left school in the previous year.
Source: National Manpower Service, *School-Leavers Surveys*.

ket. Many people have gained their jobs by being promoted within the organisation for which they are already working. This 'internal' labour market can be distinguished from the 'external' labour market, in which recruitment is from individuals not already employed by the organisation. Sociological analysis of the labour market links this division between 'internal' and 'external' labour markets to the wider conflicts of social interest which can be seen to shape the labour market as a whole.

The jobs that are available in the economy can be broadly divided into two sorts. In the 'primary' labour market jobs are relatively secure; recruitment is largely from those people already employed within the organisation; and promotion to higher jobs is possible. Even in the USA, where the labour market is believed to be so much more 'flexible' (i.e. it is easier to dis- miss people) than in Europe, this is the situation not just for many white-collar workers, but also for many manual workers who have skilled jobs in large manufacturing companies (Doeringer and Piore 1971; Piore 1985). By contrast, 'second- ary' labour market jobs are relatively insecure and do not lead to promotion. Hence, for someone in a job in the secondary labour market, the only other jobs available will be other equally dead- end jobs.

There is considerable discussion about exactly how labour markets become divided in this way (Rubery 1978). In general, US writers have tended to stress the role of employers, arguing that they divide workers on the basis of race and gender in order to weaken their bargaining power. European writers, perhaps reflecting the different European situation, have tended to argue that some workers (usually white, male and 'skilled' ones) not only benefit from a divided labour market, but actively con- tribute to creating it through their trade unions.

The division between primary and secondary labour markets explains much of the difference between women's work and men's work. Despite equal opportunity legislation, women and men usually do different jobs. Dual labour market theory argues that direct discrimination is a relatively minor cause of these differences. Far more important is the fact that women and men are concentrated in different labour market sectors (Barron and Norris 1976). Part of the reason for this becomes clear when we now turn to the supply of labour and see how men and women participate in the labour market in different ways.

For much of their lives, most women are likely to be respons- ible for 'domestic labour' in the household in which they live: it is women, not men, who do the cooking, clean the house, and above all look after both young children and older relatives. Anyone who has these obligations cannot really participate in the primary labour market, where jobs are 'full time', that is, or- ganised in terms of hours that suit men. To take just one example, 'normal working hours' include the times when children have to be fetched from school! At its simplest, so long as men manage to get out of doing a fair share of the work in the home, there is precious little chance that women will get a fair share of the good jobs outside the home. Women, in other words, are pushed towards jobs in the secondary labour market.

These constraints on women's participation in the labour market ensure that an increase in the proportion of women at work is not by itself a move towards equality. For example, in Britain a majority of all adult women are now in the labour force, and this was not the case fifty years ago. However, this increase has been almost entirely in part-time work by older married women; the proportion of women who are in full-time employment has hardly risen at all (Martin and Roberts 1984, p. 121).

Many people believe that as the Republic of Ireland has become more 'modern', so more and more women have gone out to work. Yet this is a fallacy. Firstly, unlike Britain and the USA, there has been no major increase in recent decades in the proportion of women who work: in 1951 about 30 per cent of all women were recorded as being in the labour force (Rudd 1982); in 1983 this 'participation rate' was precisely 31.5 per cent (CSO 1984). Secondly, women in the Republic of Ireland remain much less likely than women in Britain or the USA to return to the labour market after having had children. One obvious explanation for this would be the large family size in the Republic, but as the graph (Figure 1) shows, the same pattern occurs in countries such as West Germany where family size is far lower than here. It is unclear exactly what does determine these differences in women's labour market participation, but it is clear that it does not automatically increase with 'modernisation' (Hakim 1979). For whatever reason, the labour force in the Republic of Ireland consists disproportionately of single women and married men.

Women and men thus participate in the labour market in different ways. This results in *occupational segregation,* that is, women and men tend to be in different occupations ('women's work' and 'men's work'). Table 6 shows that in the Republic of Ireland women are disproportionately concentrated in profes-

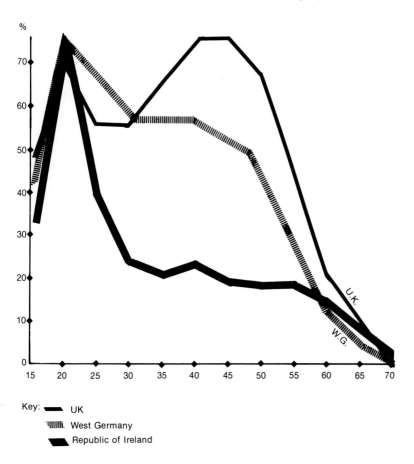

Key: ━━ UK
'‖‖‖‖ West Germany
◼ Republic of Ireland

**Fig. 1. Women's participation by age group in the labour
force ('enlarged concept'),[1] 1981.**

Source: Eurostat, *Labour Force Sample Survey 1981*, Table 17.
[1]*Note:* The 'labour force' is sometimes defined as all those with a full-time job, or
who are unemployed. However, the 'enlarged concept' defines the labour force
to also include all those who sometimes work for money (whether full or part-
time), or those who are looking for some form of paid employment.

Table 6: **Women and men at work by occupation, Republic of Ireland 1961-1983**

| | 1961 | | 1983 | |
	Women %	Men %	Women %	Men %
Farmers	10.2	22.2	2.2	16.2
Other Agricultural Workers	4.6	21.0	4.0	5.6
Manufacturing Workers	13.8	12.5	9.5	19.9
Building & Construction Workers	0.1	2.6	0.1	5.1
Supervisors of Manual Workers	0.3	0.9	0.6	1.8
Transport, Communication & Distribution Workers	3.8	8.1	3.1	9.0
Labourers & Unskilled Workers	1.1	10.7	0.3	4.9
Clerical Workers	16.3	3.9	28.2	4.7
Service Workers	30.7	7.7	23.3	10.9
Proprietors & Managers	4.3	3.6	3.0	4.3
Technical, Administrative & Professional Workers	14.7	5.8	25.2	15.8
Others	0.0	1.0	0.4	1.7
Total	99.9	100.0	99.9	99.9
N (000)	286.6	821.5	346.2	779.1
Segregation Index:	58.4		53.8	

Note: The 'Segregation Index' is calculated on the basis of a more detailed list of occupations than is shown here.
Source: Blackwell (1982), Table 4.8. Central Statistics Office, *1983 Labour Force Survey*.

sional, clerical and service work. By contrast, men are more evenly spread across the occupations. One often unnoticed result of this is that men are more likely to work only with other men than women are to work only with women: many men work in occupations where there are no women whatsoever.

The extent of this 'horizontal segregation' can be calculated from published census results and expressed in an index of occupational segregation. This is a single figure which shows the extent of change that would be needed if men and women were to be equally distributed across the occupations. It is therefore a simple way of assessing the extent to which women have achieved equality with men in the world of work: if women had gained equality with men, then in any one occupation there would be the same proportion of women as in the labour force as a whole.

For Britain, Hakim (1979) has shown that there was little change in occupational segregation from 1901 through to 1971; during the 1970s segregation was reduced slightly, but by the end of the decade, probably because of the onset of the recession, the extent of segregation had returned to that of 1971. For the Republic of Ireland Blackwell (1982, p. 52) has calculated that the overall index of occupational segregation increased slightly from 58.4 per cent in 1961 to 59.4 per cent in 1971, but that it then declined; Table 6 shows that this trend continued to 1983.

This improvement in the situation in the Republic of Ireland is certainly encouraging, but the overall index of occupational segregation is a simple and crude measure. It says nothing, for example, about the extent to which women are concentrated in the lower ranks of any one occupation ('vertical segregation'). Thus, Table 6 shows that nearly a quarter of all women (23.8 per cent) at work are in the category 'professional and technical workers'. This includes both national school teachers and nurses, who are largely women, and university lecturers and doctors, who are largely men. There are no systematic calculations of the extent of such vertical segregation available for the Republic of Ireland, but it is worth noting that Hakim found for the UK that from 1901 to 1971 the extent of vertical segregation had increased at the same time as horizontal segregation had decreased. In other words, women have gained access to more areas of work, but because few of them can work full-time over their whole working life, they are locked into the lower levels of the different occupations.

Both the supply and demand for labour are therefore not only more complex and differentiated than a simple notion of the labour market would allow, but they also often do not balance: the supply of labour exceeds the demand for labour, and there is unemployment. Here we can return to the situation of peripheral countries. One distinguishing feature of the periphery of Europe is that it has higher (male) unemployment than core countries. At any level of international economic activity, the unemployment level in West Germany will be significantly lower than in the Republic of Ireland. This is partly because peripheral countries have a low demand for labour (they create fewer new jobs), and partly because they have a higher supply of labour (a higher birth rate, and a smaller proportion of the younger age groups in full-time education).

This in turn means that peripheral European countries are countries that people leave: emigration is as central to the history of Greece or Southern Italy as it is to that of the Republic of Ireland. In the contemporary recession, however, emigration from the Republic of Ireland is also a middle-class phenomenon: while unskilled workers are not welcome anywhere, the 'Irish brain drain' is significant.

Many people who have very marketable educational qualifications emigrate shortly after they finish their education. In the recent past this was particularly the case for medical students; at the moment it is particularly true of engineering students. The latter group currently have the highest rate of emigration of all students in the Republic of Ireland (HEA 1983). It has been argued that this over-production of educationally qualified people is typical of dependent countries (Irizarry 1980); furthermore, that it is one way in which both developed societies exploit less developed societies and better off individuals exploit poorer individuals. The Republic of Ireland's population as a whole pays the taxes which subsidise our higher education. Yet if the people produced by this educational system emigrate to earn high salaries in richer countries, then any benefit from their education goes to them and to the countries where they settle, and not to those who have actually paid for it.

A sociological perspective on the labour market can also show the fallacies of some widespread contemporary beliefs about unemployment in the Republic of Ireland today. In particular, it is often argued that unemployment benefits are too high and so are destroying the incentive to work; furthermore, it is also often claimed that many unemployed are working illegally. Such arguments are not completely absurd, but they involve considerable over-simplification and exaggeration. Firstly, they ignore the fact that officially registered unemployment also under-estimates the extent of unemployment. Many people, above all many women, do not register themselves as looking for work but would accept employment if any were available. Secondly, as we have already seen, work is central to people's identity in our society. For most people to decide to be voluntarily and permanently unemployed would be to undermine their self-esteem: some people may feel that they would be better off on the dole rather than working, but it is unlikely that many of them act on such a straightforward economic calculation. Thirdly, while an unknown number of those who are formally unemployed are certainly earning money illegally, such jobs in the 'black economy' are usually a poor substitute for legal jobs: by definition they involve no statutory rights and no job security. Recent British research shows that black economy jobs taken by redundant workers were less skilled and less well-paid than the jobs they had lost (Lee and Morris, 1983). Fourthly, evidence for Britain at least suggests that in recent years the growth of unemployment has contributed to a decline in the black economy, if only because people have less money to spend on having work done for them, even if illegally (Pahl 1984, p. 93). Finally, jobs in the black economy, like jobs in the legal economy, are not equal: the skilled tradesman doing 'nixers' is in a very different situation from someone who does the occasional labouring job 'on the side'. Like jobs in the legal economy, access to black economy jobs requires skills and contacts which are unequally distributed.

Partly overlapping with the black economy as an option for the unemployed is the question of self-employment, which may or may not be legal. In all industrialised countries this has been widely put forward as one way in which unemployment can be tackled. Historically there is nothing new about self-employment growing at a time of mass unemployment: in Germany in the 1930s, for example, unemployed workers frequently attempted to open small shops and start other small businesses. While government policy stresses starting one's own business as a possible solution, this again ignores that access to the resources needed for such activity is also unequally distributed. While the media may make much of the success stories of individual new entrepreneurs, what receives much less publicity is the very high failure rate of new businesses. Equally, the extent of self-employment, like the black economy, is related to the wider social structure: dependent countries like the Republic of Ireland tend to have both a larger black economy and a larger self-employed sector than core countries — a fact which should challenge the frequent claim that this is some golden route to prosperity.

References

BANNON, M. 1982. 'The Information Society: Implications for regional development', M. Bannon and U. Barry (eds.), *Information Technology: Impact on the Way of Life*, Dublin, Tycooly, pp. 233-241.

BARRON, R. D. and G. M. NORRIS 1976. 'Sexual Divisions and the Dual Labour Market', in D. L. Barker and S. Allen (eds.), *Dependence and Exploitation in Work and Marriage*, London, Longman, pp. 47-69.

BLACKWELL, JOHN 1982. 'Digest of Statistics of Women in the Labour Force and Related Subjects', Dublin, Employment Equality Agency (mimeo).

BRAVERMAN, HARRY 1974. *Labor and Monopoly Capital: The Degradation of Work in the Twentieth Century*, New York and London, Monthly Review.

CSO — CENTRAL STATISTICS OFFICE 1984. 1983 Labour Force Survey, Dublin, Stationery Office, Pl. 2660.

CARDOSO, F. H. 1972. 'Dependent Capitalist Development in Latin America', *New Left Review* No. 74 (July/August), pp. 83-95.

COCKBURN, CYNTHIA 1983. *Brothers: Male Dominance and Technological Change*, London, Pluto.

COGAN, D. J. and RONAN O'BRIEN 1983. 'The Irish Electronics Sector: Technical manpower as an indicator of structure and sophistication', IBAR — Journal of Irish Business and Administrative Research, Vol. 5, No. 1 (April), pp. 3-11.

COOPER, C. and N. WHELAN 1973. *Science, Technology and Industry in Ireland*, Dublin, National Science Council.

DOERINGER, PETER B. and MICHAEL PIORE 1971. *Internal Labor Markets and Manpower Analysis*, Lexington, Mass., Heath.

FRANK, A. G. 1972. *Lumpenbourgeoisie, Lumpendevelopment*, New York and London, Monthly Review Press.

GERSHUNY, JONATHAN 1978. *After Industrial Society? The Emerging Self-Service Economy*, London, Macmillan.

HEA — HIGHER EDUCATION AUTHORITY 1983. *First Destina-*

tion of Award Recipients in Higher Education 1982: A composite report, Dublin, Higher Education Authority.

HAKIM, CATHERINE 1979. 'Occupational Segregation', London, Department of Employment, Research Paper No. 9.

HARRIS, LORELEI 1983. 'Industrialisation, Women and Working Class Politics in the West of Ireland'. Capital and Class, No. 19 (Spring), pp. 100–117.

HARTMANN, G., I. NICHOLAS, A. SORGE and M. WARNER 1983. 'Computerised Machine Tools, Manpower Consequences and Skill Utilisation: A Study of British and West German Manufacturing Firms', British Journal of Industrial Relations, Vol. 21, No. 2 (July), pp. 221–233.

HILL, STEPHEN 1981. Competition and Control at Work: The new industrial sociology, London, Heinemann.

IRIZARRY, R. 1980. 'Over-education and Unemployment in the Third World: The paradoxes of dependent industrialization', Comparative Education Review, Vol. 24, No. 3, pp. 338–352.

KERR, CLARK et al. 1973. Industrialism and Industrial Man (first published 1960), Harmondsworth, Penguin.

KUMAR, KRISHAN 1978. Prophecy and Progress: The sociology of industrial and post-industrial society, Harmondsworth, Penguin.

LEE, R. M. and L. MORRIS 1983. 'Informal Relations in the Job Search Behaviour of Redundant Workers', Paper read at Annual Conference of the British Sociological Association, Cardiff.

MARTIN, JEAN and CERIDWEN ROBERTS 1984. Women and Employment: A Lifetime Perspective – The report of the 1980 DE/OPCS Women and Employment Survey, London, HMSO.

McCULLAGH, CIARAN 1978. 'Development and Underdevelopment: A critical assessment of three approaches', in Proceedings of the Fifth Annual Conference of the SAI, Queen's University of Belfast, Department of Social Studies, pp. 56–64.

MURRAY, PETER and JAMES WICKHAM 1982. 'Technocratic Ideology and the Reproduction of Inequality: The case of the electronics industry in the Republic of Ireland' in G. Day et al. (eds.), Diversity and Decomposition in the Labour Market, Aldershot, Gower, pp. 179–210.

MURRAY, PETER and JAMES WICKHAM 1983. 'Technical Training and Technical Knowledge in an Irish Electronics Factory', in G. Winch (ed.), Information Technology in Manufacturing Processes, London, Rossendale, pp. 94–111.

NOBLE, DAVID F. 1979. 'Social Choice in Machine Design: The case of automatically controlled machine tools', in A. Zimbalist (ed.), Case Studies on the Labor Process, London and New York, Monthly Review Press, pp. 18–50.

OFFE, CLAUS 1976. Industry and Inequality, London, Edward Arnold.

PAHL, R. E. 1984. Divisions of Labour, Oxford, Basil Blackwell.

PIORE, MICHAEL 1985. 'Labour

Mobility: The US can be inflexible, too', *Financial Times* (8 May).

RAFTERY, JAMES 1982. 'Patterns of Taxation and Public Expenditure: Towards a corporation approach', in M. Kelly *et al* (eds.), *Power, Conflict and Inequality*, Dublin, Turoe, pp. 131–146.

ROCHE, BILL 1982. 'Social Partnership and Political Control: State strategy and industrial relations in Ireland', in M. Kelly *et al*. (eds.), *Power, Conflict and Inequality*, Dublin, Turoe, pp. 44–67.

ROTTMAN, DAVID and HANNAN, DAMIAN 1982. *The Distribution of Income in the Republic of Ireland: A study in social class and family cycle inequalities*, Dublin, Economic and Social Research Institute.

ROY, DONALD 1952. 'Quota Restriction and Goldbricking in a Machine Shop,' *American Journal of Sociology* Vol. 57 (March), pp. 427–442.

RUBERY, JILL 1978. 'Structured Labour Markets, Worker Organisation and Low Pay', *Cambridge Journal of Economics* Vol. 2, No. 1, pp. 17–36.

RUDD, JOY 1982. 'On the Margins of the Power Elite: Women in the Upper Echelons', in M. Kelly *et al*. (eds.), *Power, Conflict and Inequality*, Dublin, Turoe Press, pp. 159–170.

SEERS, DUDLEY 1979. 'The Periphery of Europe', in D. Seers, B. Schaffer and M.-L. Kiljunen (eds.), *Under-Developed Europe: Studies in Core-Periphery Relations*, Sussex, The Harvester Press, pp. 3–34.

SWEENEY, PAT 1980. 'Industrial Relations: Realities', in D. Nevin (ed.), *Trade Unions and Change in Irish Society*, Dublin and Cork, Mercier, pp. 116–130.

WALLACE, JOE 1982. 'Industrial Relations in Limerick City and Environs', (Employment Research Programme: Vol. 3), Limerick, National Institute for Higher Education.

WICKHAM, JAMES 1984, 'Dependence and State Structure', in O. Höll (ed.), *Small States in Europe and Dependence*, Vienna, Braumueller, pp. 164–183.

WILLIS, PAUL 1979. 'Shop Floor Culture, Masculinity and the Wage Form', in J. Clarke *et al*. (eds.), *Working Class Culture: Studies in History and Theory*, London, Hutchinson, pp. 185–198.

WOOD, STEPHEN and JOHN KELLY 1982. 'Taylorism, Responsible Autonomy and Management Strategy', in Stephen Wood (ed.), *The Degradation of Work? Skill, Deskilling and the Labour Market*, London, Hutchinson, pp. 74–89.

5
Stratification and Class

MICHEL PEILLON

The study of stratification focuses on social inequality. It involves, for example, ranking groups of people in terms of their income, education, power and prestige. It gives a picture of society divided into strata, that is to say in superposed levels. The study of social class, on the other hand, is the study of forces which shape society, generating patterns of inequality in the process. Patterns of inequality or stratification are thus linked to class but must not be equated with it.

One example will highlight the significance of the distinction between the study of social stratification and the study of class. Much has been written about the poor in the Republic of Ireland. Poverty has become the most glaring example of social inequality. The poor form the lowest category in the hierarchy of income. They dispose, at best, of the bare minimum in the Irish conditions of life. They are left on the margins of society, and this common fate represents the shared experience of poverty. The poor as a social category illustrate the danger of equating social stratification and social class. The poor do not form a social class and the group is made up, instead, of different fragments of class: mainly small farmers and working-class. Their exclusion from the mainstream of productive activity results from different circumstances and is accomplished in different ways. Not only do the poor occupy different positions in society, but they rarely manifest a willingness or an ability to come together as a group. Only in some urban areas do they show signs of coming together. For these reasons, the category of poor people belongs to the phenomenon of social stratification, but not to that of class-structure.

This chapter is divided in two parts. The first examines three dimensions of social stratification in the Republic of Ireland, based on material, prestige and power inequalities respectively. The second part outlines three approaches to class analysis as they have been applied in the Irish context. It presents the major features of an orthodox marxist approach and then discusses the class structuration approach which loosely derives from Weber. Finally, it outlines an approach which seeks to identify the Irish class-structure through the observed pattern of social differentiation.

Patterns of inequality

The study of stratification has traditionally focussed on the distribution, among occupational groups, of material advantages, status and power. Such a tradition is in dire need of reform, for it neglects the formation of other possible social cleavages and it ignores other dimensions of inequality (i.e. gender). But the broadening of the analysis of social stratification has hardly started and, for this reason, the following comments are confined to a conventional analysis.

Material inequality
Two figures illustrate the gap that exists within society in the Republic of Ireland. From the compilation of estate duties, it has been estimated that 1 per cent of the population owns around a third of personal wealth, while 5 per cent own about 60–63 per cent (Lyons 1975). These estimates and the assumptions on which they are based have been challenged. They give, nevertheless, an idea of the extent of wealth inequality. The Republic of Ireland is not exceptional among modern capitalist

nations, but that does not make the inequalities any less stark. At the other end of the social spectrum, Irish society contains vast pockets of deprivation. It has been calculated that in the early 1970s, about a quarter of the population of the Republic of Ireland could be considered as poor (Ó Cinnéide 1972). More recently, it has been claimed that the figure is nearer one-third (Kennedy 1981). Such figures compare quite badly with those of most European countries, although one must be aware that the number of poor is difficult to estimate (George and Lawson 1980).

A more precise picture of material inequality is given by the distribution of the national income (see Table 1; figures relating to 1980 from Thompstone 1984):

Table 1: **Distribution of national income, 1980**

% of population	Slice of gross national income
	%
Top 10	26.4
Top 20	43.9
Bottom 40	15.2
Bottom 20	4.6

However dramatic they may be, these figures (which rely on self-reported income) do not greatly differ from what is known about other industrialised societies. The share of income of the bottom 20 per cent in the Republic of Ireland may be on the lower side, but on the whole, the profile of inequality closely follows the average of the developed capitalist countries (Nolan 1977–78).

Some figures based on the 1965–66 Household Budget Survey are available and they provide a point of departure for evaluating a possible trend (Nolan 1977–78). It appears that the extent of income inequality in urban areas decreased between 1965–66 and 1974, and then rose again. Such a trend is hardly surprising, since the years 1973–74 mark the end of a period of development and the start of a long period of economic difficulties. If one compares 1965–66 to 1980, it is quite clear that the poorest 50 per cent of the population disposed in 1980 of a lesser share of the national income, while the wealthier 50 per cent had improved their relative position (Thompstone 1984).

Most industrial societies express some commitment to a decrease of social inequality, if not to its eradication. Such a commitment often signifies no more than the hope that industrial development and successful wealth creation will ease the extremes of poverty. But others envisage a more active commitment to such a goal and seek to achieve a redistribution of income through the state. Such a redistribution would be accomplished through progressive taxation and welfare allocation. Does the welfare state in the Republic of Ireland achieve the redistribution of income that it promises?

A recent survey has thrown some light on that particular aspect (Rottman et al. 1982) and Table 2 gives some of the major figures. It indicates the average weekly income for each economic class and also the balance of taxation and state transfers.

Table 2 shows the importance of state transfers for several categories of people who, like the lower working-class and the small farmers, depend on the state to supplement their insufficient income. The higher working-class and property owners are, on the whole, little affected by their relation to the state: they receive from state transfers slightly less than what they give in taxation. Only the non-property middle-classes lose a significant part of their income through their relation to the state. The reality of the welfare state in the Republic of Ireland does not correspond to the theory. One could even speak of its perverse deviation, in that a transfer of resources towards the poorer categories does occur, but the necessary resources are taken mainly from the intermediate income groups and not from the wealthier groups.

Table 2: **Average weekly direct income and the effects of state transfers and taxes by economic categories**

	Average weekly direct income	Total direct trans- fers	Total direct tax	Net effect
	%	%	%	%
Large proprietors	78.0	+1.55	-4.83	-3.28
Small proprietors	38.5	+1.90	-2.50	-0.60
Large farmers	64.3	+2.02	-1.18	+0.84
Medium farmers	45.7	+2.66	-1.27	+1.39
Small farmers	29.2	+3.93	-1.13	+2.80
Marginal farmers	18.6	+6.52	-1.13	+5.39
Higher professions	73.5	+1.34	-11.81	-10.47
Lower professions	56.6	+1.57	-9.20	-7.63
Intermediate non-manual	46.0	+2.83	-6.50	-3.67
Skilled manual	38.7	+3.64	-5.49	-1.85
Service workers	35.4	+3.76	-4.61	-0.85
Semi-skilled manual	25.0	+4.39	-4.34	+0.05
Unskilled manual	25.0	+6.82	-3.09	+3.73

Source: Adapted from Rottman *et al.*, 1982, Tables 3.1 and 3.4.

Prestige inequality
People judge each other. They hold some in high esteem and others in low esteem. They consider some occupations to be socially better than others. They see groups as being socially inferior or superior. The prestige attached to individuals or to positions in society results from such evaluations. It may represent an indication of the esteem of people for one another or, more simply, it may reflect an opinion of how desirable a particular occupation is. The attribution of prestige constitutes an evaluation; it requires passing a judgment. It signifies that people live up to held values and standards differently.

The attribution of prestige appears to be, then, a very subjective affair. Yet, it is contended that the Republic of Ireland displays a coherent pattern of prestige, implying that prestige is attributed in a consistent way. Doctors, architects or solicitors enjoy a higher status than office workers; skilled electricians or joiners are higher on the scale of prestige than unskilled labourers. Non-manual categories as a whole would enjoy greater prestige than manual occupations. Young people from unskilled backgrounds aspire to skilled positions, and many (chiefly girls) from the working-class have a very positive image of non-manual work (Ward 1967; Drudy 1975).

The Hall-Jones scale represents a general hierarchy of prestige and has been widely used in social research in the Republic of Ireland. Originally a British and urban scale, it was constructed by asking a random sample of interviewees to rank a list of occupations, and then by assigning an average score to each occupation. It outlines seven broad ranks of prestige. This scale has been used, in the Irish context, for the study of social mobility (Hutchinson 1969) and for the study of attitudes and prejudices (Mac Greil 1977). Table 3 presents a breakdown, in terms of the Hall-Jones categories, of the representative samples of the Dublin population in these two surveys.

A coherent and agreed upon hierarchy of prestige may well be a phenomenon of the past. Society in the Republic of Ireland has from the 1960s been undergoing a deep transformation. Skilled manual workers and technicians have questioned the higher prestige generally granted to office-workers (Fogarty 1969). The traditional status superiority of office-workers over manual workers has been seriously challenged (McCarthy 1973). The growing emphasis on industry has also exacerbated tensions about the relative status position of the employers and of the professional category (Fogarty 1973).

Power inequality
Political scientists have hardly been concerned with the distribution of power within the Republic of Ireland — admittedly an elusive phenomenon. However, the group of

Table 3: **Status groups in Dublin (application of the Hall-Jones scale)**

	Hutchinson (1968 sample)	MacGreil (1972 sample)
	%	%
Professionally qualified and high administrative	4.9	7.3
Managerial and executive	5.2	9.5
Inspectional, supervisory and other higher grade non-manual	8.6	13.3
Inspectional, supervisory and other lower-grade non-manual	18.6	10.3
Skilled manual and routine non-manual	33.1	36.6
Semi-skilled manual	13.0	10.4
Unskilled manual	16.6	12.9

Sources: Hutchinson (1969, Table 3); MacGreil (1977, Table 47).

people who constitute the apex of the political system, who fill the positions of political authority and make decisions on behalf of the country (TDs and ministers mainly) have themselves been quite extensively surveyed. The profile of this governing elite is well delineated. The professions and to a lesser extent, the small proprietors (mainly traders) constitute the major recruiting ground of this elite. The predominance of the professions is accentuated at the highest levels of political authority. About two-thirds of ministers since the foundation of the state have come from the professional category. Farmers are fairly represented in local authorities, but they lose ground at national level. All the other social categories are under-represented in the governing elite (Chubb 1982).

The social composition of the governing group does not give an adequate indication of the distribution of power. The governing elite represents the small group of people who are in positions of authority; who take the decisions binding on the collectivity. But this group may constitute the apparent, rather than the real, seat of power in the Republic of Ireland.

The prevailing view of the distribution of power in the Republic of Ireland, rarely explicitly formulated but implied in many comments, is one of 'institutionalised pluralism'. Pluralism indicates that diverse groups are involved in the power game and that they all exercise some kind of influence. Trade unions, farmers' organisations, business groups, a wide range of associations, etc. seek to influence state decisions and put pressure on it. Such a view emphasises the continuous negotiations that take place under the auspices of the state. It shows the interplay between a few organised forces and the state. 'Institutionalised pluralism' also means that the bargaining has been to some extent incorporated within state institutions. The accredited groups participate in many departmental commissions. They are represented in a large range of public agencies. They are consulted by Departments on relevant matters. The state, in such a perspective, responds to the pressures of different forces and takes into consideration the shifting balance of their relationships. It regulates this bargaining process by bringing it within its own institutional framework.

Another view, which suggests there is a ruling class in the Republic of Ireland, is also widely held. Such an approach, which has not been sustained in any systematic way, allows for many variations. It contends, however, that the state must be seen as the instrument through which the capitalist class and the 'establishment' exercise their domination over the Republic of Ireland; through which they secure their advantages. The state enacts the will of the bourgeoisie (namely the owners and managers of medium and large size firms), closely allied to the large farmers and the higher professions. The vigour with which the state animates an economic development based on profit-making; its refusal to envisage any other form of development; its strong backing of private property and of the advantages deriving from it; all become testimony to the capaitalist character of the state in the Republic of Ireland. This approach may acknowledge the weakness of the indigenous bourgeoisie; the state is then seen as the instrument of international capitalism and of its allies within the Republic of Ireland.

The observation of what the state is doing and of the way its activity relates to what the major forces in society seek to achieve, provides, I would contend, an effective test of the distribution of power. Such an investigation has led to the formulation of conclusions as to the distribution of power in the Republic of Ireland (Peillon 1982).

The first conclusion relates to the diversity of sources of power. Several groups are able to exercise some influence on the state; they can make their presence felt. They can force the state to respond, even if only partly and inadequately, to their needs and requirements. The power that such forces exercise is not necessarily of the same kind. For instance, the working-class constitutes a force which bears, in some ways, upon the state, along with the business class (i.e. large proprietors·and higher managers) or the commercial farmers. But their respective impact on the state is clearly different, and the bourgeoisie systematically predominates over the working-class.

It would seem that such a conclusion upholds the pluralist model which postulates a diversity of sources of power. However, one also observes in the Republic of Ireland a clear and stable pattern of predominance; one clearly witnesses a structure of domination. The business class enjoys a privileged relationship with the state, and weighs heavily upon it. Its needs and its requirements are, if not always satisfied, at least never ignored by the state. More significantly, the orientation of action of the bourgeoisie, and the orientation of the state largely coincide. The bourgeoisie can be described as a dominant class, although not a ruling class; it exercises a determining influence on the state, but it does not control it.

The analysis of the three major dimensions of stratification in the Republic of Ireland would not be complete without studying the relations that may exist between them. Does one's position in a particular hierarchy determine one's position in another? Is a wealthy group also powerful and high in status? Can power be transformed into wealth and status? Do the different patterns of inequality in Ireland coincide, or do they differ significantly?

Using a wide range of available statistics, a profile of the unskilled working-class has been elaborated (Geary and O Murcheartaigh 1974). It gives a bleak picture of lower working-class conditions and it shows the cumulation of disadvantages. The members of the lower working-class fare badly in all possible respects. They dispose of a very low income and enjoy little status. They lack power and are not likely to get a full post-primary education. The experience of unemployment is quite widespread, and their prospects of social mobility are poor. At the other extreme, advantages are cumulative. The professions seem to enjoy prestige, influence, far higher income than average and many other advantages. In that sense, the different patterns of inequality coincide.

Such a statement seems valid as long as one looks at society in the Republic of Ireland in its broader lines. A closer look, however, reveals the existence of discrepancies. The large proprietors, for instance, dispose on the whole of a higher income than most in the professional class; but they enjoy a lower status, and are hardly represented in the positions of authority (although, as we have seen, authority may not be a measure of power). Children from a shopkeeping background enjoy educational opportunities which are as good as those from proprietors and managers of larger firms, despite their lesser wealth and lower status. Such examples bring to our attention the possibility of gaps which testify to the particularity of each dimension of social inequality.

Approaches to class-structure

Sociological literature reveals a variety of approaches to the analysis of class. In the American social scientific tradition, social class typically refers to status groups identified by a common life-style. This comes close to the definition of social strata outlined above. Class, however, is better conceived as an explanatory rather than as a descriptive concept. In the European tradition it is used to explain the organisation and dynamic of society. Much of the sociological understanding of class is shaped by the continuing debate between marxist and Weberian approaches.

Capitalist social relations

For Marx, inequalities in income and wealth are the result of class divisions established within the productive processes. Whilst he recognised that there were several social classes in any particular capitalist society, he argued that capitalist societies are founded on the relationships between two social classes — the capitalist class (or the bourgeoisie) and the working-class (the proletariat). These two classes form the structure of the capitalist society. This structure is self-contradictory, as the relationships between the capitalist class and the working-class are exploitative and conflictual. The capitalist class buys the proletariat's capacity to work and turns it into capital. The latter has only its labour power to sell. Class antagonism manifests itself in a number of ways. In the economic sphere, it erupts over the distribution of wealth created; over the length of the working day; the rhythm and pace of production; discipline in the workplace. In the political field, party divisions and public policies are related to class conflicts. The dissemination of ideas, school socialisation and the control of media point to some aspects of the cultural dimension in class antagonism.

Surprisingly, no fully-fledged analysis of the class-structure in the Republic of Ireland has been presented in the marxist perspective. The latter has inspired many comments on Irish society, but they too often offer a caricature and hardly realise the possibilities of this perspective. The whole approach starts with the assertion of the capitalist character of society in the Republic of Ireland and it endeavours to identify the core of its class-structure. The dynamic of the society is accounted for in terms of the relations between the bourgeoisie and the working-class. However, the Republic of Ireland is only in the process of becoming an industrial capitalist society, and it contains residues of pre-capitalism. The presence of a large category of farmers and of small proprietors is seen as a legacy of Ireland's pre-capitalist past. Even the reluctance of the white-collar group to become identified with the 'working class' manifests an ideological resistance based on the traditional position of office workers.

Another type of analysis is also associated with the marxist perspective and it emphasises the special character of capitalist industrialisation in the Republic of Ireland. The latter does not industrialise by following the path of already advanced societies. Capitalist development takes place here in a way that suits the international pattern of capitalist development. 'Dependent capitalism' possesses definite features (Wickham 1979): assembly lines are implanted and they rely primarily on a semi-skilled and unskilled labour-force. They hardly contribute to the elaboration of an infra-structure that would sustain indigenous industrialisation. Furthermore, profit created in the Republic of Ireland is not reinvested here. Dependent capitalism leads to a strange situation, as far as the class-structure is concerned. It is said to generate a large unskilled labour-force in front of an impersonal capitalism, a sort of 'absentee bourgeoisie'.

Class structuration

Max Weber has introduced a clear distinction between three types of groupings which are to be found in society. Classes, status groups and parties correspond broadly to particular ranks within the hierarchy of wealth, status and power respectively; and there are no necessary connections between them. A class, for instance, would represent a group of people with a similar chance of obtaining a particular level of wealth, while a status group would correspond to a group of people with a similar chance of enjoying a particular level of prestige. People dispose of resources such as property, skill, education, and they compete to obtain the highest rewards for themselves. Weber asserts that material interests are not the only or even the most important source of group cohesion and life-style, for instance, matters

more in this respect. Classes represent purely economic categories and would rarely form 'real' groups. Status groups are far
more likely to engage in what he calls communal action, that is
to say, to develop a sense of solidarity and belongingness.

Weber also uses the term social class, which constitutes a
broader category than class. A social class corresponds in fact to
the cluster of classes between which social mobility is frequent
and usual. Such a view implies that a social class delimits a particular social environment, that members of a social class are
likely to develop particular ways of behaving, to share a particular life-style. It may not stretch Weber too far to consider that
social classes are for him aggregates of class which develop into
broad status groups.

The analysis of class-structure proposed by the British
sociologist Anthony Giddens (1973) has recently been applied to
the Republic of Ireland. Such an approach borrows heavily
from Weber and it presents society as a large market where
people sell relevant resources at their disposal and obtain an
income from that transaction. People possess different 'market
capacities' and command for that reason particular levels of
financial rewards.

In their application to the Republic of Ireland of such a
perspective, Rottman *et al.* (1982) have identified thirteen categories, each one corresponding to a level or a type of market
capacity. They form the basis of class formation. Several processes are involved which bring together or else clearly separate
economic classes, and so determine the shape and the boundaries of social classes. This process of formation is labelled 'class-
structuration', meaning the processes through which the class-
structure emerges and takes shape; through which some groups
of people come to have a similar experience of society; to develop
a similar life-style and to share a common culture. One major
mechanism of class-structuration is social mobility, but others
are involved. The class-structure is in that sense rooted in
economic inequality, but it is produced through other mechanisms of a social nature. Such an analysis possesses the advantage
of taking into account the variable character of the class-

structure, the degree to which a society is structured through social classes.

The process of structuration in the Republic of Ireland would result in the formation of four major social classes, each moving within its respective social space. The owners of large businesses and farmer-employers belong to bourgeoisie. The 'petite-bourgeoisie' includes all other types of property owners, from shopkeepers to marginal farmers. After that, the middle-classes of professionals, administrators and office workers use their qualification as market capacity. Finally, the working-class gather all levels of skill in manual work and unqualified non-manual work. Labour represents the market capacity of such a class.

Table 4: **Social classes in the Republic of Ireland (application of the Giddens model)**

	% of all households
Bourgeoisie (large proprietors, including large farmers-employers)	2.2
Petite bourgeoisie (small proprietors, farmers)	25.8
Middle-class (professional, intermediate and routine non-manual)	19.2
Working-class (manual and service workers)	43.9

Source: Rottman et al. (1982, pp. 24—25)

There is not much to query about the distinctions that are made or about the reality of such social cleavages. The distinctions that are not made are more troublesome. This analysis, for instance, makes a clear distinction between small business and farmers as classes (and class refers to economic categories, to groups of people possessing a different market capacity). But these categories are put together in the same social class labelled petite bourgeoisie. I would contend that small farmers and small businesses do not simply constitute different (economic) classes, but also different social classes. The same comments could apply to the distinction between large and small farmers, between professional and white-collar workers. Numerous studies have highlighted, for instance, the process of class-differentiation in rural Ireland and the deepening of *social* cleavages between two major categories of farmers (Commins *et al.* 1978).

Class differentiation

The marxist perspective possesses a great explanatory power, in the way in which all social reality is accounted for in terms of class-structure, and the latter is itself explained by the social relations of production. At the same time, the marxist perspective is always in danger of over-simplifying; of seeking to capture a complex reality in a simple model. On the other hand, Weber's approach has been praised for its richness and flexibility, for its ability to take into consideration the subtleties of a social structure. But it offers little explanation for the existence of a particular group configuration. Furthermore, social classes come to depend rather directly on material inequality; social classes are seen as deriving from classes.

Marx and Weber have much in common in fact, for they see society in terms of groups competing for scarce resources and placed within a definite pattern of power and domination. But the characterisation of the social relations of production is beyond direct observation, and the latter can only be observed indirectly, through its empirical effects. In a similar way, deciding on what constitutes the major 'market capacities' remains rather arbitrary (for there is in fact an infinity of market capacities). However, both approaches seem to agree that social classes constitute broad groups, rooted in the economic life, whose members share ways of behaving and possibly a general life-style.

'If classes become social realities, this must be manifest in the formation of common patterns of behaviour and attitude' (Giddens 1973, page 111). Such a statement provides a useful starting-point for delineating the class-structure of a society, for it points to an empirical manifestation of the class-structure on which the analysis may rest. It is possible to reconstruct the class-structure through the social differentiation that it produces, by closely observing the patterns of behaviour and attitudes that are associated with occupational groupings. Such a reconstruction overcomes the simplifications inherent in orthodox marxism and it avoids simply deriving social classes from categories of social inequality. It seeks to locate the major lines of social differentiation, and so delimit the social groupings. It admittedly provides a purely descriptive account of the class-structure in Ireland, but it may at least be sensitised by the explanatory orientation of the marxist perspective. Such an analysis has been attempted in the context of the Republic of Ireland (Peillon 1982, Part 1), and we may summarise the major conclusions.

There are three major socially differentiated groupings in the Republic of Ireland: the farmers, the working-class and a broadly defined urbanised middle-class, each with different characteristics, patterns of behaviour and attitudes. However, each grouping is itself differentiated. There exists quite a social gap between the lower (semi-skilled and unskilled manual workers) and the higher working-class (skilled manual and routine non-manual). A similar gap may divide farmers, in that small farmers have become a residual category, clearly set apart. The middle-class offers a complex picture. The bourgeoisie needs to be differentiated from the petite bourgeoisie, and professionals from office workers. Some of these distinctions do not rest on very extensive evidence; for instance, the life-styles and overall pattern of social characteristics of the bourgeoisie and the higher professionals do not dramatically differ. But the differences are significant enough to justify this kind of distinction.

Reliance on the mapping of social differentiation is not without problems: it could well be that the major lines of social differentiation do not correspond to occupational cleavages, but to that of age, gender, religion, etc. Furthermore, such an approach produces at best a description, and at worst a mere listing of the major social groupings in society. It does not contribute, as such, to the clarification of class relations. In other words, it does not define the Republic of Ireland class-structure — it only defines its elements. But in the light of what has been said about the marxist perspective, there may be some advantages in separating the two stages of the analysis (defining the elements; analysing their relations), all the more so as class relations are nowadays actualised through the state.

The picture elaborated in this way represents the framework of society in the Republic of Ireland rather than its class-structure. The concept of class, in its fullest sense, does not simply refer to categories of a hierarchy or to elements of a structure; it points to groups that become forces and are directly involved in shaping society. I would contend that only the bourgeoisie, the farmers and the working-class have developed that capacity, while the petite bourgeoisie, the white-collar workers and even the professionals do not assert themselves as autonomous forces in the making of society in the Republic of Ireland. Such a contention would clearly require elaboration. The proof of the matter rests ultimately in the capacity of a social category to develop an orientation of action.

Conclusion

Stratification and class-structure have been presented separately, as two different aspects of social reality. It is necessary to emphasise that, although distinct, such dimensions are not separate. Class-structure is perceived as the direct expression of status inequality in the Hall-Jones scale. The analysis in terms of market capacities implies, by its very definition, economic inequality. The marxist perspective reverses the relationship and presents the pattern of inequality as the outcome of the class-structure. In any case, the correspondences between stratification and class-structure are rarely direct or simple, and the analysis of their connections requires that the distinction be clearly made.

The pattern of social stratification is a complex one, involving as it does many lines of inequality and many resources or privileges that are unequally distributed. By focussing on economic, power and prestige inequalities between major occupational groups, one only views part of the picture. The reconstruction of the whole network of stratification would set each type of inequality in its proper context. The study of occupational inequality or of gender inequality is not very revealing as such. The analysis of the connections between types of inequality would give a better understanding of the way society in the Republic of Ireland is organised and functions. Such an analysis remains to be done.

Social mobility is often seen as a strategic process in the formation of social classes (see Chapter 11, also Whelan & Whelan 1984). Many other mechanisms are involved. But they still need to be identified if one is to understand how the entrenched character of the class-structure in the Republic of Ireland is produced.

References

CHUBB, BASIL 1982. *The Government and Politics of Ireland*. London, Longmans.

COMMINS, PATRICK, P. G. COX and J. CURRY 1978. *Rural Areas: Change and Development*, Dublin. National Economic and Social Council, No. 41.

DRUDY, SHEELAGH 1975. 'The occupational aspirations of rural school leavers', *Social Studies*, Vol. 4, No. 3, pp. 230–241.

FOGARTY, MICHAEL 1969. *Dispute between FUE and Maintenance Craft Unions*, Dublin, Stationery Office.

FOGARTY, MICHAEL 1973. *Irish Entrepreneurs Speak for Themselves*, Dublin, Economic and Social Research Institute, broadsheet 8.

GEARY, ROY C. and F. S. O MUIRCHEARTAIGH 1974. *Equalisation of Opportunity in Ireland*, Dublin, Economic and Social Research Institute, broadsheet 10.

GEORGE, VIC and ROGER LAWSON, (eds) 1980. *Poverty and Inequality in Common Market Countries*, London, Routledge and Kegan Paul.

GIDDENS, ANTHONY 1973. *The Class Structure of the Advanced*

Societies, London, Hutchinson.

HUTCHINSON, BERTRAM 1969. *Social Status and Intergenerational Mobility in Dublin*, Dublin, Economic and Social Research Institute, Paper 48.

KENNEDY, STANISLAUS (ed.) 1981. *One Million Poor*, Dublin, Turoe Press.

LYONS, PATRICK M. 1975. 'Estate duty, wealth estimates and the mortality multiplier', *Economic and Social Review*, Vol. 6, no 3, pp. 337-352.

McCARTHY, CHARLES 1973. *The Decade of Upheaval*, Dublin, Institute of Public Administration.

MacGREIL, MICHEAL 1977. *Prejudice and Tolerance in Ireland*, Dublin, College of Industrial Relations.

NOLAN, BRIAN 1977-78. 'The personal distribution of income in the Republic of Ireland', *Journal of the Statistical and Social Inquiry Society of Ireland*, Vol. 23, part V, pp. 59-88.

Ó CINNÉIDE, SEAMUS 1972. 'The extent of poverty in Ireland' *Social Studies*, Vol. 1, no. 4, pp. 380-400.

PEILLON, MICHEAL, 1982. *Contemporary Irish Society: an Introduction*, Dublin, Gill and Macmillan.

ROTTMAN, DAVID B., DAMIAN F. HANNAN, NIAMH HARDIMAN, and MIRIAM M. WILEY 1982. *The Distribution of Income in the Republic of Ireland: a Study in Social Class and Family-cycle Inequalities*, Dublin, Economic and Social Research Institute, Paper 109.

THOMPSTONE, KEVIN 1984, 'Income Inequality in Ireland, a Sociological Analysis', MA thesis, NIHE Limerick.

WARD, CONOR 1967. *Manpower in a Developing Community*, Dublin, An Roinn Saothair.

WHELAN, CHRISTOPHER T. and BRENDAN J. WHELAN, 1984. *The Republic of Ireland: A Comparative Perspective*, Dublin, Economic and Social Research Institute, Paper 116.

WICKHAM, JAMES 1979. 'Dependent Industrialisation and Dependent Working-Class'. *Proceedings of the Annual Conference of the Sociological Association of Ireland*, Belfast, pp. 112-115.

6
Socialisation, Selection and Reproduction in Education

PATRICK CLANCY

An expanded educational system is a distinctive feature of all advanced societies. Education, being concerned with personal development and the transmission of culture is not, of course, confined to what goes on in schools and colleges. However, a feature of modernisation has been the emergence of specialist educational institutions and it is the activities of these formal agencies which have attracted most analysis. In the Republic of Ireland, with 40 per cent of the population under the age of 20, the working of the educational system has attracted additional interest. In 1981–82 a total of 925,524 students (27 per cent of the total population) were receiving full-time education. Of these, 571,385 were attending primary schools, 309,598 were attending post-primary schools, while 44,541 were attending third-level colleges. Schooling is compulsory up to the age of 15. However, in 1981–82, it is estimated that 55 per cent of the 15–19 age cohort and 8 per cent of the 20–24 age cohort were receiving full-time education (Department of Education 1984).

This paper provides a sociological perspective on the educational system in the Republic of Ireland. The paper is divided into three sections. The first section examines a number of theoretical approaches to education, the second section examines socialisation and the production of consciousness, and the third section examines the process of selection and social reproduction.

Theoretical approaches

Most of the sociological research and analysis within the field of education has been carried out within a structuralist perspective, and this approach is followed here. Traditionally, sociologists have taken the total society as their unit of analysis and have sought to understand the contribution of the educational system to the maintenance and development of that society. This macro approach tended to leave the social processes and internal dynamics of the school unexamined. More recently, sociologists, using interpretative approaches, have turned their attention to the functioning of the school organisation and have examined the pattern of interaction within the classroom, and the nature of the curriculum through which the explicit goals of schooling are realised (see, for example, Delamont 1983).

An assertion that most sociological analysis of education can be located within a structuralist perspective should not be taken to imply that all sociologists using this approach share a common view on the role of education in society. In reality, two groups of scholars, functionalists and marxists, hold antithetical views about the functions of education in contemporary society. However, in spite of fundamentally contrary views, their approaches towards an understanding of education reveal a remarkable similarity.

Talcott Parsons, the leading exponent of structural functionalist sociology, set the agenda for many sociologists of education when he identified the 'dual problem' with which schools have to contend. Schools are simultaneously agencies of socialisation and selection. As a socialisation agency, the school is responsible for the development in individuals of the commitments and capacities which are prerequisites for their future role performance. This socialisation has both a technical and a moral component. At a technical level, schools teach the capacities and skills required for adult role performance. In an age of increasing technological sophistication society is becoming more dependent on the educational system to equip people with the range of skills necessary for the occupational world. For Parsons, the role of the school as an agency of moral socialisation is even more crucial. As a normative functionalist he insists that value consensus is essential if society is to operate effectively. Hence the significance of schooling where young people are socialised into the basic values of society (Parsons 1959).

A key value which schools teach and which is of strategic importance to society is that of achievement. Within the family the child's status is ascribed; it is fixed by birth. However, status in adult life is largely achieved; for example, an individual achieves his or her occupational role. At school, students are encouraged to strive for high levels of academic attainment and by rewarding those who do strive, the school fosters the value of achievement. The functionalist analysis suggests that the school's commitment to meritocratic principles (i.e. rewarding ability and effort) becomes the essential mechanism by which our society accepts the principle of differential rewards. Both the winners — the high achievers — and the losers — the low achievers — will see the system as equitable since status is achieved in a situation where all seem to have an equal chance.

This discussion of the way in which the norm of achievement is internalised leads us to an analysis of the school's selection function, the second element of Parsons' dual problem. The school functions as a crucial mechanism for the selection of individuals for their future occupational role in society. An important dimension of schooling is the on-going process of evaluation. Schools differentiate between pupils on the basis of their achievement. The differentiation which teachers make between students within the school prepares students for differential allocation in the labour market.

On the face of it, the strident critique of schooling which is contained in the marxist approach to education would seem to have little in common with the functionalist approach. While functionalists consider education to be an equalising force in society marxist-oriented scholars argue that education merely serves the interest of the capitalist class. The meritocratic hypothesis, with its assumption that schools are efficient ways of selecting talented people, is emphatically rejected. Instead it is argued that schools work to convince people that selection is meritocratic. It is essential for the legitimacy of the capitalist order that the population be convinced that people in high status positions deserve their positions, that they are more talented and work harder than others. Schools are an essential prop of this legitimacy. The essentially optimistic functionalist view that education is intrinsically good, that it leads to individual emancipation and self realisation, is countered by the marxists who stress its repressive features. They view the educational system as an instrument of cultural domination; its real function is best understood in terms of the need for social control in an unequal and rapidly changing social order. However, in spite of these antithetical views, and in spite of the use of very different terminology, both approaches to the analysis of education are strikingly similar. This similarity in approach is evident from an examination of the work of the American neo-marxists, Bowles and Gintis (1976).

Bowles and Gintis's analysis of the educational system begins with an assessment of the labour force requirement of capitalism. Education functions as an agency to supply appropriately educated labour power to the economy. Two modes of appropriateness are identified: firstly, the release of young men and women from the educational system at different ages and with different technical capacities and qualifications, and secondly, the production of personalities, attitudes and orientations which facilitate integration into the wage labour system with its attendant hierarchical division of labour. This latter objective is achieved through the operation of the 'correspondence principle'. Bowles and Gintis argue that major aspects of educational organisation replicate the relationships of dominance and subordinacy in the economic sphere. Thus, the social relations of schooling reproduce the social relations of production.

Notwithstanding the fundamental ideological differences between the functionalist and marxist perspectives, their broad agreement on an approach towards understanding the function of education in contemporary society provides us with an orientation which can be used to explore the working of the Irish educational system. Its role as a socialising agency concerned with the reproduction of labour power with the appropriate skills and consciousness will first be examined. Then the school's function as a mechanism of role allocation, and its contribution towards the reproduction of existing social hierarchies will be explored. In examining both of these processes, it is contended that the situation in Ireland broadly parallels that found in other capitalist countries. Hence, the main concern of the paper will be to point towards any special nuances in the Irish experience. In addition, because of the limited research on sociological aspects of Irish education, many of the generalisations advanced must be viewed as hypotheses which await verification.

Socialisation and the production of consciousness

In nineteenth century Ireland, the struggle to gain control of the national school system was explicitly a struggle to mould the consciousness of the Irish population. The British government pursued a policy of anglicisation by operating constraints on the language and culture transmitted in the curriculum. The religious denominations sought and attained the development of a religiously segregated system. This ensured the perpetuation of their particular ideologies. Social control was the main concern of those who sought to shape the system; issues of moral socialisation took precedence over issues of technical socialisation, although the latter was catered for by the inclusion on the curriculum of such subjects as needlework, cookery and laundry, manual instruction and rural science[1] (see Coolahan 1981).

The development of the national system in the Republic of Ireland since independence illustrates further the close links between education and values. The curriculum changes which were introduced after independence were inspired by the ideology of cultural nationalism. It was felt that schools ought to be the prime agents in the revival of the Irish language and Gaelic culture. The work of the infant school was to be entirely in Irish; no teaching of English as a school subject was to be permitted. For senior classes, Irish was to be the medium of instruction for history, geography, drill and singing, and all songs in the singing class were to be Irish language songs. The programme in history was to deal exclusively with the history of Ireland, the chief aim being to develop the best traits of the national character and to inculcate national pride and self-respect.

The institutionalisation of the ideology of cultural nationalism was complemented by the special position accorded to the churches in the control of education. After independence, the de facto denominational status of the school system was quickly recognised and became institutionalised. Successive ministers of education adopted the view that the role of the state in education was a subsidiary one, aiding agencies such as the churches in the provision of educational facilities. The acceptance of this principle of subsidiarity is reflected in the structure of education in the Republic of Ireland, where the degree of control exercised by the religious personnel is almost without parallel.

At the primary level, the denominational character of the educational system is reflected in the managerial system. More than 96 per cent of children of primary school-going age (4–12 years) attend state supported schools. These schools are called National Schools although the term 'national' is somewhat misleading since the schools are not owned by the state; the latter merely provides for education by assisting the other parties involved. For that reason there is a board of management (formerly a single manager) for each school. The person (or persons) recognised by the Minister for Education as manager is responsible to the Minister for the conducting of the school in accordance with the Department of Education's rules and regulations. Under these regulations the appointment of the manager normally rests with the patron (or patrons) of the school. In practically all cases the patron is the bishop of the diocese, or the diocesan trustees appropriate to the denominational character of the school concerned. Up until 1975, the normal practice was that the manager of lay Catholic schools was the parish priest of the area in which the school was situated, while in the case of schools operated by religious congregations the manager was usually the superior of the religious community. Protestant schools were managed by the rector or another Protestant clergyman. Since 1975 the single manager has been replaced by a board of management. This change has not significantly altered the power structure, since the patron's nominees constitute a majority of the board. The other members are elected parents and teacher representatives.

Notwithstanding the special difficulties experienced in some areas by the clergy and local community in providing the local financial contribution to primary education, it is generally conceded that the degree of control by the religious denominations over primary education is more than commensurate with their financial contribution. The patron and trustees are responsible for providing a site for national schools, and for making a variable contribution, averaging about 15 per cent of the capital costs, for the construction and furnishing of the school. The state pays the total salary of all national school teachers. In addition, it pays the major portion of the cost of school maintenance. This latter item has been an issue of recurrent controversy; teachers and parents have frequently complained of the inadequate financial provision by the state for school maintenance. Proposals by the Irish National Teachers' Organisation and others, however, that the total cost of school maintenance should be borne by the state or by local authorities, have not, in spite of their financial attractiveness, been supported by church authorities, as they felt that this would infringe on their managerial rights (Coolahan 1981, p. 46).

A further distinctive structural feature of the Irish system of primary education is that teachers are trained in state-supported denominational colleges of education. Thus, the provision for teacher socialisation is compatible with the requirements of a denominational system.

The structure of post-primary education in the Republic of Ireland also reflects the concern for an explicitly value-oriented education. Sixty-nine per cent of students in post-primary education attended secondary schools in 1981–82. Although almost totally financed by the state, these schools are privately owned and managed. Eighty-eight per cent of the schools are owned and controlled by Catholic religious communities (nuns, brothers and priests). The remainder are divided between those which belong to other religious denominations, and those which are either privately or corporately owned by lay Catholics. Twenty-one per cent of students in post-primary education attended vocational schools in 1981–82. These schools were established following the 1930 Vocational Education Act, and represented the first attempt to establish publicly owned schools. Vocational schools were designed to provide a qualitatively different education from that offered by the academic, and mainly middle-class, secondary schools. The curricular pattern of secondary schools was firmly fixed within the humanist grammar school tradition where language and literary studies predominated. In contrast, the vocational school emphasised practical training in preparation for skilled and semi-skilled manual occupations for boys, and commercial courses and domestic economy for girls.

The binary or bipartite system of post-primary education reflected in the secondary-vocational distinction, which remained unchallenged for more than thirty-five years, was not unique to the Republic of Ireland. However, the relative size of those two sectors was the inverse of that found in most other western European countries, where the grammar-type school catered for the minority of the post-primary school population. By the 1960s there was a growing realisation that the structure of the post-primary system in the Republic was unsatisfactory. The new policy adopted was designed to erode the academic/technical distinction, to raise the status of the vocational school and to encourage the provision of a more comprehensive-type curriculum in both secondary and vocational schools. In addition, a new form of post-primary school, initially comprehensive (1963), and subsequently community (1970), was to be established. These schools were to be co-educational, open to all classes and levels of ability, and offering a wide curriculum to match the full range of pupil aptitudes and aspirations. The desire to move away from a binary towards a more comprehensive system involved considerations of labour market needs, optimum utilisation of resources and egalitarianism. However, predictably in the situation in the Republic, the aspect which attracted most interest and considerable conflict was the question of control. This conflict was most evident with respect to the community school, which seems likely to be the growth area in the future. The community school represents a partnership between religious authorities and vocational education committees. The debate over the deeds of trust, which serve as the legal instruments of partnership, lasted for many years before agreement was reached.

From the foregoing account of the evolution and structure of primary and post-primary education, it is not surprising that most official documents on education stress the importance of the value dimension. For example, the *Council of Education Report on the Curriculum of Secondary Schools* (1962) in endorsing the existing curricular pattern in secondary schools identified the dominant purpose of these schools as the inculcation of religious ideals and values. More recently the *Teacher's Handbook* prepared by the Department of Education to introduce the new child-centred curriculum contains the following statement in its discussion on the aims and functions of primary education: 'Each human being is created in God's image. He has a life to lead and soul to be saved. Education is therefore concerned not only with life but with the purpose of life. And since all men are equal in the sight of God, each is entitled to an equal chance of obtaining optimum personal fulfilment.' (Department of Education 1971).

It might be argued however, that the apparent close correspondence between religious control and explicit value priorities does not explain many of the developments in Irish education since the early 1960s. The publication of *Investment in Education* in 1966 marks a distinct reorientation in Irish education. In the wake of the adoption of a programme for economic development, with its commitment to economic growth and export oriented industrialisation, the educational system would henceforth be assessed by its capacity to facilitate the achievement of these new economic objectives. It is noteworthy that the *Investment in Education* report was jointly funded by the OECD and the Irish government. This formal involvement of an influential international organisation in a major fact-finding and analytic report helped to reformulate objectives in education. A major preoccupation of the report was with labour market needs; it was suggested that there would be shortages of technically qualified personnel unless remedial action was taken. Concern was expressed that the post-primary curriculum was unsuited to the needs of a rapidly changing society. Other major concerns of the survey team, which were to remain on the agenda of Irish policy makers, were the value question of equality of educational opportunity and the more pragmatic issue of optimum use of scarce resources.

Since the publication of *Investment in Education* there has been a notable shift in curricular provision and take up in Irish post-primary schools. There has been a significant growth in the percetage of students taking science, business and technical subjects. It has been suggested that of all the interest groups who are seeking to redefine the purpose of post-primary schooling, it is the business and scientific sectors which have succeeded most in defining what is appropriate educational knowledge (Lynch 1981). However, the pattern of curricular change reflects more than the success of a particular interest group. The growth in the provision and take up of economically utilisable subjects on the post-primary school curriculum reflects the centrality of economic self-interest as a cultural value.

The relationship between education and economic utility is perhaps best illustrated by changes in the pattern of third level education in the Republic of Ireland. Developments over the past fifteen years have effected a radical transformation of the system of higher education. The major growth area has been the technological sector. Traditionally third level education was synonymous with university education; as recently as 1968–69 seventy-eight per cent of total enrolments in higher education were in the university sector. However, by 1980 only 41 per cent of new entrants enrolled in the university sector. Almost all of the new third-level institutions which have been developed are in the technological sector. The establishment of nine RTCs and two NIHEs, where almost all course offerings are in the fields of Applied Science, Engineering and Business Studies, testify to the trend towards vocationalism in higher education. This same trend is also evident within the universities, where the most highly valued places (as reflected in competition) are in the professional faculties. This utilitarian conception of higher education is enthusiastically endorsed by government. The chapter on higher education in the *White Paper on Educational Development* (1980) advances only one criterion by which to evaluate policy options: higher education provision must match labour market needs.

In summary, it is evident that the educational system has been designed as a socialising agency producing labour power with the appropriate consciousness and skills. While there has been a notable absence of research which seeks to specify the detailed working of this socialisation process, it would appear that developments in education in the Republic since the 1960s have reoriented the system to make it more responsive to the needs of the economy. The recent prominence given to utilitarian considerations must be viewed in the context of earlier preoccupations with more 'spiritual' values, whether they be religious or nationalistic. However, the apparent reorientation in the values which are given greatest visibility in the educational system signifies only a partial change. The educational system under colonial rule, the system after independence, and the present system fulfilled and continue to fulfil essentially similar functions. This continuity is most evident when we examine the second major function of schooling.

Selection and social reproduction

Most sociologists are interested in the school's selection function. The increased significance of the school as a determinant of future status is linked to changes in the occupational structure of our society. Several indicators help to pinpoint the magnitude of this change in the Republic of Ireland over the past sixty years. For example, in 1926 53 per cent of the workforce were employed in agriculture; by 1981 this percentage had dropped to 17. Within the non-agricultural workforce the main growth areas have been in the professional, semi-professional, managerial, administrative and other white collar occupations; the number of skilled manual workers has also increased significantly while the percentage of the workforce categorised as semi-skilled or unskilled manual has decreased. When the employment status of the workforce is examined the increase in the percentage classified as 'employees' is notable. This has grown from 45 per cent in 1926 to an estimated 76 per cent in 1983. In reviewing these and other changes Rottman and Hannan (1982) concluded that during this century in the Republic of Ireland the basic structuring principle of the stratification system has changed: the determining role of family property and inheritance has been replaced by that of wage bargaining. In the early part of this century education was not a major determinant of adult life chances; its decisive impact was confined to a small section of the middle-class who could afford private secondary and university education. By contrast, in recent years educational skills and credentials have differentiated between skilled and unskilled manual workers and between professional, managerial and other routine service workers.

Having established the close relationship between the possession of educational credentials and the attainment of high status in the occupational world, we now turn our attention towards an examination of differential educational attainment. Research findings on this issue in the Republic have replicated the findings of sociologists in other countries. Since the issue was first examined in *Investment in Education*, a succession of studies demonstrated a close relationship between social class position and educational attainment. The process of social reproduction is complete; education mediates the relationship between origins and destinations. Future occupational status (destinations) is determined by educational attainment which in turn is determined by social class of origin.

There is evidence of clear class differences in the level of educational achievement, both at the primary and post-primary stage. For example, at primary level Fontes and Kellaghan (1977) found that children from lower socio-economic groups were more likely to have problems related to literacy. At the post-primary level Swan (1978) found that 30 per cent of children of unskilled manual workers were retarded in reading compared with less than 5 per cent of children from upper middle-class groups.

Research data on class differentials in educational participation are considerably more extensive. In 1972 Rudd examined the social origin of national school terminal leavers, i.e. children leaving primary school without availing themselves of post-primary education. This group, which constituted about 15 per cent of the age cohort, came predominantly from the semi-skilled and unskilled manual and other agricultural social groups. Perhaps the most important change in Irish education over the past two decades has been the growth in participation levels beyond the compulsory years. Up to 1972 the minimum legal age for school leaving was fourteen; it was then raised to fifteen. However, an ever-increasing percentage of the age cohort are remaining in school beyond the minimum age. A recent international comparison of participation rates in full-time education for the 15–19 age group (the post-compulsory years) reveals that Ireland ranks twelfth out of 24 OECD member countries (OECD 1982). However, the overall increase in participation rates has not decreased class differentials. Rottman and Hannan (1982) have compared the social group inequalities in the participation of those aged 15–19 in 1961 with those which obtained in 1971. Comparing the respective participation rates of the Professional, Employers and Managers and

Salaried Employees group with that of the Semi-skilled, Un-skilled Manual and Other Agricultural groups, they found that the rate of increase of the latter groups (from 10 per cent to 30 per cent) was greater than the former (from 46 per cent to 67 per cent), while the absolute difference between these social groups had widened slightly by 1971. One interpretation of this finding (which is not unique to the Republic of Ireland) might be to suggest that the real beneficiaries of the introduction of free post-primary education in 1967 were the middle-classes. Post-primary education was made free in order to enable the poor to take more advantage of it but the paradoxical consequence was to increase subsidies to the affluent. More recent data on the educational attainment by social group of post-primary school leavers suggest that these inequalities continued to persist up to 1981 (Breen 1984).

Social inequalities in educational participation are most apparent at third level. In spite of an approximately four-fold increase in total enrolments in higher education over the past three decades, there is little evidence of any significant reduction in disparities between the proportionate representation of the different social groups. In the mid-1960s Nevin (1967–68) found that 7 per cent of university students were from the families of manual workers; twelve years later 11 per cent of university students came from these groups. Table 1 presents the most recent comprehensive data on the social background of new entrants to all higher education. To facilitate comparison between the size of each social group and its proportionate representation among higher education entrants, a participation ratio has been calculated. This ratio serves as an approximate measure of the degree to which each social group is 'over-represented' or 'under-represented' among third level entrants. It is observed that students from the Higher Professional group are over-represented by a factor of four while students from the Unskilled Manual group are under-represented by a factor of nine (Clancy 1982).

The persistence of marked inequalities in the attainment of valuable educational credentials raises serious questions about

Table 1: **Socio-economic status of 1980 entrants to higher education and national population under 14 years of age in 1971**

Social Groups	Higher Education Entrants 1980 %	National Population Under 14 years in 1971 %	Participation Ratio
1. Farmers	21.1	20.3	1.04
2. Other Agricultural Occupations	0.9	4.3	0.21
3. Higher Professional	11.8	3.0	3.93
4. Lower Professional	7.1	3.1	2.29
5. Employers and Managers	19.5	7.1	2.75
6. Salaried Employees	7.9	2.7	2.93
7. Intermediate Non-Manual Workers	11.1	10.0	1.11
8. Other Non-Manual Workers	5.8	11.7	0.50
9. Skilled Manual Workers	10.9	21.4	0.51
10. Semi-Skilled Manual Workers	2.7	5.5	0.49
11. Unskilled Manual Workers	1.2	10.9	0.11
TOTAL N	11,660 (a)	842,121 (b)	1.00
%	(100)	(100)	

(a) Students for whom no socio-economic status data were available have been excluded from this table in addition to foreign students and those from Northern Ireland.

(b) Children whose social group was unknown have been excluded from this table.

Source: *Clancy (1982 p. 19)*

the meritocratic assumption which underpins the public funding of education. These questions remain, notwithstanding the
conclusions reached by Greaney and Kellaghan (1984) in their
major longitudinal study. They conclude that their data suggest
that in the Republic 'the meritocratic ideal is being approached
if not quite being attained.' This conclusion has been contested,
and the study has become the focus of some academic debate
(see *Economic and Social Review* 1985). Whatever the merits of the
respective positions it would appear that, since social destinations are so closely related to social origins, the middle-classes
have perfected the process of passing on their 'achieved status'
from one generation to the next. The reproduction of achieved
status in an apparently meritocratic society seems to have replaced the inherited privileges of an ascriptive society.

Because of the persistence of the close relationship between
social class and educational achievement, much research has
been devoted to finding an explanation for this relationship.
Most attention has focussed on the differences in home background of students. Initially the focus was on differences in
material circumstances of the home, such as income, family size
and housing conditions.

While differences in material circumstances continue to be
relevant, it is noticeable that the research focus on correlates of
differential educational achievement has shifted towards an
analysis of cultural features of families which are found to have
greater explanatory power. Different patterns of socialisation
and child-rearing were closely linked to differences in educational outcomes. Some of the cultural variables identified were
manifestly relevant. These included such factors as parents' attitudes towards education, the number of books in the home and
the reading habits of parents. Other variables identified which
were not self-evidently relevant included differences in fundamental value orientations of parents and linguistic patterns of
the family (see Banks 1976).

The link between value orientations and education was
explored in a Dublin study by Craft (1974) who found that
parents' value orientations (especially mothers) served to dif-

ferentiate between those adolescents who were early leavers and those who stayed on at school beyond the minimum age. In particular, Craft found that the children of parents who were future time oriented were more likely to remain in school.

One of the most original and ultimately most controversial approaches towards explaining differential educational achievement was that developed by Bernstein (1971) in his analysis of linguistic codes. Bernstein postulated a connection between social structure, language and educability. He identified two linguistic codes, restricted and elaborated. The restricted code is a language of implicit rather than explicit meaning. The vocabulary is drawn from a narrow range while the speaker's intentions are relatively unelaborated verbally. The elaborated code, on the other hand, is a language of explicit meaning. It is a vehicle for more individuated responses and consists of more complex grammatical structures, subordinate clauses, adjectives and qualifiers. Bernstein suggests that the middle-class have access to both codes and are able to switch from one to another according to the social context. In contrast, many working-class families will be limited to a restricted code. The educational implications of this are self-evident. Since the elaborated code is the language of the school, working-class children will be at a distinct disadvantage, hence, their poorer performance. After initial approval Bernstein's thesis was challenged, most notably by Labov (1973). The point at issue is not whether the two codes are different but rather whether the restricted code is inferior.

A major implication of the research on class-linked cultural differences between families is that the experience of schooling is qualitatively different for working-class and middle-class children. In the case of the latter the transition to school is facilitated by the essential continuity of experience, whereas in the case of many working-class children the transition is characterised by an essential discontinuity. However, to pose the issue in these terms is to suggest the possibility of an alternative analytic approach. Instead of focussing on the class characteristics of those who succeed and those who fail it is appropriate to examine the class characteristics of the educational experience at which they succeed or fail. This reorientation in approach represents an important development within the sociology of education.

Most of the analysis and research on internal school processes is located within an interactionist perspective and consequently it lies outside the scope of this paper. However, it is clear that a commitment to this type of inquiry implies that what goes on within the school has an independent effect on outcomes. While this assertion appears uncontentious there has, until recent years, been very little evidence to support it. A succession of large-scale empirical studies concluded that schools had very little independent effect on attainment (Jencks 1972). By implication it did not seem to matter what type of school a child attended since educational outcomes were almost entirely determined by individual and family background characteristics. More recent research has suggested that schools do matter; they have a significant structural or contextual effect (see, for example, Rutter *et al.* 1979).

An important theoretical and substantive finding to emerge from the literature on school effectiveness is that differences in the socio-economic composition and value climate of the student body represent important contextual variables which influence individual outcomes. This is especially relevant in the Republic of Ireland at the post-primary level. The present system of post-primary education is a highly differentiated one where variations in social selectivity, prestige and academic emphasis range from those found in fee-paying secondary schools through non-fee paying secondary, comprehensive, community and vocational schools. These different school types have different retention rates and different transfer rates to higher education (Clancy 1982). While it is clear that the differential performance of the various types of schools reflects differences in individual pupil characteristics at intake, it is also certain that the social class composition of the schools has a significant effect on student aspirations and achievement, independent of the social class background of any individual student. The institutionalisation, within a system of publicly funded education, of invidious status hierarchies between different post-primary schools serves to reproduce existing status hierarchies. The willing cooperation by the state with those religious communities which operate fee-paying secondary schools demonstrates a distinct lack of commitment to meritocratic principles.

Conclusion

This paper has attempted to describe, within a sociological framework, some features of the educational system in the Republic of Ireland. It has been suggested that education involves two essential processes. The first of these involves socialisation and the moulding of consciousness, while the second involves selection and social reproduction. Of course the two processes can only be separated analytically; in reality both are compounded. While the school is involved in socialisation it is simultaneously differentiating between pupils as part of its social selection function. The interpenetration of the two processes becomes more obvious when we examine the role of education in social reproduction. In seeking to explain the intractable relationship between social class of origin and educational attainment, most analysis has focussed on differences in the socialisation patterns of families.

Notes

1   This technical socialisation was highly sex differentiated. The gender dimension, the importance of which now rivals that of class within the sociology of education, is not discussed in this paper (see Chapter 14).

References

BANKS, O. 1976. *The Sociology of Education*, third edition, London, Batsford.

BERNSTEIN, B. 1971. *Class, Codes and Control*, Vol. 1, London, Routledge and Kegan Paul.

BOWLES, S. and H. GINTIS, 1976. *Schooling in Capitalist America*, London, Routledge and Kegan Paul.

BREEN, R. 1984. *Education and the Labour Market: Work and Unemployment Among Recent Cohorts of Irish School Leavers*, Dublin, Economic and Social Research Institute, Paper No. 119.

CLANCY, P. 1982. *Participation in Higher Education*, Dublin, Higher Education Authority.

COOLAHAN, J. 1981. *Irish Education: History and Structure*, Dublin, Institute of Public Administration.

COUNCIL OF EDUCATION, 1962. *Report of the Council of Education on the Curriculum of Secondary Schools*, Dublin, Stationery Office.

CRAFT, M. 1974. 'Talent, Family Values and Education in Ireland' in J. Eggleston (ed.) *Contemporary Research in the Sociology of Education*, London, Methuen, pp. 47-67.

DELAMONT, S. 1983. *Interaction in The Classroom*, second edition, London, Methuen.

DEPARTMENT OF EDUCATION, 1971. *Primary School Curriculum: Teachers' Handbook*, Part 1, Dublin, Browne and Nolan.

DEPARTMENT OF EDUCATION, 1980. *White Paper on Educational Development*, Dublin, Stationery Office.

DEPARTMENT OF EDUCATION, 1984. *Tuarascáil Staitistiúil, 1981/82*, Dublin, Stationery Office.

THE ECONOMIC AND SOCIAL REVIEW, 1985. 'Symposium on Equality of Opportunity in Irish Schools', *The Economic and Social Review*, 16, 2, January 1985, pp. 77-156.

FONTES, P. and T. KELLAGHAN, 'Incidence and Correlates of Illiteracy in Irish Primary Schools' *The Irish Journal of Education*, Vol. XI, No. 1, pp. 5-20.

GREANEY, V. and T. KELLAGHAN, *Equality of Opportunity in Irish Schools: A Longitudinal Study of 500 Students*, Dublin, The Educational Company.

INVESTMENT IN EDUCATION, 1966. Report of the survey team appointed by the Minister for Education, Dublin, Stationery Office.

JENCKS, C. *et al.* 1972. *Inequality: A Reassessment of the Effect of Family and Schooling in America*, New York, Basic Books.

LABOV, W. 1973. 'The Logic of Nonstandard English' in N. Keddie (ed.) *Tinker, Tailor ... The Myth of Cultural Deprivation*, Harmondsworth, Penguin, pp. 21-66.

LYNCH, K. 1982. 'A Sociological Analysis of the Functions of Second Level Schooling', *Irish Educational Studies*, Vol. 2, pp. 32-58.

NEVIN, M. 1967-68. 'A Study of the Social Background of Students in the Irish Universities', *Journal of the Statistical and Social Inquiry Society of Ireland*, Vol. 21, No. 4, pp. 201-225.

OECD, 1982. *The OECD Observer*, No. 115, p. 30.

PARSONS, T. 1959. 'The School Class as a Social System: some of its Functions in American Society', *Harvard Educational Review*, Vol. 29, No. 4, pp. 297-318.

ROTTMAN, D. B. and D. F. HANNAN *et al.* 1982. *The Distribution of Income in the Republic of Ireland: A Study of Social Class & Family-Cycle Inequalities,* Dublin, Economic and Social Research Institute.

RUDD, J. 1972. 'A Survey of National School Terminal Leavers' *Social Studies,* Vol. 1, pp.61–73.

RUTTER, M. *et al.* 1979. *Fifteen Thousand Hours: Secondary Schools and Their Effects on Children,* London, Open Books.

SWAN, T. D. 1978. *Reading Standards in Irish Schools,* Dublin, The Educational Company.

7
Religious Practice and Secularisation

MÁIRE NIC GHIOLLA PHÁDRAIG

> To define 'religion', to say what it is, is not possible at the
> start of a presentation such as this. Definition can be
> attempted, if at all, only at the conclusion of the study.
> (Weber 1963, p. 1)

Newcomers to sociology often hesitate over the appropriateness
of studying religion. It may be because they view it as too sacred,
personal, and non-empirical to be studied by a behavioural
science. Or they may simply regard it as an anachronism and of
insufficient importance to warrant exploration. These two value
positions reflect the divergence with regard to doing sociology of
religion which has existed since the early days of the discipline.
The ultra positivists regarded religion as simply bad science, a
way in which simple peoples tried to explain and control natural
phenomena by such means as rites and prayers for a good har-
vest. The advance of science and the dissemination of its findings
would guarantee the erosion of the basis of religion. As it was
only a matter of time before religion would disappear, there was
no point in spending time in its study, time which could be
utilised in the analysis of some more enduring institutions.

The positivists' antipathy to the study of religion might be
expected to be endorsed within the marxist approach. Marx's
sweeping statement, 'Religion is the opium of the people', might
seem to close the door on further discussion of religion within

137

marxist analysis. But some later marxist writers developed the latent potential of Marx's work in identifying the importance of religion as part of the ideological weaponry with which the dominant ruling class maintains its sway over the subordinate class. This distinction has only recently been taken up within the sociology of religion, stimulated by the rise of liberation theology in Latin America which draws on both christianity and marxism. This new marxist sociology of religion would regard religion as a variable expression of social relationships which are generated through class conflict. The role of religion will vary according to the stage of development of a society and may in some instances act as the opium which lulls workers to accept their lot. In other circumstances religion, particularly where sectarian divisions are along class lines, and religious innovations occur, can actually act as a focus for the development of class consciousness. But as the class struggle makes progress, the significance of religion tends to decline. Sectarian divisions which occur within the proletariat, however — as is the case in Northern Ireland — can inhibit the development of class consciousness and retard the revolution (see Maduro, 1975).

The other two most seminal writers in the establishment of sociology, Max Weber and Émile Durkheim, were more influential in the development of the religious field. They were not themselves religious believers but both regarded the study of religion as a central aspect of sociology. Durkheim went so far as to regard religion as a projection of society and as a way in which people reverenced society itself. Religious norms were the ultmate sanctions and guarantee of good behaviour. They could operate even when the detection of breaches of the norms would be unlikely. His work was particularly useful in underlining the importance of ritual in bonding a community, and the role of religion in combatting alienation. Weber's work in the sociology of religion concentrated on the role of religious values, in particular where they established a climate which was hostile or positive towards enterprise and economic development. His major work, *The Protestant Ethic and the Spirit of Capitalism*, pointed to religion as an independent influence on the development of capitalism and thus has been regarded as a critique of Marx. His work on rationality as a growing feature of modern life and as incompatible with the sacred has been utilised by sociologists in the explanation of secularisation. Weber's work continues to be drawn on in the study of new religious movements.

While early sociologists had their value positions about the study of religion, religious personnel also had their value positions about the sociology of religion! The initial reactions were unfavourable; such studies were viewed as attempts to 'explain away' religion. Religious asserted that sacred phenomena could not be known by human means alone. It is true that certain aspects of religion do not lend themselves to empirical verification. We cannot, as sociologists, test the existence of God or an afterlife. But we can study what beliefs are held about such matters, and infer what the social consequences which follow from people's beliefs are. For example, fatalism and lack of enterprise are found in cultures where the religions stress the overriding importance of 'God's will' or explain everything as preordained. Nowadays, there is mutual cooperation between religions and sociologists. The major religions view sociology as offering insights which are valuable in pastoral planning, and many national churches have established their own research institutes. One such body was set up in Ireland in 1970 — the Council for Research and Development reports to a commission of the Catholic bishops on trends in religious beliefs, practice, opinions, vocation rates, etc.

Religion in Ireland

The visitor to Ireland is confronted on every side with evidence of religion — the numerous and well-attended churches, the Angelus on TV, the sober-clad clergy and religious symbols everywhere — in jewellery, in propaganda on justice and morality, in religious imagery (both devout and blasphemous) and in speech. But are the Irish a particularly religious people?

Let us examine some of the evidence.

If we take religious affiliation as our criterion, it will be seen that in 1981 93 per cent of the Republic's population were Catholics and the three main Protestant churches accounted for 3.35 per cent. Just over one in a hundred people declared they were of 'no religion'.

Table 1: **Population of the Republic of Ireland classified by religion, 1971 and 1981**

Religious denomination	1971	1981	1981 as % 1971
	%	%	%
Catholic	93.87	93.04	99.12
Church of Ireland	3.28	2.77	84.45
Presbyterian	.54	.41	75.92
Methodist	.19	.17	89.47
Jewish	.09	.06	66.67
Other stated religion	.21	.31	147.62
No religion	.26	1.15	442.31
Not stated	1.57	2.09	133.12
TOTAL	2,978,248	3,443,405	

While 97 per cent of the population have a religious affiliation, the table represents a drop of 1.6 per cent on the 1971 proportion. The main religious groups have shared in the decline, although to varying degrees; the worst hit religious group is the Jewish, at only two-thirds of their 1971 strength; Catholics are the best off at 99 per cent of their proportion in 1971. The increase in the 'not stated' category may account for some of the decline. With the net inflow of immigrants during this period, we would also expect some increase in the diversity of religious affiliation and this is reflected in almost one and a half times as large a percentage of 'other stated religions' in 1981 as compared with 1971. It is the 'no religion' group which shows the greatest increase. Although still very small in extent (1.15 per cent), it is almost four and a half times as great a proportion as in 1971.

Since the disestablishment of the Church of Ireland (Anglican Communion) in 1869, Ireland has not had an established church. This contrasts with countries such as the Scandinavian states and Britain, where the Lutheran and Anglican churches have an established civic role which is mainly ceremonial, having lost much of their political functions and power. By comparison with these countries, the 'rites of passage' (or the marking of, in particular, births, marriages and deaths) are almost exclusively religious ceremonies in Ireland, despite the lack of a formal link between church and state. While in recent years there has been a growth in the number of civil marriages (from 170 in 1971 to 454 in 1981), these still form only a tiny proportion of the total each year. Formal religion still provides the background for the more important landmarks in people's lives. For the vast majority, religion also marks the changing weeks and seasons — 91 per cent of Catholics in the Republic of Ireland attend church weekly (Nic Ghiolla Phádraig 1976) as do about 45–55 per cent of Protestants (Bowen 1983,.p. 133), and similar attendances are found in Northern Ireland. There would appear to be some relationship between the proportion of people attending church, and whether or not the group is a religious minority in each state. Catholics in Northern Ireland have a slightly higher attendance than those in the Republic, while Protestants in the Republic have a higher attendance than those in Northern Ireland (McAllister 1983). But does such a high attendance level represent a true religious commitment?

There is a great deal of continuity in religion from Northern Ireland to the Republic. All churches are organised on a 32 county basis and clergy circulate within diocesan rather than political borders. Policy decisions in all churches are made on a joint basis, while taking conditions and legislation in each area into account. In the Republic of Ireland the Catholic Church has been viewed as the moral touchstone of the nation and although there are no formal links with the state, the informal and indirect links are very significant in shaping the direction of public policy. Church and state are informally linked, above all, through the educational system, particularly at first and second levels where the vast majority of schools are run by committees 'guided by' parish clergy or by religious orders (Murphy 1980). A further important institutional link between church and state is found in the health services, where a significant number of hospitals and residential care centres are church run. While these two links have their roots in the colonial system, neither the church (for ideological reasons) nor the state (for financial reasons) is anxious to reverse the situation. Similar arrangements in relation to education and health are also found in Northern Ireland — a joint legacy of the colonial accommodation with the sectarian divisions. The decline in numbers of people entering religious orders, together with the expansion of the educational, health and welfare services, cannot but dilute the influence that clergy and religious orders have traditionally exercised in these areas. For other denominations there is also a parallel set of institutions, although of course on a smaller scale. The Church of Ireland, by far the largest Protestant religion, controls most of these institutions in the Republic of Ireland, and shows as little anxiety to divest itself of them as the Catholic Church.

While the informal ideological influence of the Catholic Church, afforded by the high levels of practice and the control of much of the education system, is substantial, active involvement in trying to influence government policy in the Republic of Ireland is said to have occurred on only a few occasions (Whyte 1971). Church intervention in matters of family care and sexual morality is regarded as legitimate, and guidance in such matters is not only accepted but sought by a large section of the Catholic population. This was evident in the 1983 referendum to amend the constitution with a view to prevent the introduction of abortion legislation. The campaign was initiated by lay people rather than clerics and it only actively involved the hierarchy at a fairly advanced stage. This exemplifies the role of lay Catholic organisations, which tend to be more conservative than the hierarchy and completely obedient to it, and tend not to make a radical critique of clerical policy as some Catholic groups in other countries do. The colonial inheritance of an underprivileged church, which had often mediated on behalf of an under-privileged people, has headed off anticlericalism at source and provided loyal, if not always uncritical, support. On matters other than sexuality and family life, there is either indifference or ambivalence regarding church intervention. For instance, the pastoral *The Work of Justice* (1977) evoked very little discussion. There is also a tendency to ignore uncomfortable church teachings which is manifestly the case in relation to the use of violence to achieve political independence and the reunification of Ireland. To match this ambivalence on the part of the laity, the church speaks with a 'plurality of voices' (Peillon 1982) which enables it to keep the pastoral lines of communication open. There is a tolerance of a range of opinions and pastoral emphases which provides for work with groups outside the mainstream of Irish society whether they be militant republicans, travellers, alcoholics etc. This flexibility is attained above all in the work of religious orders. These religious communities have a certain degree of autonomy from the local bishop and a structure which enables relatively speedy withdrawal from work which is seen as no longer an appropriate apostolate.

The minority religious groups made little contribution to public debate or to discussions of legislative proposals until the 1970s. The ecumenical movement, the parallels with the Catholic minority in Northern Ireland and a greater sense of identity with Ireland, are thought to be among the factors which have drawn them into the public arena in recent times. Their spokespersons argue consistently for a more secular and liberal state, and for a tolerance of lifestyles which depart from traditional Catholic norms. The residues of esteem for the old ascendancy class, a conscious political statement to the world in general, and Northern Ireland in particular, combine to give their spokespersons a receptive audience.

The extent to which ethnic identity is bound up with religion is an important issue in the study of religion in contemporary Ireland. Research indicates that this depends on the religious denomination; a majority of Protestants (59 per cent) deny any such association, but the nature of the ethnic identity was important for Catholics; three in five of those selecting 'Irish' or their county as their main identity saw their religious affiliation as an important ingredient in this. But more than half of those Catholics opting for Anglo-Irish/British, European/Other denied any such link with religion (Nic Ghiolla Phádraig 1976, unpublished data from this study). When social attitudes to such topics as work, authority and women's roles are compared for Protestants and Catholics, however, little differences are found (McAllister 1983).

It is useful to adopt an institutional approach to the definition of religion in Ireland as there is a high level of identification with, and participation in, formal religion. This approach does not allow for other factors, however. There is, for example, a sur-vival and coexistence of 'folk religion' and superstitions with conventional religion. Another blind-spot introduced by a con-centration on an institutional approach is the tendency to view religious organisations as cohesive bodies and to ignore the divisions and tensions that may exist. This might lead to neglecting the distinction of High Church (which stresses sacra-mental and devotional life) and Low Church (which stresses the Bible and evangelical work) in the Church of Ireland. The institutional approach also overlooks the range of opinions that exist on a variety of topics among the Catholic hierarchy — the moral condemnation of nuclear arms by Bishop Casey contrasts with the labelling of anti-nuclear policies as 'politically naive' by Bishop Newman. The institutional approach may also neglect the grounds on which members of different denomina-tions unite in common purpose, for example, the charismatic or pentecostalist movement which is organised on a fairly ecumen-ical basis; CONGOOD, the umbrella organisation for groups working for the third world; the inclusion of other christians in the previously exclusively Catholic Society of St Vincent de Paul.

The development of Ireland and secularisation

In discussions about change in religion, the model most frequently referred to in both popular debate and sociological analysis is that of secularisation. Recent attempts at legislative initiatives towards a more secular, liberal society have aroused great controversy in Ireland. Neither side disputes that such a trend is in progress. It is only the extent to which it has advanced, the instrumentality of legislation in producing it, and the desirability of this situation that they dispute. But what does the term 'secularisation' mean? A common definition of secularisation is 'The process whereby religious thinking, practice and institutions lose social significance' (Wilson 1966, p. XIV). This is seen as an outcome of modernisation or development in which a process or train of secularisation is set in motion and drawn by the twin engines of urbanisation and industrialisation. This process occurs at several levels, all of which tend to weaken the impact of religion: (a) the differentiation of institutions and roles takes place as internal divisions occur within institutions which then become autonomous organisations. Because functions are more specialised they also tend to become more compartmentalised and to have little intercommunication. Consequently religious functions are more specialised and less influential in other social spheres. For example, the medieval church was the main source of educational and social assistance provisions whereas the contemporary welfare states now supply these provisions through a multiplicity of specialised agencies; (b) the fragmentation and multiplication of religious organisations leads to a loss of plausibility for all religions and scepticism about their claims to possession of the truth; it also eventually opens the door to the option of 'no religion'; (c) rationalisation is said to occur, with the result that there is an emphasis on what is useful and pragmatic rather than on otherworldly or traditional values based on authority. For example, the success of modern medicine in controlling infectious diseases would decrease the reliance on relics, shrines and prayers for cures. These 'rational' values and lifestyles are diffused or spread from the most developed centres to the less developed, particularly through the mass communications media. Most treatments of both modernisation and secularisation depict them as one-way, irreversible and even inevitable movements along the road from traditional to modern societies on the one hand, and from sacred to secular societies on the other hand. There are many problems with these assumptions: they do not allow for other ways in which social and religious change may be introduced; for example, the impact of conquest; the possibility of religious revival movements; the use of modern rational techniques (from salesmanship to video) by evangelical groups to promote their creed. These are some of the possibilities that the theories neglect.

An examination of the religious situation in Ireland provides a critical test of the secularisation theory. As this chapter is mainly concerned with religion in the Republic of Ireland, the statistical information available is mainly about Catholics and so most of the discussion is taken up with this group. The expected consequences of modernisation for religion will be compared with the available data for the Catholic religion in Ireland.

The relationship of the Catholic Church to the modernisation process

The church played a very active part in the differentiation process during the nineteenth century. This phase was characterised by discrimination against Catholics and mutual suspicion between denominations. The main institutions set up during this period were on a denominational basis — hospitals, schools and orphanages — and these have contributed to the 'partial columnar' society on both sides of the border to this day. The term refers to the establishment of parallel and separate institutions for both religious groups. In Ireland the main divisions have been in relation to education, hospitals and welfare institutions, but in countries such as Holland, other major institutions such as the media and trade unions were also at one time organised separately for Catholics and Protestants. The first mass political mobilisation got underway in the 1820s and initially tackled the issue of Catholic emancipation. This movement received very strong church support. The differentiation process involved no conflict with the church, indeed we can trace a very great strengthening of the institutional church from this period.

One particularly public sign of religiosity is attendance at Mass, and so it tends to be used frequently in testing for secularisation. We tend to think of the Irish as particularly diligent with regard to Mass-going, and to view this as very much bound up with traditional Catholicism. But is it? In 1840 there was a priest: people ratio of only 1:3,023 and there were very few public places of worship; the ratio had improved to 1:1,500 in 1860 and continued to increase up to 1967. It has been estimated that given the number of priests and the lack of church accommodation in 1842, only 40 per cent of the population could have attended Mass on a given Sunday (Larkin 1976). However, with the church building programme, clerical recruitment and improved formation, and the introduction of Roman style devotions, Sunday Mass quickly became a universal practice. In surveys carried out in the early 1970s, over 90 per cent of the population were found to attend Mass at least weekly, a quarter of these going more frequently.

In the latter half of the nineteenth century church involvement in the nationalist cultural movements was indirect, issues concerning land reform and labour were divisive of the clergy, while the armed struggle drew clerical condemnation. The latter did not alienate the militants who compartmentalised their religious and political allegiances. In the post-independence phase, the church did not need to become directly involved in political affairs, as the politicians were almost all Catholic (there were some exceptions to this as when the hierarchy condemned proposed legislation relating to maternity and child care) (Whyte 1971). However, at a local level the clergy were major agents of social control. This period also saw a burgeoning of the lay apostolate (notably the Legion of Mary) and heavy Irish missionary activity.

The signs are mixed for religion in the current phase. Despite the fact that the population of the Republic is 93 per cent Catholic, there has been a greater consciousness of a plural dimension to society since the civil rights movement and the 'Troubles' began in the late 1960s in Northern Ireland. The introduction of a national television service in 1962 promoted empathy for alternative lifestyles. The Irish hierarchy adopted a very gradualist approach to the introduction of post-Vatican II liturgical changes and traditionalist protests have been almost non-existent despite the fact that in 1973 just 17 per cent indicated a preference for the Latin Mass. However, there have been negative signs. The vocations rate showed a continuous decrease from 1967 until 1980 when there was a slight upswing. Since the 1960s there has been a growth in material prosperity, and also an increase in social problems such as crime rates, marital breakdown and desertion, alcohol abuse etc. These factors are often cited as being associated with secularisation. Despite the fact that over half of the population attended ceremonies addressed by Pope John Paul II during his visit to Ireland in 1979 and almost all others followed the events on radio or television, there have been assertions that Ireland is becoming a secular society.

Given that the modernisation processes in our recent past have had a mixture of consequences both beneficial and retarding to religion, it remains to be examined whether these consequences can be traced in the approach to religion of contemporary Catholics.

A test of the secularisation thesis in Ireland

To test a theory of social change — secularisation — the data must be longitudinal or drawn from more than one point in time. In the absence of longitudinal data, an alternative is to do cross-sectional analysis. This is based on a comparison of religiousness of 'traditional' and 'modern' sectors at one point in time. In 1973–74 a wide-ranging study of religious attitudes, behaviour, beliefs, experiences and moral values was carried out in the Republic of Ireland.[1] This was in the form of personal interviews with 2,623 respondents sampled from the electoral registers; 79 per cent responded. Of the respondents 2,499 were lay Catholics and the analysis was largely concerned with this group. Data was also obtained on social and cultural indicators thus enabling a cross-sectional testing of the secularisation thesis (Nic Ghiolla Phádraig 1976).

The strongest aspect of religion in Ireland is religious practice. Nine out of ten Catholics go to Mass every Sunday and to Confession and Holy Communion up to three times a year. Half of those not attending Mass weekly gave reasons of lack of interest; the majority of the remainder were unable to attend through illness or work reasons. There was a statistical association between reasons given for attending Mass and frequency of attendance: the 23.4 per cent going more than weekly tended to give reasons of belief or devotion, the conformers (67.5 per cent) gave legalistic reasons (wished to fulfil church duty or avoid sin) and those going less than weekly gave reasons of habit or social pressure. Levels of devotion were somewhat lower than religious practice — 40 per cent of all respondents had family prayer at least occasionally and two in three had made some special effort the previous Lent.

Unlike most countries, levels of belief are lower than levels of religious practice. Fifty-nine per cent fully accepted all nine items which comprised an index of orthodoxy. Beliefs which were most threatening got the lowest level of support (belief in Hell and the Devil were each rejected by more than one quarter of the sample) whereas belief in God was 'accepted fully' by 95.5 per cent.

Some items were introduced to evaluate the extent to which religious experiences were found. About one-fifth replied that they had not experienced any of the items; two in three had had a 'feeling of being in God's presence' but only 31.6 per cent claimed to have had a 'feeling of having got a special message from God'.

The consoling power of religion during times of stress or trouble is often suggested as the reason for the persistence of religious belief. In order that this point of view might remain tenable, it must be shown firstly, that people do invoke religion on such occasions and secondly, that such invocation helps to allay anxiety rather than to arouse it. But for those (10 per cent) who had experienced serious trouble or problems over the previous year (for example, bereavement, serious illness, unemployment) only a tiny proportion agreed that religion had played a part in helping them to interpret or accept their problems. However, between half and three-quarters saw their religion as helpful in the achievement of a series of personal and social goals, and similar proportions claimed that in the event of a clash religion would come before other interests such as recreation, occupation or family.

In the attitudinal sphere respondents were largely supportive of various aspects of the church although there was a sizeable critical section of up to 45 per cent in some instances. A large majority, however, were happy with the changes they perceived in the church — most referring to the liturgy — and only one in three voiced specific criticisms of the church.

The social relationships in which respondents were involved were largely supportive of their religious beliefs and behaviour. Not surprisingly in a population which was 94 per cent Catholic, the opportunities for inter-faith contact were limited. Only 0.3 per cent were married to a non-Catholic and only 0.6 per cent were themselves children of mixed marriages. While one in eight claimed to have close relatives of other religious affiliations, less than half of them meet these relatives more than yearly. Almost two-thirds have only Catholics as friends. It is not surprising, then, that they perceive a high degree of similarity between their own religious beliefs and practice and those of their family, friends and colleagues (role set similarity). Twenty-nine per cent saw these groups as identical to themselves and only 16 per cent saw a high level of dissimilarity.

Attitudes to inter-faith relations were tapped by a series of items and just under half to three-quarters expressed tolerant attitudes; one-third scored high on this index and one-fifth scored low. This ecumenical indicator and other measures of inter-faith contact were negatively related to religiosity.

For Protestants in the Republic of Ireland the finding on inter-faith contact is reversed. Owing to their low proportion and small total membership overall, chance contact with another Protestant can only be one in nineteen. Although there is a certain degree of concentration of the smaller denominations in particular geographical areas, nevertheless the extent of inter-church marriages (between one in five and one in three of Protestants marrying in 1961 are estimated to have married Catholics (Walsh 1970, p. 29)) and friendships is very high for such groups. In Northern Ireland, however, the pool of potential mates and friends is large enough to sustain denominational divisions and hence the incidence of intermarriage is very low there.

To turn now to some of the more important social and cultural variables (several of which are indicators of modernisation) and their relationship to religious variables:

Sex: Males in general are regarded as being more exposed to modernisation than females. In most cases females proved to be more religious than males. This relationship is stronger for religious practice than beliefs. Women average almost 50 per cent more overconformity and have less than half the under-conformity of men.

Age: The general trend is of a strong linear relationship between age-group and religiosity. Age proves to be the best overall predictor of religious beliefs, behaviour and values. However, there is one exception to this linear relationship — the 21–25 age-group have a lower level of religiosity than the 18–20 year olds who were the youngest group. Age was equally important for both males and females.

Urbanisation as indicated by area of upbringing and area of residence: For most religious variables, rural respondents scored higher than urban ones. Area of upbringing was a slightly better predictor than area of residence. The impact of urbanisation was somewhat greater for males than for females. The effect of the modernisation indicators tended to be compound e.g. one in three young urban males were underconformers on religious practice.

Farming background: 26.1 per cent were farmers or the dependants of farmers and this group may be classified as 'traditional'.

The farming group proved significantly more religious than the non-farming, and were also more religious than other rural respondents.

Education: The categories used were primary only, vocational, secondary and third level. The relationships to religious variables were curvilinear. Those whose education finished at primary school had the highest overall level of religiosity except for practice variables. The lowest scores were for those with vocational schooling. Levels of religiosity for the secondary educated sometimes exceed and sometimes fall below third level religiosity.

Class: The overall effect of social class on religiosity is slight. When class is dichotomised into white collar and blue collar workers, the overall trend is for white collar workers to score highest on religious experience and practice while blue collar workers score highest on religious beliefs and values. Income levels had little impact on religiosity.

Emigration: 26.6 per cent of the sample had lived abroad for six months or more and were potentially exposed to a different religious ethos. In most cases the religious scores for this group were significantly lower than for those who had never been abroad. When the results were controlled for sex, age-group, educational level, area of residence and occupation, the differences in most cases remain significant.

Political affiliation: No differences were found in relation to party allegiance in this study, although a sample of males only, taken around the same time, showed that Fianna Fail supporters were more likely to be Catholic and to attend church; Fine Gael had a higher proportion of non-Catholics and Labour supporters were usually Catholics who were below average attenders (McAllister and O'Connell, 1984).

Media consumption: The actual frequency of reading newspapers, listening to radio or watching television showed little overall relationship to religious variables, but reported consumption of foreign (mainly British) media was negatively associated with religious measures. It might be expected that the relationship between use of foreign media and religiosity might simply be a reflection of other factors such as urbanisation, emigration experience, etc. But, when variables such as area of residence and age were controlled, it still remained statistically significant, although the extent of association was halved.

It may be concluded, then, that indicators of modernisation are negatively related to measures of religiosity and so provide some support for the secularisation theory, but this is not the only way in which such relationships may be understood. The approach of most Irish Catholics to their religion tends to be fairly conventional, rigid and legalistic. This applies to their approach to religious practice and also to their interpretation of moral issues. While this was a fairly satisfactory response up to the mid-1960s, the lack of a reasoned and personalised faith and ethics and the heavy reliance on authority figures like the clergy to adjudicate on moral issues, leaves them ill-equipped to face a future in which both the church and the world have changed radically (McSweeney 1980). The inertia of the old patterns still obtains and hence, on the surface, the strength of the institution is very impressive. It is, however, a vulnerable body and one in which a loss of credibility by the bishops on a single important issue could jeopardise the persistence of commitment among a majority of their flock.

Notes

1. A replication of this study was carried out in 1984 by Ann Breslin and John Weafer. There was a fair degree of continuity of results; changes were generally less than 10%, and they marked signs of both growth and decline. In the belief sphere, and also in the moral values sphere, there was a move away from absolutes and towards a less certain, although largely, orthodox stand. In religious practice, there was a decline of 4% in Mass conformity but an increase in those attending more than the minimum; while reception of Communion showed an increase, fewer attended regular Confession. Both private and family prayer showed an increase. On attitudinal matters the 1984 survey found a high degree of support for the church. Social factors showed similar relationships to religious variables as were found in 1973-74, with younger people and urban groups showing least support for religious matters.

References

BRESLIN, ANN and JOHN WEAFER 1985. *Religious Beliefs, Practice and Moral Attitudes: A Comparison of Two Irish Surveys, 1974-1984*, Maynooth, Council for Research and Development, Report No. 21.

BOWEN, KURT 1983. *Protestants in a Catholic State: Ireland's Privileged Minority*, Dublin, Gill and Macmillan.

DURKHEIM, ÉMILE 1965. *The Elementary Forms of the Religious Life*, New York, The Free Press.

IRELAND 1977. *Census of Population, 1971*, Vol. IX, Religion, Dublin, Stationery Office.

IRELAND 1983. *Census of Population of Ireland, 1981*, Provisional Results Bulletin No. 40, Table 7.

LARKIN, EMMETT 1976. 'The devotional revolution in Ireland, 1850-1875', in *Historical Dimensions of Irish Catholicism*, New York, Arno.

McALLISTER, IAN 1983. Religious commitment and social attitudes in Ireland,' *Review of Religious Research*, Vol. 25, No. 1.

McALLISTER, IAN and O'CONNELL, DECLAN 1984. 'Political sociology of party support in Ireland: a reassessment', *Comparative Politics*, Vol. 16, No. 2, January.

McSWEENEY, BILL 1980. *Roman Catholicism: The Search for Relevance*, Oxford, Blackwell.

MADURO, OTTO 1975. 'Marxist analysis and sociology of religion', in CISR International Conference for the Sociology of Religion, *Religion and Social Change*, Acts of 13th Conference, Lloret de Mar, pp. 395-401.

MURPHY, CHRISTINA 1980. *School Report*, Dublin, Ward River Press.

NIC GHIOLLA PHÁDRAIG, MÁIRE 1976. 'Religion in Ireland,' *Social Studies*, Vol. V, No. 3, 1976.

PEILLON, MICHEL 1982. *Contemporary Irish Society: an Introduction*, Dublin, Gill and Macmillan.

WALSH, BRENDAN 1970. *Religion and Demographic Behaviour in Ireland*, Dublin, ESRI Paper No. 55.

WHYTE, JOHN H. 1980. *Church and State in Modern Ireland, 1923-1979*, Dublin, Gill and Macmillan.

WILSON, BRYAN 1966. *Religion in Secular Society*, London, C. A. Watts.

WEBER, MAX 1963. *The Sociology of Religion*, Boston, Beacon.

8
Marriage and Family

CHRIS CURTIN

Marriage and the family are viewed by lay persons, political and religious powerholders and social scientists as vitally important elements of society. The significance of the family is attributable to the tasks it performs, which include bringing new members into society, caring for them and ensuring that they are socialised according to prevailing norms and values. It is also, of course, the central mechanism for the transfer of property rights and the economic and political power associated with property. Family and kinship connections also provide a basis for recruitment to positions in economic and political organisations. Given this pivotal role in society it is not surprising that the family is often at the centre of social and political debate, as individuals and interested groups argue in favour of what they regard as the ideal form of marriage and the family.

Sociologists also differ in their views on the family. The dominant theoretical perspective, functionalism, emphasises the essential functions performed by the family for society and how the smaller nuclear family unit is best suited to the needs of modern industrial societies. Marxists, starting from quite different assumptions, arrive at somewhat similar conclusions to functionalists; they argue for the 'fit' between the nuclear family and the capitalist economic system. The conflict and feminist perspectives stress the 'dark' side of the family, such as unequal division of power between husband and wife and its consequences or, as in the work of R. D. Laing, they suggest a connection between family experiences and aspects of schizophrenic behaviour. Like the lay person the sociologist finds it difficult to view the family in a value-free manner. In these circumstances we felt it best to proceed by presenting the Irish family both in its historical and comparative dimensions. We look at how families are established *via* marriage, how they develop through the life cycle and how and when they are dissolved. Comparative research allows us to see the Irish family not so much as a universal natural institution but as a socially conditioned product.

Marriage

Marriage is the 'institutional means of providing for the performance of tasks concerned with procreation, rearing and transmission, where the means concerned involve a reordering of relationships of kin groups, and/or of the persons thought to be, already or potentially, the genetic parents of children' (Harris 1983, p. 28). Though marriage appears — at least outwardly — to be the outcome of individual choice in modern society, it also represents the creation of relationships between groups and, because of its wider implications, it is governed by numerous rules and regulations. In all societies some degree of control over marriage is exercised directly or indirectly by individuals and groups other than the prospective marriage partners. Because of these rules, restrictions and controls, the range of an individual's potential marriage partners is greatly reduced. Among the most important restrictions are age, kinship, religion, property considerations and social class. Also, while many states allow marriage to be legally dissolved through divorce, others, such as the Republic of Ireland, do not.

For a marriage to be legal in Ireland, neither the man nor the woman should be less than 16 years of age. This was established by the 1972 Marriage Act. Prior to it the legal marriage age was 14 for males and 12 for females. In practice the actual age of marriage in Ireland has varied considerably over the past 150 years. K. H. Connell has suggested that pre-famine Ireland was characterised by very early marriage for males and females, particularly among the poorer classes (1950, p. 72). Post-famine Irish society was notable for postponed marriage and high celibacy rates. By the 1950s Ireland had the lowest marriage rate in Europe and very high celibacy rates, with one in four women, and one in three men, aged 55+, unmarried. The average marriage age was 33 for men and 28 for women. In Limerick in the late 1950s for example, single males gave 35 or over, and single females gave between 25 and 30, as the most suitable age for marriage. The 'late' age of marriage favoured by males reflected their view that 'marriage meant a withdrawal from life, at least a withdrawal from all that was interesting in life' (McNabb 1962, p. 32). Marriage became more popular in the Republic of Ireland in the 1960s and 1970s. The marriage rate (marriages per 1,000 population) grew from 5.5 in 1960 to 7.1 in 1970 but had reduced to 5.9 by 1982. The average age at marriage of the Irish male in 1980 was 27; it was 24 for the Irish female. Interestingly, around this time in some European countries, marriage became less popular: in Sweden in 1978, 16 per cent of all couples living together were not married, and where the male partner was aged between 20 and 24, 71 per cent were not married (Eekelaar 1984, p. 6-7).

Marriage or sexual relations between members of the nuclear or conjugal family, other than between husband and wife, is forbidden in all societies. In Ireland there is a wide range of prohibitions on inter-family marriage, based on consanguinity (blood relationship) and affinity (relationships by marriage). Of the 628 marriages recorded between 1904 and 1969 in the Connemara Gaeltacht parish studied by Kane, 59 involved consanguineous relationships between partners, including 13 first cousin and 41 second cousin marriages. There were no consanguineous marriages after 1959 (Kane 1979, p. 152). The reasons for these prohibitions include the problems of the genetic effects of inbreeding and sexual competition within the family group. Exogamy — that is out-group marriage — offers the possibility of forming alliances with other groups and families. Endogamy or in-group marriage threatens this possibility.

Marriage, as the basis of a new alliance and a means of recruiting new members to a line of descent, is most prominent and explicit in tribal and peasant societies. In post-famine Ireland, research indicates that marriage existed primarily to ensure the continuity of the family farm and to provide the labour to work it. Marriage was thus 'part of the mechanism that perpetuated the rural economy ... it established on a particular farm the nucleus of the labour that would run it, accidents apart, for a generation. Marriage was likely to be contemplated, not when a man needed a wife, but when the land needed a woman' (K. H. Connell 1962, p. 503). The typical form of peasant marriage was the 'match'. This was an arranged marriage for the son who was nominated to succeed to the family farm, and for those daughters for whom partners could be found. The main features of the match were that it was in the control of the parents and that a woman 'marrying in' should bring a dowry or fortune with her. The dowry was calculated according to the value of the land owned by the prospective groom. The in-coming dowry, which was retained by the groom's father, was used to subvent the remaining children. Ideally it was used for training them in one of the professions, but more often it was used to assist permanent emigration. A further important use of the dowry was to fortune off the groom's sister or sisters. The dowry was a necessary, but not a sufficient, condition for a match. 'Considerations of the social status[1] and reputation of the family of the prospective son or daughter-in-law also played an important role in assessing his or her acceptability' (Breen 1984, p. 286). Although Messenger reports the use of dowries on the Aran Islands in the 1960s (1969, p. 70), by this time this form of marriage had all but disappeared. That arranged marriages have not entirely disappeared is indicated by the 17th annual report of the Knock Marriage Bureau which claims to have successfully arranged, to date, 370 marriages and to have received 15,395 inquiries. The majority of applicants were, however, over 30 years old and were largely, though not exclusively, from a farming background.

In modern societies, marriage is based more on individual

choice than on parental or communal control or pressure. The ideal is that it should be based on love, emotional and physical attraction and compatibility of the prospective partners. The notion of romantic love should not, however, be equated with a random choice of marriage partner. Rather, the choice of marriage partner is free as long as the partner comes from the right social category or group. Among the important social factors here are religion, ethnicity and class. There is a continued pressure for people to marry within their own group. Families with property and material possessions have most to lose by 'wrong choices' and are consequently preoccupied with controlling their children's choice of partner.

Property is also central to another aspect of marriage, the transfer of rights to children. Marriage ensures full societal membership for children. Recognition of parentage has the consequence of enabling a child to be attributed, not merely to the society, but to a position within the society. In Ireland a child is regarded as illegitimate unless his or her parents are married at the time of his or her birth. Such a child can, however, be legitimised by a subsequent marriage of his or her parents. An illegitimate child has no succession rights to either his or her parents or relations (Shatter 1977, p. 366.).[2] Arensberg and Kimball (1968) emphasise the declassing and socially disruptive aspects of illegitimacy when they state that 'to destroy a girl's character in the countryside is to upset the pattern of family and community life by overthrowing the possibility of an orderly change in farm succession' (p. 199). By contrast, Fox (1979) states that on Tory Island illegitimacy was not 'a bar to marriage or desirability either for the mother or the child. Women with illegitimate children often married as did the children themselves' (p. 160).

Another restriction on marriage is the number of partners one may marry. Irish legal marriages are monogamous; they are unions between one man and one women. By contrast, it is possible in some societies for either a man or a woman to have more than one partner at a time. Such plural marriages are known as polygamy, of which there are two types: polygyny, in which a man may have more than one wife, and polyandry, in which a woman may have more than one husband. The former is far more common than the latter. An example of a polyandrous society is Tibet, where the rule is that brothers can be jointly married to a single wife. All husbands live in the one house with their wife. The people who practise this form of polyandry claim that it offers the advantage of making the division of property between the families of a set of brothers unnecessary (Mair 1971, p. 144). In a polygynous society, not every man will have several wives. The majority of men will have only one wife, as polygyny tends to be the 'privilege' of the wealthy.

Closely associated with the form of marriage is the pattern of residence. In contemporary Irish society the ideal, and most common, form of residence is neo-local, that is, the husband and wife leave the natal home and set up a domestic group of their own. In the past many farm families favoured viri-local residence whereby the wife left her natal group and came to live with her husband, his parents if living, and perhaps his non-inheriting brother(s). Such an arrangement would typically result in a three generational or stem family household (Gibbon and Curtin 1978, p. 429). Fox reported yet another form of residence pattern on Tory Island: a number of husbands lived, not with their wives, but in their natal homes with their mothers and/or sisters. They had what Fox refers to as 'a visiting relationship with the homes of their wives' (1979 p. 162). Of the 51 marriages on Tory Island in 1963, ten conformed to this 'visiting' pattern.

Societal roles on marital dissolution vary widely. In Ireland, under article 41.3.2 of the Constitution, the state is prohibited from enacting any law which provides for 'the grant of a dissolution of marriage'. What is permitted is 'divorce mensa et thoro', which is a judicial separation of partners but which does not allow remarriage of separated partners. Any decree of dissolution granted by the state would not, in any case, be recognised by the Catholic church. In certain circumstances — proven non-consummation of marriage in particular — the Catholic church may itself grant a dissolution and permit parties to remarry (Shatter 1977, p. 131). Arensberg mentions the practice of 'country divorce' as once existing in rural areas. An example of this practice was where a barren wife (childlessness was almost totally blamed on women) was sent back to her parents (1937, p. 92). The man could not marry again but he could give over his land to his brother in return for a fortune and a stipulation that his brother would marry and produce an heir. It is worth noting that the divorce rate (divorces per 1,000 inhabitants) has risen in the EEC countries from 0.5 in 1960 to 1.6 in 1982. The total number of divorces in the nine EEC countries increased from 125,000 in 1960 to 421,000 in 1980 (*Eurostat*, 1985). In the United Kingdom during that period, the number of divorces increased from 25,900 to 159,700, while in Italy the number of divorces decreased from 17,134 to 11,826 between 1971 and 1980 (*Eurostat*, 1984). The prediction in the United States is that close to 50 per cent of all current marriages will end in divorce (Weitzman 1981, pp. 143–144). At the same time, it should be noted that the growth in the divorce rate has been accompanied by a dramatic rise in the number of remarriages. The relationship between divorce and the instability of family life is complex; one can ask does the growing instability of the family lead to a liberalisation of divorce law or vice versa?[3]

Family and kinship

Like marriage, the family can and does take on a variety of forms. What we referred to as the 'family', husband, wife and/or children, would seem foreign to many peoples in times past, and currently in parts of Asia and Africa. It is usual to distinguish between the nuclear family, our model above, and the extended family. The latter can also, of course, come in a variety of forms. We have already referred to one type of extended family, the Irish stem family, which includes parents, one married son and his wife and/or children. However, brothers and their wives may also establish a common household as in Hindu society. This variety of extended family is the joint family; married sons live in one household with their wives and children. Such a household is controlled by the senior male patriarch.

In short, the term 'family' has different meanings in different cultures. Matters are further complicated by the fact that families are not static but rather move through stages or life cycles, from marriage to procreation, child rearing, children's departure, old age and death. Our analysis will follow the life cycle, focussing on marital roles and marital authority; child rearing and parent-child relations; departure of children and old age. We will also examine the importance and functions of wider kinship bonds and relationships.

Marital roles and authority

The main interest in marital roles has been in who does what tasks, and with whom, in the family; and in the extent to which one partner exercises control over, or makes decisions for, the other. As we shall see, these are very related issues. The traditional Irish farm family was characterised by a rigid division of labour along age and sex lines. There were clear sets of male and female tasks and these were seen to represent the natural order of things. As Arensberg and Kimball put it, 'for a man to concern himself with a woman's work, such as the sale of eggs or the making of butter, is the subject of derisive laughter, while a woman's smaller hands make it "natural" for her to be a better hand at milking cows' (1968, p. 4). This division was reflected in the different training both sexes received from an early age; as a result most of the heavy farm work was done by the male, whilst the wife dominated all activities within the household. Some of the contemporary autobiographical accounts, however, such as Thomas O'Crohan's *The Islandman,* testify to the hard physical work undertaken by women (1951, p. 3). Among the majority of Dublin families in the 1950s, women were also in charge of the domestic arena, while husbands were usually out of the home during the day (Humphreys 1965, p. 253).

Hannan and Katsiaouni's 1973 survey (1977) of 408 farm families indicates wide variations in family interaction patterns with only one-third of the families displaying the rigid division of labour which characterised farm families in the 1930s and

1940s. In the 'modern' families, husbands helped with such 'womanly' tasks as bed-making and house cleaning. It is interesting to note, however, that husbands tended to underestimate their participation in household tasks, which indicates that it is regarded by them as having a low value in the overall scheme of things. Husbands with higher levels of education and who participated in the mass media, were more likely to be involved in household tasks. What we can call situational factors also account for the level of male participation in domestic work. Where a second woman — mother or mother-in-law — was present, the level of help with household tasks was less. On the other hand, the greater the number of young children present, the higher the level of male participation (p. 97). Unfortunately, we lack a similar study for urban areas which would document the undoubted changes in the division of household labour that have taken place, particularly in situations where the wife works outside the home or where the husband is unemployed.[4] Recent work by Pahl, however, indicates that in England, households where wives have full-time employment outside the home, have the most balanced domestic division of labour (1984, p. 275).

The traditional farm family was uncompromisingly patriarchal. All major decisions on the farm and the financial area were taken by the father. Sons, even into their middle age, were given little authority and were still referred to as boys. Wives had control over whatever income they gained from such activities as the sale of butter and eggs. This tended to be a very small proportion of household income. A husband rarely consulted his wife or older children on matters of farm management. The wife, however, was free to make all decisions about the training and education of children (McNabb 1962, p. 38). Fathers were called on only to administer punishment to children whose conduct had threatened the good name of the family. Among some urban families this strong authoritarian image seems to have been less in evidence; husband and wife behaved more as 'partners' and a more democratic relationship was evident between fathers and adult children, particularly males (Humphreys 1965, p. 254). Bennett's study of Dublin street traders (1984) indicates, however, that male authoritarian attitudes are still to the fore in this group.

In the 1960s and 1970s considerable changes, even reversals, took place in household authority patterns. Some observational studies (Brody, 1973) document the total decline of patriarchalism. The more systematic results of Hannan and Katsiaouni's study indicate that there are now wide variations between families in terms of the decision-making in households. While wives continued to be most authoritative in the household, between 25 and 30 per cent of households were characterised by joint decision-making.

Child-rearing

Among the crucial societal functions of the family are reproduction and socialisation. These involve ensuring that an adequate number of children are born, and that they have characteristics and attributes needed to become full adult members of society. The demographic characteristics of families are examined in two other chapters in this book. Here we are concerned with socialisation and childrearing practices. In rural Ireland, children were desired as a means of maintaining generational continuity, as a source of labour and as insurance against old age. Arensberg and Kimball's study of Clare farms in the 1930s documents a preoccupation with 'keeping the name on the land', and indicates that women who were unable to bear children were held in low esteem. According to more recent studies generational continuity continues to be important in farming communities. These reports also suggest that, particularly in the more remote western communities, the notion of children as a hedge against old age has become increasingly important (Curtin and Varley 1984, p. 32). In the past children were important sources of labour on family farms or as farm servants. In the pre-famine period Carney has noted the connection between family life stage and the presence of servants. Households took on servants in the family formation stage, when children were below adult productivity. But as children approached adulthood, servants were let go, and as children departed the household at a later stage, servants would be taken on again as labour substitutes (Carney, 1977, pp. 41-42). In Kerry in the 1930s, Breen distinguishes two types of servant boys and girls: life-cycle servants as described above, and non-resident labourers (mainly males) who moved from position to position. Such servant boys and girls were usually the children of small farmers and labourers (1983, p. 89).

In discussing childrearing, it is usual to distinguish between early and later childhood. Childrearing in the former phase was, and is, almost the exclusive responsibility of the wife. In three generational households she would have the assistance of a mother or a mother-in-law. But this is much less likely in urban areas. Hannan and Katsiaouni's survey shows 16–17 per cent of husbands playing an active role in childrearing, and in six per cent of households husbands are as involved in this area as their wives. Research also shows that silence and passivity are desired qualities in children, and boys tend to be more valued and preferred to girls. In Limerick in the 1950s, 'girls were favoured neither by father nor mother and accepted only on sufferance. They were loved but not thought of as of any great importance' (McNabb 1962, p. 40). By contrast, Scheper-Hughes (1979) makes reference to the practice of socialising young boys, and in particular the chosen heir, into feelings of personal inadequacy to ensure that they stay at home. In later childhood the family has to share its influence with the educational agencies, peer groups, and other reference groups.

Old age

If childrearing presents its difficulties for parents, so does the departure of children. It involves major changes in parental roles, particularly for full-time mothers. Age at marriage and number of children born will, of course, leave mothers with different lengths of post-parental life in front of them. Further, where children continue to reside in the same household, or even the same locality after their marriage, mothers are very likely to be involved in the raising and rearing of grandchildren. Thus, in the Gaeltacht community studied by Kane 'neighbours or relatives are rarely asked to help with children or to babysit because the necessity does not arise. There is always someone of the house to attend to the child' (1979 p. 155). Three generational households, however, present the possibility of tension and conflict emerging between the generations, particularly between the new wife and her mother-in-law.

In the past the male patriarch tended to hold on to control and ownership of the farm until well into old age. Perhaps for this and other reasons old men were respected. In Arensberg's words, 'they live long because they have much to live for. In their own sphere of life, they are honoured; they have power' (1937, p. 107). They convened at a particular house known as the Dail where they would discuss local affairs and attempt to resolve local problems such as land disputes. That they were suspicious of the younger generation is evidenced by the fact that on transferring the farm to the heir, they insisted on a legal agreement which would ensure their financial support and a room within the household.

Generational relations continue to be a problem in some rural areas where giving up the farm leads to dependency on the younger generation and loss of voice in the local community. Recent research also indicates that as people grow old, they tend to be ignored (Brody 1973, Kane 1979). In this respect, rural Ireland has become more like urban Ireland in the decline in the range of parental control and the power of the older generations. It has also been suggested that among the new Dubliners there is considerably less veneration and glorification of the aged than among country people (Humphreys 1966, pp. 35–36).

Kinship and the wider family

So far we have discussed the family largely in terms of the narrow nuclear family unit. But family ties do of course, extend beyond this unit and hence the concept of the extended family emerges. This wider family can be based on co-residence such as was the case in the Irish stem family or the Hindu joint family. Extended family ties may also serve important functions in situations where families do not reside together, and thus the concept of kinship networks arises. The importance of extended family ties varies from society to society. In some cases, extended kin groups are the basis of organisation for many of society's activities, such as ownership of land and other strategic resources. Economics and politics are not distinguishable from kinship arrangements in many tribal societies. Kinship can also be a basis for organising religion. In the past kinship had almost a corporate status in parts of rural Ireland, as nearly all families were 'united by complicated bonds of marriage and descent ... and disloyalty to one's kinship group was felt to be a deadly crime against the group' (Arensberg and Kimball, 1968, p. 90). Kin groups are important, but not as important as neighbour-hood groups, in day-to-day mutual aid. They were of more significance and assistance in longer-term crises and difficulties and were the major emotionally supportive group at weddings, christenings and funerals (Hannan 1972, pp. 175–176).

In modern societies, kin networks are more typical than kin groups. In kin networks, the 'boundaries are different from the perspective of each individual; the individuals that are considered kin by one person are not necessarily the same as those considered kin by a close relative of this person, even though they have certain kin in common' (Leichter and Mitchell 1978, p. 18). There is, therefore, wide variation in the numbers of recognised kin, and kin with whom individuals have significant relationships.

Hannan's research in Roscommon (1972) uncovered one family who could identify and sketch in the linkages of 720 relatives. Among all families studied, the total number of relatives whose residences, names and precise linkages were fully known varied between 102 and 260. Although it has been suggested that city life tends to isolate the nuclear family from its wider kin (Humphreys 1965, p. 255), research in a middle- and a working-class housing estate in Cork indicated that 62 per cent of respondents were able to name all four of their grandparents (Gordon 1975, p. 82). The central kinship relationship in a Galway middle-class suburb was between parents and their married children. In the early years of marriage, aid usually flowed from parents to their married children and, as the parents grew older, this pattern was often reversed. The majority of married children felt a strong obligation to visit and keep in contact with their parents. Relations between siblings were characterised by a much less active concern for each other's welfare. Visiting was mainly on a yearly or special occasion basis and there was less exchanging of mutual aid. Respondents in this study had a weak relationship with their cousins and in fact nearly 30 per cent had no contact of any description with their cousins (Curtin, 1973). Finally, kinship continues to be important in recruitment to industrial and business organisations. In their contribution to this book, Donnan and MacFarlane draw our attention to the role of kin ties in Northern Ireland in providing information about jobs and providing a basis for the establishment of new businesses.

Conclusion

The family, like other social institutions, is in a process of continuous change. The 1960s witnessed an increase in the popularity of marriage; more people married and they did so at an earlier age. This change, however, has to be set against the baseline of high celibacy rates and the late age of marriage which has long characterised life in the Republic of Ireland. There is little evidence, either, of any large scale movement away from marriage as an institution. Survey research indicates that opinion is divided on the issue of the introduction of divorce, and the referendum necessary to alter the legal prohibition on divorce is unlikely to be held in the near future. Estimates on the number of couples seeking divorce vary, depending on the argument being made for or against its introduction. Yet the number of applicants for deserted wives' allowance has continued to increase. State assistance on a short-term basis to deserted or unsupported wives was introduced under the Social Welfare Supplementary Welfare Allowances Act 1975. This Act facilitated the provision of short-term relief for a wife until she could instigate maintenance proceedings, or until she became entitled to a deserted wives' allowance. The 1976 Family Law Act granted jurisdiction to a variety of courts to bar either spouse from entering the family home where they deemed it necessary. The introduction of this legislation is in itself an indicator of the increasing level of family stress and marital breakdown.

Some of the changes in the structure and functioning of the family are clear-cut, others complex and multi-directional. A definite pattern is the decline of large three generational households. On the other hand, recent census evidence for the Republic shows that the nuclear family of husband, wife and children accounts for only forty-five per cent of all households, while single persons accounted for seventeen per cent, and a lone mother with one or more children accounted for 6 per cent of households (Census, 1981, Vol. 3). Within the family the pattern of change in roles and relationships is also complicated. The increased participation of married women in the labour force has undoubtedly resulted in changes in the household division of labour and power structure. At the same time recent urban and rural research indicates the persistence of a traditional division of labour. Parent-child relations would also appear to be in a fluid state, particularly in later childhood, as parents and children negotiate their roles rather than acting out roles according to definite culturally prescribed positions. The position of the elderly has also altered with a decline of the extended household, though modern communications have facilitated contact among kinfolk living in different places. Irish society, as the other chapters in this book show, has experienced dramatic changes since the 1960s. The family, facing towards the individual and towards society, is a crucial mediator and barometer of these changes.

Notes

1   In Greece, the dowry also acted as a means of increasing the social prestige of the family, and because urban sons-in-laws were highly sought after, farmers were willing to give larger dowries in such marriages (Friedl 1971, p. 136).

2   If the proposals set out by the Minister in the document, *The Status of Children*, become law, they will effectively end the differential legal treatment of persons born outside and those born inside marriage. Children born outside marriage will, however, continue to have a separate status in law (p. 6).

3   For two different views on the implications of introducing divorce to the Republic of Ireland, see W. Duncan *The Case for Divorce in the Irish Republic* (1979) and W. Binchy *Is Divorce the Answer?* (1984).

4   Preliminary findings from research carried out on family kinship in Ennis, Co. Clare by Colm Ryan, indicates that a very rigid household division of labour is still dominant. Activities such as cooking meals, making beds, or house cleaning were almost exclusively done by women.

References

ARENSBERG, C 1937. *The Irish Countryman*, American Museum Science Books Edition, New York.

ARENSBERG, C. and KIMBALL, S. 1968. *Family and Community in Ireland*, Cambridge, Mass. Harvard, Harvard University Press.

BENNETT, D. 1984. 'Maggie Feathers and Missie Reilly: Hawking Life in Dublin's City Quay' in C. Curtin *et al.* (eds.). *Culture and Ideology in Ireland*, Galway, Galway University Press.

BINCHY, W. 1984. *Is Divorce the Answer?*, Dublin, Irish Academic Press.

BREEN, R. 1983. 'Farm Servant-hood in Ireland, 1900-40', *The Economic History Review*, 2nd series, Vol. XXXVI, pp. 87-102.

BREEN, R. 1984. 'Dowry Payments and the Irish Case', *Comparative Studies in Society and History*, Vol. 26, No. 2, pp. 280-296.

BRODY, H. 1973. *Iniskillane: Change and Decline in the West of Ireland*, London, Allen Lane.

CARNEY, F. J. 1977. 'Aspects of pre-famine Irish Household Size: Composition and Differentials' in Cullen, L. M. and Smouth, T.C. (eds.) *Comparative Aspects of Scottish and Irish Economic History*, Edinburgh.

CURTIN, C.A. 1973. 'Kinship in a Middle Class Housing Estate'. Unpublished MA thesis, University College, Galway.

CURTIN C.A. and VARLEY, A. 1984. 'Children and Child-hood in Rural Ireland' in *Culture and Ideology in Ireland*, Galway, Galway University Press, pp. 30-45.

CURTIN, C.A., KELLY M. and

O'DOWD, L. 1984. *Culture and Ideology in Ireland*, Galway, Galway University Press.

CONNELL, K.H. 1950. *The Population of Ireland, 1750–1845*. London, Oxford University Press.

CONNELL, K.H. 1962. 'Peasant Marriage in Ireland: Its structure and development since the Famine', *Economic History Review*, second series, Vol. 14, April, pp. 504–523.

DUNCAN, W. 1979. *The Case for Divorce in the Irish Republic*, revised edition, 1982, Dublin, Irish Council for Civil Liberties.

EEKELAAR, J. 1984. *Family Law and Social Policy*, London, Weidenfeld and Nicholson.

EUROSTAT, 1984, 1985. *Demographic Statistics*, European Communites Statistics Office: Luxembourg.

FOX, R. 1967 *Kinship and Marriage: An Anthropological Study*, London, Penguin.

FOX, ROBIN, 1979. 'The Visiting Husband on Tory Island', *Journal of Comparative Family Studies*, Vol. X, No. 2, pp. 163–190.

FRIEDL, E. 1971. 'Dowry, Inheritance and Land Tenure' in J. Goody (ed.), *Kinship*, London, Penguin.

GIBBON, P. and CURTIN, C. 1978. 'The Stem Family in Ireland', *Comparative Studies in Society and History*, Vol. 20, No. 3, pp. 429–453.

GORDON, M. 1975. 'Some Aspects of Urban Irish Kinship'. Proceedings of the Second Annual Conference, Dublin, 4–5 April 1975, Sociological Association of Ireland.

GOVERNMENT PUBLICATIONS, 1985. *The Status of Children*, Dublin, The Stationery Office.

GOVERNMENT PUBLICATIONS, 1981. *Census of Population* Vol. 3, Dublin: The Stationery Office.

HANNAN, D. 1972. 'Kinship, Neighbourhood and Social Change in Irish Rural Communities', *Economic and Social Review*, Vol. 3, No. 2, pp. 163–189.

HANNAN, D and KATSIAOUNI, L.A., 1977. *Traditional Families? From Culturally Prescribed to Negotiated Roles in Farm Families*, the Economic and Social Research Institute, Dublin, paper No. 87.

HANNAN, D. 1978. 'Patterns of Spousal Accommodation and Conflict in Traditional and Modern Farm Families', *Economic and Social Review*, Vol. 10, No. 1, pp. 61–84.

HANNAN, D. 1979. *Displacement and Development: Class, Kinship and Social Change in Irish Rural Communities*, the Economic and Social Research Institute, Dublin, paper No. 96.

HARRIS, C.C. 1983. *The Family and Industrial Society*, London, George Allen & Unwin.

HUMPHREYS, A. 1965. 'The Family in Ireland' in M. R. Nimkoff (ed.) *Comparative Family Systems*, Boston, Houghton Mifflin Company.

HUMPHREYS, A. 1966. *New Dubliners: Urbanisation and the Irish Family*, London, Routledge and Kegan Paul.

KANE, E. 1968. 'Man and Kin in Donegal: A Study of Kinship Functions in a Rural Irish and an

Irish-American Community', *Ethnology*, Vol. 7, pp. 245–258.

KANE, E. 1979. 'The Changing Role of the Family in a Rural Irish Community', *Journal of Comparative Family Studies*, Vol. X, No. 2, pp. 141–162.

KELLY, J. 1980. *The Irish Constitution*, Dublin, Jurist Publishing Company.

LEICHTER, H. E., and MITCHELL, W. E. 1978. *Kinship and Casework*, New York, Columbia University Press.

MAIR, L. 1971. *Marriage*, London, Pelican Books.

McNABB, P. 1962. 'Social Structure' in *The Limerick Rural Survey*, J. Newman (ed.), Tipperary, Muintir na Tire Publications.

MESSENGER, J. 1969. *Inis Beag, Isle of Ireland*, New York, Holt, Rinehart and Winston.

O'CROHAN, T. 1951. *The Islandman*, London, Oxford University Press.

PAHL, R. 1984. *Divisions of Labour*, London, Basil Blackwell.

RYAN, C. 'Family, Kinship and Work in a Working Class Estate in Ennis, Co. Clare', PhD thesis (uncompleted), University College, Galway.

SCHEPER-HUGHES, N. 1979. 'Breeding Breaks Out in the Eye of the Cat: Sex Roles, Birth Order and the Irish Double-Bind', *Journal of Comparative Family Studies*, Vol. X, No. 2, pp. 207–226.

SHATTER, A. 1977. *Family Law in the Republic of Ireland*, Dublin, Wolfhound Press.

WEITZMAN, L. J. 1981. *The Marriage Contract: Spouses, Lovers and the Law*, New York, The Free Press.

Part II

Social Structure and Institutions: Northern Ireland

Introduction

This section opens with an account by John Coward of the demographic characteristics of the population of Northern Ireland. In this chapter Coward documents the major population changes which have occurred since the late 1960s. He points out that, unlike the Republic of Ireland, Northern Ireland did not experience population growth between 1971 and 1981: high migration loss and declining fertility rates are identified as the major factors contributing to this. Fertility levels in Northern Ireland are still unique. They stand roughly half way between those in Britain and those in the Republic of Ireland. The trends in fertility in both parts of Ireland, however, are downward. Coward also examines a variety of other demographic patterns and trends in Northern Ireland. He analyses social class and religious differences in family size and emigration; differences in mortality rates between Britain and Northern Ireland; and differences between Northern Ireland, Britain and the Republic of Ireland in the age structure of the population.

While Coward analyses the implications of demographic change, Liam O'Dowd examines the implications of industrial change. Using a conflict model, he argues that Northern Ireland is no longer an industrial society built around manufacturing industry. De-industrialisation has taken place with the decline of traditional industry and the failure of many factories established by multi-national corporations. There has been a corresponding expansion of service employment in all sectors, especially in the state sector. Like the Republic of Ireland, there has also been a decline in the proportion of the population engaged in farming. However, the proportion of self-employed in farming in the Republic of Ireland still remains considerably higher than in Northern Ireland. O'Dowd goes on to point out how the expansion of state and service employment frequently did not result in the creation of full-time jobs; part-time employment has been a feature of post-industrial society, with women constituting the main body of the part-time work-force. Finally, he analyses religious and regional differences in employment patterns — observing that the two are not unrelated.

The third chapter in this section on Northern Ireland is an analysis of stratification and mobility patterns by Robert Miller. After presenting a brief introduction to the concept of stratification, Miller proceeds to examine the reasons why class position and religious affiliation are uniquely interwoven in Northern Ireland. The third, and major part of the chapter is devoted to an analysis of mobility patterns within the given class structure. The author's main conclusion is that social mobility trends in Northern Ireland are broadly similar to those in the Republic of Ireland and in England and Wales. The main source of difference between Northern Ireland and the others, however, is that Northern Ireland people of all (five) classes of origin are more likely to move into working-class first jobs than people elsewhere.

Unlike Miller, Dominic Murray relies on ethnographic research to explain the dynamics of Northern Ireland's education system. After a brief outline of the provenance and development of the educational system, the author proceeds to elaborate his main thesis: that segregated education in Northern Ireland is the product of the explicit wishes of both Catholic and Protestant groups. Integrated education, therefore, is not a realistic option, as both groups want to retain their distinctive cultural traditions. Through the use of evidence collected from a participant observation study, he goes on to show how symbol systems are used in both Catholic and Protestant schools to reinforce cultural identities which are not only different but are also antagonistic. He concludes by suggesting that cultural misunderstandings, which are reinforced by segregated education, should be addressed by the development of educational programmes which do not presuppose integration.

The final chapter in this section examines the role of religion within Northern Ireland society. John Hickey's principal contention is that, with the advent of industrialisation, Northern Ireland society has not experienced widespread secularisation as has been the case in Britain, for example. He presents statistical evidence on religious practices in Northern Ireland and Britain to substantiate this claim. Hickey's explanation as to why religion persists, involves two themes: he suggests that it is a function of the interdependence of political and religious interests on the one hand, and the mutual defensiveness of Catholic and Protestant 'world views' on the other. He concludes by suggesting that, while 'religion has gone through the processes associated with modernisation', in so far as it performs a more restricted role in society, it nevertheless remains a pervasive force 'in the sphere of politics and group interaction'.

9
Demographic Structure and Change

JOHN COWARD

Northern Ireland's demographic characteristics display many features that are of sociological interest as well as having important implications for socio-economic change and planning. Some of these characteristics, such as relatively high rates of natural increase and emigration, are broadly similar to those displayed by the population of the Republic of Ireland while others, such as recent trends in the birth rate, are more akin to the population of Britain. However, in other respects, certain characteristics, such as the levels of fertility and nuptiality, fall between the levels attained by the populations of the Republic of Ireland and Britain. This chapter examines some of these major demographic features, focussing on population change, the components of population growth, nuptiality and family size, emigration and population composition. Particular emphasis will be given to recent trends and, where possible, some of the major socio-economic differentials will be highlighted. The chapter concludes by briefly summarising some of the more important social, economic and political implications of these demographic characteristics.

While the study of Northern Ireland demography is of much potential interest, problems of data availability and reliability ensure that some features can only be examined in a rather cursory manner. Indeed, detailed demographic data are rather limited compared with many other areas. Firstly, for example, the amount of published information on vital statistics (a major data source for demographic analysis) is particularly limited compared with Britain. Secondly, the number and scope of detailed social surveys has been, until recently, somewhat limited. Thirdly, the recent 1981 Census of Population (another standard source for demographic study) encountered problems of non-response and under-enumeration which make it difficult to use for detailed study.[1] However, on a more optimistic note, it should be emphasised that some of the previously mentioned data sources are expanding in scope and detail. Thus increasingly detailed published vital registration data have become available recently, while more social surveys have been carried out since the mid 1970s. The Policy and Planning Research Unit at Stormont has recently introduced (since 1983) the Continuous Household Survey which is broadly similar to the General Household Survey in Britain (a major source for social and demographic research), while the Northern Ireland Housing Executive surveys have also generated a considerable amount of detailed socio-economic and demographic information. Hopefully, these contributions will form the basis for further detailed socio-demographic surveys.

Population change and distribution

While the individual components of population change — fertility, mortality and migration— will be analysed in later sections, some broad features of population change and distribution are considered in this section. The trends in the components of population change are summarised in Figure 1 and Table 1 and several major features are of interest. Firstly, the total population of Northern Ireland has, with the exception of the intercensal decade 1971–81, generally increased over each intercensal period since 1926 (Table 1). Secondly, the growth in population is attributed solely to the relatively high rates of natural increase and has occurred despite the continuous outflow of population due to net migration loss (Table 1). Thirdly,

Table 1: **Variations in population change 1926–81**

| Inter-
censal
period | Population at
end of period
(000s) | Average annual rate per
1000 population | | |
		Population change	Natural increase	Emigration
1926–37	1,280	+1.7	5.8	4.1
1937–51	1,371	+4.9	8.5	3.6
1951–61	1,425	+3.9	10.5	6.6
1961–66	1,485	+8.2	13.4	5.2
1966–71	1,536	+5.9	10.1	4.2
1971–81*	1,534	–0.1	7.0	7.1

*1981 estimate derived from Compton (Compton and Coward 1983).
Source: *Annual Reports of the Registrar General.*

there have been considerable variations in the intensity of
natural increase and migration over the last fifty years. It can be
seen that population change during the most recent inter-censal
decade 1971–81 was markedly different from that of the earlier
decade 1961–71. The rate of natural increase dropped during
the 1970s as the result of an intensification of the decline in births
which had started in 1964, while this period also witnessed a
substantial increase in the level of net migration loss. The main
consequence of these trends is that the population of Northern
Ireland either declined or remained more or less static during
the 1970s (it is impossible to be precise because the exact extent
of under-enumeration is not known). On the basis of the figures
utilised here, derived from Compton (Compton and Coward
1983), it is apparent that the population slightly declined
between 1971 and 1981 — an unprecedented feature in
Northern Ireland for an inter-censal period.

   Northern Ireland's population is unevenly distributed with
approximately half of the population in the Belfast region and
only one-third in the western half of the province. This basic
pattern has generally become more accentuated over the last
fifty years as many western areas have declined in population
while many eastern areas have grown. Generally speaking, the

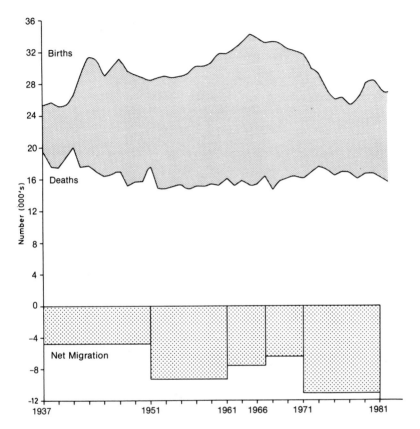

Fig. 1. **Variations in births, deaths and net migration (migration refers to inter-censal periods).**

poorest and most isolated rural areas have experienced the greatest population losses. The dominant feature of change in the last twenty years has been the decline of population in the Belfast District Council Area as a result of redevelopment, suburban growth and the troubles. Between 1971 and 1978, for example, Belfast's population declined by 19 per cent, with particularly large reductions in the older inner city areas (Harrison 1981). However, rapid growth has occurred in many parts of the Belfast suburbs and beyond, as well as some of the towns (particularly Antrim, Ballymena and Bangor) in the east of the province. Generally speaking, then, the dominant factor influencing variations in population change within Northern Ireland has been that of migration rather than natural increase.

Fertility, marriage and family size

The level of fertility in Northern Ireland has generally occupied a position roughly midway between that of Britain and the Republic of Ireland. This is reflected in Table 2 where the birth rate in Northern Ireland (17.5 in 1981) stands in contrast with Britain (13.0) and the Republic of Ireland (21.0). Higher fertility in Ireland is due to the particularly high rates of marital fertility rather than to high illegitimacy ratios (Table 2). Compton (1982) has suggested that the distinctive Irish and British fertility patterns overlap in Northern Ireland, associated with the Catholic and Protestant populations respectively, and that this accounts for Northern Ireland's intermediate position. The following section examines variations in the birth rate in Northern Ireland and also considers two of the major components that affect the birth rate — proportions married and marital fertility.

While the birth rate in Northern Ireland has remained higher than in Britain throughout this century, the general trends in the rates have been similar. The rise in the birth rate, starting in the early 1950s, has been attributed to the greater relative affluence of the post-war generation of parents compared with their

Table 2: **Selected measures of fertility 1981**

Index	Britain	Northern Ireland	Republic of Ireland
Birth rate	13.0	17.5	21.0
Marital fertility rate*	77.1	119.9	156.3
Illegitimacy ratio (%)**	12.7	7.0	5.4

*Legitimate births per 1,000 married women aged 15–49.
**Illegitimate births as a percentage of all births.

own parents (who had lower fertility during the 1930s) and reached a peak in 1964. From 1964 to 1977 the number of births declined sharply in Britain and Northern Ireland (although the decline was less marked in Northern Ireland) and the 1977 birth rate represents the lowest ever attained in these areas. In contrast, the birth rate in the Republic of Ireland fluctuated over the period 1964–77, but remained at relatively high levels. The sharp decline in the birth rate since the mid 1960s has been attributed to the higher material aspirations of this generation of parents, coupled with various socio-economic changes such as the increasing participation of married women in the labour force, increasing female emancipation and also the availability of a greater range of efficient forms of contraception. The number of births increased somewhat between 1977 and 1980 (partly reflecting changes in age structure as a result of the higher birth rates of the previous generation) but has subsequently fallen again (Figure 1).

The relatively high birth rate in Northern Ireland compared with Britain has been attained despite the occurrence of lower proportions married. The general trend, however, has been one of moving away from the Irish pattern of late marriage and

Table 3: **Proportions of females ever-married in Northern Ireland**

| Date | Proportions ever-married (%) | | |
	20–24	*45–49*	*15–49*
1926*	20.1	62.1	43.6
1937	22.7	63.3	45.5
1951	29.1	68.1	54.0
1961	38.6	72.0	58.8
1971	46.7	85.0	64.1
1981**	43.3	89.5	63.5

*In this year cohorts were 20–24, 45–54 and 15–54.
**Subject to possible error: see footnote 1.
Source: *Censuses of Population.*

relatively high celibacy. These changes are depicted in Table 3 in terms of the proportion of females ever-married, which have generally increased over the last fifty years. The changes have been most marked at younger ages, indicative of the trend towards earlier marriage, and occurred most rapidly over the period 1951–71. This latter feature perhaps reflects the declining proportion of the population engaged in agriculture (where the average age at marriage has been relatively high), higher incomes and the increasing urbanisation of the population. However, the decline between 1971 and 1981 in the proportion of females ever-married at ages 20–24 may well reflect a greater delaying of marriage as a result of increasing material expectations coupled with worsening economic conditions, as well as a greater incidence of informal unions through cohabitation. Within Northern Ireland, the Catholic section of the population has generally displayed lower nuptiality than that of non-Catholics and this feature remains applicable to the most recent period of study (Table 4).[2]

There is little information on 'mixed' marriages in Northern Ireland. A special tabulation from the 1971 census indicates that

Table 4: **Variations in females ever-married at ages 20–24 and 45–49 by main religious groupings 1971 and 1981**

| | Females ever married (%) | |
| | Aged | Aged |
Year and group*	20–24	45–49
1971		
Catholics	40.4	78.5
Non-Catholics	50.2	87.4
1981		
Catholics	36.7	86.0
Non-Catholics	46.6	90.7

*Of those stating a religion.
For data sources: see footnote 1.

only 2 per cent of all marriages were mixed (Lee 1979), although a province-wide survey of married couples in 1983 indicates a somewhat higher figure of 4.5 per cent.[3] This low incidence of intermarriage reflects the low level of social integration between Catholics and Protestants as well as the large absolute and relative size of the minority Catholic population (Walsh, 1970). There are, however, variations in the proportion of mixed marriages within Northern Ireland and survey evidence relating to some of the rural and small town populations of northern Antrim and Londonderry indicate levels several times higher than the average.

While nuptiality and extra-marital fertility in Northern Ireland have generally remained below the level of that of Britain, the relatively high fertility is a product of the substantially larger average size of family. For example, census data for 1971 show that the average size of completed family in Northern Ireland was 3.2 children compared with 2.2. for Britain. The corresponding figure for the Republic of Ireland was 4.0 children. Larger family sizes in Northern Ireland compared with Britain can be attributed to a variety of factors including the lower levels of modernisation and industrialisation, greater proportions engaged in agriculture, the particular strength of Catholicism, the relatively small size of the middle-class and the more limited development of the women's movement (Coward 1980, Compton, 1978).

Two major sources of variation in family size are evident within Northern Ireland — social class and religion. Thus, data on completed family size in 1971 indicate that for both Catholics and non-Catholics there is, generally speaking, an inverse relationship between socio-economic grouping (as defined by occupation of husband) and family size. The separate socio-economic grouping of those engaged in agriculture (farmers, farm managers and agricultural labourers) is also associated with relatively large family sizes (Fig. 2). This gradient of variation is broadly similar to the trends displayed in England and Wales, although for the latter the smallest families occur amongst those social groups where the husband's occupation is skilled non-manual (Fig. 2). The generally low fertility of those social groups in the non-manual occupations is a common (although not universal) occurrence and is generally attributed to the perceived higher relative costs of childbearing coupled with greater long-term planning and greater contraceptive efficiency amongst these groups.

The Catholic-Protestant fertility differential in Northern Ireland is particularly large and, on the basis of the marriage cohort depicted in Figure 2, amounts to approximately two children for each social group. The family sizes of non-Catholics in Northern Ireland are of course far closer to the averages for England and Wales overall, although they are still higher in Northern Ireland (Fig. 2). The Catholic-Protestant fertility differential is also reflected in differences in the birth rate, where recent estimates indicate that the Catholic birth rate is approximately 50 per cent greater than that of Protestants (Compton 1982). The high fertility of Northern Ireland Catholics reflects not only the continued strength and influence of the Catholic church within Northern Ireland but also a considerable sense of attachment to the church on the part of the Catholic population, and hence a greater inclination to follow the church's teaching regarding family life. Recent church attendance figures, albeit rather crude indicators of religiosity, indicate particularly high levels amongst Catholics (Moxon-Brown 1983). In addition, the occupational profile of Catholics in which relatively large proportions are engaged in manual (high fertility) occupations (Aunger 1975) as well as the lower overall levels of social mobility (a factor often associated with lower fertility) amongst Catholics (Miller 1979, 1983) will also influence the high fertility of the Catholic population overall. The role of minority status has also been investigated as a possible influence on the high fertility of Northern Ireland Catholics (Coward 1980, Kennedy 1973). More recently, in 1983, a fertility survey was carried out in Northern Ireland and the initial results indicate that there is still a marked difference between Catholics and Protestants (as well as differences within the Protestant denominations) and that there has been a quite

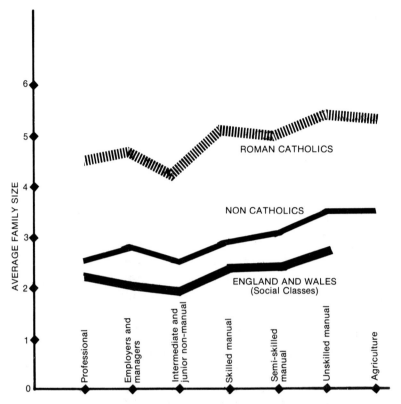

Fig. 2.   **Variations in family size by religion and socio-economic grouping 1971.**

considerable reduction in the fertility of the Catholic population in particular (Compton *et al.* 1985).

Variations in family size by other socio-economic factors are less clearly discernible owing to lack of data, but there is evidence from 1971 census data to indicate that the participation of married women in the labour force is associated with relatively lower fertility for both Catholics and Protestants (Compton 1982), although the nature of the precise causal links are less easy to establish. Furthermore, an analysis of ideal family size amongst Northern Ireland husbands indicates a preference for smaller families within each of the main denominations amongst the young, those engaged in non-manual occupations and those with tertiary education (Coward 1981).

Emigration and migration loss

Apart from high fertility, the other population characteristic for which Ireland is renowned is that of the relatively high levels of emigration. The loss of population through net out-migration has been an all-pervasive feature of the Northern Ireland population and has generally consisted of young adults moving to Britain. The essential motivating factor has been economic, reflecting the lack of suitable employment opportunities in Northern Ireland in the secondary and tertiary sectors. The importance of emigration within Northern Ireland is indicated by a province-wide survey in 1968 where 36 per cent of respondents claimed to have given thought to emigrating from Northern Ireland (Rose 1971). However, while emigration is a topic of considerable relevance in terms of its causes, consequences and implications, lack of detailed information prohibits anything but a rather cursory analysis.[4]

It is evident from Table 1 that the rate of population loss was particularly high over the 1970s, reflecting the severe economic problems of Northern Ireland and the effects of the troubles. Annual estimates of migration over the 1970s show particularly high rates in the early 1970s (Table 5) and this is probably a reflection of the intensity of the troubles then (although it is not known how many have left as a direct result of intimidation or rather the general desire to avoid living in areas of civil disturbance).

The lower rates of the later 1970s reflect the more recent difficulties of finding employment in recession-hit Britain. The 1970s was also a period when, for the first time since partition, inter-censal migration rates from Northern Ireland were higher than those from the Republic of Ireland (Table 6). Indeed, while this period was characterised by particularly high out-migration from Northern Ireland, the 1970s represented a period of net inflow to the Republic of Ireland (see Chapter 2).

Table 5: **Annual estimates of net migration 1971–81**

Period	Net-Migration*
1971/72	7,500
1972/73	12,484
1973/74	11,000
1974/75	16,000
1975/76	8,900
1976/77	8,200
1977/78	7,500
1978/79	5,700
1979/80	5,900
1980/81	6,200

*Movements to and from the Republic of Ireland only partially covered.
Source: *Abstract of Statistics 1983* (HMSO, Belfast).

Table 6: **Inter-censal rates of net migration for Northern Ireland and the Republic of Ireland**

Inter-censal period*	Net migration per 1000 population per annum	
	Northern Ireland	Republic of Ireland
1926–37	−4.1	−5.6
1937–51	−3.6	−7.0
1951–61	−5.5	−14.1
1961–71	−4.7	−4.7
1971–81	−7.1	+3.9

*1926–36 and 1936–51 for the Republic of Ireland
Source: Northern Ireland — see Table 1; Republic of Ireland — *Census of Population 1981*, Volume 1

The preponderance of young adults among migrants can be seen from the recent census data for England and Wales concerning movement over the period 1980–81 classified by place of birth. Of those migrants born in Northern Ireland, approximately two-thirds were aged 20–44 while only 10 per cent were older than 45. The sex ratio of migrants was more or less even and some 20 per cent of migrants were aged 15 or less, indicating the dominance of fairly young families in the migration process.

Little information is available concerning socio-economic and religious differentials in migration. Various researchers have shown that Catholics have generally comprised the majority of emigrants, representing some 58 per cent of out-migrants in the period 1937–51 (Barritt and Carter 1962) and between 60 and 65 per cent in the period 1951–71 (Compton 1982). On this basis, therefore, the rate of out-migration amongst Catholics is considerably higher than that for Protestants. Little hard evidence is available concerning the most recent denominational differences in migration: Browne (1978) has suggested that Protestant rates may have increased because in times of recession it is only the highly skilled or qualified (more likely to be Protestant) who can move with ease. However, Compton (1982) argues that such a trend could have been compensated by the greater movement of Catholics to the Republic and therefore suggests the differential has probably remained largely unaltered over the 1970s. It is also difficult to speculate on the 'brain drain' effects of movement, as past trends in migration have presumably consisted of individuals with all ranges of technical and educational expertise. However, research over the 1970s (Osborne et al. 1983) indicates that a sizable proportion of Northern Ireland graduates move away from the province (either by migrating after having qualified in Northern Ireland or by qualifying and remaining in Britain) and on this basis there has been a net loss of those with higher education qualifications.

Mortality

Mortality levels in Northern Ireland are essentially similar to those in Britain and the Republic of Ireland, with all areas displaying relatively low mortality. The lack of major fluctuation in the number of deaths (and also the death rate) depicted in Figure 1 does, however, obscure certain major features, the most notable being the steady increases in life expectancy over much of this century. Thus life expectancy (a measure which, unlike the crude death rate, takes account of age structure) at birth for females increased from 55 to 75 between 1925-27 and 1979-81. However, there have not been major changes in life expectancy over the last fifteen years: indeed, it can be noted that male life expectancy at birth declined somewhat during the early 1970s. These increases in mortality were most marked at ages 20-34 and probably reflect the higher incidence of traffic accidents as well as an increase in violent deaths associated with the troubles.

Although essentially similar, life expectancy at birth in Northern Ireland is somewhat lower than that of England and Wales. In 1980, for example, this differential amounted to 2 years for males and 1.8 years for females. Such differences, which are reflected in the particularly high mortality rates through heart disease in Northern Ireland, can be attributed to a variety of economic, social and lifestyle factors which partly reflect the lower levels of living and greater extent of poverty in Northern Ireland, as well as differences in diet and smoking habits. It is also possible that the high degree of out-migration from the province is selective of healthier individuals, although lack of data renders this suggestion difficult to verify.

While most developed countries have attained relatively low levels of mortality they are also associated with varying mortality levels by social grouping such as that the more affluent groups generally have lower mortality. Such differences have declined through time, but still represent significant variations. These general features are likely to be applicable to the Northern Ireland population and indeed a study of mortality in the Belfast urban area (Pringle 1983) emphasises that the considerable spatial variations in mortality are strongly associated with the variations in social class structure. Furthermore, variations in infant mortality (often used as a general indicator of socio-economic conditions) in Northern Ireland in 1974 indicate the presence of considerable variations by social class of father, with the rate for social class V more than double that of social classes I and II (ACIM 1980). Similarly, on a regional basis, the highest levels of infant mortality in Northern Ireland are generally found in the least prosperous areas, particularly some areas in the west of the province. These social and spatial variations are undoubtedly a reflection of varying levels of living, although the association between infant mortality and high parity births (the latter being associated with class and region) will also contribute to the overall differences.

Population composition

Some features of population composition such as social class, occupation and education are discussed in other chapters. This section will briefly examine two aspects: the basic demographic characteristic of age structure and also the cultural attribute of religion.

The age structure of the population of Northern Ireland, reflecting past trends in fertility, mortality and migration, is in some respects different from that of Britain and more akin to that of the Republic of Ireland. The main difference concerns Northern Ireland's younger population, which is a result of the past trend of relatively high fertility. In 1981, for example, approximately 28 per cent of the population were aged less than 15, compared with 21 per cent in Britain and 30 per cent in the Republic of Ireland. Similarly, only 14 per cent were aged over 60, compared with 20 per cent in Britain and 15 per cent in the Republic.[5] The other main feature of Northern Ireland's age structure is the relatively small size of the group aged 20–39, reflecting the history of high emigration. However, the age structure is subject to change and it is apparent that the youthfulness of Northern Ireland's age structure has declined recently as a result of the declines in the birth rate. Furthermore, the declines in the birth rate (coupled with the long-term increase in life expectancy) will lead to relatively large proportions of the population in the elderly (60+) age groups.

The denominational composition of the Northern Ireland population is of considerable socio-demographic relevance. As noted earlier, denominations differ in terms of marriage, fertility and emigration patterns. The main differences are those between the Catholic and Protestant populations (the latter mainly comprised of Presbyterians and Church of Ireland), although certain differences also occur within the Protestant groups. In terms of relative size, the proportion of Catholics in the Northern Ireland population has changed little over the last fifty years, increasing from 35.5 per cent in 1926 to 36.8 per cent in 1971. The major feature here is that the high natural increase of the Catholic population (a function of the high birth rate) has been off-set by high levels of out-migration and consequently the relative proportions have changed little. It is more difficult to estimate the figure for 1981 because 19 per cent of the population did not state their religion at the recent census. However, Compton (1985) suggests a proportion of 38.2 per cent on the basis of estimated natural increase and migration during the 1970s. In relative terms, large proportion s of Catholics occur in many of the western parts of the province and in the District Council Areas of Moyle in the north-east and Newry and Mourne in the south. In absolute terms, large numbers of Catholics are found in the Belfast Urban Area, although here constituting a minority overall.

The future religious balance of the Northern Ireland population is of considerable social and political relevance, although it is, of course, difficult to anticipate both the overall and the inter-denominational differences in fertility and emigration. Thus on the basis of rates of natural increase at 1977 levels and emigration at levels of the period 1971–77 (with Catholics constituting 60 per cent of emigrants), Compton (1982) estimates that a Catholic majority would be attained by the middle of the twenty-first century. This date would be brought forward some fifteen years if emigration dropped to relatively low levels. On the other hand, it is likely that Catholic fertility will continue to decline beyond the levels for the late 1970s and in this case, other things being equal, a Catholic majority in Northern Ireland would be an unlikely event. However, the future level (and religious composition) of emigration is the other crucial factor in this equation and is particularly difficult to estimate. It is apparent that there remains considerable scope for varying scenarios regarding the numbers game in Northern Ireland.

The distribution of the population by religious denomination is particularly important at those finer, more local, scales of analysis at which much social interaction occurs. Thus research on Belfast indicates that the extent of segregation of housing has been quite high over this century and has recently increased in intensity (Boal 1982). There was, for example, a sharp increase in the extent of segregation in Belfast (at the street level) between 1969 and 1972 and a reduction in the overall extent of residential mixing (Boal 1982). This reflects the considerable movement of families to Protestant or Catholic enclaves at the beginning of the recent troubles (Darby 1976). However, Poole (1982) emphasises that there is a considerable range of variation in the segregation of housing throughout the towns and cities of Northern Ireland, and the high degree of residential segregation in Belfast, Londonderry, Armagh and Lurgan is not replicated to the same degree in other urban areas. Little is known about the overall extent of residential segregation in rural areas, although Harris's (1962) micro-study of a rural area near the border suggests a quite marked degree of residential segregation.

Conclusion and implications

This chapter has attempted to summarise the overall demographic characteristics of the population of Northern Ireland as well as outlining some of the more important variations by social class, religion and area of residence. Apart from the immediate demographic importance of such characteristics, many of these features are of relevance in a wider social, economic and political arena. Indeed, the various implications of such demographic characteristics may be divided into two groups embracing, firstly, certain general demographic features that have repercussions in many developed societies and secondly, those that are particularly pertinent to Northern Ireland. Of the former, the socio-economic implications of several demographic factors can be emphasised involving, for example, the various consequences of an aging population; the problems of maintaining service provision in rural areas which have undergone considerable population losses; the problem of balancing the demand for jobs with population change and also planning the varying demand for education provision in relation to changes in age and class structure. Recent (1978 based) population projections for Northern Ireland anticipate moderate increases in population to the end of the century and if borne out, these will have important implications for the overall distribution of population as well as the demand for employment, housing and service provision.

The second group of factors are of relevance in that they relate to the particular characteristics of Northern Ireland society. Thus, various studies of the Northern Ireland problem, such as Darby (1976) and Boal and Douglas (1982), emphasise the importance of population characteristics as one of a set of factors of direct relevance. These include population distribution (especially in terms of denominational segregation); population movement (particularly in relation to intimidation and 'forced' movement during the troubles); the relative and absolute sizes of the Catholic and Protestant populations; social integration (as seen in terms of residential segregation and the incidence of mixed marriages); past, present and future inter-denominational growth rates (particularly the differentials in fertility and emigration) and the relationship between demographic structure and such social problems as unemployment. Moreover, Poole (1983) has outlined how spatial variations in ethnic violence in Northern Ireland can be related to certain sociodemographic factors, such as the relative and absolute sizes of the Catholic population and the extent of residential segregation.

Thus, demographic factors have considerable relevance to the study of society in Northern Ireland. The subject should therefore continue to receive detailed attention from researchers and, hopefully, available data sources will continue to improve in terms of their scope and quality.

Notes

1   The problem of under-enumeration of the 1981 Census of Population reflects the resistance to the Census associated with a campaign of civil disobedience. It is, of course, difficult to assess the degree and nature of the problem of non-enumeration: the Registrar General (1983) estimated an undercount of approximately 19,000; the Policy and Planning Research Unit at Stormont has suggested a much higher figure of 74,000 while Compton suggests a figure of 40,000. See Morris and Compton (1985). Compton's analysis indicates that the extent of under-enumeration was particularly marked amongst the population aged less than 19 and, to a lesser extent, those aged 20–49. In some respects an undercount of the population of between 1 and 5 per cent may not seem excessive (all censuses contain at least some minor inaccuracies) but the fact that the under-enumerated population is unlikely to constitute a representative cross-section across the Northern Irish population ensures that any detailed analysis of the census data will be a hazardous task.

2   These data on religion are subject to error because of the non-response to the question on religion at the censuses of 1971 and 1981 (9 and 19 per cent respectively). The figures will be correct if the rates of non-response were similar by marital status, but unfortunately such information is not known.

3   'Mixed' marriages were defined from the census tabulation in terms of a family where the current religious denomination of one partner was Catholic and the other was non-Catholic. Mixed marriages occur, of course, within the Protestant denominations but these are of less demographic and sociological importance. Apart from the problem of non-response to religion in the 1971 census, the figure of 2 per cent is likely to underestimate the extent of mixed marriages and a wider definition, based on the religious background of each partner (rather than current religion), would be more appropriate. This is reflected in Hickey's work (1984). The author is grateful to Dr M. Poole for advice on this matter and for providing estimates of the extent of mixed marriages in North Antrim and Londonderry from unpublished survey material.

4   Recent estimates of migration have been based on a variety of data sources including the transfer of National Insurance records, the transfer of National Health Service records and The International Passenger Survey. Apart from the problems of accuracy inherent in such sources, little information is available on the characteristics (and motivations) of migrants. Moreover, there is very little information on cross-border movement. Net migration loss can be inferred from census and vital registration data (see Table 1) but this only refers to inter-censal periods and again, little or no information is available on the characteristics and attitudes of migrants.

5   These estimates of age structure for 1981 are based on adjusted census data derived by Compton (Compton and Coward 1983).

References

ADVISORY COMMITTEE ON INFANT MORTALITY AND HANDICAP IN NORTHERN IRELAND, 1980. *You and Your Baby,* HMSO, Belfast.

AUNGER, E. 1975. 'Religion and Occupational Class in Northern Ireland', *Economic and Social Review,* Vol. 7, pp. 1-23.

BARRITT, D. and CARTER, C. 1962. *The Northern Ireland Problem: A study in Group Relations,* Oxford, Oxford University Press.

BOAL, F. 1982. 'Segregation and mixing: space and residence in Belfast', in F. Boal and N. Douglas (eds.) *Integration and Division: Geographical Perspectives on the Northern Ireland Problem,* London, Academic Press, pp. 249-280.

BROWNE, B. 1978. 'Emigration shifts Balance in the North', *Hibernia,* Vol. 42(16), p. 10.

COMPTON, P. 1976. 'Religious affiliation and demographic variability in Northern Ireland', *Transactions, Institute of British Geographers* Vol. 1(4), pp. 443-52.

COMPTON, P. 1978. 'Fertility differentials and their impact on population distribution and composition in Northern Ireland', *Environment and Planning,* Vol. 10, pp. 1397-1411.

COMPTON, P. 1982. The demographic dimension of integration and division in Northern Ireland, in Boal, F. and N. Douglas (eds.) *Integration and Division: Geographical Perspectives on the Northern Ireland Problem,* pp. 75-104.

COMPTON, P. 1985. 'An evaluation of the changing religious composition of the population of Northern Ireland', *Economic and Social Review,* Vol. 16(3), pp. 201-224.

COMPTON, P. and COWARD J. 1983. The development and present structure of the population of Northern Ireland. Conference Paper, British Psychological Society (N.I. Branch) Health and Vulnerability in Northern Ireland, December 1983. Unpublished.

COMPTON, P., COWARD, J., and WILSON-DAVIS, K. 1985. 'Family size and religious denomination in Northern Ireland,' *Journal of Biosocial Science* (forthcoming).

COWARD, J. 1980. 'Recent characteristics of Roman Catholic fertility in Northern and Southern Ireland', *Population Studies,* Vol. 34(1), pp. 31-44.

COWARD, J. 1981. 'Ideal Family Size in Northern Ireland', *Journal of Biosocial Science,* Vol. 13(4), pp. 443-454.

DARBY, J. 1976. *Conflict in Northern*

Ireland: the Development of a Polarised Community, Dublin, Gill and Macmillan.

DOUGLAS, N. and BOAL, F. 1982. The Northern Ireland problem, in Boal, F. and Douglas, N. (eds), *Integration and Division: Geographical Perspectives on the Northern Ireland Problem*, London, Academic Press, pp. 1–18.

HARRIS, R. 1972. *Prejudice and Tolerance in Ulster: a Study of Neighbours and 'Strangers' in a Border Community*, Manchester, Manchester University Press.

HARRISON, R. 1981. Population change and housing provision in Belfast, in P. Compton (ed), *The Contemporary Population of Northern Ireland and Population Related Issues*, Belfast, Queen's University, Institute of Irish Studies.

HICKEY, J. 1984, *Religion and the Northern Ireland problem*, Dublin, Gill and Macmillan.

KENNEDY, R. 1973. 'Minority group status and fertility: the Irish,' *American Sociological Review*, Vol. 38, pp. 85–96.

LEE, R. 1979. Interreligious courtship in Northern Ireland, in M. Cox and G. Wilson (eds) *Love and Attraction: An International Conference*, Oxford, Pergamon, pp. 167–169.

MILLER, R. 1979. Occupational mobility of Protestants and Roman Catholics in Northern Ireland, *Fair Employment Agency for Northern Ireland*, Research Paper 4.

MILLER, R. 1983. Religion and occupational mobility, in R. Cormack and R. Osborne (eds), *Religion, Education and Employment:*

Aspects of Equal Opportunity in Northern Ireland, Belfast, Appletree Press., pp. 64–77.

MILLER, R. and OSBORNE, R. 1983. Religion and unemployment: evidence from a cohort survey, in Cormack, R. and Osborne, R. (eds), *Religion, Education and Employment: Aspects of Equal Opportunity in Northern Ireland*, Belfast, Appletree Press, pp. 78–99.

MORRIS, C. and P. COMPTON. 1985. 'The census of population in Northern Ireland', *Population Trends*, Vol. 40, pp. 16–20.

MOXON-BROWNE, E. 1983. *Nation, Class and Creed in Northern Ireland*, Aldershot, Gower.

OSBORNE, R., CORMACK, R., REID, N. and WILLIAMSON, A. W. 1983. Political arithmetic, higher education and religion in Northern Ireland, in R. Cormack and R. Osborne (eds), *Religion, Education and Employment: Aspects of Equal Opportunity in Northern Ireland*, Belfast, Appletree Press, pp. 177–200.

POOLE, M. 1982. Religious Residential Segregation in Urban Northern Ireland, in F. Boal and N. Douglas (eds), *Integration and Division: Geographical Perspectives on the Northern Ireland Problem*, London, Academic Press, pp. 281–308.

POOLE, M. 1983. The demography of violence, in J. Darby (ed). *Northern Ireland; the Background to the Conflict*, Belfast, Appletree Press, pp. 151–180.

PRINGLE, D. 1983. Mortality, cause of death and social class in the Belfast Urban Area, 1970, *Ecology of*

Disease, Vol. 2(1), pp. 1–8.
REGISTRAR GENERAL
NORTHERN IRELAND, 1983.
The Northern Ireland Census 1981: Summary Report, HMSO, Belfast.
ROSE, R. 1971. *Governing without*

Consensus, London, Faber.
WALSH, B. 1970. *Religion and Demographic Behaviour in Ireland,* Dublin, Economic and Social Research Institute, Paper No. 55.

10
Beyond Industrial Society

LIAM O'DOWD

Contemporary social change and development confronts social
scientists with an enormous paradox. It seems, on the one hand,
to indicate unprecedented social progress, on the other to
portend social conflict and destruction. There are signs that a
new and more interdependent world system is coming into existence, one which is based on new technologies of communication,
production and military power under the aegis of giant multi-
national corporations and the major super-powers. Yet this
emerging 'global village' seems to generate wealth for the few
and poverty for the many; it juxtaposes food mountains in the
EEC with mass starvation in Africa; the 'high' technology of
'Silicon Valley' and 'Star Wars' with the primitive technology
of subsistence agriculture. Increasingly, therefore, the major
theories of social change (for overview, see Chapter 4) have been
forced to recognise the great inequities, diversity, and uneven-
ness of comtemporary social development. These become
manifest in the persisting, and often growing, inequalities
among states, geographical regions, classes, the sexes, ethnic and
racial groups.

Theories of development and change can be divided into two
crude categories with regard to how they come to terms with
these divisions and inequalities. Firstly, modernisation theories
see the latter either as characteristics of 'traditional', undevel-

oped societies or as defects in the development process which can be corrected. Modernisation theorists emphasise above all the achievements and potential of the 'western path to development' with its origins in the first industrial revolution in western Europe. They see capitalist entrepreneurs, investing money in new technology and producing commodities for profit in the market place, as the driving force of a process which proceeds through several stages. These include the mechanisation and commercialisation of agriculture, industrialisation and urbanisation, and finally, the post-industrial service economy. This is a theory of *diffusion*. The path to development (conceived as modernisation) is via the diffusion of technology, entre-preneurial skills, and capital to undeveloped countries and regions. There are 'strong' and 'weak' versions of modernisation theory. The 'strong' thesis links modernisation with evolution and progress, often seeing it as natural and inevitable. It links its basic economic components to a much wider range of social changes such as the emergence of western style nuclear families, the work ethic, secularisation, pluralism and representative democracy. The 'weak' thesis agrees with the primacy accorded to economic and technical change but does not necessarily link them to the other changes listed above. It recognises that tradi-tional forms may survive and be adapted to new requirements (for fuller account see Webster 1984).

The second set of theories incorporates theories of imper-ialism, the world system, dependency and underdevelopment. While they seldom question the material benefits deriving from modernisation they see its attendant inequalities and uneven-ness not as characteristics of 'traditional society' or as correct-able side-effects, but rather as endemic to the whole process. Thus the development of the so-called advanced regions directly generates underdevelopment in peripheral regions and third world countries. The key process of change is seen as *domination* and *exploitation* rather than diffusion — a domination rooted in the history of western imperialism and colonialism and one which continues today via the activities of multi-national corporations and their sponsoring states.

In general, the second set of theories has found more acceptance in third world countries and, to some degree, in state
socialist systems, especially in poorer countries and those most
adversely affected by western domination. Their greatest
impact in the 'West' has been academic and critical — in
questioning the assumptions, empirical validity, and policy
implications of 'modernisation' theories (see Frank, 1971). In
particular, they have succeeded in highlighting the underdevelopment of peripheral regions in Western Europe and
North America.

Social change and development in Northern Ireland provide
an interesting test of both approaches. In many ways the
existence of the province as a separate political unit is a testimony to the impact of uneven development. The Belfast region
was an integral part of the first industrial revolution in the
United Kingdom. Since 1920, however, the UK has lost its
industrial pre-eminence and Northern Ireland has been transformed from one of its most to one of its least industrialised
regions. It is a high unemployment, high social deprivation
region marked by sharp internal disparities. Yet, as in the
Republic of Ireland, development strategy remains identified
with modernisation theories, i.e. with the view that the diffusion
of entrepreneurial skills, technology and capital investment are
the keys to economic growth. Even more significantly, the
assumptions behind modernisation theory have a certain com-
monsensical plausibility. As in other advanced countries, it
seems clear that the standard of living of the vast bulk of the
population has increased dramatically over the past sixty years.
Higher incomes, less onerous employment, better diet and social
services, along with the advent of cars, televisions and other
appliances all coexist with a staged movement of people out of
agriculture and manufacturing into the service economy. The
links between 'development' in Northern Ireland and underdevelopment elsewhere seem obscure.

In this chapter, I consider some data on changing employment patterns in the light of the theories discussed above.
Employment statistics must be distinguished from the occupa-

tional statistics discussed elsewhere (Chapter 11). They relate to economic sectors which may comprise different combinations of occupations. Thus, employment totals for manufacturing will include managerial and other white-collar workers as well as skilled and unskilled manual workers. Employment statistics do indicate however, the changing significance of the different production sectors, although they omit unpaid housework and jobs in the informal or 'black' economy.

Social change and development will be described under three broad headings:

1. changes in broad employment patterns since the 1950s
2. de-industrialisation and the impact of multi-national corporations
3. the emergence of a state-dependent service economy.

The implications of these developments will be considered in turn for:

(a) the different experiences of male and female workers
(b) the changing location of jobs
(c) Catholic–Protestant differences.

Changing employment patterns

At first glance, the broad employment changes in the province seem to mirror the experience elsewhere in advanced industrial countries as portrayed by modernisation theories. Table 1 demonstrates the major historical shift away from agriculture and manufacturing towards service employment.

Table 1 excludes the self-employed but the decline in the latter from 107,800 in 1950 to 75,750 in 1979 corresponds with patterns in other advanced countries. Farmers continue to account for the bulk of the self-employed although they have shown a slight decline from 75 per cent to 66 per cent of the total self-employed in the period 1950–79. In the same period those in self-employment declined from 20 per cent to 13 per cent of the total in civil employment (self-employed plus employees).

Comparison with the Republic of Ireland is instructive, even allowing for the difficulties of comparing a nation-state with a

Table 1: **Percentage of employees in employment in the main industrial sectors in Northern Ireland, 1952–83***

	1952 %	1971 %	1983 %
Agriculture/Forestry/ Fishing	6	3	2
Manufacturing (including Construction)	53	45	27
Services	41	52	71
Number	466,000	473,241	464,370

*Some problems of strict comparability across time do not vitiate the basic trend.
Sources: Isles and Cuthbert (1957, p. 63); Department of Manpower Services (DMS) Gazettes; Department of Economic Development (DED), unpublished statistics.

'region'. At Partition, both parts of Ireland were 'open economies' heavily dependent on exports. Northern Ireland, however, depended much more heavily on manufacturing exports, whereas the Republic of Ireland relied mainly on agriculture. Since then, and especially since 1960, both areas have pursued modernisation strategies, albeit relatively independently of each other. The main aim in Northern Ireland was to diversify the manufacturing base of the economy and to offset the decline of the traditional engineering and textile sectors. In the Republic of Ireland the main aim was to build up manufacturing industry to combat emigration and the large scale movement of people out of subsistence agriculture. By the 1960s both areas were seeking to come to terms with international free trade, the EEC and a world economy increasingly dominated by large multi-national corporations. Although the history and structure of employment in each area was rather different, the 'development' strategies adopted were similar. They included the state sponsorship of multi-national investment in manufacturing, the encouragement of greater mechanisation and efficiency in agriculture and in traditional manufacturing. Table 2 suggests that despite different starting points, there are now clear signs of convergence between both parts of Ireland in terms of the broad sectoral composition of civil employment (employees plus the self-employed).

The contraction of agricultural employment has been more marked in Northern Ireland, although the gap is narrowing between both areas. Sheehy *et al.* (1981) have noted that in both areas, agricultural production takes place largely on owner-occupied farms staffed mainly by family labour while there has been a long run convergence in the types of agriculture practised. The expansion of the service sector has been marked in both areas mainly owing to the growth of public sector employment. This growth has not been an explicit part of modernisation strategy which has tended to focus on the more directly productive sectors.

In Northern Ireland, however, the expansion of the (mainly state) service sector has been more dramatic than in the

Table 2: **Civil employment in the main industrial sectors as a percentage of total employment in Northern Ireland and the Republic of Ireland**

	1973 %		1981 %	
	NI	*Republic*	*NI*	*Republic*
Agriculture	8.5	24.6	7.5	17.5
Industry	38.5	30.7	26.9	31.3
Services	53.0	44.7	65.6	51.2
Total	100.0	100.0	100.0	100.0
Manufacturing (Industry minus Construction)	29.4	20.5	20.8	20.5

Source: Bradley and Dowling (1983, p. 40).

Republic of Ireland (see Table 2), where the thrust of development strategy has been towards manufacturing employment. Here a major historical shift seems to have occurred. As Table 2 indicates, manufacturing employment accounts for the same proportion of total employment in each area. Given that the Republic of Ireland has twice the number of employees as Northern Ireland overall, it is now clear that for the first time this century the bulk of manufacturing employment is south of the Border. It is in the transformation of the Northern Ireland manufacturing industry that the ambiguous effects of modernisation strategy can be seen most clearly.

De-industrialisation, development strategy and the impact of multi-national corporations

De-industrialisation (defined as the loss of manufacturing employment) has been the most visible component of socio-economic change in Northern Ireland. Abandoned linen mills and engineering works in inner Belfast and other towns, as well as empty factories in the new industrial estates built in the 1960s, bear testimony to the nature and extent of its effects. In 1960, Stormont was on the brink of initiating a more active regional development strategy. Northern Ireland still had a substantial manufacturing base which was highly specialised and unstable. The revival of regional strategy in Britain and heavy redundancies in engineering and shipbuilding in the early 1960s precipitated government action. The particular administrative structure in the province, combined with considerations of sectarian geography and opposition from powerful local interests in traditional firms, all shaped the implementation of the new strategy (see O'Dowd *et al.* 1980).

At first, the new strategy appeared to be successful. It assumed that 'development' depended on the diffusion of capital, technology and new skills to Northern Ireland from the more advanced industrial economies — the Matthew and Wilson plans of the 1960s built in a spatial dimension. In line with the conventional wisdom of the time, 'growth centres' were designated from which it was expected that 'development' would be diffused to the rest of the province.

The key vehicle of economic modernisation was to be state-sponsored multi-national corporations. These did facilitate one of the prime aims of the industrial strategy — the diversification of manufacturing employment. Table 3 suggests the limits of this process, however. Dependence on particular sectors was slow to disappear although the table does obscure the full extent of diversification within sectors. Within the shipbuilding and engineering sector, for example, employment in shipbuilding and marine engineering declined dramatically from 24,648 in 1960 to approximately 6,000 in 1984 (DMS Gazettes, 1978–79, DED statistics). Employment in the long-established engineering plants in Belfast, such as Mackies, Shorts, Sirocco, also contracted and was partially replaced by employment in the new electrical and instrument engineering factories which were being attracted to the province. Similarly, the decline in the textile/clothing sector masks the dramatic disappearance of the traditional textile sector (notably linen). Textiles employed only 11,000 people in 1983 compared to 74,000 in 1952. Clothing

Table 3: **Percentage of overall manufacturing employment in major industries in Northern Ireland, 1952–84**

	1952 %	1965 %	1971 %	1984 %
Shipbuilding/ Engineering	26	22	21	27.5
Textiles/ Clothing	51	42	39	28.5
Total	77	64	60	56.0
N	161,480	110,883	102,176	56,040

Sources: Isles and Cuthbert (1957, p. 63); Department of Manpower Services Gazettes 1978-9; Unpublished Department of Economic Development statistics.

employment has been halved in the same period from 33,000 to 15,000 (Isles and Cuthbert 1957, p. 63, DED statistics).

A closer look at the textile sector illustrates many of the ambiguous effects of economic modernisation. In the early 1950s the linen industry employed over 60,000 people in over 400 factories dominated by small local family concerns. Employees were mainly female, working for low wages in bad conditions (Steed 1974; Dohrs 1950). As early as 1959, one of the main links of linen manufacture with other forms of local production was broken. Flax had virtually ceased to be grown. The complex of small family firms failed to come to terms with new marketing conditions and with the rise of the international synthetic fibres industry. The latter was not to remain a purely external threat. Between 1960 and 1973, the promotion of the synthetic fibres industry in Northern Ireland became a major part of industrial strategy. Some of the world's largest producers were attracted to Northern Ireland, despite opposition from local linen interests. The result here, as elsewhere, was that the new firms accelerated the closure of the traditional plants. They were capital intensive, operated as part of world-wide organisations, and provided alternative, relatively well-paid, and high skilled employment, in contrast to the traditional linen sector. A small number of large multi-national plants, such as Courtaulds, ICI, and Enkalon, moved away from the old sites of linen employment to new growth centres such as Carrickfergus, Antrim and Coleraine.

The new sector had a much larger component of white collar employment and a much higher proportion of male workers and Protestants (the new factories were located in predominantly Protestant areas). Ownership was in the hands of the multi-national companies rather than the local family firms. Above all, the synthetic fibres firms proved much less durable than linen manufacture. From a peak of 9,500 jobs in the early 1970s, employment has now reverted to the early 1960s level of 1,000-2,000. The major cause was branch plant closure after 1979 owing to unfavourable oil prices and the availability of cheap Third World labour.

While the story of the textile/synthetic fibre sector is not representative, it is indicative of the nature of socio-economic 'development' after 1960. Regional strategy in Northern Ireland, as in the Republic of Ireland, involved high levels of job loss as well as new job creation. The multi-national companies began to impose a new international division of labour on the global economy. Production processes became more fragmented and more geographically mobile and were moved to countries and regions which offered the best long-term prospects in terms of cheap labour, access to markets and raw materials, cooperative labour unions and governments. Significantly, however, it was largely production units which were located in peripheral economies such as Ireland. Research and development functions and often key marketing functions were retained in the multi-national companies' country of origin which was generally the US, Continental Europe or Japan. In this context, inter-state and inter-regional competition for new jobs became fiercer as states became more heavily involved in facilitating and subsidising incoming firms.

Changes in manufacturing employment have not been the result of some natural evolutionary process; they have been increasingly influenced by state, i.e. political and administrative, decisions. Between 1946 and 1982 state agencies 'promoted' 170,000 manufacturing jobs in Northern Ireland of which 137,000 actually came into being (NIEC-40, 1983, p. 16). Of these only 40,000 (40 per cent of total manufacturing employment) remained in 1982. In addition, the state financially 'maintained', or promoted via small industries, another 82,000 jobs between 1971 and 1983, of which 46,000 remained in 1983 (NIEC-47, 52, 1985). The vast bulk of manufacturing industry is state-aided in Northern Ireland. Even so, employment is becoming more volatile and less durable (NIEC-40, 1983). The average duration of state assisted jobs under all schemes ranges between three and four years (NIEC-52, 1985 p. 33).

Regional industrial strategy, after some initial success, has faced a mounting crisis since the early 1970s. Accelerating de-industrialisation has led to much higher unemployment. Foreign investment has fallen, partly as a result of greater competition from Third World countries, and also from the more prosperous regions of the advanced countries. Above all, however, the impact of the 'troubles' reduced the willingness of multi-national companies to come to Northern Ireland. A number of high cost, high risk ventures, notably De Lorean and the Lear Fan Jet company, were promoted in the late 1970s only to end in spectacular failure. In stark contrast to the 1960s, Northern Ireland succeeded in promoting only one-fifth of the jobs promoted by the Republic between 1970–78 (NIEC-40, 1983 p. 54). To compound the problem several major multi-national company plants closed after 1979, adding to the steady loss of jobs elsewhere in the manufacturing sector (see O'Dowd 1985).

The accession to power of a Conservative government in 1979 seemed to further threaten Northern Ireland's manufacturing sector. The Conservative government is ideologically committed to curbing state intervention and expenditure and to encouraging the 'free play of market forces'. Interpreted literally, this could decimate manufacturing in Northern Ireland. Industrial policy has been re-oriented to encouraging small local entrepreneurs. While many more small businesses have started, they create relatively little employment and large manufacturing plants still dominate the sector. In the circumstances, most of the prospects for employment creation seem to be in the service sector — where the state plays an even more prominent role.

A state-dependent service economy

Despite the importance of the service sector (see Table 1 above), the growth of state service employment and expenditure has taken the form of a series of incremental policies and reactions rather than a coherent strategy. The generation of high levels of unemployment, the impact of the 'troubles' and the administration of the British welfare state under direct rule have all shaped the emergence of a state-dependent service economy in Northern Ireland. Since 1974, public expenditure in Northern Ireland has increased at twice the rate of that in Britain as a whole (NIEC-42, 1984 pp. 9-10).

It is in the area of direct job creation, however, notably in the education and health services, that the impact of the state sector has been visible. In 1979 the state directly employed 40 per cent of all employees — reaching 46 per cent in 1983. The increase in public sector *services* employment (by far the most important part) has been estimated at an average of 2,700 jobs per annum over the period 1960-78 — a growth rate which more than doubled to 6,000 per annum in the latter part of this period (NIEC-23, 1981 p. 37). All public sector employment increased by an average of 6,800 per annum between 1974-79, levelling off to a growth of 1,400 per annum under the Conservative government since then. In this last period, there are even signs of decline, especially in male public sector jobs.

This expansion in state employment and public expenditure, however, needs to be qualified. While it may moderate the unevenness and inequalities generated in the overall development process it also reflects them: (1) it has not prevented a doubling of unemployment between 1970-79 and a further doubling between 1979-82; (2) much of the increase in public expenditure is in legally automatic social security payments (unemployment assistance) which accounts for 33 per cent of the

Table 4: **Part-time workers as a percentage of all workers in Northern Ireland, 1971-81**

	1971	*1978*	*1981*
	%	%	%
Male	4.8	6.6	7.5
Female	19.0	32.2	34.5
Total	10.3	17.5	19.6
N	48,623·	88,130	95,127

Sources: Department of Manpower Services Gazettes; Department of Economic Development statistics.

total; (3) the rise in state and other service employment has largely meant a rise in part-time employees, of which the vast majority are women. Part-time workers doubled between 1971–83, increasing at a rate of 5,644 per annum between 1971–78 and subsequently by 2,332 per annum. As Table 4 shows, a growing proportion of women workers are part-time.

Male and female employment patterns

The growth of women's part-time jobs is one indication of the increasing significance of women generally in the Northern Ireland labour force. They have increased from 36 per cent of all employees in 1952 to 46 per cent in 1983, and they account for 55 per cent of all employees in the public sector — the only expanding area of the economy (DED statistics). The modern history of female employment in Northern Ireland has been substantially different from that in the Republic of Ireland and many British regions. As Table 5 shows, a high proportion of women have historically worked in full-time manufacturing jobs, notably in linen. With the latter's demise, there has been a major shift towards service (often part-time) jobs. Thus the socio-economic changes detailed above have had more far-reaching consequences for women than for men.

Table 5: **Percentage distribution of all female employees among the main industrial sectors (male figures in brackets)**

	1952	1971	1983
	%	%	%
Manufacturing	55 (39)	35 (37)	16 (27)
Services	44 (40)	63 (45)	82 (61)
Agriculture/Construction	1 (21)	2 (18)	2 (12)
	100 (100)	100 (100)	100 (100)

Sources: Isles and Cuthbert (1957, p. 63); Department of Manpower Services Gazettes; Department of Economic Development statistics.

Female employment still falls within a much narrower range than men's, however. Women tend to be employees rather than employers; they accounted for 46 per cent of all employees in 1981 and only 10 per cent of the self-employed. Female jobs are much more likely to be part-time, periodic and to fall within a much narrower range of (mainly service) industries — especially in the lower paid sectors such as distribution, health, education and clerical work. With the growth of the public service 'caring' services, women are increasingly paid for work they previously did in the home. Here the jobs continue to carry some of the stigma and low status of 'purely domestic' duties.

Growth in female employment does not necessarily reduce 'official' unemployment figures. Instead, it may merely increase female activity rates (defined as the percentage of women of working age actually in, or available for, paid employment). This has happened in Northern Ireland. Compared with the Republic of Ireland, married women are approximately twice as likely to be in paid employment, although the situation has been rapidly changing in the Republic with the dramatic increase in the proportion of married women working (NIEC-23, 1981 p. 6; Hutchinson and Sheehan 1983, pp. 43–4). It seems likely, moreover, that the extent of women's paid work is not adequately reflected in official employment statistics, just as reluctance or ineligibility to register reduces women's actual unemployment rate. Despite the increase in female paid work, technological innovations such as the 'electronic office' may constrict women's employment opportunities in the future, when falling birth-rates, postponed marriage and changed attitudes to married women workers may push more women on to the job market. There are also signs that high male unemployment rates are another factor increasing female activity rates.

The location of employment and unemployment

The major changes in employment patterns are clearly visible from the aggregate statistics, yet such aggregates obscure a central feature of socio-economic change — its uneven spatial pattern. In Northern Ireland, population and economic activity were historically concentrated in Belfast and its surrounding area. Location of industry has an enhanced importance in Ulster, given the highly durable mosaic of Protestant and Catholic territories which have their roots in the plantations. This mosaic has been modified, reconstituted and altered by successive waves of socio-economic development and by the partition of Ireland. Table 6 demonstrates, in crude terms, the current uneven distribution of population, economic activity and unemployment. While manufacturing industry has been crucial, historically, in shaping the locational pattern, the growth of the service and state sectors has not led to much re-

Table 6: **Percentage distribution of population, employment and unemployment by location in Northern Ireland, 1981**

	Greater Belfast Region	Rest Northern Ireland	Total
	%	%	%
Population	65	35	100
(Catholics)*	(46)	(54)	(100)
(Non-Catholics)*	(74)	(26)	(100)
Employees	71	29	100
(Manufacturing)	(75)	(25)	(100)
(Service)	(73)	(27)	(100)
(Agricultural)	(36)	(64)	(100)
(Construction)	(65)	(35)	(100)
Unemployment (1984)	59 (50)**	41 (50)**	100

*The religous population figures are subject to two qualifications. Nineteen per cent failed to answer the religion question in the 1981 census. Some Catholics refused to provide any census returns. This had important local effects especially in west Belfast. The figure for Catholics in the Belfast region may therefore be somewhat understated.
**Figures in brackets refer to unemployment in 1973/74.
Source: Northern Ireland, 1981 Census and Department of Economic Development.

distribution of population or economic activity away from the dominant Belfast region. While recent industrial closures have raised unemployment rates in areas such as Carrickfergus, Antrim and Newtownabbey, rates remain significantly higher west of the Bann.

The main locational changes over the last twenty years have occurred *within* the Belfast region. Here there have been two main features. Firstly, manufacturing employment more than halved in Belfast between 1959 and 1981. The decline has been continuous but uneven, being concentrated mainly in inner, west and north Belfast. The collapse of linen manufacture and the contraction of traditional engineering were the main causes. Secondly, between 1959 and 1971 there was a substantial growth in manufacturing employment in the new suburbs of Belfast (Lisburn, Newtownabbey, Bangor) and in the growth centres such as Antrim, Ballymena, Carrickfergus and Craig-avon, to which incoming multi-national companies were directed by the regional strategy of the time. In the 1959–71 period some new, if somewhat shortlived, factories were set up in Enniskillen, Newry, Strabane and Derry. Coleraine was the only town outside the immediate Belfast region to show a rela-tively durable increase in manufacturing employment. After 1971, however, a decline set in in nearly all areas (O'Dowd 1980, p. 46). The closure of large multi-national employers in synthetic fibres and tyre manufacture affected Carrickfergus, Craigavon, Antrim and Derry. The whole basis of post-war regional strategy had been undermined and the large numbers of people who had moved to the suburbs and the growth centres now began to experience high unemployment. The state response was to reverse regional policy by seeking to address the 'inner city problem' in Belfast which the previous strategy had helped to create. Housing rehabilitation, and an attempt to encourage small businesses via the Belfast Enterprise Zone, sought to counter the long-term effects of employment contrac-tion, civil conflict and depopulation in the inner city. The effects to date have been rather limited, as the unemployment figures show.

While Northern Ireland has had higher unemployment rates than any other region in Britain throughout the post-war period, the provincial rate has always masked huge variations in terms of area, gender and sectarian categories within the province. In 1976, a government report formally recognised the major and most durable aspect of spatial inequality in the province. It referred to 'a virtually dual economy' comprised of the western and eastern parts of Northern Ireland. West of the Bann, to which west Belfast might be added, contained the areas of the most durable hard core unemployment. Average male earnings were also much lower in the west, and its record of attracting new industry was much inferior (*Economic and Industrial Strategy for Northern Ireland* 1976, pp. 20–22). Unemployment has increased more rapidly in the east in absolute and relative terms over the last decade, but the gap still exists (Map 1, Table 6). However, the widest disparities are within the Belfast area itself, at least in terms of unemployment rates. West and north Belfast (especially the Catholic areas) have unemployment rates between three and four times those in the south and east of the city (*New Ireland Forum* 1983, p. 19).

Protestant and Catholic differences

It is impossible to analyse spatial disparities without reference to the sectarian differences which critically determine the social significance of space. These interact with class. Working-class areas in Belfast and the larger towns are the most segregated, but in every part of Northern Ireland the sectarian headcount is of local political significance. Catholics live disproportionately in west Belfast and in the west of the province, in areas with high unemployment rates and little access to new employment. Between 1960 and 1973, multi-national companies established their plants largely within the Belfast region which is overwhelmingly Protestant (see Map 1). Inner Belfast lost over a quarter of its population as people moved (including some Catholics) to the suburbs and the growth centres being developed by the regional planners in the 1960s.

Map 1

Unemployment rates/Ratio of other denominations to Catholics in 1981.

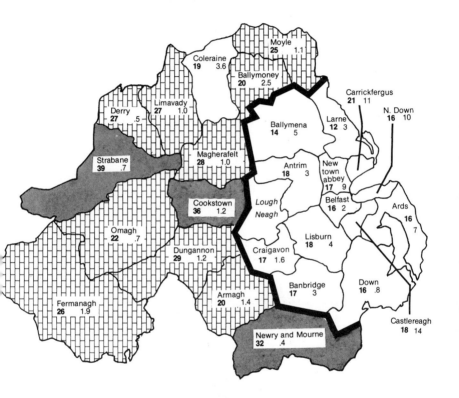

Unemployment Rates

- 30% and over
- 20–29%
- Under 20%
- Belfast Region Boundary

Bold figure — 1984 Unemployment rate (U.R.)
Light figure — Religion Ratio (R.R.)
Other denominations: Catholics

Catholics reversed this process however, when, in response to the 'troubles', they moved back to west Belfast, i.e. to the most de-industrialised part of Northern Ireland. Even prior to this, the shortlived success of regional strategy had done little to improve the relative employment position of Catholics. In 1971, after the unprecedented success in attracting multi-national companies to the province, Catholics were two and a half times more likely to be unemployed than Protestants, despite their much higher emigration rates. Overall unemployment has increased by over three and a half times since 1970, and since 1971 Protestants have also experienced mass unemployment. Yet, remarkably, the margin of Catholic disadvantage has been scarcely reduced. In 1981 Catholics were still 2.3 times more likely to be unemployed than Protestants. The major gap remains in male unemployment rates. Catholic females have slightly improved their position mainly owing to the expansion of state (especially part-time) employment (see Table 7).

Table 7: **Protestant* and Catholic unemployment rates, 1971–81 (percentages)**

	1971		1981	
	Protestant	*Catholic*	*Protestant*	*Catholic*
	%	%	%	%
Males	6.6	17.3	12.0	30.0
Females	2.4	4.9	10.0	17.0

*Protestant here refers to all religious denominations other than Catholic.
Source: *Northern Ireland Census, 1971; Northern Ireland Census 1981.*

The relative disadvantage of Catholics is associated with a number of factors — geographical location, an unfavourable occupational and class profile (see chapter 14), and uneven distribution in the industrial sectors. They are further disadvantaged by their over-representation in recession-prone industries such as construction, clothing and footwear, and transportation. Within these industries they are disproportionately employed in semi-skilled and unskilled manual jobs. On the other hand, Catholics (especially males) are under-represented in more stable highly skilled industries such as engineering and electricity provision (*Fair Employment Agency* 1978). Perhaps more significantly, they are very under-represented in banking, financial services, in the upper echelons of the civil service and at the managerial level in the major industries.

Explanations for Catholic-Protestant differences are a matter for sharp political debate, partly reflected in the social science literature. Crude notions regarding the 'Protestant ethic', Catholics' unwillingness to work, inferior qualifications, high fertility rates and discrimination have all been advanced and challenged in turn. Whatever the merits of the arguments, there is a large measure of consensus among researchers about the highly durable and systematic structural inequality between Catholics and Protestants — an inequality that has remained despite the 'modernisation' and the restructuring of the last three decades (see, for example, Cormack and Osborne 1983; Hepburn, 1982; Whyte 1983).

Summary and conclusions

Radical changes have occurred in Northern Ireland employment patterns over the last thirty years. A heavily state-dependent service economy has emerged, accompanied by a substantial increase in part-time female employment and the unemployment of over one-fifth of the total workforce. Production and employment have moved progressively out of local control to multi-national corporations and the Westminster government. While Northern Ireland is still far removed from the status of a developing Third World country, it has become an increasingly dependent, underdeveloped economy despite attempts at economic modernisation. Economic growth and technological change do not seem to have fulfilled the expectation of some modernisation theorists. Furthermore in Northern Ireland at least, there are few signs of societal consensus, convergence, secularisation or political pluralism.

The relative failure of 'modernisation' in this sense is perhaps due to the fact that the old disparities and inequalities of the first industrial revolution have been refurbished and reshaped by contemporary social change. Economic disparities between Northern Ireland and the rest of the UK, and within Northern Ireland itself — between males and females, east and west, Catholics and Protestants — continue to have sharp political and cultural significance. The employment profile of the various social classes may have changed, but the threat of unemployment and other forms of social deprivation remain largely working-class phenomena.

The prevalence and persistence of uneven development and social inequalities lend credence to theories of dependency and domination. The latter stress the interaction between political and economic power. This is supported by the key role of the state in peripheral economies like Northern Ireland — in the short and medium term, state policy is decisive for local employment prospects. Yet state policy can only influence rather than determine the operation of the global economic system and the decisions of multi-national corporations and other investors. Technological developments, seldom under state control, may be beginning to destroy jobs in the most buoyant employment sectors — state services. Employment in Northern Ireland shipbuilding, engineering and textiles is continually threatened by international energy prices and trading agreements, as well as by cheap, docile labour forces in developing countries. The high-technology route to competitiveness means fewer jobs.

Finally, this chapter has concentrated on employment patterns because having a job is still the key to an adequate standard of living. There are, of course, many fanciful visions of a workless automated society of the future — an 'Athens without slaves'. Such an eventuality would seem to demand at the very least an effective means of redistributing wealth from those remaining in paid employment or directly controlling capital and high technology. Despite the central role of the British state in maintaining employment, welfare services, and social control in Northern Ireland, it has proved either unable or unwilling to reverse the various patterns of social inequality associated with its development strategy. The Northern Ireland case is a sharp reminder that power and control may often lie outside the territorial boundaries of particular states and regions. Yet questions of who controls, and who benefits from, the modernisation process must be answered if an alternative and more equitable form of development is to be found beyond industrial society.

References

BRADLEY, JAMES F. and DOWLING, BRENDAN 1983. *Industrial Development in Northern Ireland and in the Republic of Ireland*, Belfast and Dublin, Cooperation North, pp. 90.

CORMACK, R. J. and OSBORNE, R. D (eds) 1983. *Religion, Education and Employment: Aspects of Equal Opportunity in Northern Ireland*, Belfast, Appletree.

DOHRS, F. E. 1950. 'The Linen Industry in Northern Ireland', Chicago, unpublished PhD. dissertation, North-Western University.

ECONOMIC AND INDUSTRIAL STRATEGY FOR NORTHERN IRELAND, Report of a Review Team, 1976. Belfast, HMSO.

FAIR EMPLOYMENT AGENCY 1978. *An Industrial and Occupational Profile of the Two Sections of the Population in Northern Ireland*, Belfast, Fair Employment Agency.

FRANK, A. G. 1971. *The Sociology of Development and the Under-development of Sociology*, London, Pluto Press.

HEPBURN, A. C. (c. 1982). *Employment and Religion in Belfast, 1901-71*, Belfast, Fair Employment Agency.

HUTCHINSON, R. W. and SHEEHAN, J. 1983. *Economic Indicators in Northern Ireland and the Republic of Ireland*, Belfast and Dublin, Cooperation North.

ISLES, K. and CUTHBERT, N. 1957. *An Economic Survey of Northern Ireland*, Belfast, HMSO.

NEW IRELAND FORUM, 1983. *A Comparative Description of the Economic Structure, North and South*, Dublin, Government Publications Office.

NORTHERN IRELAND ECONOMIC COUNCIL (NIEC) 23, 1981. *Employment Patterns in Northern Ireland, 1950-1980*, Belfast, NIEC.

NIEC 40, 1983. *The Duration of Industrial Development Assisted Employment*, Belfast, NIEC.

NIEC 42, 1984. *Public Expenditure Priorities: Overall Review*, Belfast, NIEC.

NIEC 47, 1985. *The Duration of LEDU Assisted Employment*, Belfast, NIEC.

NIEC 52, 1985. *The Duration of Industrial Development Maintained Employment*, Belfast, NIEC.

O'DOWD, L. 1985. 'The Crisis of Regional Strategy: Ideology and the State in Northern Ireland', in G. Rees et al. (eds.) *Political Action and Social Identity: Class, Locality and*

Culture, London, Macmillan, pp. 143–165.

O'DOWD, L. et al. 1980. *Northern Ireland: Between Civil Rights and Civil War*, London, Zed Press.

SHEEHY, SEAMUS J. *et al.* 1980 *Agriculture in Northern Ireland and the Republic of Ireland*, Belfast and Dublin, Cooperation North.

STEED, G. P. F. 1974. 'The Northern Ireland Linen Complex, 1950–70', *Annals of the Association of American Geographers* Vol. 64, pp. 397–408.

WEBSTER, A. 1984. *Introduction to the Sociology of Development*, London, Macmillan.

WHYTE, J. H. 1983. 'How much discrimination was there under the unionist regime, 1921–68?', in T. Gallagher and J. O'Connell (eds.), *Contemporary Irish Studies*, Manchester University Press, pp. 1–35.

11
Social Stratification and Mobility

ROBERT MILLER

Social stratification can be thought of as the enduring, vertical division of 'valued social goods'. Stratification is social when individuals agree as to which goods have value: the possession of land, wealth, a high income, power (political or otherwise), knowledge, social standing or whatever. It is the recognition that different individuals and groups possess unequal amounts of 'valued social goods'; that the divisions have stability and tend to persist over time; and that these divisions of possessions can be seen as arranged vertically in layers analogous to geological strata that leads us to call the divisions *stratification*.

Dimensions or types of social stratification serve as the primary criteria for identifying many of the groups or categories of people in society. For instance, the central position given by many of the authors in this volume to social classes or socio-economic groupings stems from some classes or socio-economic groupings enjoying disproportionate amounts of both the economic 'goods' that define their existence and of virtually all other types of stratification 'goods'. Furthermore, other groupings considered important within a society, such as the sexes, age cohorts and racial, ethnic or religious groups, derive much of their salience from their generally high or low positions along dimensions of stratification. For example, the differences between the sexes are differences of power as well as biology. A woman who finds herself suddenly in

221

possession of a large enterprise upon the death of her businessman husband finds herself in an anomalous position. With regard to age, the young are legally barred from whole categories of basic citizenship rights, such as control of property or the right to vote, until they attain their maturity. The elderly experience a similar withdrawal of rights through such normally unquestioned practices as mandatory retirement, which can result in a severe restriction in income, or being required to re-qualify for a driving licence. Racial, ethnic and religious differences lose much of their significance when not buttressed by stratification differences. Thus, the study of social stratification is central to sociology. This chapter focuses particularly on economic aspects of social stratification in Northern Ireland.

The province is a unique case with regard to economic social stratification in at least two ways. Firstly, the development of the north of Ireland has been along more industrial lines than that of the rest of the island, resembling more the sequence of events followed in the north of England or south-west Scotland. Liam O'Dowd's chapter describes in some detail this sequence since the partition of Ireland. At the same time, the agricultural sector of the economy has remained important, causing Northern Ireland to retain resemblances to the Republic of Ireland. This persistence of a significant rural component means that on many social and demographic indicators the province occupies a position intermediate between Britain and the Republic of Ireland as detailed in John Coward's chapter. As such, Northern Ireland constitutes a special case that informs the understanding of social stratification in both islands. Secondly, the working of the Protestant/Catholic division through the economic structure of the province provides much of the substance to the claim that Northern Ireland represents a special case of 'ethnic relations' of interest to sociology generally.

The sectarian division

The roots of the present sectarian division in Northern Ireland extend back to the 'plantations' of the early seventeenth century.

Large numbers of Scots and English of all social classes came, or were brought, into the province of Ulster in a process of colonisation not unlike that being followed in the New World. The plantation of an augmented County Coleraine by the city of London, resulting in the name Londonderry being applied to the city of Derry and then to the whole county, constitutes perhaps the best known example. A more extensive settlement of lowland Scots in counties Down and Antrim had begun even prior to the plantations further to the west, and was then developed further. This colonisation, almost four hundred years ago, created the present sectarian stratification of the economy. 'The Catholic Irish remained. . . . but in conditions which emphasised their suppression' (Darby 1983, p. 14).

In the eighteenth century, the north of Ireland began to develop a class structure distinct from the rest of Ireland. Belfast arose as a centre of commerce with its base in the linen industry. The reasons why the north-east began to develop are debatable — the popular depiction of the 'natural industry of the Protestant people' does not in itself constitute sufficient explanation. The farming methods of the new settlers may have been more efficient than those of their predecessors, and more food was probably being produced for sale rather than consumption. The 'Ulster custom' in land tenancy, where tenants had a (legally undefined) right to a saleable interest in their holdings has been suggested as being of importance. Tenants stood to gain something from improvements to their holdings either while occupying the property or through higher compensation if they left. The increased amount of capital in circulation from these factors would raise the prospects for industrial development. In any case, the growth of the linen industry with its exports to English and colonial markets brought in finance and led to a demand for machinery which was produced by a local engineering industry (Beckett 1966; Darby 1983, pp. 15–18). With finance, a shipping tradition and local engineering, a modern ship-building industry followed. Protestants dominated the skilled work in all the new industries, as well as the middle-classes that arose from these industries or existed to support them. These elements, centred around the manufacturing sector, existed alongside other middle-class groups such as doctors, lawyers and like professionals who served the general populace, as well as the landowners, small merchants and businessmen, which were common to all Ireland. In short, before partition the north-east of Ireland had developed an occupational structure dominated by Protestants and distinct from the rest of the island.

O'Dowd and McCullagh in this volume, and many authors elsewhere, document the subsequent decline of the 'traditional' industries of shipbuilding, engineering and linen, their eventual faltering replacement by new industry and the associated patterns of unemployment.

The interplay of religion and occupational structure persists into the present day. Aunger's influential analysis of the 1971 Census indicated: 'a marked tendency for Protestants to dominate the upper occupational classes while Catholics are found predominantly in the lower classes'. Looking at non-manual occupations, Aunger noted that in 'the professional and managerial class, it is apparent that the occupations filled by Catholics are largely those which respond to the felt need of each religious group to have certain services provided by their co-religionists… By contrast, professional and managerial occupations providing services required by the whole community rather than by a specific religious section, are very disproportionately Protestant … Catholics are located in the social services while Protestants are disproportionately represented in finance and industry.' Among manual workers, Protestants are more likely to be located in 'higher status' industries (industries enjoying higher rates of pay, more stable employment and skilled work). Furthermore, Aunger notes an interaction between religion and sex where 'occupations which can be identified as strongly Protestant tend to be male, while a significant number of those identifiable as disproportionately Catholic tend to be predominantly female … While a nurse may be a Catholic, it is more likely that the doctor will be Protestant.' Only among Catholics were the majority of non-manual workers women (Aunger 1983, pp. 27–41).

Many commentators accept the basic parameters of Aunger's

analysis, while not necessarily agreeing on the explanations for their existence. Following on from that acceptance, many assume that the general trend in religious differences is moving towards a lessening in their scale and distinctiveness (see, for example, Jenkins 1984, pp. 26-27). Unfortunately, direct examination of this assumption through a replication of Aunger's 1971-based analysis using the 1981 Census data is not feasible. The large proportion of people who opted not to reply to the religion question in the latest census produces a substantial margin of error no matter what strategy is adopted to handle the incomplete reporting of religion. Available evidence, however, indicates trends in the religious segmentation of the occupational structure contrary to the popular assumption of general improvement.

Hepburn, comparing employment and religion in Belfast between 1901 and 1951, found that 'The disadvantageous position which Catholics had increasingly slipped into during the second half of the nineteenth century was not alleviated during the first half of the twentieth... The proportion of Protestants who were in Class IV/V (semi-skilled and unskilled manuals) declined, while that of Catholics probably increased, so that an already substantial differential between the two religious groups widened significantly' (Hepburn 1983, p. 62). Miller (1983, pp. 70-76), in an analysis of religion and inter-generational occupational mobility, noted that the differences in Protestant and Catholic mobility, advantageous to Protestants, could be attributed solely to changes in the occupational distribution of the sons' generation compared to that of their fathers. The sons of Protestants tended to dominate the non-manual classes while Catholics were located proportionately more in the manual classes, especially in the unskilled manual group. While this result in itself must be viewed with caution since the occupational distribution of fathers cannot be assumed to represent directly any one distinct point in the past, it points with the other studies to an increasing clarification of the occupational division between religions.

Bew, Gibbon and Patterson (1979) found evidence for widening, rather than stable or shrinking, occupational differences between Protestants and Catholics when comparing the 1971

Census with pre-partition census data. Cormack and Rooney, in a detailed comparison of the religious distribution of occupations in the 1911 and 1971 Censuses conclude that 'The period of economic expansion in the 1950s and 1960s provided the best opportunity to redress the past pattern of Catholic disadvantage ... That opportunity was lost, and the moment has passed'. They also see the new industries of the last decades as differentially benefitting Protestants (Cormack and Rooney, n.d.).

Some authors have attempted to assess the extent to which the disproportionate unemployment of Catholics can be attributed to the effects of lower socio-economic status and demographic differences between Protestants and Catholics (Compton 1981, 1982; Doherty, 1981, 1982). That is, that apparent differences between the religions taken as representing a legacy of discrimination or disadvantage for Catholics, such as a higher rate of unemployment, in fact only reflect other, more fundamental and non-discriminatory differences. Factors such as the larger average size of Catholic families, or proportionately more Catholics being located in the rural portions of the province 'west of the Bann' are seen as going a long way toward explaining religious differentials. A comprehensive investigation following this multi-variate approach found, however, that when looking at the determinants of the individual occupational standings of men, religion continued to exert a relatively small but significant independent effect to the advantage of Protestants and to the disadvantage of Catholics even when the effects of '... start of career, educational attainment, social background and population size of the community of origin' had been controlled. Furthermore, the same model eliminated as significant factors present geographical location, residence or origin in the more rural and disadvantaged west of the province, the size of the families of origin and procreation, 'ambition' and geographic mobility (Miller 1981). That the persisting advantage in favour of Protestants occurred in the individuals' own careers indicated an active process rather than merely a passive replication of pre-existing patterns. Kelley and McAllister (1984), while reporting a similar multi-variate analysis that emphasised

the importance of background in explaining a substantial portion of Protestant advantage, also located persisting disadvantages for Catholics in income and among Catholics born into
'élite' families.

So, while occupational differences and the average earnings
'shortfall' between Northern Ireland and the rest of the United
Kingdom have lessened (Simpson 1983), available evidence
does not show a congruent lessening of religious differences.
Similarly, a decline in the 'traditional' and 'new' industries
associated particularly with Protestant employment has not resulted in the erosion of the religious differential in unemployment hypothesised by some (Byrne 1980). (For instance, to use a
source different from those cited elsewhere in this volume, a
large-scale sample survey carried out in 1980 by the Policy
Planning and Research Unit, Department of Finance and Personnel (N.I.) reported a Catholic unemployment rate almost
three times higher than that for Protestants (Economic and
Spatial Planning Ltd 1984).)

A case study of 'fair employment'

A case study illustrates the dangers of uncritically adopting the
assumption that 'things' must be getting 'better' as far as
religious differences in occupational distributions are concerned. The Fair Employment Agency for Northern Ireland, a semi-
autonomous body set up in the mid-1970s to combat religious
discrimination in employment, carried out an investigation of
the Northern Ireland civil service. Since the study concerned itself with a major employer in the public sector that had been expanding in recent decades and was based on employment data
generated in 1980, well after the imposition of direct rule, it is
highly relevant to the issues discussed above.

The results of this lengthy and complex enquiry can be summarised briefly. The Agency found that 'the proportion of
Roman Catholics ... was less than the proportion in the working
population'. and that, 'Roman Catholics are not adequately represented at the key policy-making levels of the Northern

Ireland Civil Service.' The Agency immediately qualified these findings, however, by pointing out that, 'During the 1970s the number of Roman Catholics entering has increased substantially ... in particular during the last five years of the decade'. It went further by claiming that religion 'was not a statistically significant factor ...' affecting the salary levels '... for those Roman Catholics recruited since 1968', and for senior staff, that 'between 1973–1983, the proportions of Roman Catholics amongst Principals, Deputy Principals and Staff Officers have all shown marked increases' (*Fair Employment Agency* 1983). The Agency adopted findings in conformity with the assumption that religious differences are lessening over time, and gave the civil service a 'clean bill of health'. It concluded that any observed disparities in the present were a legacy of the 'bad old days' prior to direct rule. Interestingly, and in spite of their own conclusions, the Agency also recommended that the Northern Ireland civil service should establish a 'monitoring system' to 'match and extend' the FEA investigation (*Fair Employment Agency* 1983, p. 66).

What the Agency failed to report, however, was that all of the qualifications to its originally critical findings had been inserted into the report after the original submission of the investigation, that the qualifications came from analyses produced by the civil service itself and not from the Agency's investigation (in fact, the civil service analysts had been upgraded to the status of 'Specialists who assisted the Agency' (in investigating themselves!). It failed to specify that these 'qualifications' were included over the objections of internal FEA personnel and consultants involved in the investigation, and that the version of the final report that was eventually published disagreed in important aspects with the reports submitted by the Agency's own consultants. In particular, the reports of the Agency consultants had found the existence of promotion anomalies favouring Protestants in lower, *recently* appointed grades (*Institute of Manpower Studies* 1982) as well as at higher grades, and pointed out that the most significant disparities in salary level occurred among 25 to 34 year-olds and *not* among the older age categories (Miller

1985, pp. 118–122). These are hardly the findings one would expect if religion had ceased to make any difference to careers after 1968. Promotion projections also predicted a developing promotion blockage where Protestants appointed into the expanding civil service in the late 1960s and early 1970s were shown to have slightly more seniority than Catholics appointed over the same time span. The significance of this was that the Protestant group was more likely, through the operation of seniority, to replace a 'lump' of soon-to-retire upper-level civil servants who themselves were a relic of the previous expansion of the civil service immediately after World War II. Once in, the relatively young new appointees could be anticipated to remain there well into the next century. The current pattern of Catholic under-representation at senior levels could be anticipated to reproduce itself over some decades even in a situation of complete equality of promotion. Finally, the figures for 1973 and 1983 that showed 'marked increases' in Catholic senior staff resulted from exercises carried out within the civil service and do not correspond easily with the figures for senior staff generated by the Fair Employment Agency's own 1980-based data. (As one cynic put it, the only way to make the 1980 figures agree with those found by the civil service three years later would be to assume a remarkable rate of conversion to Catholicism among senior civil servants. A more plausible explanation is that the civil service and the Agency used differing procedures for allocating religion. The Fair Employment Agency allocated religion on the basis of secondary schooling. The procedure used by the civil service itself, however, is not reported.) Nevertheless, it is to the Northern Ireland civil service's credit that, despite the Fair Employment Agency's investigation, it seems to have taken cognizance of the problems posed by a 'promotion blockage' that affects the religious groupings differently, and is seriously going ahead with implementing the recommendation for a system of monitoring.

Besides providing a telling verdict on the credibility of the Fair Employment Agency, the history of the civil service investigation and its results have a larger significance. The study demonstrates the dangers in naively assuming that patterns of inequality set up in the past are withering away of their own accord. It does so using recent information from a major employer that could be generalised to other branches of the large public sector in Northern Ireland. The, by now largely irrelevant and counter-productive (for social policy), debate about 'how much "discrimination" *was* there under the Unionist regime?' shows signs of evolving into a debate on 'how much "discrimination" *is* there under direct rule?'

Social mobility: its significance and definition

The study of social mobility, far from being the 'stupid bourgeois problematic' claimed by one critic (Poulantzas 1975, p. 33), is central to an understanding of social stratification. Many of the 'founding fathers' of sociology concerned themselves with mobility issues. For instance, when Marx and Engels asserted in the *Communist Manifesto*, that 'The lower strata of the middle class — the small tradespeople, shopkeepers ... all these sink gradually into the proletariat', they were making a statement of group downward mobility. Pareto argued that the long-term stability of a society required a 'circulation of élites', since the mobility of gifted individuals into a ruling group would revitalise it. Sorokin also emphasised the importance of mobility for societal stability owing to its drawing up the most intelligent and effective, and claimed that the upwardly mobile made the most efficient repressors (Sorokin 1959). Numerous more recent commentators have echoed their predecessors by claiming that a real chance of mobility serves to co-opt potential trouble-makers by redirecting their efforts toward individual striving rather than altering the system as a whole. Others see high rates of mobility as reducing the likelihood of class-based politics by mixing people of diverse origins.

Contrarily, mobility has also been depicted as a radicalising force in politics with such diverse examples being cited as the thwarted upward mobility of the bourgeoisie giving rise to the French Revolution, and the growth of the Nazi Party being stimulated by a lower middle-class losing its position through inflation (see Heath 1981, for a discussion of these issues). Similarly, it has been suggested that a 'new Catholic middle-class', brought into being by educational reform after World War II, provided the impetus behind the civil rights campaign in Northern Ireland. Commentators have also attributed the conservatism of Northern Ireland Protestants to their relatively advantaged position being seen as under threat from Catholic upward mobility. (These examples have been included to show how mobility issues can intersect with broader concerns and not necessarily because they are empirically valid). The results of studies of social mobility can inform social stratification theory generally by confirming (or failing to confirm) empirically the existence of distinct strata or classes between which movement is relatively restricted (Giddens 1973, pp. 107–112). Furthermore, the liberal concern with 'equality of opportunity' meshes well with the perspectives of many mobility researchers and has been informed by their often critical findings. The study of social mobility is one of the most empirically developed areas of sociology, and Northern Ireland possesses, along with the Republic, several mobility datasets of high quality.

Social mobility may be defined as the movement of individuals or groups from one point on a dimension of social stratification to another. The dominant trend of mobility research has been to use data from large sample surveys to assess the mobility of males along a hierarchy of occupational stratification. One should note that the table and the figure following both conform to this traditional focus by concerning themselves with the mobility of men only, using data collected by survey in the winter of 1973/74. Therefore, the generalisation of the findings to the whole population of Northern Ireland can only be undertaken with caution. The study of social mobility until very recently can be viewed as an example (one out of many) of 'sexism in sociology'. For instance, the term most commonly used when reporting the mobility of women has been 'marital mobility'. 'Marital mobility' compares the occupational status of a woman's *father* with that of her *husband*; that is, the woman has no independence but exists solely adjacent to some male. While there are serious conceptual and methodological difficulties that need surmounting in order to incorporate women adequately into mobility analyses (see, for instance, the debate in recent issues of *Sociology*, 1983–84), real progress is being made. An examination of the labour mobility of women in both parts of Ireland using the same datasets from which these figures for men have been derived is underway.

Occupation is classified in the table below by an adaptation of the Hope-Goldthorpe schema developed by the Nuffield College, Oxford mobility study of England and Wales. The 'service' categories refer to professionals, administrators, managers, proprietors of large enterprises and supervisors of non-manual employees. 'Routine Non-Manual' consists of clerical workers and sales personnel. The 'Proprietor' category refers to owners/employers in small enterprises. 'Farmers' includes farm managers and 'Skilled Manual' includes foremen and technicians. (See Erickson, Goldthorpe and Portocereo 1979, for the original use of this adaptation and Goldthorpe and Hope 1974, for a complete discussion of the Hope-Goldthorpe occupational schema.) The occupational strata have been arranged from 'high' to 'low' in order to ease the presentation of results. One must note, however, that the Nuffield team considers their 'class schema' to be a set of distinct categories and explicitly rules out an interpretation that assumes the occupational categories make up a scale of income, social standing, attainment or any other means of rating occupations.

Father to son mobility

The top numbers in the cells of Table 1 are percentages that sum to 100 down each column. That is, looking down a column, the percentages tell us what proportion of people in an occupational category originated in each of the eight strata. For instance, of the 174 men in the 'Upper Service' group, 18.4 per cent had fathers who were also in the 'Upper Service' group. Percentages developed in this manner are sometimes called 'inflow percent-

Table 1: **Father's occupation by occupation of son; column percentages and disparity ratios***

	Son's occupation, 1973								
col. % ratio Father's occupation	Upper service	Lower service	Routine non-manual	Proprietor	Farmer	Skilled manual	Semi-skilled and unskilled	Agri. worker	% (N)
Upper service	18.4 9.0	6.5 6.0	3.4 1.1	1.8 1.1	1.5 6.5	1.8 0.4	1.0 0.2	0.0 0.0	3.3 (77)
Lower service	13.2 5.0	17.1 6.0	4.7 1.1	0.9 0.4	0.0 0.0	2.8 0.5	2.0 0.3	2.3 1.4	4.4 (102)
Routine non-manual	8.0 2.0	10.6 2.5	15.0 2.3	8.2 2.6	1.0 2.2	6.8 0.8	3.6 0.3	0.0 0.0	6.6 (152)
Proprietor	13.8 2.3	11.1 1.7	13.7 1.4	26.8 5.7	2.0 3.0	7.8 0.6	6.3 0.4	2.3 0.6	9.8 (227)
Farmer	9.8 0.7	13.1 0.9	13.7 0.6	25.9 2.4	91.1 59.5	10.1 0.4	15.4 0.4	57.0 6.8	22.4 (518)
Skilled manual	19.0 1.5	21.6 1.6	20.1 1.0	20.9 2.1	0.5 0.3	30.4 1.2	20.5 0.6	7.0 0.9	20.8 (480)
Semi-skilled and unskilled	16.7 1.0	17.6 1.0	26.5 1.0	13.2 1.0	2.0 1.0	34.4 1.0	42.5 1.0	10.5 1.0	27.1 (626)
Agricultural worker	1.1 0.3	2.5 0.7	3.0 0.6	2.3 0.8	2.0 5.2	5.8 0.8	8.8 1.0	20.9 10.1	5.5 (128)
%	7.5	8.6	10.1	9.5	8.8	26.1	25.6	3.7	100.0
(N)	(174)	(199)	(234)	(220)	(203)	(602)	(591)	(86)	(2,309)

*Males aged 18–64 in 1973. Father's occupation taken at time of son's first full-time job; son's occupation is present occupation or, if not in work, previous job held (Miller 1984).
Source: *Determinants of Occupational Status and Mobility in Northern Ireland and the Irish Republic,* SSRC Grant HR 1430.

ages', depicting as they do the origins of everyone who has moved into an occupational group. Looking at the origins of the 'Upper Service' group, which could be considered a broadly defined élite, we see that the origins of this 'élite' are very diverse. While over half had non-manual fathers, over one-third had manual origins with the 'Skilled Manual' group actually contributing more sons to the 'Upper Service' group than that group did itself. If this is an élite, it is an élite that is not closed to entry from outside. The 'Lower Service' strata is even less closed. Aside from the 'Proprietor' group, the other non-manual strata in fact have more members originating in either of the manual categories than they do in their own stratum. 'Farmers' make up the most closed group, with over 90 per cent the sons of fathers. The manual strata have much less diverse origins. Almost two-thirds of both the 'Skilled' and the 'Semi-skilled and Unskilled' originate in one of the manual categories.

These results broadly agree in their form with those reported for the Republic of Ireland (Hout and Jackson 1984; Whelan and Whelan 1984) and England and Wales (Goldthorpe 1980). Northern Ireland falls between the Republic of Ireland and England and Wales in its amount of gross mobility, showing more mobility than the Republic of Ireland but somewhat less than England and Wales. The Republic of Ireland differs most significantly in the much greater closure of its 'élites'. (Preliminary results from the CASMIN Study (Comparative Analysis of Social Mobility in Industrial Nations) confirms the position of Northern Ireland as intermediate between the Republic of Ireland and England and Wales).

'Inflow percentages' in themselves, however, do not tell the complete story and in fact obscure important features in the mobility table. The total numbers in each of the eight strata vary (for instance, there are 626 'Semi-skilled and Unskilled' fathers but only 77 'Upper Service' fathers) and, furthermore, the total numbers in each stratum vary across generations (for example, the 77 fathers in the 'Upper Service' category grow to 174 'Upper Service' sons). These 'structural effects' make some patterns of mobility more likely than others; for example, because there are more people of semi-skilled and unskilled manual origin than of any other category, one naturally expects to discover generally more people throughout the table from that category than from any of the other, smaller categories. Secondly, since the numbers in the strata vary across generations, and fathers are in a one-to-one correspondence with sons, a shrinking category will mean that some sons must have moved out to other categories. If a category has expanded (for instance, there are over twice as many sons in the service groups as there were fathers) some sons from other categories must have moved in. The second number in the cells of Table 1, called the 'disparity ratio' provides a means of controlling for the first of these structural effects — the problem of some categories of origin being much larger than others. (A more effective method of control for both this problem and the latter structural effect of shrinking or expanding strata, log-linear analysis, is not given here owing to its complexity and considerations of space. (See Miller 1983 for such an analysis of Northern Ireland mobility data.) A disparity ratio tells us the relative chances of men from different origins getting into a destination stratum (see Heath 1981, pp. 260–263). In Table 1, the chances of those of 'Semi-skilled and Unskilled' origin have been set at one and the relative chances of all the other origin strata can be compared to that of the 'Semi-skilled and Unskilled'.

Looking at the relative, rather than absolute, chances that people of different origins have of moving into the 'Upper Service' category, one discovers a radically different perspective from that shown by the inflow percentages. Those of 'Upper Service' origin can boast of a ratio of 9.0 compared to the 1.5 for the 'Skilled Manuals'. So, even though more men in the 'Upper Service' stratum come from 'Skilled Manual' origins, the odds of an 'Upper Service' man remaining in the stratum are six times higher than the odds of a man of 'Skilled Manual' origin moving up into the stratum. Looking down the 'Upper Service' column, one sees that while the odds for moving into the 'Upper Service' stratum are higher for all the non-manual groups than for the manual and agricultural categories, none approaches the level of inheritance of the 'Upper Service' stratum itself. The élite that appeared open, in terms of inflow percentages, begins to look more exclusive when one examines relative chances. The 'Lower Service' group shows a very similar, though somewhat less exclusive pattern of ratios. The 'Routine Non-Manual' group shows a more evenly dispersed pattern of relative chances, while 'Proprietors' shows a high degree of inheritance within their own stratum and is the only non-agricultural group exhibiting a relatively large influx from 'Farmer' origin. The extremely closed nature of the origins of farmers is reflected in their enormous disparity ratio. (The size of the ratios for the 'Farmer' column, however, should be read with some caution as they are inflated by the small number of semi-skilled and unskilled origin upon whom the basic ratio of 1.0 is set. The high ratios for farmers of 'Agricultural Worker' and 'Upper Service' origins refer in fact to only 4 and 3 men respectively.) The 'Skilled Manual' stratum takes most of its members from within the working-class. The 'Semi-skilled and Unskilled' themselves are perhaps most notable for having a large proportion who have remained in the same stratum as their fathers and for having relatively fewer from 'Skilled Manual' origins than might be anticipated. 'Agricultural Workers' show a pattern of remaining distinct from non-agricultural occupations and, as might be expected, a high ratio of agricultural workers from 'Farmer' origins. Neither these disparity ratios nor the inflow percentages displayed above should be taken as depicting the mobility table completely. Taken together, what they do is indicate simultaneously both absolute and relative rates of mobility and immobility.

Intra- and inter-generational mobility

Comparing the present occupation of sons directly with that of their fathers does confound two separate phenomena. On the one hand, we have the effects of individuals' social origins or backgrounds upon their current social positions. This can be called inter-generational mobility, since the father's job indexes a person's origin status in the previous generation. On the other hand, a person has also reached his or her present position through their own efforts, independently of any advantage or disadvantage incurred from their origin. This form of mobility may be recorded as the movement between a person's first and present jobs and is called intra-generational or career mobility. While the effects of origin obviously can persist beyond a person's first job, a diagram like Figure 1 below, showing the pathways of men from different origins through first jobs to present occupational positions, goes a long way towards separating intra-generational from inter-generational mobility. The eight strata of Table 1 have been collapsed into five categories in order to keep the diagrams from becoming hopelessly complex. 'Upper' and 'Lower Service' combine into a single 'Service' category. 'Routine Non-Manual' and 'Proprietors' amalgamate to form an 'Intermediate' group and the 'Skilled' and 'Semi-skilled and Unskilled' manual categories are collapsed together into a 'Working' class group.

   Looking first at Part (A) of the figure (the 122 men of 'Service' origins), one notes that 30 per cent move directly into 'Service' level jobs when they start work. Considering the types of jobs that go into making up the 'Service' group, the most likely scenario is that of men obtaining a higher educational qualification that allows them to move directly into a professional type first job. The stability of their careers is clear in that of this 30 per cent, practically all (29 per cent of the total), still possess service level jobs in their present occupation. The second feature of note for those of service origin is the extent of 'counter mobility', moving temporarily out of an origin status only to return to it later. Of those who moved down into a lower first job at the intermediate or working-class levels, large proportions (18 and 13 per cent respectively) returned to the service level in their present occupations. The hypothesis of 'counter mobility' is further supported when one notes that the considerable portion who fell to 'Intermediate' first jobs did not continue on down into the working-class in their current job. Also, those who went into 'Working' first jobs were much more likely to move all the

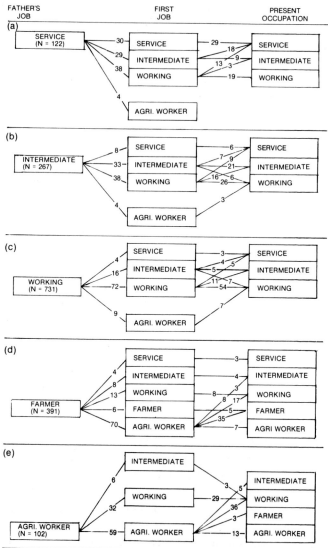

Source: 'Determinants of Occupational Status and Mobility in Northern Ireland and the Irish Republic,' SSRC Grant HR 1430.

Fig. 1. 'Three point' mobility patterns: flows (in percentages) from classes of origin of men aged 30 to 65, 1973. Flows of less than three per cent are not shown.

way back up to the 'Service' level rather than the shorter distance to an 'Intermediate' present occupation. It is reasonable to anticipate that with time even larger proportions of those of service origins regain their former status. If there is truth in the myth of the boss's son who starts at the bottom in his dad's enterprise and, to no one's surprise, rises to its head, we find it here.

Part (B), the 267 men of 'Intermediate' origins, confirms the conclusions reached above while at the same time highlighting the lower position of the 'Intermediates'. Here, direct entrants to 'Service' occupations make up a smaller proportion of the total (8 per cent), but the stability of a career with a service beginning persists. While more move down into working-class first jobs and 6 per cent of those in 'Intermediate' first jobs also go on down into the working-class, 16 per cent of those of 'Intermediate' beginnings experience 'counter mobility' back to their group of origin.

The largest group, the 731 men of working-class origin, also show the greatest amount of stability between father's job, first job and present job. Almost three-quarters (72 per cent) move into working-class first jobs and, of these, over half (54 per cent of the whole group) are still in working-class jobs at present. Aside from the direct entrants into 'Service' jobs, the most likely option for the remainder is 'counter mobility' back into the working-class by the time of their present job.

The diagrams for those of agricultural origin demonstrate the radical separation of the mobility patterns of those of farm origin from the rest. For the 391 of 'Farmer' origin, 70 per cent were 'Agricultural Workers' in their first jobs (contrasted to, at most, 9 per cent of those from non-agricultural origins). That half of these men become farmers in their present occupations and that they make up the majority of present farmers (only 6 per cent of those of 'Farmer' origin were farmers in their first jobs) demonstrates the importance of what can be presumed is direct farm inheritance. Further evidence for direct inheritance of the farm after a period of work as a labourer on it comes from the diagram for those who do not have a farm to inherit — those of 'Agricultural Worker' origin. Here, while the majority (59 per cent) also had first jobs as farm workers, only 3 per cent of the total are farmers in their present jobs (compared to 40 per cent of those of 'Farmer' origin). Those who move out of either group into non-agricultural first jobs do not return to agriculture in significant numbers. Practically all of the agricultural labourers who move out end up in working-class jobs. While the majority of 'Farmer' origin who leave agriculture altogether also end up in the working-class, significant proportions either enter directly into the 'Service' category or move directly into the 'Intermediate' group. The diagrams of the three urban origin groups also affirm the one-way pattern of movement out of agriculture. The 'Farmer' category does not appear at all among these urban diagrams and, while some of non-agricultural origin did move into agricultural work as a first job, this category has evaporated by the time of present job.

Overall, Figure 1 highlights important patterns in mobility for each of the origin groups. The much higher odds of those of service origins moving into service jobs themselves, as found in Table 1, can be seen to come from two phenomena. Firstly, the service categories are able to use the educational system to their benefit through placing a large proportion of their progeny directly into high-level jobs. Secondly those of service origin are likely to experience 'counter mobility' back into a service level job if they do move out. The 'Intermediate' origin categories are truly intermediate in that, while they enjoy better chances of moving into high level occupations than manuals or those of farm origin, they do distribute their progeny throughout all of the three urban groups in roughly equal proportions. The persistence of working-class origins can be seen in the large proportions who either remain within the working-class throughout or who return to it in their present jobs. Finally, the separation of the agricultural occupations from the rest, the importance of farm inheritance and the one-way movement out of agricultural origins into the working-class, appears in the diagrams for those of agricultural origins. These results for Northern Ireland generally agree with findings for England and Wales (Goldthorpe 1980, pp. 50–54), Dublin (Whelan and Whelan 1984, pp.

48-54) and the Republic of Ireland (from equivalent tabulations for the Republic generated by the author). Northern Ireland, while broadly coinciding with other parts of the two islands as to the extent and patterns of its mobility for men, does differ in some respects. The main source of difference between Northern Ireland and the others is that the Northern Ireland data show more movement from all five levels of origin into working-class first jobs. It is to be hoped that further comparative analyses will describe the areas of convergence and divergence and will move toward substantive explanations of their causes.

References

AUNGER, E. A. 1983. 'Religion and Class: An Analysis of 1971 Census Data', in R. J. Cormack and R. D. Osborne (eds.), *Religion, Education and Employment*, Belfast, Appletree Press, pp. 24-41.

BECKETT, J. C. 1966. *The Making of Modern Ireland 1603-1923*, London, Faber and Faber.

BEW, P., P. GIBBON and H. PATTERSON 1979. *The State in Northern Ireland: 1921-1972*, Manchester, Manchester University Press.

BYRNE, D. 1980. 'The Deindustrialization of Northern Ireland', *Antipode*, Vol. II, No. 2.

COMPTON, P. A. 1981. 'Demographic and Geographical Aspects of the Unemployment Differential between Protestants and Roman Catholics in Northern Ireland', in P. A. Compton (ed.), *The Contemporary Population of Northern Ireland & Population-Related Issues*, Belfast, Institute of Irish Studies, pp. 127-142.

COMPTON, P. A. 1982. 'The Demographic Dimension of Integration and Division in Northern Ireland', in F. W. Boal and J. N. H. Douglas (eds.), *Integration and Division: Geographical Perspectives on the Northern Ireland Problem*, London, Academic Press, pp. 75-104.

CORMACK, R. J. and E. ROONEY n.d. 'Religion and Employment in Northern Ireland 1911-1971', manuscript.

DARBY, J. 1983. 'The Historical Background', in J. Darby (ed.), *Northern Ireland: The Background to the Conflict*, Belfast, Appletree Press, pp. 13-31.

DOHERTY, P. 1981. 'The Unemployed Population of Belfast', in P. A. Compton (ed.), *The Contemporary Population of Northern Ireland and Population-Related Issues*, Belfast, Institute of Irish Studies, pp. 115-126.

DOHERTY, P. 1982. 'The Geography of Unemployment', in F.

W. Boal and J. N. H. Douglas (eds.), *Integration and Division: Geographical Perspectives on the Northern Ireland Problem*, London, Academic Press, pp. 225–248.

ECONOMIC AND SPATIAL PLANNING LIMITED, 1984. 'The Northern Ireland Labour Mobility Survey: Final Report', St Albans, Economic and Spatial Planning Limited.

ERICKSON, R., J. H. GOLDTHORPE and L. PORTOCARERO 1979. 'Intergenerational Class Mobility in Three Western European Societies: England, France and Sweden', *British Journal of Sociology*, Vol. 30.

FAIR EMPLOYMENT AGENCY 1983. 'Report of an Investigation by the Fair Employment Agency for Northern Ireland into the Non-Industrial Northern Ireland Civil Service', Belfast, Fair Employment Agency for Northern Ireland.

GIDDENS, A. 1973. *The Class Structure of the Advanced Societies*, London, Hutchinson.

GOLDTHORPE, J. H. 1980. *Social Mobility & Class Structure in Modern Britain*, Oxford, Clarendon Press.

GOLDTHORPE, J. H. and K. HOPE 1974. *The Social Grading of Occupations: A New Approach and Scale*, Oxford, Clarendon Press.

HEATH, A. 1981. *Social Mobility*, Glasgow, Fontana.

HEPBURN, A. C. 1983. 'Employment and Religion in Belfast, 1901–1951', in R. J. Cormack and R. D. Osborne (eds.), *Religion, Education and Employment*, Belfast, Appletree Press, pp. 42–63.

HOUT, M. and J. A. JACKSON, 1984. 'Dimensions of Occupational Mobility in the Republic of Ireland', Paper presented to the Budapest meeting of the Social Stratification Committee of the International Sociological Association, Budapest, 10–12 September 1984.

INSTITUTE OF MANPOWER STUDIES 1982. 'Report of an Investigation by the Institute of Manpower Studies into the Non-Industrial Northern Ireland Civil Service', Belfast, Fair Employment Agency for Northern Ireland.

JENKINS, R. 1983. *Lads, Citizens and Ordinary Kids: Working-class Youth Life-styles in Belfast*, London, Routledge and Kegan Paul.

KELLEY, J. and I. McALLISTER 1984. 'The Genesis of Conflict: Religion and Status Attainment in Ulster, 1968', *Sociology* Vol. 18, No. 2, pp. 171–190.

MARX, K. and F. ENGELS 1848. 'Manifesto of the Communist Party', in L. S. Feuer (ed.), *Marx & Engels: Basic Writings on Politics and Philosophy*, Garden City, New Jersey, Doubleday & Company, Anchor Books.

MILLER, R. L. 1981. 'A Model of Social Mobility in Northern Ireland', in P. A. Compton (ed.), *The Contemporary Population of Northern Ireland and Population-Related Issues*, Belfast, Institute of Irish Studies.

MILLER, R. L. 1983. 'Religion and Occupational Mobility', in R. J. Cormack and R. D. Osborne (ed.), *Religion, Education and Employment*, Belfast, Appletree Press, pp. 64–77.

MILLER, R. L. 1984. 'Unemployment as a Mobility Status', Paper presented to the Budapest meeting of the Social Stratification Committee of the International Sociological Association, Budapest, 10-12 September 1984.

MILLER, R. L. 1985. 'Fair Employment in the Civil Service: Report of an Investigation into the Non-Industrial Northern Ireland Civil Service', *L'Irlande Politique et Sociale*, Vol. 1, No. 1.

ROBINSON, P. 1982. 'Plantation and Colonisation: The Historical Background', in F. W. Boal and J. N. H. Douglas (eds.), *Integration and Division: Geographical Perspectives on* the *Northern Ireland Problem*, London, Academic Press, pp. 14-48.

SIMPSON, J. 1983. 'Economic Development: Cause or Effect in the Northern Ireland Conflict', in J. Darby (ed.), *Northern Ireland: The Background to the Conflict*, Belfast, Appletree Press, pp. 79-109.

SOROKIN, P. A. 1959. *Social and Cultural Mobility*, London, Collier-Macmillan.

WHELAN, C. T. and B. J. WHELAN 1984. 'Social Mobility in the Republic of Ireland: A Comparative Perspective', Dublin, Economic and Social Research Institute, Paper No. 116.

12
Educational Segregation: 'Rite' or Wrong?

DOMINIC MURRAY

Before attempting an analysis of the segregated nature of schooling in Northern Ireland, it is important to be aware of the educational structures and context within which it operates. Overall control of the education system is exercised by the Department of Education located in Belfast. This control is dispensed at local level by five Education and Library Boards which have responsibility for the educational and library services of schools in different areas of the Province: Belfast, Western, North Eastern, South Eastern and Southern. Education is compulsory from the ages of five to sixteen.

Primary schooling

There are 1,123 primary schools in Northern Ireland, attended by over 200,000 pupils. Children generally enter the primary sector at 5 years and continue there until the age of 11. One factor which distinguishes the system from that in England is the persistence of the 11+ examination. This is basically a selection procedure which pupils undergo in their final year at primary school. It is on the basis of results attained in this examination that decisions are taken with regard to the child's subsequent second level educational experience. Several attempts have been made to increase parental and teacher involvement in the transfer process. These have proved somewhat less than successful and there is evidence of a preference for traditional and objective test measures being employed as a means of assessment of academic ability and as predictors of future performance.

Post-primary schooling

The 1947 Education Act N.I. proposed a tripartite system of education — Grammar, Secondary Intermediate and Technical Intermediate. It did not, however, provide for the alternative of Comprehensive schools as did the 1944 Act in England. Basically, Grammar schools catered for the academically gifted children (or those whose parents could afford to pay fees). Secondary Intermediate schools were to be attended mainly by those children who were 'unsuccessful' in the 11+ examination. Technical Intermediates were seen as appropriate for those wishing to pursue commercial or practical courses.

Significant blurring of these discrete functions has taken place since 1947. While Grammar schools have continued to concern themselves with academic aspects of education, the curriculum of the Secondary Intermediate schools has changed and broadened considerably over the years. Sutherland (1973, p. 22) claims that Secondary Intermediate schools 'responding to the demands of pupils, parents and teachers, have moved away from the original model of a four-year general, examination-free education for "average" pupils.' The majority of Secondary Intermediate schools now cater for commercial and practical subjects and also prepare some of their pupils for CSE examination and GCE 'O' and 'A' levels. The word 'Intermediate' has been dropped from their title.

Technical Intermediate schools suffered badly as a direct result of the broadening of the curriculum in Secondary schools. A decision was taken in 1957 to phase them out thus leaving only the Technical Colleges of which they had formed a part. These now remain as Institutes of Further Education. Wilson (1982)

Table 1: **Percentage distribution of students in post-primary schools by school type**

	Grammar %	Secondary Intermediate %	Technical Intermediate %	Total places in Second Level Education
1950	67.3	19.4	13.3	34,448
1955	59.1	29.0	11.9	44,661
1960	38.6	56.1	5.3	84,129
1965	37.0	59.9	3.1	106,377
1970	35.1	64.6	0.4	130,929

Source: Wilson, 1982

claims that as a result there now remains a bipartite system of post-primary education in Northern Ireland (Table 1).

Returning to Comprehensive schools, the only school officially designated as such is sited in the new town of Craigavon. Nonetheless, consideration has been given to the concept on several occasions. The 1964 White Paper *Educational Development in Northern Ireland* raised the question of whether the prevailing system should be continued or replaced by a new system based on some form of Comprehensive school. In its 1973 report, *Reorganization of Secondary Education in Northern Ireland*, the Seventh Advisory Council recommended that a declaration of intent should be made to eliminate selection as soon as possible through a restructuring of the educational system. In 1975 and 1976 the Department of Education issued further proposals for the introduction of non-selective post-primary schooling. In 1977 the Government formally announced its intention to eliminate selection at 11+ and to introduce a Comprehensive system. Nineteen seventy-eight saw the Conservative party returned to power in Britain. Almost immediately it 'shelved' the plans for the introduction of a Comprehensive school system in Northern Ireland. The issue has rarely been raised since.

Third level provision

Approximately 12.8 per cent of the relevant age group attend higher education institutes (or degree courses) in Northern

Ireland. Until 1984 there were two universities — the New University of Ulster at Coleraine and the Queen's University of Belfast. There also existed a polytechnic (Ulster College) with its main campus at Jordanstown. This institution differed from its counterparts in England mainly with regard to the number of degree courses offered. In 1980, from example, 69 per cent of its full-time students were engaged on undergraduate programmes.

The Chilver review of Higher Education (1982), commenting on the polytechnic, stated that 'it may have overextended itself in some areas' and suggested 'a period of consolidation and a halt on further extension'. Osborne and Cormack (1984) comment wryly that the Government's response was to announce the merger of the polytechnic with the New University of Ulster! In 1985 this merger has become a reality. It remains to be seen, however, how successful this 'marriage' (unique in British educational history) will prove to be.

Further education

From 1957, largely as a result of losing their Intermediate component, technical colleges began to provide commercial and pre-apprenticeship courses for sixteen-year old school leavers and thus provide 'Further Education'. In fact provisions exist which allow pupils to transfer to Further Education colleges at the age of fourteen or fifteen. However, Wilson (1982) argues that this latter provision is likely to be discontinued since 'a policy document (DENI 1982) has indicated that the Department would prefer to see pupils remaining in secondary school until 16'.

Typically, further education colleges offer courses leading to GCE, City and Guilds and RSA. This is done either through full-time courses or by accommodating students on release from apprenticeships or involved with Youth Opportunity Programmes.

Thus far, this chapter has presented empirical data on the structures of the contemporary educational system in Northern

Ireland. However, what makes the system unique is that almost every sector (with the exception of Higher and Further Education) is characterised by segregation on religious grounds (Table 2). It is to the development and nature of this segregated character that the remainder of the chapter is addressed.

The development of segregation

Segregated schooling in Ireland is by no means restricted to the Northern part of the island. In fact, long before the inception of Northern Ireland as a separate political entity in 1921, there existed a national system of schooling which was divided quite rigidly along religious lines.

This national system, established in 1831, was conceived as a non-denominational structure to afford the same educational advantages to all classes of professing christians without interfering with their particular religious opinions. Despite this laudable aspiration, certain aspects immediately caused problems. In the first place it was proposed that religious education should be excluded from the secular day and secondly, that all clergy were to have full access to the schools.

Table 2: **Primary and second level schools in Northern Ireland**

	Controlled (Protestant)	Maintained (Catholic)	Total
Primary	592	531	1,123
Secondary	92	90	182
Grammar	47	32	79

Source: Adapted from Darby *et al.* 1977, pp. 19–20

Generally speaking, the Catholic hierarchy took most exception to the former, while the latter proposal caused considerable disenchantment among many Protestant clergy. It was, *inter alia*, these early misgivings which sowed the seeds of division in formal education in Ireland. Quite rapidly a segregated system developed catering for Protestant and Catholic children in separate schools, usually under the management of the local parish priest or minister. This segregation was quite rigid by 1921 when the first government of Northern Ireland was established. Segregated education was thus an inheritance of that government rather than its issue.

In 1921 Robert Lynn submitted a report to the first Minister of Education for Northern Ireland, Lord Londonderry. It proposed that three classes of elementary schools be set up:

Class I — those built by local authorities or the Ministry of Education or those handed over to the Ministry by previous managers (known as 'controlled or state schools')

Class II — those schools with management committees composed of four representatives of the former managers and two of the local government authorities (known as maintained schools)

Class III — those schools whose managers wished to remain independent of the local government authorities (known as voluntary schools).

Financial aid to each type of school was in direct proportion to the degree of involvement of governmental authorities on their management committees.

Originally, being deeply resentful and suspicious of the new governmental order in Northern Ireland, the Catholic population in general (and school managers in particular), steadfastly resisted any governmental influence in their schools. Thus all Catholic schools became Class III or 'Voluntary' establishments. In fact it was not until 1967, when an amendment Act produced increased financial incentives to managers for them to allow one-third of their management committees to consist of government representatives, that the Catholic hierarchy moved from their abstentionist position. When satisfied that the relative independence of their schools would be preserved, they agreed to the new proposals and by the mid-1970s the vast majority of Catholic schools had become Class II or 'Maintained' establishments.

On the Protestant side (the implied homogeneity is justified in the educational context), while there was greater identification with government authority, significant reservations existed about the original proposed educational structures. Their concern arose mainly from Lord Londonderry's insistence that religious instruction be excluded from the secular day, that teachers could not be compelled to teach it and that teachers should be appointed at local government level.

The Protestant churches were just as insistent as the Catholic church that government authorities should provide for bible instruction; that teachers should teach it; and that teachers should *not* be appointed at local government level but rather by a central committee. With regard to the latter point, the main concern was that in areas with a Catholic majority in local government, Catholic teachers might be appointed to Class I schools. A clarion call to Protestants at the time was that 'the door is thrown open for a Bolshevist or an atheist or a Roman Catholic to become a teacher in a Protestant school' (*Sunday News*, 1980). It is not clear whether this statement represents a hierarchy of repugnance, but it does give an indication of the prevailing reservations at that time. In fact, by 1925 only 10 (out of 2,000) elementary schools had transferred to state control.

In subsequent years various concessions were made to the Protestant churches with regard to their concerns about educational structures. These concessions were enshrined in the 1930 Education Act which Lord Craigavon described as an assurance that '... it will be absolutely certain that in no circumstances whatever will Protestant children ever be in any way interfered with by Roman Catholics'. The passing of this particular Act allayed the bulk of Protestant anxieties. As a result, the joint education committee of the three main Protestant churches expressed the view that the 'Protestant character of the state is (now) reflected in state schools'. By 1937 50 per cent of Protestant elementary schools had transferred authority to the Ministry of Education. By 1970 almost all

Protestant schools had done so, to become Class I or controlled schools.

At the present time, at primary and post-primary level, it is justifiable to refer to schools attended by Catholic children as 'Maintained' and those attended by Protestant children as 'State' or 'Controlled'.

The nature of segregation

Even the most cursory study of the development of segregated schooling in Northern Ireland demonstrates that *all* of the main churches fought rather hard and persistently to ensure that their various expectations and aspirations were protected within the separate institutions. There is nonetheless a common belief both in Northern Ireland and abroad that the integration of schools is made impossible owing to some kind of intransigence on the part of the Catholic hierarchy alone. It is true that this church has consistently been more outspoken in defence of its own schools. However, Gallagher (1978, p. 33) claims, 'As long as Catholicism has insisted and still insists on its special role in education, so long the rest are absolved from any requirement to articulate their position radically'.

Furthermore, it is difficult for the various Protestant churches to publicly defend Protestant schools, when officially no such institutions exist[1]. They are rather referred to as 'State' or 'Controlled' schools. However, one point should be made very clear here. At every level (apart from official nomenclature) state schools are Protestant establishments. There is ample historic and contemporary evidence to support this claim (see Murray 1983, 1985). This fact must be stated clearly and unambiguously since, without an acceptance of 'what is' rather than what is 'purported to be', there can be no productive dialogue with regard to possible integration or any other aspect of schooling. In fact, as will be discussed later, it is exactly this lack of frankness with regard to the disparate educational aspirations and expectations which has tended to sterilise debate on the social and cultural aspects of education in Northern Ireland.

In this context, the advent of the Astin report (1979) has engendered the most public defence of state schools by the Protestant clergy for forty years. (The Catholic defence has always been public.) The report was leading to a restructuring of the management of schools and the main Protestant churches were concerned that their representation (as transferrors) was being reduced on management committees. Of even greater concern was the implied increased secularisation of state schools.

The response of the 1982 Synod of the Church of Ireland gives a flavour of this concern:

> The term state school has come into popular use but controlled schools are not state schools ... they are church related schools ... attended by Church of Ireland children and other Protestants.

and again;

> But let there be no mistake — we in the Church of Ireland are just as concerned about the identity, ethos and moral and spiritual values of the controlled school as are the Trustees about the maintained [Catholic] sector ... We transferred our schools under conditions which guaranteed, in the generally accepted language of 52 years ago, Protestant teachers for Protestant pupils. (*author's parenthesis*)

These claims raise a vital point. The educational debate in Northern Ireland is *not* between religious schools and secular, or 'Godless' ones. It is rather between religious schools of different denominations — basically Protestant and Catholic. For this reason, analogies drawn with England or America are inappropriate and not very useful. It may also be the reason why some of the analyses by outside observers may, on occasion, seem rather simplistic.

The regular (and almost ritual) social surveys on segregated education which appear mainly in the British press are a good example of this. These invariably purport to show that there is a large majority of the population of Northern Ireland in favour of integrated education. I believe, and again it is important to state it clearly, that this simply is not the case.

Generally speaking, Protestant parents see controlled schools as Protestant in character and as such serving well the needs of their children. As Gallagher (1977, p. 40) puts it:

> they [Protestant parents] know what they want and don't want for their children. And bible-based religious instruction is a must and they believe that they are more likely to get it in a segregated school (of a Protestant kind of course) than in a Catholic one. *(First parenthesis by the author, second parenthesis original text.)*

The Catholic desire for their own schools has always been consistent and predictable (see Philbin 1975; Daly 1980; Conway 1971; O Fiaich 1979). Why then do the various surveys invariably demonstrate a majority in favour of integrated schooling? One reason may be that many Protestants, despite their expressed desire for a church-related state system of education, continue to claim that these establishments are non-denominational. Thus, for them, integration is simply a case of Catholic schools joining the state system. This perception will obviously inflate a positive response to the integration question.

Secondly, to be asked a question about integration is akin to being asked if you have stopped beating your wife (or husband!). It now seems to be axiomatic that segregated schools are socially pernicious and divisive (which has never been demonstrated). Thus, while there may be a sincere desire for segregation, there may also be the fear that a forthright statement of this may well brand one as a bigot.

Thirdly, and perhaps most importantly, the concept of integrated schooling has never been adequately defined. Would it mean for instance the access of all clergy? Would it mean the abolition of prayers before and after class? Would the Angelus be outlawed? Would we forbid the children to sing 'God save the Queen' or 'Faith of our Fathers'? What about the celebration of St Patrick's Day or Commonwealth day? Where would we stand with regard to history teaching? Where would we train our unemotional (or emasculated) teachers? Which flags should be flown? Which prayers said? Which games played? Which songs sung?

Some of these questions may seem banal. But they are not! They are the realities of separation. Without an appreciation of their importance to the various cultural groups in Northern Ireland there can be no hope of advancing our understanding of the relationship between educational experience and cultural difference, social division and community conflict.

Schools and conflict

Darby (1976, p. 114) has presented evidence of a strong body of opinion which would argue that the conflict in Northern Ireland is not primarily religious in character. This is a debatable point and the arguments which have accompanied it have tended to be complex and, indeed, circular. The relationship between religion and culture in the province is so close that they are taken as almost synonymous. Most Protestants subscribe to a Unionist/British political ideology and maintain their own cultural traditions, attitudes and values which are largely a function of an English or Scottish identity. Most Catholics on the other hand aspire, to varying degrees, to a nationalistic ideal and possess a set of values and traditions emanating from and identifying with an Irish heritage.

More importantly, in the context of this chapter, is the fact that not only does religion determine one's cultural membership but also the school one attends. With regard to the relationship between schools and conflict, it should be noted that although segregated schools in Northern Ireland may offer differing cultural experiences within them, they are seldom defended for this reason. They exist mainly as a result of religious conviction. On the other hand the social problems of the province are argued to stem mainly from cultural and political differences. It would seem to be misleading therefore to lay the blame for community conflict at the portals of segregated schools.

However, the equating of religious composition with political and cultural aspiration allows schools to be neatly presented in terms of cause rather than effect. This is not to suggest that segregated schools in Northern Ireland do not have a reproductive effect with regard to social and cultural difference. In fact there were many examples of such influence observed during research in both types of school. However, two points should be made at once.

In the first place, I would argue that the influence of segregated schools in this context has consistently been overestimated. Commentators such as Skilbeck (1976) who describes teachers as 'naive bearers of sectarian conflict' and Spencer (1974) who claims that the religious identities fostered in the two church school systems form the basis of national identities, seem to elevate the influence of schools, in terms of causality, to an unrealistic level. Such comments epitomise an all-too-common approach which seems to accept the pernicious effect of segregated schooling as 'a given' and subsequent discussion proceeds at this axiomatic level.

Secondly, and perhaps of more importance, is the fact that we cannot (or should not) equate difference with division. I have argued elsewhere (Murray 1983, p. 145) that the problem of segregated schools, with regard to community division and conflict, lies not so much in the fact that they reflect differing cultures but rather in the meanings which are attributed by observers to the manifestation of cultural affiliation.

In the context of social conflict, difference itself is of less importance than intolerance of difference. Thus, in more stable societies than Northern Ireland (for example Holland), segregated schooling can and does exist relatively uncontentiously. In these societies pluralism may be natural and desirable. However, in Northern Ireland, cultural difference is seen as being synonymous with political aspiration. These aspirations are not only different but they are also antipathetic and mutually exclusive. It is for this reason that Northern Ireland society has difficulty in handling difference. But, does it necessarily follow from this that we should try to abolish difference, in this case, segregated schools? The point is that during ten years' research within and about segregated schooling I have observed myriad examples of differing influences, biases and behaviour but very rarely have I seen intolerance or intransigence being encouraged.

At the same time this same period of research has highlighted one area in which a valid criticism can be made of segregated schools. It seems that the majority of them are content to inform or encourage or foster one element of culture only (very broadly, Nationalist or Unionist). In this way the children are being denied half of their inheritance. Not enough is being done in schools to make children sensitive to, and tolerant of, cultural and political differences. I believe it will be much more fruitful to address this particular aspect of schooling than to argue endlessly in terms of cause and effect.

Nonetheless, this whole notion of causality or the socialising influence of schools continues to be debated at length in Northern Ireland. This debate usually takes place in the context of whether segregated schools should be seen in terms of causes or effects of social conflict. Readings which should prove informative in this regard include: Akenson (1973) who states that 'it is probable that the segregated school system exacerbates inter-group frictions'; Darby (1976) who argues that 'it is foolish to claim that community divisions are created by its institutions'; Robinson (1971) and Russell (1972) who attribute differing social responses and attitudes to separate (and different) school experiences; Murray (1983) who claims that divisions in society owe less to segregated education than to the perceptions of the society in which it is operating; Greer (1972) and Magee (1970) who comment respectively on the influence of differing religious and history teaching in segregated schools.

However, Salters's work (1970) on the differing attitudes of Catholic and Protestant children highlights a difficulty common to all of the research cited above — that it is difficult (if not impossible) to isolate the school's influence on social attitudes and behaviour. Such information is vital if one is to either criticise or defend segregated schooling. Unfortunately, as yet, it is not available.

It is possible that the only way in which such information will be forthcoming is for researchers to spend long periods inside segregated schools observing the pattern of influence within them. This is partly what I have attempted to do. In the context of the differing experiences undergone by pupils within their segregated schools, space restrictions here dictate an acceptance of their disparate religious emphases without further comment. This analysis will therefore concentrate on the differing cultural biographies of the children in their separate institutions.

Ethnographic findings

The data informing this analysis has been collected in several ways. In the first place, 152 schools were studied by means of questionnaires in an attempt to gain a general profile of school practice in Northern Ireland. This general profile was used to facilitate a more interpretative approach within nineteen schools situated in the North West of the province. This latter approach entailed frequent visits to the schools to enable observation and interview to be carried out. One of the conclusions of the research (see Darby et al. 1977) was that 'perhaps a real understanding of the dynamics of school life can only be provided by an intensive study of a single school'.

This particular suggestion prompted a third mode of research, i.e. participant observation within two of the nineteen schools. This entailed spending six months, full-time, in each. I kept the same hours as teachers, took classes, supervision and games. Throughout this period I was engaged in observing and recording phenomena related to such aspects of school life as culture, character and ethos (see Murray, 1982). While this aspect of research was carried out in primary schools only, the 'Schools Apart' project gathered data from primary, secondary and grammar schools.

This prolonged participation and observation suggested that cultural considerations formed a significant part of the hidden (and sometimes formal) curriculum of the schools. In addition, identity seemed to exist as a covert pedagogy in both establishments with ritual and symbols being the visual aids which facilitated learning.

It must be said at once that symbols are very important in Northern Ireland. At a very basic level, they let you know 'where you stand'. Such 'cues' are useful since at any social gathering individuals will attempt to determine the religious affiliation, and hence political and cultural aspirations, of the others. There is nothing remiss in this process. It is simply a means of avoiding possible embarrassment. The more visible the symbols displayed the more this identification process is facilitated.

It is also important to note therefore that, for the individuals or groups displaying them, a symbol can construct a framework of meaning which goes far beyond its objective self. The memorial plaque in the Protestant school was a good example of this. On it were recorded all the names of past pupils who had fought in 'The Great Wars'. These men had fought in defence of the country of the present pupil population and were being honoured for doing so. In addition, the school was required to display the 'Union Jack' daily outside. The school was, therefore, quite naturally, demonstrating its identity with the state and thus, the establishment. The large papal flag draped in the assembly hall of the Catholic school is another case in point. This was a clear proclamation to pupils, teachers and visitors of the catholicity of the school — its *raison d'etre*.

These, and many other symbols displayed in both schools were clear and natural manifestations of the values and attitudes of individuals within each establishment. However, in a culturally divided country, the demonstration of symbols tends to be of less impact than how they are perceived and reacted to. Individuals, not being privy to the meaning structures of those for whom the symbols are constructed, must therefore interpret their display at a superficial level. By their very nature, symbols must be clearly visible. In Northern Ireland, however, visibility can be perceived as provocation.

The flag flying outside the Protestant school which might be seen as a cultural symbol was in fact perceived by Catholic teachers very much in religious terms. They saw it as emphasising the religious composition of the school. It was not only Protestant, but was exclusively so, presumably because no Catholic would concur with the displaying of such an emblem.

Protestant teachers, observing the religious symbols in the Catholic school tended to relate these to 'Catholic Ireland' which was equated with a united Ireland. For them, therefore, the overt emphasis on Catholicism was in fact a political acclamation. This would seem to have important implications in a segregated society since, although the Catholic hierarchy may defend their schools on religious grounds, many Protestants perceive them to be strongly political in nature.

This raises another crucial point. In the educational context it is not of concern that symbols are displayed singly by each type of school. It is rather their combined or cumulative effect which is significant. In this sense the segregated schools themselves are symbolic of the attitudes, values and aspirations of each cultural group. They exist not just as Catholic and state establishments, but rather as separate institutions which parents perceive as being most likely to provide an appropriate ethos, or cultural milieu, for their children. Their existence, therefore, should be seen in terms of the fulfilment of a perceived need rather than a determinant of that need. It is this point more than any other which minimises the feasibility of their integration.

The cultural milieu thus provided allows children to learn the trappings of their identity. For example, Bishop Philbin (1975) in extolling the virtues of the interdependence of home, school and church in 'the christian formation of the young' requests that children should be asked to 'wear school uniform to add to the visual effect'. It is interesting to note in this context, that all of the primary schools in the area in which my research was carried out wore a green uniform. Again this was seen by Protestant teachers in the area as a very strong political message. A subsequent observation in the researched Catholic school suggests that this perception may not be too far from the truth. In this school the football team wore a Glasgow Celtic strip for all home matches and all away matches against other Catholic schools but changed to less evocative attire only when playing away to Protestant schools. The point could not have been lost on the children. It certainly was not on visiting Protestant teachers!

On another occasion in the same school both primary 1 classes were watching a video recording of a schools programme on television. When the schools programme finished the tape continued running to display a sports programme which presumably had been recorded some time earlier. The sports began with the playing of the British national anthem. As soon as it became clear what the music was, both teachers ran forward shrieking and laughing to switch the television set off. This action was greeted with laughter and some applause from the pupils. It should be noted that many of these pupils were less than five years old, which may give some credence to the claim by several teachers that the attitudes and identity of the children are formed at home. It hardly confirms the other claims by these teachers that the school has a minimal effect on the attitudes of pupils. Such cues, delivered by individuals whom these young children hold in high esteem, must have a major influence on how they will react when confronted with similar symbols in the future.

These formative experiences contrasted starkly with those observed in the Protestant school. On Commonwealth day, for example, the whole of assembly was devoted to this topic. A letter from the Queen was read out to the pupils by the principal. He also delivered a brief eulogy about the Commonwealth. One of the ministers present gave a homily about the Queen and the good works she carried out for her subjects. The proceedings closed with a request from the principal that, to show their loyalty, everyone should sing a verse of 'God save the Queen'. Assembly broke up amid a festive atmosphere and all pupils from primary 1 to primary 7 were united with teachers and clergy in a common identity within a Commonwealth family.

These few examples of rituals and symbols are cited in an attempt to give a flavour of the cultural ethos of both schools. They are neither specially selected nor untypical of the general day-to-day experiences within the establishments. In fact observation in the two schools, carried out over one full academic year, clearly demonstrated that each reflected and nourished differing cultural expectations and aspirations. This is to be expected. However, the trouble with segregated schools, in connection with community conflict, may well be that no effort seemed to be made to make pupils aware of the sensitivities of any cultural group different from their own.

Many Catholics, for example, find it incomprehensible that anyone should support the union with Britain. This is seen as an identification with a colonial power which has consistently demonstrated nothing but avarice and derision towards the people of Ireland. This may not actually be formally taught in Catholic schools (although in some cases it may well be) but little is done to inform the position. This is not to suggest that there should be any compromise of ideals. *Justification* of the Unionist position is not being recommended but simply an *explanation* of it.

On the other hand, there has been much discussion recently of the alienation of Catholics in Northern Ireland. The impression may be given that it is a new phenomenon. In fact it is far from new, though the events of this past 16 years have thrust it into prominence. One way of understanding it is to perceive it in terms of the relative, and disparate, institutional responses to the display of the cultural symbols of 'each side'.

An attempt has already been made to show that cultural symbols are not only learned in schools but also that their meanings are learned to be cherished. However, one cultural group in the province has total freedom to display the symbols which they hold dear while, at the same time, significant restrictions are imposed on the other group from doing the same thing. This can cause severe community friction which generally occurs as a result of the enforcement of the *Flags and Emblems Act* (N.I.) and is epitomised perhaps by the lengths to which the present establishment will go (sometimes with the most disastrous consequences) to ensure that no Republican symbols are displayed at the funerals of Republican activists.

In Northern Ireland, the cultures cherished both in schools

and beyond are not only different, but also antipathetic. Any demonstration of one is seen as an assault on the other. Dr Paisley (1985) demonstrates this:

> I think that the tricolour in the majority of instances is flown as an act of defiance and in disrespect of the British sovereignty in this part of the island. Unionists see this as a defiance of the constitutional position.

Such a view is as legitimate as is the Catholic perception of Unionism. However, when it results in the curtailment of the freedom of expression or identity of another group, then the alienation of the group thus deprived is almost inevitable.

Obviously there is more to alienation than the relative freedom to display cultural symbols. However, symbols, as manifestations of identity, are very important in Northern Ireland and these are nurtured (if not planted) in the segregated schools. Since some symbols are perceived by the Northern Ireland establishment as signs of stability and others as seeds of sedition, it may well be that in this particular context there is a direct link between separate schooling and community conflict.

Conclusion

It would seem that in the segregated schools of Northern Ireland culture is caught rather than taught. It would also seem that mutual comprehension loses out on both counts, since little effort is made to explain the values held by other cultural groups. This may be indicative of realism rather than isolationism. It may be frustrating to encourage tolerance and understanding within schools if there is little displayed in society as a whole.

At the moment it can be said that the two main cultures in Northern Ireland are mutually exclusive because of the contrary political aspirations of both. However, it is also true that exclusiveness and intolerance are exacerbated by a mutual ignorance which schools do little to redress.

The political aspects are ones for others to address but at the level of schools, one point should be made very clear. There is an obvious need for more meaningful contact between children of all creeds and cultures. This has been said many times before but I believe that a preoccupation with the concept of integration has actually impeded progress in this direction. In the first place it is not realistic — schools are segregated for religious reasons and will continue to be so irrespective of whatever political solutions are imposed or accepted.

Secondly, the whole notion of integration puts people off. It would entail too much compromise from each group. Thus there tends to be an avoidance of activities in schools which are seen as some kind of thin edge of an integrationist wedge. These are the very activities which are essential if each side is to comprehend the other. It is now time that we gave up notions of integration and instead worked towards achieving a cultural milieu which would make its implementation superfluous.

Notes

1   It is appreciated that some schools exist in Northern Ireland which are both officially and *de facto* Protestant. They are so few in number as to cloud rather than clarify the issues being discussed.

References

AKENSON, D. H. 1973. *Education and Enmity: the Control of Schooling in Northern Ireland 1920–1950*, London, David and Charles.

ASTIN REPORT (1979). *The Report of the Working Party of the Management of Schools in Northern Ireland*, HMSO, Belfast.

BELL, R. (1973). *Education in Great Britain and Ireland*, An Open University Source Book, London, Routledge and Kegan Paul.

CONWAY, Cardinal William (1971). *Catholic Schools*, Dublin, Communications Institute of Ireland.

DALY, Bishop Edward (1980). 'Integrated Education', *Network*, The Journal of the Association of Teachers of Cultural and Social Studies, Vol. 1 No. 2.

DARBY, J. (1976). *Conflict in Northern Ireland*, Dublin, Gill and Macmillan.

DARBY, J., D. MURRAY, D. BATTS, S. DUNN, S. FARREN and J. HARRIS (1977). *Education and Community in Northern Ireland: 'Schools Apart'?*, Coleraine, New University of Ulster.

DEPARTMENT OF EDUCATION (NORTHERN IRELAND) (1982). *Towards a New Policy for 15-18 Year Olds in Full Time Education*, Bangor, DENI.

GALLAGHER, E. (1977). 'A Protestant Rationale of Segregated Education' in *Segregation and Education: Conference Report*, Derry, Magee College.

GREER, J. (1972). *A Questioning Generation*, Church of Ireland Board of Education.

MAGEE, J (1970). 'The Teaching of Irish History in Irish Schools,' *Northern Teacher*, Vol. X, No. 1, Winter.

MURRAY, D. (1983). 'Education and Conflict' in J. Darby (ed.), *Northern Ireland: A Background to the Conflict*, Belfast, Appletree Press.

MURRAY, D. (1985). *Worlds Apart: Segregated Schooling in Northern Ireland*, Belfast, Appletree Press.

MURRAY, D. (1982). 'A Comparative study of the culture and character of Protestant and Catholic schools in Northern Ireland, *DPhil thesis*, Coleraine, New University of Ulster.

Ó FIAICH, Cardinal Tomás (November 1979), *Irish News*.

OSBORNE, R. and R. CORMACK (1984). 'Higher Education: North and South', paper presented to the ESRC-sponsored conference, *Social policy in Ireland: North and South*, The Queen's University, Belfast.

PAISLEY, I. (1985). *Sunday Tribune* January 1985.

PHILBIN, BISHOP WILLIAM (1975). Pastoral letter.

ROBINSON, A. (1971). 'Education and Sectarian Conflict in Northern Ireland', *New Era*, 52, 1.

RUSSELL, J. (1972). *Some Aspects of the Civic Education of Secondary schoolboys in Northern Ireland*, Northern Ireland Community Relations Commission.

SALTERS, J. (1970). 'Attitudes towards Society in Protestant and Roman Catholic schoolchildren in Belfast', *unpublished master's thesis*, Queen's University, Belfast.

SKILBECK, M. (1976). 'Education and Cultural change', *Compass*, The journal of the Irish Association for Curriculum Development, Vol. 5, No. 2.

SPENCER, T. (1974). Comments to a Meeting of the Belfast Education and Library Board, cited in *The Education Times*, February 1974.

SUNDAY NEWS (1980), August 16. Extracts from papers released under 30 years' law by the Public Records Office, Northern Ireland.

SUTHERLAND, M. (1973). 'Education in Northern Ireland' in Robert Bell (ed.) *Education in Great Britain and Ireland*, London, Routledge and Kegan Paul, pp. 19–26.

WILSON, J. A. (1982). 'Developments in Secondary and Further Education in Northern Ireland', paper read at the British Education Research Association conference, St Andrew's Scotland.

13
Religion in a Divided Society

JOHN HICKEY

Religion in Northern Ireland should occupy an important position in any sociological study of the society. Any observer of the scene in Northern Ireland, or any reader of the many books, pamphlets, articles and essays which have been produced on Northern Ireland since 1968, will be aware that the terms 'Catholic' and 'Protestant' carry an importance and significance here which is rare in western societies. There has been much debate over exactly what these titles mean in political and sociological terms and to what extent membership of one or other of these groups actually influences social behaviour. This chapter attempts to shed some light on this problem and to help to explain why religion is so central to the analysis of the social structure of Northern Ireland. This process will involve some comparisons with other societies where religion is not so obviously an important element of the social structure. In this regard it can be demonstrated that, among western countries, only in the United States and the Republic of Ireland is membership of a religious organisation regarded as of comparable importance. In most European countries, including Britain, religion does not seem to hold anything like so central a position in the concerns of their citizens as it does here. There is only space in this chapter to state this fact, and to refer readers to the works relating to other countries in the brief bibliography at the end.

One exception must be made, however, in order to enhance our understanding of Northern Ireland by employing a comparative perspective. Northern Ireland's links and physical proximity to Britain make it both necessary and desirable to take some account of the situation of religion in that country so that we can make some assessment of the distinction between the two societies. The differences shown will, in turn, assist us to make some estimate of how far the processes of 'secularisation' and 'modernisation' have proceeded in Northern Ireland as compared to another society with which it has ties. The concepts of secularisation and modernisation will be more fully explained later in this chapter. It is sufficient to observe briefly now that both concepts may be linked and related to the comparative significance of religion in the lives of the members of a given society. In this respect their application to the study of Northern Ireland should become evident as the main theme of the chapter develops.

The first obvious task is to look at what the situation in both societies actually is, in terms of both membership of religious organisations and, equally important, religious practice. 'Religious practice' here is defined as attendance at church or chapel, with some emphasis, which will be explained later, on the regularity and frequency of that attendance. It should be pointed out at this stage that there are always difficulties in interpreting figures and percentages like those cited below. This is a problem with all statistics gathered from surveys and applies particularly to religion. The data given, however, are all that are available. Provided they are used carefully, they can provide an acceptable base for generalisations.

Religious membership and practice

The 1981 census of Northern Ireland gave a total population of 1,488,077. Although filling in the census form is required by law there were, in fact, a number of non-returns, estimated variously at between 19,000 and 74,000 (see Coward's chapter). Unlike

the census forms of England, Scotland and Wales, the Northern
Ireland form contains a question asking the religion of each
member of the individual household. It is not however, compulsory to answer this question and in the 1981 census 19.0 per cent
of the population of Northern Ireland did not, in fact, answer.
This compares with 9.4 per cent of the population surveyed in
the preceding census of 1971. Non-respondents may be
unevenly distributed, of course, among the denominations and
between the believers and non-believers. Compton, for
example, has estimated that Catholics constitute 38 per cent of
the total population (see Coward's chapter) compared to 28 per
cent of those who responded to the religion question. What is
clear is that, on the basis of the census figures, we can be sure of
only the religious affiliation, or lack of affiliation, of 80 per cent
of the total population of Northern Ireland. This is, nevertheless, a very significant proportion of the population and
sufficient to give us a general picture of membership of religious
organisations.

Table 1:

Religion	Total membership	% of total population*
Catholic	414,532	28
Presbyterian	339,818	23
Church of Ireland	281,472	19
Methodist	58,731	4
Other	112,822	8
Not Stated	274,584	19
TOTAL	1,481,959	100

*Figures have been rounded up to nearest whole number. The Northern
Ireland Census, 1981. (Belfast, HMSO).

The 'other' figure in the religion column comprises sixty-one
groupings of which fifty are christian. The largest of these is the
Baptist with 16,375 members and the smallest is the United
Church of Canada with a total membership of ten. There are

also a number of non-christian groupings with the Hindus being the largest at 830 members, followed by the Mohammedans with 608 and the Jews with 517. A total of 1,995 people declared themselves as being either atheists, agnostics or free thinkers.

The figures speak for themselves and there is no need for an elaborate commentary on them. It is worthwhile to note however, that the membership levels are extremely high in Northern Ireland compared with most other European countries. This will become clearer when we make a comparison with Britain. Figures concerning membership alone, though, are not enough to provide a basis for conclusions on the significance of religion in everyday life. We have also to get some indication, at least, of the extent of religious practice among members of these organisations. In this regard the census returns do not help us because there are no questions on the form relating to the frequency or regularity with which people attend church or chapel. We have then to look to surveys which have been carried out, to try to discover how seriously people take their church or chapel membership. The results of two such surveys are quoted below. Richard Rose (1971, p. 496) conducted a survey, which took in the whole of Northern Ireland, in which he asked his respondents the question, 'How often do you go to church for services or prayer?' The responses were as follows:

Table 2: **How often do you go to church for services or prayer?**

	Protestant %	Catholic %	Total %
Daily	1	8	4
More than once a week	6	25	14
Weekly	39	62	48
At least monthly	18	1	11
Occasionally/hardly ever	30	2	18
Never	5	1	4
Not applicable	1	1	1
TOTAL	100.0	100.0	100.0

The same question was asked by the present author in a survey conducted more than ten years later in a community located in County Londonderry (1984, p. 129). This produced the following responses:

Table 3: **How often do you go to church for services or prayer?**

	Protestant %	Catholic %	Other %	Total %
Daily	1.3	6.0	0.0	3.0
More than once a week	5.3	19.0	43.0	10.4
Weekly	30.4	59.0	14.0	40.2
At least monthly	28.3	4.0	0.0	18.5
Occasionally/ hardly ever	31.7	7.0	0.0	21.5
Never	2.4	6.0	43.0	6.1
Not applicable	0.6	0.0	0.0	0.3
TOTAL	100.0	100.0	100.0	100.0

When interpreting these results one point in particular has to be borne in mind: the Catholic church places great emphasis on regular weekly attendance at mass and so a Catholic feels obligated to go to church every Sunday if he or she wishes to be regarded as a properly 'practising' member of the church. The Protestant churches on the other hand, do not put anything like so much emphasis on weekly attendance at church, so the Protestant does not feel under the same pressure as a Catholic in this regard. In order to make a fair comparison between the two groups in terms of practice, the figures down to and including the 'At least monthly' column should be taken into account.

On this basis the figures indicate that, though there is some evidence of decline, a substantial majority of both Protestants and Catholics can be regarded as practising their religion regularly. The percentage among Protestants — approximately 65 per cent — is smaller than among Catholics — approximately 90 per cent — but both groups demonstrate a remarkably high level of religious practice compared with other societies.

This last statement can be demonstrated by comparing the situation in Northern Ireland with that in Britain where both membership of religious organisations and practice of religion is not on the same scale as in Northern Ireland. David Martin shows (1967, Chapter 2, pp. 34–51) that there has been a decline in Britain of both membership and practice in the years since the first decade of the twentieth century. The Church of England, for example, which is regarded as the staple Protestant religion in England, has lost ground in terms of the practice of its members. The church is divided into two major provinces, those of Canterbury and York. In 1967 twenty-seven million persons resident in those provinces were baptised into the Anglican community. Of these twenty-seven million baptised, one-third were confirmed, i.e. nine million people. When we come to estimating religious practice, however, we need more precise indicators than either Baptism or Confirmation. The minimum measure generally accepted, in terms of the Church of England, is reception of the Sacrament of Communion at the two major feasts of the church, i.e. Christmas and Easter. This is not a very stringent demand but, even so, the figures indicate that only 5 per cent of those baptised into the Church of England receive communion at Christmas and just 6 per cent at Easter.

These facts show that in the major church in England religious practice is at a much lower level than in Northern Ireland. There are other Protestant denominations and sects in Britain called as a group the 'Free Churches'. We can only look at the more prominent of these to see if they are undergoing the same process as the Church of England. Between 1910 and 1966 the Methodist Church in Britain declined from a membership of 1,168,415 to one of just over 700,000. Other churches have undergone the same process of decline. The Baptist Church in Britain, for example, has lost membership to the extent that it has gone down from around 400,000 to approximately 280,000 in the same period. At the same time, membership of the Congregationalists, the first group in the Free Churches to make its mark in England and Wales in the sixteenth century, has declined from 456,613 to about 200,000.

Smaller groups like the Unitarians, the Presbyterian Church of England, the Calvinistic Methodists, the Salvation Army and the Society of Friends have all experienced an element of decline of the same order as the bigger churches. They now between them number some 350,000 members. Taken altogether, the Free Church membership in Britain stands at almost 1,750,000. Of these, just under 25 per cent go to church each Sunday, under 40 per cent attend at least once a month, and less than 60 per cent go to church 'now and again'.

There remains the Catholic community in Britain to be taken into account. It is difficult for a variety of reasons, to arrive at any precise figure regarding the total membership of this group, but the most reliable estimate has come from Spencer (1965). He gives the total Catholic population of England and Wales as 5.6 million, a figure which has been largely confirmed by the results of market research and public opinion samples (Hickey 1967, pp. 12-13). This would make the membership of the Catholic Church in England and Wales second only to that of the Church of England and more than twice that of all the Free Churches combined. The figures relating to religious practice among Catholics, while higher than those in relation to the Church of England, still do not compare with the levels in Northern Ireland. Forty per cent of Catholics attend church weekly while 60 per cent claim to go to church most Sundays. Seventy per cent of the total membership say that they receive communion at Easter and Christmas.

All in all, Martin (1967, p. 43) claims that the data available relating to the Church of England, Catholic and Free Churches indicate that in Britain as a whole, 15 per cent of the total population are in church or chapel each Sunday, 20 per cent every two Sundays, 25 per cent every month, 40 per cent every 3 months and 45 per cent every year. The contrast with Northern Ireland where, as we have seen, 65 per cent of Protestants and 90 per cent of Catholics claim to attend church or chapel at least once a month, is striking. We shall be looking for reasons for this difference in the remainder of this chapter and using the concepts of modernisation and secularisation to explain it.

Membership of religious organisations in Northern Ireland and the consequent religious practice is not restricted to one particular social group or social stratum within the society. Religion permeates the whole social structure and its influence is manifest in most aspects of life of the members of that society. It is true that membership of a particular religious body is associated with certain sections of the society. Evidence has been produced (Hepburn, 1982 and 1983) that Catholics, for instance, are concentrated in the lower and middle socio-economic groups with a minority emerging into the upper group. By the same token, Presbyterianism is seen as appealing largely to the lower-middle and middle groups with the Church of Ireland drawing its members from the lower and upper sections of the society. The picture as a whole shows that religious affiliation and practice is an important element in the lives of all groups in Northern Ireland.

The persisting influence of religion

It is clear that both in historical terms and in contemporary life religion has persisted as a major factor in Northern Ireland. This fact has brought with it a whole range of consequences for the social structure, and these are dealt with at various stages throughout the other chapters of this book. It is sufficient just to mention some specific points here. Because religion has such social influence, the clergy, priests or ministers of the various groups play a significant role in Northern Ireland. They are persons of consequence and are able to exercise an authority which their counterparts in other societies could not aspire to. As a result their influence is evident in politics, either through direct participation as elected members of Westminster, the European Parliament and at Stormont, or through the statements of Catholic clergy on political issues and events. Clerical influence on another major social institution — the family — is apparent through their pronouncements, for instance, on matters relating to birth control, divorce, abortion and homosexuality, pronouncements which are listened to and followed by a large proportion of the practising members of both Protestant and Catholic groups. Perhaps their most obvious impact however, is on education in Northern Ireland (see Murray's chapter). In this regard all we need to do here is to emphasise again the control that the Catholic clergy have over one section of an almost totally divided system, and the control that the Protestant clergy have in the operation of the other.

The questions now to be addressed are how and why the influence of religion upon Northern Ireland society affects the political and social structure of this deeply divided part of the world. Some attempts to provide answers to these questions may be found in the present author's work cited in the bibliography (1984, Chaps. 3 and 4). Briefly, we may say that Protestantism in Northern Ireland reflects virtually the whole tradition of Protestantism in the United Kingdom since the Reformation. This tradition is expressed through all the major groupings — the Church of Ireland, Presbyterian, Methodist and Baptist — and the remaining smaller groups mentioned earlier. All of these organisations, despite their doctrinal differences, regard themselves as allies in the face of the Catholic religious tradition and have common membership in other groups like the Unionist parties and the Orange Order. Their traditions and their appeal to their membership have endured much longer than those of their counterparts in the rest of the United Kingdom.

The reasons for this may be found in the fact that, although Protestants in Northern Ireland regard themselves as 'British' by culture and tradition, their society has not had, in certain vital areas, the same experiences as the mainland United Kingdom. Its economy has not developed at the same rate, it has not experienced the same working-class political and trade union movements and it has not been exposed to the shifts and developments in political and social ideology which have occurred 'across the water'. Above all, it has been unique in experiencing fifty years of one-party rule. This one-party rule has itself been unique in that it has been sustained by a combination of the religious and the political. The political has been expressed through the Unionist party which has existed on the single issue of maintaining a Protestant dominion and the union with Britain. In this sense it has been primarily a defensive rather than an innovative government. The religious element has been provided by support of the Unionist party from the combination of the Protestant creeds outlined above.

No other part of the United Kingdom has experienced a politico-religious tradition such as this. The nearest rather crude parallel would be the links between religion and government in sixteenth and seventeenth century England, where it was possible to identify allegiance to Rome with disloyalty to the state. It would not be profitable, however, to push this comparison too far. English governments of the time were concerned with very different internal problems and external pressures from the Stormont government. Northern Ireland is a small society where the majority are largely descendants of people who were established there by a mother country in order to defend her interests, at a time when religion was a crucial *political* consideration. But the problem now is not to defend the interests of the mother country but to defend themselves and their homeland. The Protestants in Northern Ireland still see the problem in the terms in which their homeland was established: Catholics are still the enemy because Catholics seek to overthrow the state, to deprive them of their homeland. Politics then, becomes a simple matter of protecting the Protestant homeland, and Protestantism remains the religion which it was in early post-Reformation England — a bulwark against the imperialism of Rome on the one hand, and a defence of the christian faith against the errors of popery on the other.

The culture in Northern Ireland is unique in this regard. Politics in the North is not politics exploiting religion. That is far too simple an explanation; the actual relationship between these two institutions is much more complex. It may be maintained, in fact, that it is more likely to be a case of religion inspiring politics than the reverse. In this respect we have a situation more akin to the first half of seventeenth century England than to the last quarter of twentieth century Britain. One sociological perspective then on Northern Ireland would be to see the Protestant group as a beleaguered people who are determined to defend a tradition and a homeland that they see as under constant threat. Viewed from this angle we observe a society which has all the external trappings of a modern, urbanised, class-structured group but which basically has one major division around which all others cluster — religion.

This is in contrast to other western societies where the processes of 'modernisation' and 'secularisation' are more advanced than in Northern Ireland. In such societies the existence of the state is generally beyond question: some form of open democracy in political institutions is taken for granted; the members of the society feel reasonably secure in pursuit of their personal and economic goals; and as a result of all this, these same members have the basic self-confidence to allow the existence of 'deviant' groups within their midst, providing the latter do not seriously challenge the bases on which this self-confidence exists. In such a context it becomes extremely difficult to envisage a situation where religion, with its apparent 'otherworldly' connotation, may become a serious ground for suspicion and mistrust. Religion in such societies becomes merely a mark of individuality, a private idiosyncrasy, a memory of ethnic tradition or a means of comfort and protection against the demands of life. It is certainly not a reason to be deflected from the serious business of life, still less a cause of conflict which results in death and destruction.

Two world views

Protestants and Catholics differ in their views and interpretations of christianity and christian doctrine. These differences affect the 'world view' of the members of these groups and consequently have repercussions on the political and social systems of the society in which they are located. Let us take as an example the doctrine of the individual's access to grace. The Catholic doctrine, that grace is to be achieved through prayer and the sacraments but particularly the latter, has substantial social implications. If the sacraments are essential — baptism, penance, the eucharist (mass), etc. — the person who administers them becomes of crucial importance. Such a person must be chosen and consecrated — hence the need for a priesthood. The role of the priest is to bring grace, through the sacraments, to the people. Initially such a priest was an itinerant who combined preaching with his sacramental duties, but as the number of converted grew and became geographically widespread it became necessary to introduce an element of organisation into these activities. As a result, then, of the doctrine of sacramental grace and the function of the priest as its indispensable mediator we now have the social organisation of parishes and dioceses and an educational system of schools and colleges governed by an ordained clergy of various ranks, which is the familiar appearance of the Catholic Church. In late twentieth-century Northern Ireland what this means in effect is that the Catholic clergy have reached a point where, through their sacramental role, they control parishes and a school system, and exercise a high degree of influence over their lay members. Because of this, the social organisation of Catholicism appears monolithic to an outside observer. The fact that this 'monolithic' organisation is commonly assumed to support the Nationalist political cause makes the division between Protestants and Catholics deeper and more enduring.

The Protestant stance on this doctrinal issue of achievement of grace is very different. The Church of Ireland has to some extent followed the tradition of Catholicism in terms of its interpretation of grace through the sacraments, but it has not pursued its implications in terms of endowing its priesthood with anything like the other's status in terms of religious and social authority. The other Protestant churches have a contrasting tradition. For them there is no need of the priest as an intermediary; the duty of the minister of the gospel is to preach in order to prepare the individual for direct contact with the Divinity, and it is through this contact that grace is achieved. There is no need, therefore, for a highly structured clerical organisation dominating its lay members and holding over them the threat of denial of access to grace. Such an organisation is in fact regarded as a threat on two levels: it is assumed to deny the right of the individual to approach God directly, and it is seen as also capable of exerting a powerful if concealed influence over the *political* institutions of the society in which it operates.

There is then a distinct difference between Protestants and Catholics as to what constitutes being a christian, and the difference has considerable social implications. The Catholic defines being a christian as belonging to a powerful organisation with a clearly defined hierarchy of authority, an authority which may be exercised in all spheres of life, spiritual, political, social and economic. The Protestant on the other hand, defines christianity in a much more individual manner. Being a christian does not necessarily demand the ministrations of a priesthood, or membership of a large, powerful, authoritarian organisation. The Protestant's aim is unity with his or her fellows on the basis of a consensus among believers. Any progress towards unity among Protestants should be based upon mutual recognition and acceptance among people who differ widely from one another. The Protestant clergyman is not the opposite number of the Catholic priest but shares authority with his congregation so that there is a very high degree of participation in the life of the Protestant church. Protestants of all churches would wish to see themselves as voluntary participants in a united movement aimed at establishing the 'City of God' (Smyth 1974, pp. 28-30). In direct contrast to Catholicism, Protestantism in Northern Ireland looks to the continued existence of the Northern Ireland state to protect its integrity — an external factor which operates as a unifying force amongst Protestants — through the Unionist political parties.

Modernisation and secularisation

Religion and religious belief systems, then, contribute to the social and political divisions in Northern Ireland. Some attempt must be made to try to understand why this can happen here when elsewhere in the United Kingdom, as has been shown, religion does not seem to occupy anything like such a central position in society. It is at this stage that we turn to the related concepts of modernisation and secularisation. The concept of 'modernisation' is used by sociologists to help in the analysis of social change. In general terms, 'modernisation' is the process within a society which marks the transition from a traditional folk form of structure to that of the complex social organisation associated with urban, industrialised societies. The major instruments of modernisation are the development of industrialisation and urbanisation. The former involves the growth of mass production, the development of heavy industries, the spread of factory work and the consequent destruction of old patterns of work and the creation of new ones. The latter results in the growth of towns and cities located close to the industries and involves a movement of people from rural areas into rapidly growing urban areas. So the society undergoes a change from one style of life adjusted to rural surroundings, to another which is located in an urban setting.

Modernisation does not just affect the economic side of life. Changes also take place in government, religion, education and the social structure, including the structure of the 'family'. The whole culture of the society undergoes change and that means shifts and developments in knowledge, beliefs, values, self-conception and ways of life in general. Beliefs and values, of course, relate directly to religion and we are here concerned with the effects that modernisation may have on religion within a society. These effects are summed up in the concept of 'secularisation', a process which may be related to modernisation. This concept is a difficult one and the question of its application to contemporary urban society is hotly debated by sociologists (see, for example, Martin, 1978, and Wilson, 1966 and 1979). In a broad sense, secularisation implies a shift in the bases on which people build their norms and values. This shift is from a 'sacred' base, founded on received doctrines, dogmas and traditions, to a 'secular' base founded on the principle of scepticism and the need to question all received wisdom. The change implies that most people in society no longer hold in unquestioning respect traditional patterns of norms and beliefs but prefer instead to adopt rational and utilitarian attitudes which allow them to adjust and change to meet the demands of life. It is this development which is used as an explanation for the decline in church membership and religious practice which has been experienced by many western societies including the example we have given — Britain. It is claimed that this decline has occurred because the values of the members of those societies are increasingly based on 'secular' rather than 'religious' principles. As a result, secularisation has produced a situation where religion has simply become a private concern for some individuals rather than a matter of public importance which impinges on social life generally.

Northern Ireland, as a society, has been subjected to 'modernisation' in the same way that other societies have, but with certain major exceptions. We have to bear in mind the fact that, although the process of modernisation affects all the institutions in society, it does not do so uniformly. That is, the process of change may take place more rapidly in one institution than it does in another. To use a simile, modernisation is not like a 'wave' which strikes all institutions together, carrying away the superstructure and leaving behind a foundation on which they all build anew at the same rate. It is more like a series of wavelets which rapidly overwhelm some institutions but only weaken the bases of others. So, change in the economy of a society may proceed very rapidly, while change in its political institutions is much slower and change in religion slower still. If we apply this concept to Northern Ireland, we can see that the economy has experienced a degree of modernisation, going back to the late eighteenth century when urbanisation and industrialisation began to develop in Britain generally. The effects of these changes are obvious in Northern Ireland today. In politics change has been much slower. The normal political concerns of people in other western societies are not those of people in Northern Ireland where politics have been concentrated on the linked unchanging issues of nationality and religion.

Religion itself is the one institution which has most successfully resisted change and the process of secularisation as we defined it. The evidence relating to membership of religious bodies and religious practice quoted at the start of this chapter indicates that a very substantial majority of the population still regard religion as an important element in their lives. Religion has not gone through the processes associated with secularisation. It is not carrying out a progressively more restricted role in the functioning of society. It has not become a purely private affair and retreated into the depths of the personal lives of individuals. On the contrary, it still pervades this society, particularly in the sphere of politics and group interaction, in the sense that it was assumed to have pervaded all societies in the past. In this regard we may repeat what was said at the start of this chapter: religion must play an important part in any sociological analysis of Northern Ireland, for it is the strength of the religious survival here which has marked off this society from most of the other modernised societies in the western world.

References

ACQUAVIVA, S. S. 1979. *The Decline of the Sacred in Industrial Society*, Oxford, Blackwell.

BERGER, P. L. 1969. *The Social Reality of Religion*, London, Faber and Faber.

GLOCK, C. and STARK, R. 1973. *Religion and Society in Tension*, New York, Rand McNally.

GREELEY, A. M. 1972. *Unsecular Man: The Persistence of Religion*, New York, Delta.

HEPBURN, A. C. 1982. *Employment and Religion in Belfast, 1901–1971*. Belfast, Fair Employment Agency.

HEPBURN, A. C. 1983. 'Work, Class and Religion in Belfast, 1871–1911', *Irish Economic and Social History*, Vol. X, pp. 33–50.

HICKEY, J. 1967. *Urban Catholics*, London, Geoffrey Chapman.

HICKEY, J. 1984. *Religion and the Northern Ireland Problem*, Dublin, Gill and Macmillan. New York, Barnes and Noble.

MARTIN, D. 1967. *A Sociology of English Religion*, London, Heinemann.

MARTIN, D. 1978. *A General Theory of Secularization*, Oxford, Blackwell.

ROSE, R. 1971. *Governing without Consensus*, London, Faber and Faber.

SMYTH, REV. M. 1974. *Sectarianism – Roads to Reconciliation*, Dublin, Three Candles Press.

SPENCER, A. E. C. W. 1965. 'The Demography and Sociography of the Catholic Community of England and Wales', (*Downside Symposium*).

WILSON, B. 1966. *Religion in Secular Society*, London, Penguin.

WILSON, B. 1979. *Contemporary Transformations of Religion*, Oxford, Clarendon Press.

WRIGHT, F. 1973. 'Protestant Ideology and Politics in Ulster', *European Journal of Sociology*, Vol. XV, No. 2, pp. 213–280.

Part III
Issues and Processes in Irish Society

Introduction

This section draws together a number of chapters which are varied in both theme and sociological perspective. Although the issues and processes which are examined are crucial within any society, the examples used here are primarily from the Republic of Ireland and Northern Ireland. In many ways these chapters serve to illustrate the richness and diversity of the theoretical and methodological approaches which have developed in Irish sociology.

It is, of course, difficult to draw a neat dividing line between social 'structures' and 'processes'. This is clearly demonstrated by the first of these chapters. Gender divisions are fundamental to all societies, although not all societies perceive them as an 'issue' worthy of public debate. Over the last twenty years, sex differences and inequalities have become an extremely important issue in Ireland. The processes by which these differences and inequalities are produced and maintained have increasingly been a focus for research among social scientists. In her chapter on the social dimension of sex roles, Pauline Jackson takes a conflict approach to the study of gender. She illustrates the process through which women's productive role in agriculture disappears because of the way official statistics of the *Farm Management Survey* are assembled; women's labour is thus subsumed within the household. Indeed, even within sociology itself, the importance of gender differences has been distorted by the concentration on the family as the unit of analysis. Turning to education, Jackson argues that the initial educational advantage held by girls is lost between leaving school and entering the labour market or higher education. Her analysis of the labour market points out that women are disadvantaged with respect to working conditions, pay and seniority.

Official statistics are again subjected to scrutiny in the chapter by Michael McCullagh. This is an interpretive account of the way in which certain 'facts' or 'realities' are constructed by the categories and definitions used in official statistics. Unemployment in Northern Ireland is used to illustrate the argument. McCullagh examines the relationship between (a) the changing definitions of unemployment; (b) the composition and distribution of the registered unemployment; and (c) unemployment analyses and policies.

McCullagh considers the historical evolution of the concept of unemployment in Northern Ireland, with particular emphasis on the role of the state in creating an official category of the 'unemployed' during the inter-war period. The chapter goes on to explore the way in which the 'official' definition of unemployment has determined the flow of statistical data on unemployment in contemporary Northern Ireland. The author concludes that academic analyses of unemployment, and policies for dealing with it, have been greatly influenced by the official statistics. He suggests that both could benefit from a closer scrutiny of the way in which these statistics are compiled, and the meaning of unemployment as portrayed by them.

In her chapter, Ellen Hazelkorn draws our attention to another crucial, and some would say very Irish, phenomenon — clientelism. Taking a marxist approach to the topic, she argues that, far from being exclusive to the Irish political process, clientelism can be observed in other societies, notably Italy and Greece. The persistence of clientelism can be linked to Ireland's social and economic dependency. Indeed, Hazelkorn argues, clientelist relations have been actively encouraged and institutionalised by the state, and have been used as a method of inhibiting the development of class politics.

There is no doubt that the issue introduced by Ciaran McCullagh has become a major preoccupation in Irish society: crime has become the centre of one of the great 'moral panics' of our time. McCullagh begins by defining crime and deviance and then proceeds to examine patterns of crime in the Republic of Ireland over the last two decades. Having outlined theories which help explain the persistence of crime he then assesses the applicability of these theories to the Irish context. Finally, he looks at the response of Irish society to crime, especially as regards policing and prisons and argues that these have not been a particularly successful response to crime.

Many of the ills of Irish society, including crime, have been laid at the door of urbanisation. In spite of this, urbanisation and its effects remain a topic which is largely under-researched in Ireland. Thus, the chapter by Kieran McKeown on urbanisation in the Republic of Ireland is a most useful contribution. McKeown applies a conflict theory of society to the study of the urban environment. Firstly, he describes the main characteristics of urbanisation in the Republic. He then goes on to analyse the process of urban planning and development and the conflict of interests which arises in that process. The third part focuses on the housing and neighbourhood conflicts which have occurred in urban areas in the Republic of Ireland over the past few years. He predicts that as the population of the Republic continues to grow throughout the 1980s, these conflicts will continue and may even increase in intensity, as the presssure for new urban development and the competition for desirable houses and neighbourhoods increases.

In the next chapter we have a change of focus; our attention turns from urbanisation to some of the most important features of rural life in Northern Ireland. Hastings Donnan and Graham McFarlane offer insights, based upon ethnographic research, to show the extent to which different rural identities have been maintained, or have changed in significance over the last thirty years. They illustrate this by showing how the phrase 'you get on better with your own' is used in Northern Ireland rural life to refer variously to kinship groupings, class and religious identities. They suggest that daily life in rural Northern Ireland is based on a complex interplay of these identities, and their analysis assesses the importance attached to different identities in different geographical areas. The way people have recourse to these identities in their response to the 'troubles' or to violent incidents is presented. The authors point out, however, that in rural areas different sets of relationships cross-cut one another, leading to a constant state of flux in one's interactions and demanding a negotiation between different identities and relationships.

If the 'troubles' in Northern Ireland present difficulties of response to ordinary people, this is no less the case for the media. In the final chapter, Mary Kelly uses the conflict in Northern Ireland as a case study in order to examine the images and explanations of the conflict offered by the British and Irish media. Using an approach which has its roots in marxism, she attempts to elucidate why some images rather than others have come to prevail. Coverage of the Northern Ireland conflict by television and newspapers is examined and she argues that the role of the media has been to translate the dominant political definitions of the situation into words and images.

14
Worlds Apart — Social Dimensions of Sex Roles

PAULINE JACKSON

The gender concept

The study of gender concerns the social relationships between men and women: how they are socially constructed and reproduced from generation to generation. Gender is a newcomer to the body of sociological knowledge. The arrival of the gender concept in sociology was like the introduction of a powerful telescope. Looking at social structures through the 'gender lens', familiar realities — like social class, family, race and power — could be perceived in a quite different way.

The founding fathers of social science were not particularly interested in gender. Indeed it is noteworthy that there seem to be no founding mothers in sociology (Abraham 1973). The focus on gender was stimulated by feminist writings and the broader women's movement. Soon it became apparent that sociology, like the other social sciences, had been developed historically with only one of the genders in view (Giddens 1982, p. 128). The study of gender seemed to undermine naturalistic interpretations of the world. Naturalism is a way of looking at the world about us. It involves acceptance of social structures like the family as unchanging and essential ways of living. In the case of gender, naturalism leads us to imagine that the social division of roles between the sexes, the sexual division of labour between work and home or among occupational skills are an immutable and fixed state of affairs — a sort of natural and even morally desirable order. Naturalistic tendencies in sociology confused what 'ought to be' with what 'is' — mixing together ethical and sociological analysis.

Equipped with a concept of gender, sociology is able to develop an understanding of areas like human sexuality and biological reproduction which has been all but ignored until the late sixties. Oakley (1980, p. 2) argues:

> There has been very little in the way of a sociology of childbirth so far; what the study of reproduction has overwhelmingly lacked is the appreciation of its social character. Everything that is done to, and by, women having babies has a cultural base — from the preference of American doctors for forceps and of their Swedish counterparts for vacuum extraction as alternative ways of getting a baby out.

Thus, naturalism greatly understated the differences in sexual behaviour, childbirth practices and child rearing, for example, stressing instead the patently physiological, and hence universal, character of these activities (Harris 1981, p. 62). The emergence of the gender concept, therefore, began to reveal the importance of culture in the reproduction of differences between the roles of men and women. It exposed to scrutiny behaviour hitherto regarded as taboo, private or more appropriate to other sciences like medicine and theology. In Ireland progress has been slow. The principal research institutions have yet to undertake sociological research on sexuality or biological reproduction.

The absence of an adequate treatment of domestic work, child care and biological reproduction in contemporary sociology is paralleled in the sphere of paid employment. Kergoat (1982) has criticised some contemporary sociological studies of social class for focussing exclusively on the male components of the working-class. She writes:

male concepts have played the role of a rear view car mirror where one's view depends entirely on adjustments to the mirror; women workers remain somehow lost in a 'dead angle' of the sociological car; they are not visible.

She goes on to comment that when women workers do become sociologically visible, it is usually as asexual beings, their productive and reproductive roles having been artificially separated. An example of how women's productive role can disappear, when gender is not taken into account, arises in agriculture, which is a central sector of the economy in the Republic of Ireland (see chapter 3 by Commins).

In the Republic of Ireland tens of thousands of individuals live in farm households and earn their living from agriculture. The households can take many forms: husband, wife, children; unmarried brothers and a sister; or grand-uncle and nephew. Every year 2,000 farm householders are interviewed for an important state survey of agriculture called the Farm Management Survey. Information from the survey is used in agricultural policy-making and it provides information on size of farm, type of agriculture, labour employed, and incomes for households. Labour employed on the farm is measured in 'labour units'. The method devised to conceptualise a 'labour unit' involves weighting the labour of men and women in different ways. All the labour units are then added up to give a measure of household labour. The method involves assumptions about the volume and value of work carried out by women and men and by boys and girls on farms. In other words, it makes assumptions about the division of labour in agriculture. To be included in the survey in the first place, a household must employ 0.9 of a 'labour unit' in farming. Table 1 below shows how the Farm Management Survey method works.

One is struck at once by the conceptualisation of labour in male terms; females even where included are measured in these terms. The gradations are fine; thus a young man and women of 17 years old are given separate and unequal weightings; a woman who works alone on a farm, for example, a

Table 1: **Definition of a labour unit**

One labour unit is a male over 18 years of age working full-time on the farm. For males under 18 years and for females the adult male equivalents are:

Males 16–18 years	3/4
Males 14–16 years	1/2
Females over 16 years	2/3
Females 14–16 years	1/2

Source: Heavey, J. F., Harkin, M. J., Connolly, L., and Roche, M., *Farm Management Survey*, Dublin. An Foras Taluntais, 1983, page 3.5.

widow, cannot be included in the survey since her labour is less than 0.9 of a labour unit; the labour of wives working full-time alongside their husbands, for example, in dairy farming, is given an inferior value to the labour of their husbands. It may be that the methodology is well tested and corresponds in part to the sexual division of labour in agriculture, but this is not clarified in the research report. Furthermore, the increased necessity for farm accounts may involve wives doing more farm-related work than previously — this might not be included in the survey where the labour unit is defined as 'working on the farm'.

By using an apparently neutral measure — the 'labour unit', and grossing up all the units in a farm household, gender disappears inside the household. The Farm Management Survey has the potential to yield extraordinarily interesting information on the sexual division of labour in Irish agriculture over time; this potential is blocked at the level of method and no amount of interpretation of its ninety Tables can undo this problem.

The methodology of the Farm Management Survey illustrates a point about gender in research methods. It is a problem that one encounters repeatedly and the Farm Management Survey is not atypical in this sense. So extensive is the gender subordination of women in publicly used statistics that the use of the gender concept in research design is becoming increasingly important as a criterion for evaluating what is 'good' research in sociology.

The importance of the gender concept becomes clearer when we look at specific social structures which we experience in our lives, such as the family, education or work. In the remainder of this chapter, these social structures will be examined to see what gender issues they raise.

The family and gender

Many sociologists have adopted a commonsense view of the family as 'the basic unit of society'. This commonsense view is written into the Constitution of Ireland (1937) as a separate Article; as a fact with which most people might agree. Bottomore in his guide to problems in sociological literature (Bottomore 1971, p. 168) has this to say:

> one fact stands out beyond all others that everywhere the husband, wife and immature children constitute a unit apart from the remainder of society ... the individual nuclear family is a universal social phenomenon.

Giddens (1982, pp. 121–140) summarises some of the contemporary critiques of the treatment of family in sociology, including the type of generalisation in Bottomore's statement. Going outside of sociology for a moment, we find that studies in the fields of both anthropology and history suggest that the nuclear family in countries like France may not be a twentieth century phenomenon as suggested by sociologists. Anthropologists would argue that a unit containing husband, wife and immature children is only one of several forms of family life that may be found across the globe. Tillion (1966), in a landmark study of the Touareg peoples of North Africa, illustrates the rich complexity of tribal units which embrace large numbers of kin as a single functioning unit.

In the absence of a notion like gender, or an analytical approach to power in the family, sociology has had difficulty in coping with change in institutions like the family. Changes in gender relations inside the family were sometimes conceptualised as generating new social entities in such books as *The Captive Wife* (Gavron 1969) or *Mothers Alone* (Marsden 1973) or *Dual Career Families* (Rapoport 1983). More recently, Oakley (1980) has succeeded in bringing sociology beyond the limited view which considered changes in family life as deviance from the normative concept of family, with its male head-of-household cum breadwinner and his stay-at-home wife. The new interest in internal family relationships and sex roles has generated new terms now incorporated in sociology. The arrival of gender into the sociology of the family posed the question of the different and often unequal relationships between husbands and wives.

Feminist writings (cf. Gardiner, Himmelweit and McIntosh 1980) have employed the concept of patriarchy to explore the connections between family structure and economic production and to examine gender relations inside family units. Patriarchy is a particular formulation of the gender concept. It constructs gender hierarchies, inside of which women are subordinate to men. It shows us how the hierarchies reproduce themselves inside diverse social structures like church, work and political life. Patriarchal relations can be transmitted by both women and men as Belotti (1975) demonstrates in an amusing Italian study of gender influences in the socialisation of small children. She found that from the earliest months parents had clearly delineated expectations of the gender roles and attributes of their children and instilled them diligently.

Indeed gender expectations can reach back to the pre-natal stage in the sexual preference of parents for boy or girl babies. New reproductive technologies can now enable parents to 'choose' the sex of their children using the amniocentiesis technique (Arditti, Duelli Klein and Minder 1984). In India it is used by women to choose abortion where the test shows that they will give birth to a female.

By over-concentration on the family as a basic unit of analysis, the component parts of the family tend to get neglected — namely its gender composition and the relationships between the two sexes inside the family. As a result, when changing relationships inside the family became of interest to sociologists, these changes were often examined for the disruptive effects they might have on the family as a 'basic unit of society'. Wars and economic restructuring are just two of the more obvious factors which impinge on the division of sex roles inside the family, transforming the relations of the family adults to production.

In Ireland, studies of family life and kinship networks (Arensberg and Kimball 1940) and relations (Hannan 1979) have been undertaken which have focussed respectively on the unchanging and modernising features of the Irish family. While they have recognised the pervasiveness of male authority and have stressed the complementarity of male and female roles within the family, they have failed to utilise the notion of patriarchy. This failure has led to the popularisation of an image of the family as an autonomous unit, impervious to gender differences and inequalities.

This discussion has looked at families only from the point of view of adult relationships. From the point of view of children, it is inside the family that culture, religion, attitudes and values, behaviour and most importantly, speech and language, are informally learnt. In this sense, the family is an important social structure for what may be called cultural reproduction — the transmission of a whole complex of behaviour and attitudes from one generation to the next, from one gender to another. This process can be unconscious and silent, involving imitation, and listening. It can equally be explicit — by scolding, punishment and other forms of control and pressure. Family structures are the first social institutions in which individuals experience gender differences. Here children informally learn gender-moulded expectations in behaviour, speech, dress and attitude.

Besides cultural reproduction, the family is also the first place where children learn to accustom themselves to the gender division of labour between so-called productive and non-productive work; between paid work and unpaid domestic work. For girls in particular this can be a first apprenticeship for their later entry into the world of work as service workers. In the words of one of Angela McRobbie's respondents in her investigation of the culture of femininity (1978, p. 100):

> Me brother doesn't do a thing in the house. He makes a mess and I clean up after him. He doesn't even make his own bed, he waits for me mum to do it when she gets in from her work.

In the family, the organisation of housework, childcare, heavy/light work, clean/dirty work closely fits the sexual division of labour which children will encounter later in employment. In formal structures like the school system, the unspoken gender differentiated learning of the home is reinforced in a more systematic way during the most formative period of a person's life, their youth.

Some of the tasks of unpaid domestic labour have now been automated (washing machines) or socialised (nurseries) or turned into products (convenience foods) but in each case, this involves greater expenditure of money and the family remains the essential unit for their co-ordination and management. As for cultural reproduction, here the situation is quite different; the family is not alone. Other institutions like the mass media, the churches and the education system play distinctive parts in reproducing and creating attitudes and values, including the reproduction and creation of gender differences. In the next section, the importance of gender to just one of these institutions — education — is examined in more detail.

Gender and education

Not one but several gender issues arise in the education system: the gender of pupils and students in different types of schools and colleges; the gender content in curricula and in subject choice and provision in schools. Gender arises in teacher promotion and careers, and also in student performances as measured by examinations. Some of these instances interconnect with each other reinforcing gender as a factor in the education system. This does not imply that gender differences in the education system function necessarily to the detriment of girls and women — in some cases they operate in their favour, but this advantage seems to be lost when we examine women's participation in third level education and in the labour market.

The role of gender in the education system can be seen by looking at just some of the ways it arises at different points in the system. First the gender of primary school teachers will be touched on. At post-primary level, the type of school attended and the subject choice by pupils seem to have a gender dimension. At third level, gender differences in the careers of academics and in types of college and courses pursued illustrate the gender issue overlapping with the labour market — this latter issue is discussed in a later section.

The Primary School

The primary school system, from a pupil's point of view, revolves around the relationship between a single teacher and his or her pupils over the period of a school year. The primary school teacher teaches all subjects and is physically present with his or her pupils all of their working day. The early years at school, junior and senior infants and first class, prepare children for more formal learning in delineated subject areas like arithmetic or Irish. Educationally, these early years are crucial to later intellectual development, concerned as they are with the development of language, concentration, manual dexterity, oral expression and number concepts, to name but a few educational objectives. These are the years when infants are more likely to be taught by a woman than by a man teacher. The reason for this is not because these important early years are valued more and, as such, are entrusted to the more highly valued teachers — women. Rather, the division of labour in the family, where women take on the care of young children, is continued in the school, and thus younger children remain initially in the care of women. Recalling that child care is not paid within the family, this would suggest that responsibility for infants' class, like child care, is not a high status task.

Women outnumber men among national school teachers by a

ratio of 3:1 in the Republic of Ireland. Yet men teachers are more likely to teach grades 2 to 6 than infants or first class. As role models and authority figures, the gender of a primary school teacher is a factor in the allocation of class responsibility for the two age-groups. The woman-maternal figure is appropriate, under this schema, to infants' classes and the male-authority figure to older pupils. For the pupils this is undoubtedly a reassuring continuity of the division of power in the homes to which they return after school. For women teachers, on the other hand, the gender factor in promotion to posts of increased responsibility and income is a source of frustration. In 1981 the Employment Equality Agency and the Irish National Teachers' Organisation commissioned an investigation of the gender factor in primary school teachers' promotion. (Some 1,438 teachers co-operated in the study (Kellaghan 1983)). The study found that although women outnumber men among national school teachers, men teachers were five times more likely to be promoted to school principal than women. Furthermore, male teachers who had taught grades 2–6 were at an advantage over their women colleagues with experience of infants' class teaching. We see therefore that at primary school level, gender is a factor in the allocation of teachers to the different classes of children and is closely related to promotion. From the point of view of the children, the gender factor at primary school level sustains the maternal/paternal division of roles which children experience outside the school environment, preparing them for new gender distinctions which they will confront at post-primary level.

The Post-primary School

Post-primary schooling is a sex segregated experience for most Irish school pupils. About 44 per cent of pupils attend mixed sex schools (Tansey 1982, p. 28). But co-education is not the only measure of 'mixed' schooling since there are three different types of post-primary schools: secondary, vocational and community/comprehensive. Each has a distinct history, organisation and educational ethos. Again the proportions of boys and girls in these three 'streams' of schools varies as Table 2 below illustrates.

Table 2: **Distribution of post-primary students by gender and school type**

| | Secondary | | Vocational | | Community/ Comprehensive | |
	N	*%*	*N*	*%*	*N*	*%*
Male	86,200	43.4	39,300	66.9	13,076	53.1
Female	112,500	56.6	19,400	33.1	11,536	46.9
Total	198,700	100	58,700	100	24,612	100

Source: *Tansey 1982, p. 27.*

Table 2 enables us to see some interesting differences in the distribution of boys and girls between schools. At secondary schools, which are the more academic stream, girls outnumber boys. In the vocational schools, which are more practical and technical, boys outnumber girls and indeed the proportion of girls attending these schools has been falling over the last two decades. In community type schools, the proportion of boys and girls is the nearest to balanced.

Disproportionately concentrated in secondary schools, girls actually outperform boys. Girls stay on longer at school to complete the senior cycle of the secondary school curriculum. More girls than boys present themselves for the leaving certificate examination. We can say that girls come out of school better educated than boys. In their participation in the final years of second level schooling, Irish girls surpass, by far, their sisters in the other nine member states of the European Community (Eurostat 1984, p. 3).

There is, however, a significant difference between boys' and girls' schools in their curricular provisions. Boys' schools make better provision for science and technical subjects. The effects of this can be seen by looking at the examination subjects which boys and girls undertake in the leaving certificate. In 1980 biology was a 'girls' subject. Among biology candidates, 67 per cent were girls; in technical drawing 99.4 per cent of the candidates were boys; in home economics 94 per cent of the candidates were girls while in higher mathematics 74 per cent of the examination candidates were boys. Again, in physics, 86 per cent of leaving certificate candidates were boys (Tansey 1982, p. 30). This polarised and sex-segregated rate of subject take-up reflects the different curricula offered in boys' and girls' schools. However, subject availability and timetabling is only part of the story. When subjects are both available and timetabled in such a way that girls and boys can make choices, the types of choices they make are different. Boys tend to choose the more technical subjects and girls tend to choose subjects related to the Arts and Humanities (Hannan et al. 1983). These choices may be inspired on the part of girls by their specific gender-typed expectations of themselves and their place, if any, in the labour market.

Gender and Third Level Careers
There have been important changes in the gender composition of students entering third level education. Smyth (1984) has made a summary of these changes, drawing on a study by Clancy (1982) which reviewed a whole range of social and educational factors affecting participation in higher education. The modernisation of third level education has exacerbated rather than diminished gender differences between men and women. While women make up 48 per cent of entrants to the university sector of third level education, they make up only 38 per cent of new entrants to the technological sector. Colleges of education are predominantly 'female zones' with 84 per cent of their entrants being women.

Let us recall for a moment the concept of social class. Children whose fathers are manual workers or farm labourers form a tiny proportion of university entrants. So the students we are speaking about are mostly from more privileged social class backgrounds. Gender differences in educational opportunity do not fade away as one passes up the social class hierarchy, they merely become more subtle and difficult to see.

In terms of student enrolment in the different university faculties, there has been a gender equalisation in the students entering degree courses leading to the liberal professions. Increases are notable in Law, Science, Dentistry, and Veterinary Medicine. Nevertheless, the largest percentage of women entering university join the Arts faculty, which is consistent with their streaming by school and subject choice at post-primary level.

While the gender composition of students entering selected university faculties tends to equalise, the overall distribution of women and men between the different third level sectors is unlikely to alter dramatically. The technological sector — the most gender imbalanced — is also a sector highly favoured in government policies for science and technology development. These policies in turn will contribute to the expansion of departments and faculties where women are already poorly represented as students and academic staff.

Entering the third level sector, students are entering a world where, as at primary school level, gender is a factor in the distribution of teaching jobs. In the universities, just 1 per cent (four women) of professorship posts, 6 per cent of the associate professor jobs and 7 per cent of senior lecturer jobs are held by women. In colleges managed by vocational education committees, the situation is worse. An examination of eight VEC colleges outside of Dublin (Smyth 1984) could not locate a single woman principal or senior lecturer.

The higher education sector plays an important part in the construction of knowledge: through research, through cultural explorations and critiques, and by supplying graduates to the leading decision-making branches of the state and private industry. The interaction of class and gender at this point ensures, therefore, the dominance of a narrow range of social class interests, and among these interests, a perception of the world through the eyes of the predominant viewer: the male intellectual. Sociology itself cannot be exempt from this process. It is not an island of goodness in the rough sea.

In summary, it is at primary school level that children are first exposed to gender differentiated models of authority. Women are a majority among primary school teachers and yet their numerical superiority does not seem to manifest itself in decision-making posts in the schools in which they function. Women are a minority in the technological sector of third level education as both students and staff. There is no reason, going by the primary school experience, to expect changes if they were to suddenly become a numerical majority there. The concept of gender in sociology is about exploring such paradoxes by examining the social relations embodied in social structures, and by analysing how they are reproduced by personnel, be they women or men.

In this brief perusal of some of the gender issues which arise in the educational system, one can see that the gender concept enables us to follow the different educational 'careers' of boys and girls. Passing through the educational system, the distribution and performance of boys and girls between and within schools and colleges shifts first in favour of girls and then in favour of boys. It is at the age of 18 years, between leaving school and entering the labour market or higher education that girls lose their educational advantage and remain disadvantaged in the labour market.

Gender in the labour force

In analysing men and women in the labour market, gender is an extremely useful tool. It enables us to understand the different positions men and women occupy. If we look at the different proportions of men and women (of working age) in the labour market — that is at work, or unemployed seeking work — we find that 75 per cent of men of working age are in the labour market but only 31 per cent of women are (CSO 1984, pp. 19–20). This strong difference disappears, however, if we focus on certain age and marital status groups. For example, there is scarcely any difference between the labour force participation of young unmarried men and women aged 20 to 24 years: here 87 per cent of young men and 86 per cent of young women are at work or seeking work (CSO 1984, 19–20). The big gender differences emerge between older men and women, and particularly among the married people, when women drop out of the labour market, for example, on the birth of a child. Up to 1973 a marriage bar prevented women in the public service from staying in their jobs after marriage. Many left work prior to its removal and have never returned. It was not until 1977 that all employers were prohibited from discriminating against married women by an anti-discrimination Act. Table 3 below shows some of the differences between the participation of men and women of different marital status in the labour force.

Table 3: **The labour force participation of men and women aged 15 and over according to their marital status, 1983**

	Men %	Women %
Single	68.5	56.3
Married	83.6	19.6
Separated (including divorced)	79.9	40.9
Widowed	27.5	10.8
Total	75.3	31.5

Source: Central Statistics Office, *Labour Force Survey 1983*, Dublin, 1984 Tables 8A and 8B.

In Table 3 we see that the labour force participation (LFP) of single women is lower than for single men. This is partly explained by girls staying on longer at school between 15 and 18 years of age. The LFP of married women and men is quite different with just under 20 per cent of married women in the labour force. The LFP of men in the divorced and separated category is not very different from married men but there are important differences among women. Separated (including divorced) women have twice the rate of labour force participation of married women. However, the numbers recorded in the separated and divorced categories are relatively small and detailed conclusions cannot be drawn from them.

Among men and women in the labour force and at work, there are differences in working conditions. For example, a majority of industrial shift workers are men while a majority of home-workers and part-time workers are women. If we define part-timers as all those working less than 30 hours a week, we find that 71 per cent of part-time workers are women (CSO 1984). Part-time workers are less protected by social and labour legislation than full-time workers, so more women than men find themselves in somewhat precarious working conditions. Yet, for married women with children part-time work may be the only choice possible if suitable child-care facilities are not available after school closing hours.

In industry, the majority of workers are men (80 per cent). In agriculture only a very small proportion of reported workers are women. This may, as mentioned earlier, be partly the results of gender bias in agricultural labour force statistics. It is in service employment of all kinds that we find women working, as professionals in nursing, teaching and social work; in offices as secretaries and clerks; and in commerce, banking, insurance and retail outlets. Some 42 per cent of service workers are women and this proportion is increasing (CSO 1984, Table 18). Where women and men do find themselves in the same sector of the economy and even the same branch of manufacturing they do not share the same occupational position. In the engineering industry, for example, 80 per cent of bookkeeping jobs are held by women but only 2 per cent of technological and 4 per cent of technical occupations. Even on the engineering shop floor where women are a minority, 66 per cent of assembly line workers are women (AnCO 1983, pp. 32–35).

The gender differences in occupation, working conditions and branch of industry all contribute to a highly gender segregated division of labour at work, and account, in part, for the earnings differences between men and women. No contemporary statistics are available on earnings in the service sector by sex, where most women are employed, but hourly earnings data are available for industry. In manufacturing women earned about 68 per cent of the male hourly earnings in 1981 and the gap between men's and women's earnings continued to widen during the eighties. This might be due to redundancies among women in the better paying branches of industry as well as to the weak effect of annual wage rounds on low paid women workers.

More and more women of working age are entering the labour force, particularly young married women in the 25–34 age group. As Burke remarks (1984, p. 48):

> If the participation of Irish women in employment was to match that of the rest of Europe, there would be almost 100,000 more women in employment in Ireland.

Gender raises issues at all points of the labour market and yet is often ignored in labour market studies. The concentration of women into a narrow range of occupations is an element of gender segregation and while the single sex education of girls does not function neccessarily to their disadvantage, the single sex employment of women has few redeeming features. In a sense, the narrow subject choices of girls at post-primary level may be a rational perception of their future position in the labour market as white collar employees. Yet interesting discrepancies do occur. The science subject, biology, is a 'girls' subject (Hannan 1983, p. 116) which might suggest a departure from the humanities in subject choice among girls. Alternatively, the usefulness of biology as a subject in applying for entry to the nursing profession may influence its frequency in girls' choices of leaving certificate subjects. In this sense the popularity of biology may merely reflect a more efficient route to a traditional career rather than an innovative path to a non-traditional occupation. A consequence of the use of the gender concept in examining the labour force is the realisation that the places occupied by men and women are so different and separate that they cannot easily substitute for one another. Thus rising unemployment among men does not mean that these same men can, or will, take jobs as routine factory operatives or clerical workers. Conversely, extensive industrial training of already well-educated girls will not necessarily add to their employment prospects.

Conclusions

> Sociology has been in its modes of thinking, method-ologies, conceptual organisation and subjects of inquiry, one of the most sexist of academic disciplines, embodying in largely uncritical fashion the structure and value of the existing social order (Oakley 1980, p. 71).

In this sense, sociology has reflected the dominant social values as expressed in everyday life; the media, education and other social institutions tend to see existing gender differences as natural and unproblematical. These values have infused sociol-ogy until recently. This chapter has illustrated some of the implications of ignoring gender differences in sociological analy-sis. Systematic, and generally male, bias is evident in the choice of both research tools and of areas of study. The result has been an inadequate and uncritical understanding of areas such as the family, education and work. In the process, women have been relegated to subordinate, limited or invisible roles.

While progress has been slow in Ireland, the balance has begun to be redressed. Women's studies programmes and publications have included contributions and participation from sociologists (Maguire 1985; Lynch 1985) while sociology in Ireland has begun to confront gender issues (Rudd 1982; Harris 1984; Curtin et al. 1985). A focus on gender is not sufficient for sociological analysis; it must be related to other forms of social relations such as class, race and ethnicity. The brief discussions of family, education and labour force contained in this chapter suggest, however, that a comprehensive and critical appraisal of the existing social system is not complete without the study of gender.

References

AnCO the Industrial Training Authority, 1983. *Manpower Survey 1981*, Dublin, AnCO.

ARENSBERG, C. A., S. KIMBALL 1940. *Family and Community in Ireland*, Harvard, Harvard University Press.

ABRAHAM, J. H. 1973. *Origins and Growth of Sociology*, London, Penguin.

ARDITTI, R., R. DUELLI KLEIN and S. MINDER (eds.) 1984. *Test Tube Women*, London, Pandora Press.

BELOTTI, G. B. 1975. *Little Girls*, London, Writers and Readers.

BOTTOMORE, T. B. 1971. *Sociology — A Guide to Problems and Literature*, London, Allen and Unwin.

BURKE, H. 1984. 'Continuity and Change — the Life cycles of Irish Women in the 1980s' in *The Changing Family*. Family Studies Unit, Dublin, University College Dublin.

CENTRAL STATISTICS OFFICE, 1984. *Labour Force Survey 1983*, Dublin, Government Publications.

CLANCY, P., 1982. *Participation in Higher Education: A National Survey*, Dublin, Higher Education Authority.

CURTIN, C., P. JACKSON and B. O'CONNOR. *Gender in Irish Society*, Galway, Galway University Press (forthcoming).

EUROSTAT, 1984. *Statistical Bulletin, Education and Training*, No. 1, Luxembourg.

GARDINER, J., S. HIMMELWEIT and M. MACKINTOSH 1980. 'Women's Domestic Labour' in E. Malos, *The Politics of Housework*, London, Allison and Busby.

GAVRON, H. 1969. *The Captive Wife*, London, Penguin.

GIDDENS, A. 1982. *Sociology — A Brief but Critical Introduction*, London, Macmillan Press Ltd.

GUILBERT, M. 1966. *Les Fonctions des Femmes dans l'Industrie*, Paris, Mouton.

HANNAN, D. 1979. *Displacement and Development: Class, Kinship and Social Change in Irish Rural Communities*, Dublin, ESRI, Paper No. 96.

HANNAN, D., R. BREEN, B. MURRAY, D. WATSON and N. HARDIMAN 1983. *Schooling and Sex-Roles: Sex Differences in Subject Provision and Student Choice in Irish Post-primary Schools*. Dublin, ESRI, Paper No. 113.

HARRIS, L. 1984. 'Class, Community and Sexual Divisions in North Mayo' in C. Curtin, M. Kelly and L. O'Dowd (eds.), *Culture and Ideology in Ireland*, Galway, Galway University Press.

HARRIS, O. 1981. 'Households as Natural Units' in K. Young, Carol Wolkowitz and R. McCullagh, *Of Marriage and the Market*, London, CSE Books.

KELLAGHAN, T. 1983. 'Equality in Primary Education' in *Tuarascail*, Dublin, Irish National Teachers' Organization, No. 9, pp. 94–96.

KERGOAT, D. 1982. 'Plaidoyer pour une Sociologie des Rapports Sociaux', Communication to the Xth World Congress of Sociology, Mexico.

LYNCH, K. 1985. 'Gender Issues in Education', paper to the UCD Women's Studies Forum. Research Seminar, Dublin, Unpublished.

McROBBIE, A. 1978. 'Working Class Girls and the Culture of Femininity' in *Women Take Issue*, Birmingham, Centre for Contemporary Cultural Studies.

MAGUIRE, A. 1985. 'Power — Now You See It, Now You Don't' in Liz Steiner-Scott (ed.) *Personally Speaking*, Dublin, Attic Press.

MARSDEN, D. 1973. *Mothers Alone — Poverty and the Fatherless Family*, London, Penguin.

OAKLEY, A. 1972. *Sex, Gender and Society*, London, Temple Smith.

OAKLEY, A. 1974. *The Sociology of Housework*, London, Martin Robertson.

OAKLEY, A. 1980. *Women Confined — Towards a Sociology of Childbirth*, London, Martin Robertson.

RAPOPORT, R. and R. 1983. 'Dual Career Families Re-examined', in Mike O'Donnell, *New Introductory Reader in Sociology*, London, Harrap.

RUDD, J. 1982. 'On the Margins of the Power Elite — Women in the Upper Echelons', in M. Kelly, L. O'Dowd and J. Wickham (eds.), *Power Conflict and Inequaltiy*, Dublin, Turoe Press.

SMYTH, A. 1984. *Breaking the Circle — the Position of Women Academics in Third Level Education in Ireland*, Dublin, Department of Education.

TANSEY, J. 1982. *Schooling and Sex Roles*, Dublin, Employment Equality Agency.

TILLION, G. 1966. *Le Harem et Les Cousins*, Paris, Editions du Seuil.

15
The Social Construction of Unemployment in Northern Ireland

MICHAEL McCULLAGH

The frequency with which unemployment is debated within Northern Ireland gives some indication of its importance as a contemporary social issue. Politicians, trade unions, churches, employers' organisations, the media, community groups, academics and others continually refer to the 'unemployment crisis' (Morrissey 1984) and discuss its causes and consequences. To a large extent this debate is informed by the unemployment statistics which are published regularly by governments. In historical and comparative terms these statistics demonstrate that Northern Ireland is a high unemployment society. As diagram 1 shows, the official figure of registered unemployment in Northern Ireland is considerably higher than the UK average, which in turn compares unfavourably with the European Economic Community (EEC) average[1]. Indeed, the diagram shows that Ireland, both North and South, topped the EEC unemployment league in both 1974 and 1984. Other countries which had unemployment rates above the EEC average in 1984 were the Netherlands, Belgium, Italy and the UK. Of these the Netherlands and the UK went from below average to above average levels between 1974 and 1984.

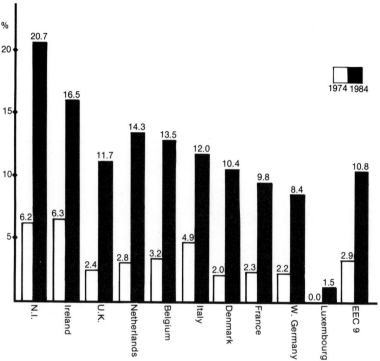

Dia. 1.   **Unemployment rates in EEC countries: 1974–84***
(percentages).

Source: *Eurostat*, 1985, Department of Economic Development
(NI).

*All 1984 figures refer to April.

   Furthermore, unemployment is not evenly spread *within*
countries. Diagram 2 illustrates the uneven distribution of unemployment throughout Ireland. From this it can be seen that
regions in the Northern part of the country, including Donegal,
have unemployment levels which are well above the average for
the country as a whole. The highest levels of all are in inner
Belfast and outer west Belfast, which both have unemployment
rates more than 2.5 times the overall average. It must be noted
that since 1981 unemployment in Dublin and the Republic of
Ireland as a whole has risen substantially.

Dia. 2. **Distribution of unemployment rates throughout Ireland.**

Source: *New Ireland Forum* 1983, p. 19 (derived from 1981 Census).

Figures such as this are, quite naturally, a matter of some concern within Northern Ireland. However, in drawing international comparisons such as the above, it is important to bear in mind exactly what is being compared and the nature of the data which are used. The problems of making international comparisons have been fully discussed in the literature (see Sorrentino 1981) and there is not sufficient space to review them here. However, the discussion of the social construction of unemployment statistics within Northern Ireland raises similar issues.

There exists a broad consensus within Northern Ireland about the meaning of unemployment and the validity of the official statistics which quantify it. Some maintain that official unemployment statistics understate the 'real' level of unemployment because of under-registration by groups such as females and young people on training schemes. Others allege the opposite, seeing official statistics as exaggerating the actual level of unemployment because they include an unknown number of people who are 'doing the double' and therefore not really unemployed (see Trewsdale 1980 for a scholarly attempt to estimate the real level of unemployment in Northern Ireland). Despite these qualifications, official statistics are generally accepted as a fairly accurate reflection both of the amount of unemployment and its internal composition and distribution (i.e. who the unemployed are and where they live). The official definition of the category of 'unemployed' has become virtually synonymous with the commonsense view. Yet underlying this official definition is a whole series of assumptions about work and non-work, and a long history of struggle by different social groups over the right to be recognised as unemployed. In order to understand fully the significance of this struggle, and the consequences which it has had for the theorising of unemployment, it is necessary to examine the historical background to the emergence of official unemployment statistics. This chapter sketches out the origins of official unemployment statistics in Northern Ireland and it also examines the social and political processes which lie behind their production. Finally, it considers the consequences which the existence of an official category of unemployment has had, for both analyses of the causes of unemployment and social policies aimed at its alleviation.

The origins of the modern concept of unemployment

The emergence of the modern concept of unemployment can be traced to the National Insurance Act, 1911. This marked the introduction of a system whereby employers, employees and government paid contributions into a central fund and those workers covered by the scheme thereby became entitled to draw benefits for a period when unemployed. Initially the National Insurance system covered a very limited number of workers in a small number of industries, but it was gradually extended during subsequent decades to cover all employees for all of the year. Provision for those workers who existed outside of the National Insurance system had always been much less secure. Throughout most of the nineteenth and early twentieth centuries they were catered for under the 1834 Poor Law Act, which provided the workhouse as a place of last resort for the able-bodied destitute. In the 1920s and 1930s this was gradually replaced by the provision of unemployment assistance for those without insurance cover, although guaranteed financial cover for all members of the population did not arrive until the 1948 National Assistance Act. This was replaced in turn by non-contributory, means-tested supplementary benefits in 1966.

The advent of the National Insurance system is important for three reasons. Firstly, it marked the transfer of responsibility for the alleviation of unemployment from the trade unions and friendly societies to the state. Secondly, it heralded the beginning of the definition of unemployment as a legal category and in doing so it afforded to the state significant control over both the definition and the statistical flow of information on unemployment. Finally, it began an era in which the struggles of the unemployed came increasingly to focus on the state and its willingness/unwillingness to make provision for the unemployed.

It is important to stress that official statistics of the registered unemployed are not an absolute category, but rather have been created as a by-product of increasing state intervention during the twentieth century. The continual refinements and extensions which have been made to the National Insurance system since 1911 have not happened automatically but rather have emerged from an historical process of social conflict. Official unemployment statistics should be viewed, therefore, as the end product of a social process of negotiation and struggle between various social groups which were (and are) seeking to establish their claim to the status of officially unemployed. The state has played a central role in mediating this process and in conferring legitimacy on the unemployment status of some groups.

One way of illustrating how official unemployment statistics are socially negotiated is to examine in detail the workings of the National Insurance system. Unemployment statistics are drawn from the numbers claiming benefit under the National Insurance schemes (plus, of course, those unemployed persons who, because they fail to qualify under the National Insurance Acts, draw supplementary benefit under the Social Security Act). Whilst it is possible to examine how the system works in the present, a much clearer view can be obtained from an examination of how the process worked in the past. This is because it is possible to obtain access to much more substantial information about the administration of the schemes in the past, and particularly the manner in which they were manipulated by government for political ends. The next section looks in some detail at the working of the National Insurance system in inter-war Northern Ireland, a period which provides a particularly good example of the social construction of unemployment statistics.

Inter-war Northern Ireland: a case study

Unemployment was a major political problem of successive governments in inter-war Northern Ireland. Overall during the 1920s and 1930s officially registered unemployment averaged around 23 per cent, with a high point of approximately 28 per cent in 1931 and 1938 respectively. As will be seen below, it is highly likely that these figures greatly understated the real level of unemployment.

The political crisis which unemployment prompted stemmed from the simple fact that the Northern Ireland governments could not afford to keep pace with the unemployment policies being pursued in the rest of the UK (at least not without a major expansion in taxation which was strongly opposed on ideological grounds). At the same time they felt obliged to do so for reasons of internal politics. The Minister of Labour, Mr Andrews, illustrated this latter point quite well when he argued that parity with Britain was essential to 'prevent the establishment of a Socialistic Labour Party here' (Public Records Office of Northern Ireland (PRONI), CAB 9C/3, 8th January 1924).

From the outset then, the government of Northern Ireland had committed itself to a policy which was beyond its financial resources. There is considerable evidence that, as a response to this problem, the government routinely manipulated the regulations governing eligibility for unemployment benefit so as to debar large numbers of legitimate claimants. Those disallowed were compelled to turn to the Poor Law for assistance or, as was more likely, to private charities such as St Vincent de Paul. Another alternative was emigration. The result in any case was the exclusion of large numbers from official statistics of registered unemployed persons.

It is interesting to note that historians and political scientists almost unanimously endorse the view that parity was actually achieved by Northern Ireland governments. Harbinson (1973, p. 137) argued that 'In social security he [i.e. Prime Minister Craigavon] secured for the community a system identical to that in Britain'. Buckland (1979, p. 150) similarly claimed that 'Unemployment benefit always operated on the same basis as in Britain'. This interpretation is endorsed to a greater or lesser extent by other historians and commentators[2].

It is argued here that such an interpretation is seriously deficient and that it conveys a misleading image of the treatment of the unemployed at that time. The deficiency stems from either:

(a) a failure on the part of the writers to consider conflicting evidence from organisations and individuals of the period who opposed the dominant government view or (b) the fact that the writers over-concentrated on comparisons of National Insurance *legislation* in Northern Ireland and Britain but failed to consider the manner in which this legislation was implemented. This latter point is crucial to an understanding of the evolution of National Insurance schemes as it was in this area that the opportunity for departing significantly from British practice arose.

With regard to this first point, there existed a substantial amount of opposition in the inter-war period to the official claim that parity with Britain had been achieved. The most consistent opponent of government propaganda in this respect was the Independent Labour MP, Mr Jack Beattie, who frequently challenged the parity claim in the Northern Ireland Parliament. For example, Mr Beattie said: 'The unemployment statistics are false because British regulations do not apply in Northern Ireland.' (N.I. Hansard, Vol. VI, c. 358). And 'unfortunately no such thing as uniformity exists between N.I. and G.B. with regard to insurability. In Ireland it is a name and a name only and in the working out it is different.' (N.I. Hansard, Vol. XXI, c. 236).

Mr Beattie was supported in these claims by Mr Joe Devlin, the leading Nationalist MP of the period, who claimed in the Northern Ireland Parliament that: '60,000 are recorded as being unemployed but I believe that if you fully explored the whole situation, got to the bottom of it, and secured accurate figures, the numbers would be nearer 100,000' (N.I. Hansard, Vol. XI, C. 911). Similar claims were made by a wide range of trade unions and unemployment pressure groups at that time (these are fully recorded in a file in the PRONI, CAB 9C/1/2).

The emphasis on comparing National Insurance legislation between Northern Ireland and Britain provides the second deficiency of conventional historical interpretations of unemployment in inter-war Northern Ireland. As noted above, this ignores the practical dimension of the manner in which policies were implemented. Discretion was a particularly important feature of National Insurance schemes in the 1920s and 1930s. This meant that claimants were not automatically entitled to unemployment benefit, but had to satisfy a number of conditions before receiving benefit. By far the most important of these was the obligation on claimants to prove that they were (a) genuinely seeking work and (b) normally in insurable employment. The definition of each of these conditions was extremely vague, thus facilitating manipulation of the rate of debarment of claimants. The vast majority of those disallowed were refused under these two clauses.

It is difficult to obtain comprehensive statistics on the numbers of unemployed in Britain and Northern Ireland who were refused unemployment benefit and consequently excluded from official statistics of the registered unemployed. However, some figures are available from the records of the Ministry of Labour and from answers to questions in the Northern Ireland parliament. These show a disallowance rate in Northern Ireland which ranged from 18.5 per cent to 40 per cent in the 1920s and 1930s compared with an average for Britain of around 10 per cent (N.I. Hansard, Vols. XI, C. 807, XIV, C. 479, XIII, C. 134 and PRONI CAB 4/132, and Deacon 1978, p. 162). In part this result was achieved by the requirement that unemployed claimants in Northern Ireland, in order to satisfy the genuinely seeking work clause, were obliged to obtain letters from employers stating that they had sought employment. In Britain, it was only required that claimants furnish a list of employers whom they had visited. Further evidence of a disparity between the two regions can be seen from a Northern Ireland Ministry of Labour memorandum which pointed out that it would be impossible to implement new UK guidelines for the tightening up of the administration of the National Insurance schemes *because this is already routine practice in Northern Ireland.* (PRONI, CAB 4/286/10, 24 June 1931). In other words administration of National Insurance was already much harsher in Northern Ireland than in Britain.

One obvious conclusion from the above is that official unemployment statistics for inter-war Northern Ireland greatly understate the real level of unemployment, and that this occurred to a greater extent in Northern Ireland than in Britain. It is important, however, to consider the general lesson which can be drawn from this detailed example. This is that unemployment statistics were a by-product of a socio-political process of conflict in which various social groups, with different degrees of power and influence, sought to impose their own definition of unemployment. The Northern Ireland Government itself was clearly the main interest-pursuing group.

National Insurance legislation provided the overall framework but it had sufficient flexibility to allow for major variations in the manner in which it was implemented. That flexibility allowed governments in Britain to vary their responses to the demands of the unemployed in accordance with the degree to which they posed a threat at any given time. For Northern Ireland governments it resolved a basic problem facing the nascent state; i.e. the fact that parity with Britain was deemed to be politically necessary but was beyond its financial resources. The discretion which was so central to National Insurance in the inter-war period enabled successive Northern Ireland governments to depart significantly from average British standards whilst retaining the rhetoric of parity. This renders unemployment statistics from the period highly suspect.

Unemployment statistics: the post-war period

The groundwork for the present National Insurance/Supplementary Benefit system for alleviating unemployment was firmly laid in the inter-war period. However, it was the Welfare State legislation of the immediate post-war period which formally ended the Poor Law. Briefly, this legislation firmly established a two-tier system based on unemployment benefits dependent on insurance contributions, and a back-up system of National Assistance (known as Supplementary Benefit from 1966) for those who either had not paid sufficient contributions or who had exhausted their entitlement to unemployment benefit. All unemployed who were claiming benefit (whether they received it or not) were obliged to register as unemployed and this formed the basis of official unemployment statistics. Because National Assistance was provided as an absolute entitlement to all those eligible for it, the scope for discretion in the administration of unemployment policies was greatly reduced in the post-war period.

Because of these changes, the degree to which unemployment statistics can be arbitrarily manipulated by governments is not as great today as in the inter-war period. However, allegations of deliberate misrepresentation of statistics continue to be made. Many have alleged that youth training schemes perform a cosmetic function in that they remove large numbers of unemployed young people from the official unemployment register. The net effect of such schemes may well be to reduce by over 50 per cent the numbers of under 18 year olds registering as unemployed (McCullagh 1984).

Others point out that the present National Insurance regulations encourage under-registration by females. McWilliams (1984, p. 54), for example, shows that between October 1982 and 1984 female unemployment in Northern Ireland fell by approximately 2,000 whilst male unemployment increased by 6,000 in the same period. She attributes the fall in the numbers of registered unemployed females to the introduction of stricter questioning of female claimants, particularly with regard to their availability for work.

Another way in which official statistics understate the real level of unemployment is in excluding part-time workers. Under the 'Full-Extent Normal' clause, those who have worked on a part-time basis for over half the previous twelve months are no longer classified as unemployed on those days they are not working. This rule particularly affects the right of married women to unemployment benefit. A recent development has been the exclusion from the unemployment register of some workers who are employed for only part of the year during that period they are out of work. A good example here is ancillary staff in educational institutions who may be laid off for as much as sixteen weeks a year but who are now deemed by the Department of Health and Social Services to be on 'unpaid leave' during that time and therefore not available for work.

Yet another example of 'tinkering' with the official unemployment statistics occurred in October 1982, when the government announced that in future published statistics would only include those unemployed people actually in receipt of unemployment or supplementary benefit. Previously official unemployment statistics had been made up from all those 'signing-on' as available for work, whether in receipt of benefit or not. This change reduced the numbers of officially recognised unemployed people in Northern Ireland by about 10,000, and particularly affected unemployed people whose spouses were working and who had exhausted their own right to unemployment benefit. It is interesting to note that one of the proposed 'Fowler amendments' to the unemployment benefits system is that unemployment benefit should only be payable for six months instead of the current 312 days. This would further increase the numbers of unemployed people who are excluded from the official statistics because they do not receive either unemployment or supplementary benefit.

In 1983 a further innovation was that people over sixty years of age could continue to receive benefit but were no longer included in the unemployment count. This removed between one and two thousand from the register of unemployed. In the same year a three-month waiting period was introduced for school-leavers during which time these young people were unable to claim benefit, thus placing them in a state of legal limbo — being neither school-children, employees or unemployed. A further regulation has also been introduced which debars many part-time students from claiming supplementary benefit unless they had been receiving benefit for the three months prior to the commencement of their course. This was designed to dovetail neatly with the first regulation and amounted in effect to double discrimination against school-leavers. At a stroke these new rules have removed thousands of unemployed people from the official unemployment statistics.

These examples, from both past and present, illustrate a general process. In periods of economic recession and high unemployment the right of certain groups to the status of 'unemployed' is called into question. The social groups particularly at risk are females, young people, the old, part-time workers and students. All have been disproportionately affected by recent financial cutbacks and the related tightening-up of regulations regarding eligibility to unemployment benefit. In a sense, therefore, these groups could be viewed as an 'industrial reserve army'. In periods of high demand for labour they are actively encouraged to participate in the workforce (a good example of this is provided in Northern Ireland by the Haughton Report of 1969 which recommended ways of enticing married women to re-enter the workforce). In periods of recession the process is reversed and National Insurance/Supplementary Benefits regulations provide a mechanism by which the state attempts to exclude members of these groups from the labour market.

So although the National Insurance/social security system has the primary function of administering financial relief to the unemployed, it can be seen that it has an important secondary function with regard to defining the position of social groups. It is clearly not a coincidence that the social groups most at risk are those with the least amount of social power.

The effects of official definitions on attitudes

So far it has been argued that state unemployment schemes have served not only to define unemployment in a certain way but also have had important consequences for the citizenship rights of some social groups. The flow of statistical information on unemployment has had other, less obvious, influences and these will now be briefly considered.

Firstly, state statistics have emphasised unemployment as a 'people-problem'. Official employment and unemployment statistics chart the movement of people into and out of employment and a wealth of information is available about the breakdown of unemployment by sex, age, industry and region. There are no comparable official statistics which chart the flow of capital into and out of investment and no detailed information is available about under-used (in the sense of failing to create employment) capital resources such as those tied up in financial speculations.

Furthermore, there has been a tendency for unemployment to be conceptualised as a phenomenon affecting not people in general, but the working-class in particular. In modern capitalist societies the work ethic is applied very selectively. It is possible to be in a state of 'worklessness' throughout one's life without being labelled as 'unemployed'. As Westergaard and Resler (1975, p. 180) note: 'Property confers immunity from it (i.e. the work ethic). There are no penalties for being work-shy if one has money.'

So at one extreme of society are the least powerful groups on the margins of the labour force. For them access to the status of 'unemployed' is double-edged. On the one hand, it entitles them to certain benefits, although as we have seen these benefits may be changed or withdrawn. On the other, it carries a certain stigma which is often accepted by the unemployed person himself/herself. At the other extreme of society are the wealthy. They can remain workless whilst at the same time avoiding the stigma of being termed 'unemployed'.

This emphasis on unemployment as a phenomenon affecting mainly working-class people can result in the view that unemployment is caused by the inadequacies of the people who are unemployed. In Northern Ireland in the 1960s, for example, a recurrent theme in government statements and policies was that persistently high unemployment in certain regions was a result of immobility of labour owing to the parochial attitudes of those living there. The main thrust of government unemployment policy at that time was to restructure employment in Northern Ireland, both in terms of the type of employment provided and where it was located. Central to that policy was the creation of the new city of Craigavon to which the unemployed from the south and west of the province were supposed to migrate for work. When the Craigavon project failed, blame for its failure was automatically attached to the unemployed themselves, as the following quotation from one of Northern Ireland's leading journalists (a typical view from the period) illustrates: 'Craigavon could succeed provided that those people raise their standards and behaviour and at least acquire the intelligence to appreciate the importance of what Craigavon is offering them.' (*Belfast Newsletter*, 8 July 1976).

As this example shows, there is a tendency for unemployment to be conceptualised as a phenomenon affecting, not people in general, but certain types of people in particular. Because the statistics show that unemployment is higher among some groups, policies are constructed to alleviate the alleged deficiencies of these groups (for example, mobility grants, retraining schemes). The persistence of unemployment can then be seen as a 'failure' on the part of those with high unemployment to respond positively to the policies. The problem with this thinking is that it is one-sided and circular. It is based on an initial assumption that because unemployment is higher in certain areas, the cause of that higher unemployment must lie in the characteristics of the people who live in those areas. The 'solution' then is to move the people or change their characteristics. If these policies fail to solve the unemployment problem then this is seen as support for the original theory that immobility or lack of skill is the cause of unemployment.

Social scientists frequently analyse official unemployment statistics in order to construct statistical 'profiles' of the unemployed. Indeed, official statistics actively facilitate such an approach by compartmentalising the unemployed into age, sex, regional, and industrial categories. There are a number of reasons why using unemployment statistics in this way can actually constrict sociological analysis.

The first is that the state controls the flow of statistics and therefore determines which categories are deemed to be relevant. In Northern Ireland there is a significant debate currently in progress about the different unemployment experiences of Catholics and Protestants. Whilst this is seen by sociologists as a relevant area of study (see chapters by O'Dowd, Miller and Coward), official unemployment statistics do not provide a breakdown of unemployment by religion. Hence sociologists are compelled either to use alternative sources such as the Census or to improvise by comparing 'Catholic' and 'Protestant' areas. In this case, then, it can be seen that sociological research has proceeded in spite of the limitations of official unemployment statistics.

The second way in which unemployment statistics can constrict critical analysis is best illustrated by way of an example. Official statistics inform us that the unskilled manual workers are particularly prone to unemployment. This has led some to propose special educational/training measures specifically for the unemployed. It has led others to 'explain' their higher unemployment experiences in terms of the individual weaknesses of the unskilled. The latter view is informed by an implicit uncritical acceptance of the assumptions which underlie the statistics. These measure a person's employment status at a *given moment in time*. They say nothing about the number of hours normally worked by the various groups when in employment. We know from a wide range of sources that the unskilled have a longer working week and in many instances a longer working life than other groups in higher social strata. Hence, when contrasted *over a lifetime*, it is likely that the unskilled manual workers actually work more hours per lifetime than many sections of the non-manual workforce. The over-representation of the former in the unemployment statistics illustrates clearly the difference between 'unemployment' and 'worklessness'. The group most likely to experience unemployment according to the official statistics may in fact work more hours per lifetime than any other social group. This clearly shows that the evolution of official unemployment statistics has merged smoothly with existing inequalities in the distribution of life-chances and with the dominant image which is projected of the stratification system. Groups such as the unskilled, the unqualified, and manual workers appear disproportionately in unemployment statistics, not because they do less work than other groups but because they are less able to legitimate their 'worklessness' within an unequal labour market. Females face a broadly similar problem with regard to their involvement in housework and child-rearing.

Conclusions

The word 'unemployment' first came into popular usage in the late nineteenth century. Since that time it has been moulded by state unemployment schemes and has acquired a highly specific, sharply defined legal meaning. State intervention has defined not only the numbers of unemployed but also those officially recognised as being unemployed at any given time. Despite their shortcomings these statistics are an important source of data for social scientists. With careful use they can provide information on the extent of need arising from the shortage of employment. In addition, studying the processes by which these statistics are constructed can reveal insights into the way in which society works. The examples above have demonstrated the relevance of changes in economic, political and social conditions to the definition of unemployment.

The recent upsurge of interest in the problem of unemployment in Northern Ireland and the debate which has ensued, almost invariably relies on an uncritical or only partly critical acceptance of these official statistics. Whilst it is perhaps inevitable that social scientists cannot ignore such a major source of data, it is important also that we continually remind ourselves of the nature of that data and of its limitations. This chapter has demonstrated, through the use of historical and contemporary sources, that official unemployment statistics reflect the outcome of a conflict between the state on the one hand and the various groups which comprise the population on the other. As such, the statistics express in a concrete form the unequal distribution of material resources in a stratified society. To use them uncritically is to risk constructing an analysis which incorporates the very assumptions which it is the task of sociology to expose to critical scrutiny.

Notes

1. The Organisation for Economic Co-operation and Development (OECD) regularly publishes international unemployment statistics which have been standardised to allow for differences in methods of compilation in the various countries. This enables more precise comparison to be made, but unfortunately Northern Ireland is not included in the standardised tables. For further information on international unemployment trends, and the technical problems in making international comparisons, see ILO (1984, pp. 441-444).
2. See also, Harkness (1983, p. 32), Lawrence (1967, p. 162), Wallace (1971, p. 119), Budge and O'Leary (1973, p. 145), Clifford (1983, p. 124) and Morrissey (1984, p. 76).

References

BUCKLAND, P. 1979. *The Factory of Grievances: Devolved Government in Northern Ireland 1921-1939*, Dublin, Gill and Macmillan.

BUDGE, I. and O'LEARY, C. 1973. *Belfast Approach to Crisis: A Study of Belfast Politics 1613-1970*, Macmillan, St Martin's Press.

CLIFFORD, A. 1983. *The Poor Law in Belfast*, Belfast, Athol Books.

DEACON, A. 1978. *Genuinely-Seeking Work: A study of Unemployment Insurance in Britain 1920-1931*, London, LSE, PhD.

EUROSTAT, 1985. *Employment and Unemployment*, Luxembourg, Eurostat.

HARBINSON, J. 1973. *Ulster Unionist Party 1882-1973*, Belfast, Blackstaff Press.

HARKNESS, D. 1983. *A History of Northern Ireland*, Dublin, Helicon Press.

HAUGHTON REPORT, 1969. *The M.A.F.E. Haughton Report on the Employment and Training of Women in N.I.*, Belfast, Ministry of Health and Social Services.

I.L.O., 1984. *Yearbook of Labour Statistics*, Geneva, International Labour Organisation.

LAWRENCE, R. J. 1967. *Government of N.I.: Public Finance and Public Services 1921-1964*, Oxford, Clarendon Press.

MORRISSEY, M. (ed.) 1984. *The Other Crisis: Unemployment in N.I.*, Belfast, Polytechnic Series.

McCULLAGH, M. 1984. 'Youth Unemployment and the Ideology of Control in N.I.' in C. Curtin, M. Kelly and L. O'Dowd (eds), *Culture and Ideology in Ireland*, Galway University Press.

McWILLIAMS, M. 1984. 'Women and Unemployment' in M. Morrissey (ed.) *The Other Crisis: Unemployment in N.I.*, Belfast, Polytechnic Series.

NEW IRELAND FORUM, 1983.

A Comparative Description of the Economic Structure and Situation, North and South, Dublin, Stationery Office.

SORRENTINO, C. 1981. 'Unemployment in International Perspective in B. Showler and A. Sinfield (eds), *The Workless State: Studies in Unemployment,* Oxford, Martin Robertson.

TREWSDALE, J. 1980. *Unemploy-ment in Northern Ireland 1974–1979,* Belfast, Northern Ireland Economic Council.

WALLACE, M. 1971. *Northern Ireland: Fifty Years of Self-Government,* Newton Abbot, David and Charles.

WESTERGAARD, J. and H. RESLER 1975. *Class in a Capitalist Society: A Study of Contemporary Britain,* London, Penguin.

16
Class, Clientelism and the Political Process in the Republic of Ireland

ELLEN HAZELKORN

The image of the politican intervening on behalf of constituents to help obtain government and/or other benefits to which they may or may not be legally entitled, is a traditional 'folk-tale' of political life in the Republic of Ireland. Or is it? This chapter seeks a deeper understanding of the complex nature of clientelism. It examines the reasons for its persistence, and its implications for the political process and class formation in Ireland. The first section will briefly define the term, while the second will consider the range of Irish studies on the subject. Sections three and four will offer a theoretical explanation of the phenomenon, relating its persistence to questions of political development and class conflict.

Clientelism

A model of clientelism can be constructed from the various studies of the subject. Broadly, the model would incorporate the following characteristics: 1) the establishment of strong personal bonds between two individuals of unequal power and usually of unequal socio-economic status, known as the patron and the client; 2) these bonds, voluntarily entered into, derive their legitimacy from mutual benefits that each expects to gain, for example, access to subsistence, protection, influence, information or votes; 3) while the interdependency of the patron and client is complex and long-term, it does not mean that the client is completely at the mercy of the patron; 4) the effect is that inter-class linkages are stressed, while intra-class solidarities, which stress (political) action via class, are de-emphasised; and 5) the political and social impact of such bonding is to conserve the power held by dominant social classes within society (see Caciagli and Belloni 1981; J. Chubb 1981b; Lemarchand 1981; Macciocchi 1973; Mouzelis 1978a).

Put simply, Irish clientelism involves individuals who seek out their TD, or similarly placed 'élites', in order to acquire some benefit or service which they feel they would not receive by their own, or their group's efforts. 'Transactional relations' involve a motive of seeking profit or advantage for oneself and differs qualitatively from 'moral relations' which unite individuals according to a common ideology (Bax 1976, p. 68).

There are two forms of clientele ties: *patronage*, which dispenses first order resources, for example land, jobs or money, and *brokerage*, which dispenses second order resources, for example contact with people who control the (first order) resources directly (Boissevain 1974, p. 147). Brokers are middlemen[1] or intermediaries. A question is often raised as to whether brokerage can produce 'clients' in the manner typified by clientelism. According to Komito, brokerage is 'the basis of clientelist links, and clientelist links are the building blocks of a clientelist system, but brokerage alone does not create clientelist politics' (1984, p. 176). The difference is whether or not long-term moral or instrumental links or bonds are established that dominate the entire political system; only then can clientelism be said to exist. Finally, it must be quantifiable, most particularly in terms of votes.

Many studies have used modernisation theory to explain clientelism, thereby associating it with traditional societies of Asia and Africa. In these societies, social relationships are usually hierarchical, deferential and kinship-based. Modern society, however, is said to bring about the displacement of the family and familial bonds to be replaced by wider social ties which, in urbanised environments, are associated with trade unions, societies, clubs, associations, etc. Social reorganisation is thought to be mirrored in political activity, with political parties divided on ideological grounds. Thus, modernisation theory basically argues that societies tend to travel along a particular path of development, as typified by Western society. As they do so, they acquire more and more features of 'modernity'. Crudely put, industrialisation begets urbanisation which begets social polarisation and political formations. Clientelism, which thrives on personalistic bonds formed in small social spheres, is hence seen to be theoretically antagonistic to modern society with its large social and economic conglomerates (see Huntington 1971; for criticisms of modernisation theory, see Tipps 1974).

While modernisation theory stresses the incompatibility of clientele and class relations, some recent studies of clientelism suggest the opposite. Not only do these studies stress the ability of clientelism to change its character as the society develops, but they also show that class/horizontal modes of political integration can continue to coexist with clientelism, alternating with it in political importance. Judith Chubb's study of Italy (1981a) further suggests that left-wing or marxist politics — as represented by the electoral victory of the Communist Party (CPI) in Naples — has found it extremely difficult to replace political clientelism. Neo-marxist studies further argue that clientelism has 'slowed down or actually prevented the political organisation and the ideological coherence of the economically dominated classes' (Mouzelis 1978b, p. 17; Flynn 1974). In other words, clientelism is a particularly 'effective mechanism for the maintenance of the status quo' (Mouzelis 1978b, p. 134; O'Connell 1982).

These last studies provide some important references for an analysis of clientelism in the Irish context; we will return to them later. At this juncture, we can outline two basic approaches to the study of clientelism: 1) transition from traditional familial or hierarchical relationships to class-oriented linkages or 2) resurgence/maintenance of clientelistic ties in the face of dominant class or ethnic objectives.

Irish clientelism

Irish studies of clientelism have considered many of the issues outlined above, although rarely with any theoretical expertise. In the main, they have been descriptive and historic rather than analytic or theoretical (see O'Connell 1982). Basil Chubb's 1963 article set the scholastic parameters by establishing the centrality of clientelism for an understanding of the Irish political process. It was followed within the decade by his textbook on Irish government (1970, 1982). His assessment of politicians as those who 'go about persecuting civil servants' on behalf of constituents, was based largely upon consideration of cultural and historical factors that had moulded a 'general pattern of people's attitudes and beliefs about, and their knowledge of, politics and political phenomena ...' (1970, p. 43; Garvin 1982, p. 176). Within this framework, he focussed upon the influences of Britain, nationalism, Catholicism, a dying peasant society, authoritarianism and anti-intellectualism. These factors, coupled with the country's smallness and rurality, had fashioned a society where priests and politicians reigned and reinforced intellectual and political passivity. Institutional centralisation and bureaucratisation provided clientelism with its *raison d'etre*.

> For generations, Irish people saw that to get the benefits that public authorities bestow, the help of a man with connections and influence was necessary. All that democracy has meant is that such a man has been laid on officially, as it were, and is now no longer a master but a servant (Higgins 1982, pp. 114-115).

Implicit in Chubb's account were two points which have provided the baseline for Irish clientelist studies ever since. Firstly, Chubb argued that popular pursuit of a politician's aid for state or other benefits was really unnecessary; politicians for their part had only encouraged the view as a means of amassing electoral advantage (Komito 1984, p. 177). Secondly, he assumed that the process of modernisation, which was visibly in progress, would forcibly change this, and other, traditional practices.

The later works of Mart Bax (1970, 1976) and Paul Sacks (1976) pursued the general line of enquiry posed by Chubb, although they disagreed as to whether the politicians' intervention actually worked. On this point, Bax's experience, in Munster during an election campaign, suggested that 'a politician's interferences can have good results ...' (1976, p. 77). The wider a politician's own and his or her party's political and personal network, the greater would be his or her ability to acquire information and reap the desired benefits. In the electoral stakes, Fianna Fáil's lengthy periods in government, as well as its unique organisational strength, has allowed it to exercise an influence over constituents/clients well beyond that approachable by either Fine Gael or Labour until recently. Nevertheless, for Bax the major conflict was not inter-party but intra-party. The extensiveness of a TD's brief, coupled with relatively long absences from his or her constituency, had necessitiated the appointment of a 'broker's-broker' or local agent. Over time, the latter began, intentionally or not, to develop his or her own clientele network, often out-polling his or her colleague at the next election. For Sacks, intra-party feuding was partially minimised by the creation of personal bailiwicks or political 'no-go' areas. On the issue of whether the politician/patron could actually deliver on promises, Sacks was sceptical:

> Over the course of time, the countrymen[2] have come to possess an exaggerated view of the power of their most frequently utilized advocates — the local party politicians. And the parties systematically cultivate this misconception with a deft bit of legerdemain which one might call imaginary patronage, that is, by providing the appearance of aid to their constituents when their actual influence in acquiring such aid is limited (1976, p. 7).

How can these studies explain clientelism's persistence if its real effects are often unclear? Chubb's study had clearly doubted the ability of clientele links to survive the onslaught of modernisation. In contrast, Bax asserts that the cultural traits — to which Chubb had traced the origins of clientelism — would enable clientele relations not only to resist the threats posed by modernisation but to ensconce themselves in the fabric of Irish urban political life as well (1976, pp. 194–195). Similarly, Sacks explained the persistence of Blaney's 'machine' in terms of a political culture born of 'real' historic and economic conditions (1976, p. 212). Indeed, it was the strength of these traditional values that enabled clientelism to remain, while many of the material conditions had altered fundamentally. Gibbon and Higgins (1974) and Komito (1984) have also pointed to this paradox within modernisation theory, using studies of Wicklow and Dublin to illustrate both the persistence of clientelism and its extension to urban areas from its traditional rural base.

Thus there has been a broad agreement as to clientelism's durability, which has cast doubt on the cruder versions of modernisation theory. Instead, emphasis has been placed upon cultural features which have in turn reproduced a particular form of political behaviour. It is this behaviour more than anything else, it is argued, that has sustained clientelism as a prominent feature of the political process.

The following five themes have characterised these studies:

(a) Most studies have seen ideas and culture as important explanations for clientelism. In Sacks' view, 'It is the countryman's[3] set of ideas about the nature of the political process that makes machine politics possible in Ireland' (1976, p. 7). A further factor is the tendency towards authoritarianism, buttressed by a highly moralistic climate, which has encouraged a passive or non-participatory role by citizens in the political process. Surveys reveal that only 42 per cent of Irish adults felt they could do something about a national law, compared with 62 per cent in the UK and 75 per cent in the USA. Of these, over three-quarters of the adults questioned sought a solution to their own grievances through their politician (Raven 1976, pp. 26–33; Hart 1970).

(b) The impression that solutions to, or advice about,

problems is the task of politicians has been encouraged by the overly bureaucratic and centralised nature of the state itself, at both national and local level. The excessive 'red tape', multi-centred departments, and the lack of published and easily-digested information about social benefits has necessitated the intervention of knowledgeable patrons. This development has not been restricted to the working-class, who might be more likely to seek such interventions. Sections of the petíte bourgeoisie and bourgeoisie have likewise been driven to seek the assistance of politicians to secure telephones, road developments, grants, etc. Komito argues that in this context, brokerage politics have 'fulfilled useful administrative functions' while allowing the politician to maintain a watchful eye over the 'provision of state benefits' (1984, p. 189).

(c) Integral to this process of bureaucratisation and centralisation has been the manner in which national parliamentary institutions and political practice have rein-forced a very narrow definition of the parliamentarian. The cabinet has emerged as the dominant power, with opposition and government back-benchers reduced to a routine and mundane role. Hence, few politicians would seek to define themselves as legislators, preferring the image of representing or 'servicing' their constituents. Chubb's initial assertion that deputies spend their time in clinics and letter-writing has been substantiated by more recent research (Roche 1982).

(d) The local and parochial concerns of national politicians are further reinforced by the fact that almost three-quarters of them simultaneously perform functions as local authority coun-cillors (Zimmerman 1978). The annals of Irish election history are filled with examples of politicians defeated by party col-leagues because they had failed to maintain necessary local con-tacts. Government's centralised and bureaucratic approach to local government has been partly a reaction to and reinforce-ment of politicians' self-interest and indifference to the wider local issues. The prospects of returning more power to local poli-ticians must be viewed in the light of the controversies over the abuse of planning and development controls in local government, one of the few areas where councillors can exercise political muscle. In turn, it is scarcely surprising that politicians see local government as merely a necessary rung on the political ladder.

(e) Intra-party rivalries have been accentuated by the partticular form of proportional representation — the single transferable vote in multi-seat constituencies — used in Ireland. While granting a theoretically more democratic choice to voters, it places party candidates in direct competition with each other as well as with political opponents. Thus, it affects party behaviour within and outside the Dáil by giving more significance to local issues than to national questions or political debate.

An unsatisfactory feature of these studies has been their tendency to concentrate too heavily upon descriptive and historical phenomena rather than seeking to explain or assess clientelism's origins, its mechanisms of social control or its relationship to the broader questions of political power (see Flynn 1974). What is missing is an understanding of the manner in which clientelism has a 'coercive, exploitative character' (Higgins 1982, p. 117), and how it has been reinforced and reproduced by the state, resulting in the masking and deflecting of conflict. Neo-marxist studies are useful here, as they see the state not as a mere amalgam of 'neutral' institutions, but the arena of class conflict.[4] In Antonio Gramsci's work (1971), the capitalist state forms and organises society on a broad front through political, moral and intellectual leadership. It performs three crucial functions with regard to social classes: 1) it organises the dominant classes; 2) disorganises the dominated classes; and 3) re-aligns other non-dominant classes (Held and Krieger, 1984). The Irish experience illustrates the manner in which clientelism, combined with nationalist symbols and rhetoric, imposes a 'way of life' through which the state can be experienced as representing society's 'general interest', and as the guardian of the universal vis-à-vis private individuals (Poulantzas 1973, p. 214). In this context, class issues are marginalised and seen as inappropriate. It is to a consideration of the relationship of clientelism to class and the political process that we now turn.

Political developments

The 1974 study by Gibbon and Higgins links the survival of clientelism to the form of economic development called 'petty-capitalism'. For them, clientelism's persistence has to be understood in the context of uneven economic and political development (p. 43). This unevenness has meant a weak industrial and social infra-structure, and a poor dispersal of existing resources. The extensive, and perhaps exaggerated, reliance upon the state to help or directly provide essential resources to virtually all social classes has thus helped underpin clientelism in Ireland.

Political debate in the Republic of Ireland has largely been defined by nationalism since the formation of the Free State in 1922. This has meant that deliberations on the existence and/or credibility of the Northern Ireland state, as well as arguments about the centrality of unity for political and economic development in the Republic of Ireland, have always remained dominant. The tide of populist nationalism was initially led by a united bourgeoisie, under the Sinn Féin banner. It successfully undermined Labour's early efforts to arouse debate on even limited social and economic reforms. After Fianna Fáil's entrance into Dáil Eireann in 1927, such concerns were easily marginalised by the highly politicised debate that ensued between Cumann na nGaedheal/Fine Gael and Fianna Fáil (Whyte 1974; Mair 1977, 1979; Hazelkorn 1983).

The main political protagonists were not non-ideological but anti-ideological. Fianna Fáil's hegemony[5] was constructed on an alliance of petit-bourgeois economic nationalism and popular social reform. Sustaining an image of itself as classless, it appealed to the Irish nation, urban and rural, above class divisions. Politics were not to be concerned with social conflict; they came to be perceived as a contest between Fianna Fáil and the rest; the Irish nation and the British; Catholicism and socialism. Thus nationalism, combined with traditional clientelism, over the decades became a particularly effective way of maintaining the status quo. While nationalism endeavoured to transcend class and social conflict, clientelism has introduced and reinforced the image of an aggrieved individual seeking aid from elected and/or well-positioned élites.

The first Cumann na nGaedheal government sought to minimise state intervention in the economy. This allowed Fianna Fáil to present a 'radical' response to unemployment and poor housing. which gave it a permanent image of being more in touch with what the people wanted. Over time, it established a particularly extensive and successful network of grants, housing, welfare payments and contracts as the means to political power. It forged an enduring alliance with large sections of the working-class. Furthermore, because of the underdeveloped nature of the economy, public expenditure, dispersed by politicians, has been influential in constructing key clientele links; Fianna Fáil's ties with the petíte bourgeoisie in general, and the building sector in particular, is a case in point. The construction industry is of crucial importance to the economy; a point underscored by the party's electoral strength amongst heavily unionised workers in that industry. In addition, a wide range of social groups depend upon a healthy construction industry for their livelihood; speculators, artisans, suppliers, architects, engineers and those who would seek to gain by acquiring better and more accommodation, new factories and work-places (Chubb 1981b). The significance of these political class alliances is evidenced by their durability. As Fianna Fáil's home base among the small farming and traditional petíte bourgeoisie began to vanish in the face of the capitalisation of the economy and increased competition, the old links forged in the 1930s and 1940s have endured. Since the 1970s, the challenge to Fianna Fáil's hegemony by Fine Gael must be understood in part by the latter's efforts to construct competing class alliances, and by its successful copy of the former's clientelist structure. Where Fianna Fáil had (by virtue of its governmental longevity) been able to control, unchallenged, lucrative public expenditure and appointments, Fine Gael, through its coalition with the Labour Party, has been able to build up its own following.

Class and clientelism

Clientelist networks work well in Ireland precisely because the
level of services, and access to information about them, is
particularly low. As studies in Italy have shown, the individual
assumes that there is 'no alternative but to seek a particularistic
solution to his problem' (Chubb 1981b, p. 80). While the
majority of queries concern housing, they also involve health
benefits, employment and education. The introduction of
examining boards in the late 1920s for public sector employment eliminated the worst excesses of jobbery, but political ties
are still important and publicly visible, especially for public
sector promotions. It is, to a very large degree, a moot point
whether the patron's intervention actually produces the desired
results; the crucial factor is less the immediate benefit than the
long-term relationship. Moreover, the desirability of seeking
intervention through a politician has been reinforced by the
state itself: housing lists, releases from prison, and grants payable are, for example, often channelled through local politicians
(an important reason in itself to hold down a local authority post
simultaneously with a parliamentary one). It is then up to the
individual to decide which politician and party was responsible.
The 1980 administration of Charles Haughey institutionalised
the practice further by appointing state personnel to deal with
ministers' 'clinic queries' so as to avoid weakening crucial
clientele links with the resultant electoral defeats. 'Suffice it to
say ... that every action of the state, of the local authority, of
related agencies generates a source of clientelist communication. They help create the illusion of assistance' (Higgins 1982,
p. 123; see Collins 1985).

Clientelism in Ireland, theoretically at least, has not operated
unchallenged. The trade union movement, for example, has
had an impressive history, unionising 57 per cent of the workforce, a figure higher than its more industrialised neighbours.
Significantly, however, it has consistently been unable to ensure
electoral support for its own political party. Labour Party
support among the working-class has remained far below that

given to Fianna Fáil, although not Fine Gael. A key explanation for this phenomenon must be located within Fianna Fáil's carefully constructed political leadership, through which it has more ably portrayed itself as acting in the interests of the working-class than Labour itself. Its extensive clientele network is partly responsible for this; there are examples of people who have sought solutions to work-related grievances through their politician rather than their union. Often, the unions are themselves to blame for this political ambiguity; they have, for example, facilitated clientelist practices, especially within the local/public sectors, by failing to press hard enough for recruitment and promotional procedures free from political interference.

The emergence of the Irish Farmers Association (IFA) is a unique example of an explicitly class-conscious organisation in Ireland. Unlike the trade union movement, which is often split between industrial, craft, private and public unions, the IFA acts coherently and unambiguously. It fearlessly confronts the government and the EEC on any issue it sees as being against its (class) interests. Its voting strength has been fashioned into an effective political weapon. Yet, its growth and success has never sought to challenge the traditional clientelist structures; instead, the IFA has neatly supplemented these links with more modern forms of political activity.

For modernisation theory, the examples of the unions and the IFA would be paradoxical; the emergence of 'class'-based organisations should ultimately supplant clientelist ones. Studies by Nicos Mouzelis on Greece and Judith Chubb on Italy illustrate, however, that class and clientele relations can coexist. While class links might appear stronger at times, traditional relationships do not disappear and continue to perform a significant political function. In this regard, these works depart from both modernisation theory and classical marxism. The former denies any link between class and politics. The latter often views political cleavage, too mechanistically, as a direct outgrowth of class divisions. Significantly, both approaches fail to see clientelism as a dynamic political form.

In Ireland, radical changes in the economy and society have forced changes within clientelism. It is no longer merely a rural phenomenon, for instance. The image of the traditional patron as the post-famine gombeen-man or rural money-lender has been transformed into the modern politician, whose occupation is most likely to be that of teacher, publican, auctioneer, farmer or shopkeeper. Equally, the image of the client 'tied' by electoral allegiance to a particular patron is less appropriate. The client's ability to exercise choice does not, however, negate the existence of assumed reliance on the patron for desired resources or information, it merely introduces the concept of competition. Indeed, politicians often refer to their clinics as the source of their stance on a particular issue; a process which puts the clinic at the centre of the Irish political process.

Clientelism's signifiance stems from its role as a particular mode of 'dependent integration' — a means of integrating the mass of the population into the political system without simultaneously threatening the status quo (Mouzelis 1978b, p. 139). Its persistence is necessitated by the social and political conflicts that are associated with capitalist societies, and the advent of mass politics. Clientelism is thus a feature of the capitalist state itself. It is not merely another name for corruption; rather, it is a way in which the ruling class can appear to represent the interests of society as a whole and not just themselves (Gramsci 1971; Therborn 1978). It ensures that incipient (class) conflict can be redirected through acceptable channels which emphasise the role of individuals and not groups or classes. Insofar as this is the dominant mode of political organisation, class or mass mobilisation is that much more difficult to achieve. Put more succinctly, clientelism has helped to keep the working-class outside the sphere of active politics, while it has encouraged an image of politics that is anti-ideological and issue-oriented. The effect has been to retard the political development and consciousness of the economically dominated classes.

Few Irish studies have sought to examine the implications of clientelism. The 1974 Gibbon and Higgins article does draw attention to some key aspects of the Irish political process which they deduce from clientelism:

These include: the character of both major parties as vertically-integrated inter-class alliances; a lack of serious ideological differences between these parties; a comprehensive localism in national politics; a statistically-attested extremely low degree of public confidence in the ability of ordinary citizens to collectively influence local or national governmental action; an absence of interest-groups or public campaigns in national politics; the dominance of national and local politics by the personal clienteles of politicians; and the constant recurrence of corrupt practices in local government (1974 p. 30).

The effect is, however, more class related. In Ireland, there are scant instances of mass or even class mobilisation; the PAYE campaign of the late 1970s was one such instance, but the clear inability to win any concessions, coupled with its quick dissipation, is an indication of labour's powerlessness. In contrast, the IFA has been extraordinarily successful in acquiring many of its demands; indeed during a period of heightened consciousness over taxation, partly due to the trade unions' campaign, the IFA has managed to actually reduce its taxation burden. Here, the contrast with labour should not obscure the IFA's position as a fraction of the dominant class.

If clientelism is a mechanism for manipulating political disorganisation among the dominated classes in society, is it then a permanent feature of the Irish political process? Again, the Italian study of Judith Chubb is interesting. In Palermo, economic underdevelopment and social fragmentation underpin clientelism; hence, meaningful change can only come about through a national programme of economic development. To achieve this, the development of alternative sources of economic goods outside political control, and the creation of an industrial working-class 'even if subject to clientelistic control in the short-run', would be crucial (1981b, pp. 84–85). The Greek experience should caution us, however, against placing too much emphasis on economic development. Moreover, the increasing dominance of the capitalist mode of production in Ireland has not been accompanied by any noticeable weakening in clientele ties. There is a growth of cynicism and alienation from politicians and the political process, but political debate has not shown any significant alteration in style, content or ideological level. Since 1980, party differences have seemed to revolve around economic policy. Yet, more often than not, 'bread-and-butter' issues are translated into clientelist terms as the parties compete via promises about car tax, rates, or grants to women in the home. The Workers' Party and sections of the Labour-left have occasionally succeeded in raising debate onto a more ideological plane, but change will not be easy or automatic. For them to operate in constituencies through clinics could be politically disastrous in the long-term; suggestions that their councillors/TDs can be as effective as others in acquiring services or information will likely reinforce the traditional vertical/clientele links, and negate the horizontal/class ties which they ideologically favour.

In Ireland, clientelism is not merely a cultural or historic feature of rural life now appendaged onto the urban political scene. Nor has its existence and persistence been merely the result of successful interventions by politicians. Rather, through clientelism, the state has actively sought to deflect incipient conflict by channelling it instead into well-established clientele networks, controlled by parties of the dominant classes. Clientelism is institutionalised within the very fabric of the state, and reinforced by a consistent effort to exclude questions that refer to class differences. In this manner, protest is curtailed and the status quo enforced.

Notes to chapter 16

1, 2, 3, 6, 7. The use of sexist terms here is necessitated by their use in the work of the original authors.
4. Broadly, pluralist/democratic political theory sees the 'state' as the institutions of government, to which all citizens have equal access. Marxism challenges this classic position and argues that the 'state' is the instrument through which the political power of the economically dominant classes is exercised.

5. The term 'hegemony' is given its fullest development by the Italian
marxist, Antonio Gramsci (1971). Briefly, it combines the concepts of
political dominance and leadership, the latter implying popular consent.

References

BAX, MART 1970. 'Patronage Irish style: Irish politicians as brokers', *Sociologische Gids*, Vol. 17, pp. 179-191

BAX, MART 1976. *Harpstrings and Confessions*, Assen, Van Gorcum and Co.

BOISSEVAIN, JEREMY 1974. *Friends of Friends: Networks, Man ipulators and Coalitions*, Oxford, Blackwell

CACIAGLI, MARIO and FRANK P. BELLONI 1981. 'The "New" Clientelism in Southern Italy: the Christian Democratic Party in Catalonia', in S. N. Eisenstadt and René Lemarchand, (eds.), *Political Clientelism, Patronage and Development*, London, Sage, pp. 35-56

CHUBB, BASIL 1963. '"Going about Persecuting Civil Servants": The Role of the Irish Parliamentary Representative', *Political Studies*, Vol. 10, No. 3, pp. 272-286

CHUBB, BASIL 1970. *The Government and Politics of Ireland*, Oxford, Oxford University Press

CHUBB, BASIL 1982. *The Government and Politics of Ireland*, 2nd Edition, London, Longman

CHUBB, JUDITH 1981a. 'Naples Under the Left: The Limits of Local Change', in S. N. Eisenstadt and René Lemarchand (eds.), *Political Clientelism, Patronage and Development*, London, Sage, pp. 91-124

CHUBB, JUDITH 1981b. 'The

Social Bases of the Urban Political Machine: the Christian Democratic Party in Palermo', in S. N. Eisenstadt and René Lemarchand (eds.), *Political Clientelism, Patronage and Development*, London, Sage, pp. 57-90

CLAPHAM, CHRISTOPHER 1982. 'Clientelism and the State', in Christopher Clapham (ed.), *Private Patronage and Public Power: Political Clientelism and the Modern State*, London, Frances Pinter, pp. 1-35

COLLINS, C. A. 1985. 'Clientelism and Careerism in Irish Local Governments: the Persecution of Civil Servants Revisited, *Economic and Social Review*, Vol. 16, pp. 273-286.

FLYNN, PETER 1974. 'Class, Clientelism, and Coercion: Some Mechanisms of Internal Dependency and Control', *Journal of Commonwealth and Comparative Politics*, Vol. 12, Part 2, pp. 133-156

GARVIN, TOM 1982. 'Theory, Culture and Fianna Fail: A Review', in Mary Kelly, Liam O'Dowd, and James Wickham (eds.), *Power, Conflict and Inequality*, Dublin, Turoe, pp. 171-185

GIBBON, PETER and MICHAEL D. HIGGINS 1974. 'Patronage, Tradition and Modernisation: The case of the Irish "Gombeenman"', *Economic and Social Review*, Vol. 6, pp. 27-44

GRAMSCI, ANTONIO 1971. *Pris-*

on *Notebooks*, London, Lawrence and Wishart

HART, IAN 1970. 'Public Opinion on Civil Servants and the Role and Power of the Individual in the Local Community', *Administration*, Vol. 18, No. 2, pp. 375-391

HAZELKORN, ELLEN 1983. 'The Political Ideology of the Irish Labour Party, 1912-1932', unpublished.

HELD, DAVID and JOEL KRIEGER 1984. 'Theories of the State: Some Competing Claims', in Stephen Bornstein, David Held, and Joel Krieger (eds.), *The State in Capitalist Europe*, London, Frances Pinter, pp. 1-20

HIGGINS , MICHAEL D. 1982. 'The Limits of Clientelism: Towards an Assessment of Irish Politics', in Christopher Clapham (ed.), *Private Patronage and Public Power: Political Clientelism in the Modern State*, London, Frances Pinter, pp. 114-141

HUNTINGTON, SAMUEL 1971. 'The Change to Change; Modernization, Development and Politics', *Comparative Politics*, Vol. 3, No. 3, pp. 283-322

KOMITO, LEE 1984. 'Irish Clientelism: A Reappraisal', *Economic and Social Review*, Vol. 25, No. 3, pp. 173-194

LEMARCHAND, RENÉ 1981. 'Comparative Political Clientelism: Structure, Process and Optic', in S. N. Eisenstadt and René Lemarchand (eds.), *Political Clientelism, Patronage and Development*, London, Sage, pp. 7-32

MACCIOCCHI, MARIA ANTONIETTA 1973. *Letters from inside the Italian Communist Party to Louis Althusser*, London, New Left Books.

MAIR, PETER 1977. 'Labour and the Irish Political Party System Revisited: Party Competition in the 1920s', *Economic and Social Review*, Vol. 9, No. 1, pp. 57-70

MAIR, PETER 1979. 'The Autonomy of the Political: the development of the Irish Party System', *Comparative Politics*, Vol. 11, No. 4, pp. 445-465

MOUZELIS, NICOS 1978a. 'Class and Clientelistic Politics: the Case of Greece', *Sociological Review*, Vol. 26, No. 3, pp. 471-497

MOUZELIS, NICOS 1978b. *Modern Greece*, London, Macmillan

O'CONNELL, DAVID 1982. 'Sociological Theory and Irish Political Research', in Mary Kelly, Liam O'Dowd and James Wickham (eds.), *Power, Conflict and Inequality*, Dublin, Turoe, pp. 186-198

POULANTZAS, NICOS 1973. *Political Power and Social Classes*, London, New Left Books

RAVEN, J. *et al.* 1976. *Political Culture in Ireland: The Views of Two Generations*, Dublin, Institute of Public Administration

ROCHE, RICHARD 1982. 'The High Cost of Complaining Irish Style', *Journal of Irish Business and Administrative Research*, Vol. 4, No. 2, pp. 98-108

SACKS, PAUL M. 1970. 'Bailiwicks, Locality, and Religion: Three Elements in an Irish Dail Constituency Election', *Economic and Social Review*, Vol. 1, No. 4, pp. 531-554

SACKS, PAUL M. 1976. *The Donegal Mafia*, New Haven; Yale University Press

THERBORN, GORAN 1978. *What Does The Ruling Class Do When It Rules?*, London, New Left Books/Verso.

TIPPS, D. C. 1974. 'Modernization Theory and the Comparative Study of Societies: A Critical Perspective', *Comparative Studies in Society and History*, pp. 199–226

WHYTE, JOHN H. 1974. 'Ireland: Politics without Social Bases', in Richard Rose (ed.), *Electoral Behavior: a Comparative Handbook*, New York, Free Press/Collier Macmillan

ZIMMERMAN, J. F. 1978. 'Role Perceptions of Dual Office Holders in Ireland', *Administration*, Vol. 26, No. 1, pp. 25–48

17
Deviance and Crime in the Republic of Ireland

CIARAN McCULLAGH

It is one of the inconveniences of discussing deviance that we must begin with what are very difficult questions. These are about how we define our area of study. If we wish to go shooting elephants it is a great help, not least to rhinoceroses, if we know what an elephant looks like. With deviance it is the same. If we wish to study the phenomenon we need some indicators of it. With elephants it is relatively easy. They have after all a distinctive style of imbibing liquid that would cause comment at most dinner tables. Deviance by contrast does not have such readily distinguishing characteristics. By its nature it tends to defy easy classification.

The simplest definition of deviance is that of David Matza. He says (1969, p. 10) 'to deviate is to stray, as from a path, or a standard'. But what paths and what standards? In sociology it is generally assumed that the relevant path is the social rules or norms of the society (see, for example, A. Cohen, 1966). But this in turn assumes there is a commonly shared and generally accepted set of social rules in society. This is not self-evidently the case.

Particular social rules which appear to have universal acceptability turn out on inspection to be somewhat limited in applicability. It might, for example, appear to be the case that every-

344

body is against stealing. Yet there is a range of activities in society that look suspiciously like stealing but which do not appear to be regarded as wrong. Over-estimating travel expenses, borrowing office equipment, taking objects that fall off the backs of lorries and other forms of 'five-finger discount' are technically acts of theft yet they do not provoke the moral outrage that 'borrowing' a car without the owner's permission does. This is despite the higher rate of return of 'borrowed' cars. They may not always be returned to the same place or in the same condition but about 75 per cent of stolen cars are recovered.

Equally while there is agreement that certain kinds of behaviour, such as child-battering, are definitely deviant, this consensus may not extend to other kinds of behaviour like homosexuality and family planning. Here the degree of consensus may vary by age or by social location. So there are considerable uncertainties involved in the definition of deviance. However, many sociologists go on to argue that these uncertainties are not unlimited. The means of resolving the difficulties of definition is to talk about the 'authoritative resolution' of the law (Matza, 1969). Some acts of deviance are regarded as sufficiently harmful to society to be forbidden by the state. Thus we can limit our discussion of deviance to those acts of social rule-breaking that are prohibited by the laws of the state.

As a tactic this has a number of important advantages. It provides us with a clear range of behaviour ('criminal acts') and a distinct group of people ('criminals') to study. It has other advantages too. For example it sensitises us to the notion that only some social rules have the backing of the law and it opens up for study the process by which some rules rather than others achieve this distinction. It does not necessarily follow that acts of behaviour which are penalised by legal sanctions are more serious or cause greater degrees of social harm than acts which are not so penalised.

The poisoning of people with strychnine is an offence against the criminal law, the potential poisoning of people by the discharge of various forms of effluent is a breach of civil law, the potential poisoning of people through the contamination of their food by antibiotics is limited by a state regulation while the poisoning of people with the lead content of petrol fumes is not penalised at all. Yet the differences in the way these acts are treated have important social consequences, most notably in terms of the stigmatisation of the people who perform these acts. We have a vocabulary which designates people prosecuted under the criminal law (suspect, defendant, criminal, prisoner, ex-offender). There is no comparable vocabulary to deal with people who deviate but not in ways defined as criminal. How many 'ex-antibiotic regulations offenders' do you know.

Confining our study of deviance to the study of crime in this way raises questions about the process of law-making in society. Why do some acts of rule-breaking come to be defined as violations of criminal law while others do not? As we have argued, it is not necessarily related to the degree of social harm of particular acts. Is it, therefore, in terms of who in society is most likely to commit these acts or who is likely to suffer most from these acts? In other words, does the law reflect the interests of some sections of the population to a greater extent than those of other sections? As we shall from now on confine our attention to acts and people who violate the criminal law, it is essential to remember that this discussion is structured by the ways in which laws are made in society.[1]

Extent and distribution of crime in the Republic

The Extent of Crime
Crime became a matter of public concern in the Republic during the 1970s. This concern was reflected in politics. In the 1969 general election crime was not an issue; by 1977 it had become one. The major parties promised to declare 'war on crime' so as to 'ensure that the citizen is safe from marauders'. It may seem odd to ask if this growing concern has any basis in reality, but in the United States the fear of crime has grown at a faster rate and is now, according to Warr (1980), a more substantial problem than the actual incidence of crime. How much crime is there in our society?

Data about crime in Ireland are contained in the annual reports of the Garda Commissioner. Table 1 is drawn from these reports. It shows the number of indictable offences reported to the Gardai and the number and percentage of such offences in which criminal proceedings were commenced, i.e. the detection rate, for various years from 1961 to 1981.

Three points can be drawn from this table. The first is that there has been a fivefold increase in the total amount of crime over the period. The bulk of this increase occurred after 1966. This can be seen most clearly with property crime i.e. 'offences against property with violence' and 'larcenies etc'. Both of these categories doubled in size between 1966 and 1971. 'Offences against property with violence' almost doubled again between 1971 and 1976 and there was a further large increase in larcenies between 1976 and 1981.

The second point is that these increases have been accompanied by declines in detection rates. These declines are most evident for property crime. Again the key period of change is 1966 to 1971. In 1966, 73 per cent of 'offences against property with violence' and 60 per cent of 'larcenies' were detected. In 1971 the respective figures were 51 per cent and 40 per cent. In both cases the rates have continued to decline since 1971 in a less dramatic, but still substantial, fashion. By contrast the detection rates for 'offences against the person' like murder and assault and for 'other indictable offences' have remained very high.

The final point is that, while there has been a substantial increase in the amount of crime, the major types of crimes still involve the illegal acquisition of property. In 1961 93 per cent of all crime was property crime. In 1981 it was 96 per cent. This predominance of property crime is a feature of most industrialised societies. In Britain, for example, almost 96 per cent of crimes in 1971 were against property, while in the United States the figure was almost 88 per cent (Taylor, Walton and Young 1973).

Overall then, this data would suggest that there are grounds for the increased concern about crime in Ireland. The level of all types of crime has increased substantially, particularly since the

Table 1: **Number of indictable offences reported to Gardai and number and percentage detected, in various years, from 1961–1981**

Offence categories		1961	1966	1971	1976	1981
1. Offences against the person	No. reported	701	1,132	1,256	1,714	2,478
	No. detected	646	1,060	1,128	1,546	2,174
	% detected	92	94	90	90	88
2. Offences against property with violence	No. reported	3,186	4,957	10,654	20,903	28,916
	No. detected	2,439	3,624	5,444	9,152	11,181
	% detected	77	73	51	44	39
3. Larcenies etc.	No. reported	10,623	12,631	24,929	31,540	57,642
	No. detected	6,473	7,535	10,103	11,583	19,089
	% detected	61	60	41	37	33
4. Other indictable offences	No. reported	308	309	942	225	364
	No. detected	280	291	825	201	310
	% detected	91	94	88	89	85
TOTAL	No. reported	14,818	19,029	37,781	54,382	89,400
	No. detected	9,838	12,510	17,518	22,482	32,754
	% detected	66	66	46	41	37

NOTE: Offence categories are those used in Garda statistics. Category (1) includes murder, manslaughter and assault, (2) includes burglary, house-breaking and robbery, (3) includes larceny from the person, of cars and from shops, (4) includes miscellaneous offences such as perjury and indecency.

mid-1960s. Now, as then, however, property crime is by far the most prevalent type.

The increase in crime: real or illusory?

Garda statistics on crime would suggest major changes in the level of crime. But there are questions that can be raised about the reliability of crime statistics. These questions arise from the results of victim surveys. In such surveys, members of the public are asked if they have ever been victims of crime and if so, have the crimes been reported to the police. These surveys suggest that there is a considerable amount of crime which goes unrecorded. One such survey was done in the Republic between October 1982 and October 1983. It is estimated that, for example, the number of incidents of burglary for the period was slightly over 40,000 and the number of car thefts was 34,000 (Breen and Rottman, 1985 p. 2). Yet Garda statistics for the nearest calendar year, 1982, only record 16,558 residential burglaries and 21,936 incidents of car theft.

These findings are similar to those of victim surveys in the United States and in Britain (see Box 1981, for a summary). In these countries failure to record all crime is explained in terms of the unwillingness of the public to report all crime, and in terms of the failure of the police to record all incidents of crime reported to them. The reluctance of the public to report crime is in turn explained by either the tolerance level in the community for particular offences, the degree of confidence people have in the police and the level of inducement to report offences. This latter factor includes insurance, where claims for loss require a police report.

Breen and Rottman, however, found that the rates of reporting offences in the Republic are high. 'Members of the Irish public', they argue (1985 p. 3), 'are generally more likely than residents of Britain to report victimisation incidents to the police'. Discrepancies between official statistics and victim surveys may therefore be explicable in terms of the recording practices of the Garda. The overall impact of the results of such victim surveys on the study of crime must be to induce caution in our treatment of official statistics on crime.

The social characteristics of offenders
Garda statistics on crime do not include any information on the social characteristics of people who commit crime. The major source here is Rottman's research (1984, pp. 191–205) on a particular group of offenders — those apprehended for indictable offences in the Dublin metropolitan area in 1981.

The most striking characteristics of this group of about 20,000 people were their largely male, working-class status, their youthfulness, the early ages at which they left school, and their high level of unemployment. These findings, when linked to the previous discussion on patterns of crime, are in line with those of other countries (see, for example, Bilton *et al.*, 1981, p. 571). They suggest that most crime is committed by young unemployed working-class males against property in urban areas.

However, a number of reservations must be entered about these findings. The data on which they are based had important limitations: they did not include, for obvious reasons, those who commit non-reported crime; they did not include those forms of social injury which are not violations of the criminal law. As both of these categories stand, it is likely that crimes and forms of social injury committed by middle- and upper-class people may be understated, thus introducing a class bias into our knowledge of offenders. Studies of those arrested are also limited by low detection rates, which mean that those offenders who are not arrested are not included. As middle-class offenders may have greater resources through which they can evade arrest, there is scope for class bias here too. What this means is that the characteristics of offenders identified in such studies may be more adequate as indicators of vulnerability to arrest than of propensity to commit crime.

The victims of crime
Our knowledge about the victims of crime is also limited to one major study — Breen and Rottman's victim survey (1985). It found that in general, the households most at risk of crime were those in urban areas, especially Dublin, those headed by a

person under 30, and in terms of socio-economic status, those of the self-employed. The victimisation risks for crimes such as burglary were lower for the old than for any other age group. However, in considering such findings it is well to bear in mind that the effects of being a victim of crime may not be the same for everyone. In this sense the old may be least able to bear the material and psychological effects of crime.

Explaining crime in the Republic of Ireland

In this section we examine sociological explanations of crime and we will deal almost exclusively with property crime. There are two types of explanation of crime in sociology: the first is concerned with the explanations of crime rates in society, the second is concerned with explaining why particular groups in society have a greater propensity to commit crime than others. Put another way, the first type of explanation is concerned with the increase in criminal opportunities in society, the second with explaining why certain people take advantage of these opportunities.

Theories of rates

The first type explains crime rates in terms of their relationship to other social changes. This is the strategy in Rottman's work on crime in Ireland (1980). The concurrence of increases in crime with other major social changes constitutes his point of departure. The relevant changes are in the age structure of the population, and in the level of material affluence produced by industrialisation and reflected in the increase in urbanisation. The age structure is important because males in the age group 15–24 are, according to criminologists, the group most involved in crime. Any expansion in this age group, such as that which occurred here in the 1960s and 1970s, will be reflected in an increased incidence of crime. As the supply of potential criminals increased, industrialisation has increased the range of objects that can be stolen — television sets, motor-cars, and money. This combination of increased criminal opportunities and an increased supply of potential criminals produced, almost inevitably, an increase in crime.

Theories of motivation
While such theories are useful in the way in which they link structural change and crime, they leave, as Rottman puts it (1980, p. 77), 'a vital question unanswered: why do people take advantage of the new opportunities for criminal activity?' This is the question which the second type of explanation attempts to answer. It examines how the workings of society generate or produce criminal motivations in certain sections of the population. Within this general type there is a variety of theories. We shall consider three — that of Robert Merton, that of radical criminologists and that of labelling theorists.

Robert Merton's argument (1938) is that certain kinds of society systematically produce crime and deviance. He separates out two central elements in a society. The first is the cultural structure, or the culturally defined goals of society. These goals are shared, initially at least, by all members of a society. They are implanted in socialisation and it is to the attainment of these goals that people organise their behaviour and activity in society. The second element is the social structure, or the institutionalised means, by which the goals of society are to be achieved. So not only are there goals in a society that people are expected to achieve but there are also proper means of achieving these goals.

Merton argues that in a well-regulated society, goals and means are integrated in that they are both accepted by, and available to, all in the society. However, in many societies the legitimate means of achieving the goals are not available to all. In such societies those who wish to achieve the goals, but who are denied access to the means, adapt to this situation. The most significant adaptation is what Merton calls the innovatory response. Working-class people have internalised and accepted the cultural goals of the society but are denied access to legitimate means of achieving success. For example, they are cut off from the upper reaches of the educational system and as a result find themselves faced with a future of low status and low paying work. Crime represents for them an alternative means of achieving the goals of society. So in a society where the possession of property is the primary aim this inevitably produces high rates of property crime among those with little access to legitimate means of obtaining it, i.e. the working-class.

Crime, however, is not the only form of adaptation. People may also react in a ritualistic fashion by rejecting the goals but continuing to live by the rules of society. They may also adapt by rejecting both the goals and the rules in what Merton calls the retreatist solution. This is the response of drug addicts, vagrants, suicides and alcoholics. Finally, people may reject the rules and the goals and try to create a new kind of society with new cultural and social structures.

Merton's analysis can be usefully applied to the Republic of Ireland. We know that the working-class are excluded from many parts of the education system (see Rottman and O'Connell 1983). We know also that the education system is the major allocator of positions in the occupational world, so they are also cut off from the better occupations in the country. They find themselves either in low paying jobs or else excluded from the labour force through unemployment. In a society which respects high occupational achievement and high monetary rewards, success in conventional terms is not a realistic option for them. It is not surprising then to find the high representation of working-class individuals among 'property' criminals. Merton's analysis has the further advantage in the Irish context in that it sees crime as only one response to social inequality. The high levels of heroin addiction and of other forms of solvent abuse among working-class people are also responses to social inequality.

Merton's analysis has been criticised on many grounds (see Clinard 1964). One important criticism is that Merton does not tell us how the disjunction between goals and means emerges in a society. This does not constitute a notable difficulty for those who adopt a marxist perspective on crime and deviance generally. According to this view, the origins of crime and deviance are to be found in the nature of, and the contradictions in, capitalist societies. Taylor, Walton and Young (1973) have developed this proposition. They argue that social problems can be divided into two kinds. The first are those that spring from human diversity such as prostitution, drug-taking and homosexuality. Capitalist society cannot tolerate these forms of diversity because (with their hedonistic overtones) they threaten to undermine the work ethic. So it designates them as crimes. The second kind of social problems are those that flow from the material inequalities that are intrinsic to capitalist societies. The sources of most forms of conventional property crime are simply the inequalities of income, wealth and opportunity in capitalist societies. Because of its nature as a social and economic system capitalism systematically and inevitably generates inequality and as a consequence systematically generates crime. The disjunction between ends and means is not an accidental or a transient feature of capitalist society but an essential part of it.

Thus for such criminologists it is capitalist society that is crimogenic. It is the kind of society that promotes the right to own property while simultaneously depriving an entire class of the possibility of having any. Jock Young (1975) suggests that people who are 'victims' of capitalism in this way have a number of options. They can become what he calls determined creatures allowing themselves to be brutalised by the system. In the process they will become submerged in drink and drugs. They can play the capitalist game and enter the battle for material accumulation. They can steal from the rich, which, while seen as a crime by capitalist society, is a political act. Crime is seen here as a form of resistance to, and subversion of, capitalist society. Finally, they can ignore the other options and join the struggle for a socialist society.

There are therefore important similarities between the arguments of Taylor, Walton and Young and of Robert Merton. They see the nature of society as facilitating crime and deviance. They also see a range of possible responses to inequality in society, one of which is crime. However, there is a crucial difference between the two arguments. For Merton the disjunction between ends and means in a society is one that can be rectified.

Social reforms which widen the opportunities available to the working-class but which do not fundamentally alter the nature of the society are the solution to crime. For marxists, however, major social transformation is necessary in order to create social and productive arrangements that would abolish crime. The replacement of capitalism by socialism is a necessary stage in the reduction of crime in society.

In contrast to these theories, the labelling perspective locates the sources of deviant behaviour in the institutions in society that are designed to control crime (see Becker 1963). For them a distinction between rule-breaking and deviance is critical. Rule-breaking behaviour is widespread in society. For example, studies of juveniles show that most have committed offences for which they could have been arrested. Yet only some come to the notice of the police and only some have their acts labelled as criminal or deviant. Labelling theory argues that it is in what happens to those who are singled out in this way that the sources of further criminal behaviour lie. In other words, it is in the process by which the police, the courts and the prisons select out and process some of the rule-breakers in society that the motivation to further crime can be located.

It happens like this. Being officially registered as a criminal has important social-psychological implications. No longer is the person seen as just like anyone else. This differentness is emphasised for him by the way he is treated. He[2] finds himself in a prison-cell without his shoe-laces and belt, he finds himself in a court-room where he is now simply the accused in the dock, he finds himself in prison stripped of his clothing, reclothed in a prison uniform and his hair cut. From being John Murphy to others he has become prisoner no. 3180. In this situation he finds it difficult to maintain his sense of himself as being like everybody else. The concrete events he is undergoing deny him that possibility. He is also cut off from people like family and friends who would support his self-identity. In such circumstances he may accept the new identity that is being forced on him. He may come to see himself as a criminal and act accordingly.

The extent of the difficulties produced for an individual by changes in the way society views him should not be underestimated. For example, being labelled a 'criminal' changes the way others view his past. Incidents in his life now become redefined as symptoms of incipient delinquency. The criminal label in society also carries with it a series of auxiliary traits that are assumed to be naturally linked to it. If one is a 'criminal' one is also tough, aggressive and dangerous. People react to labelled individuals as if they had all of these traits. How many criminals do you have as friends? Finally, a 'criminal' finds himself excluded from situations that might help him lose the criminal label. He is, for example, no longer considered suitable for certain kinds of employment. The accumulation of pressures to become what one is labelled is intense.

We argued earlier that rule-breaking was common in society. How then is only some of it selected and reacted to? Labelling theorists would see it as a matter of chance. But the operation of chance is influenced by certain factors. Other things being equal, the visibility of rule-breaking influences the attention it receives. Glue-sniffing in the street is more likely to be reacted to than dope-taking in a private residence. The power of the rule-breaker and the social distance between him and the police is also important. Contrast the reaction to students' behaviour in rag-week with the reaction to the same behaviour from a group of skin-heads. Thus, some groups in society — the less powerful and those who use the streets more as living space — are more vulnerable to official reaction and labelling.

It is difficult to assess the utility of this perspective in the Irish context. There is only one published study in this tradition, O'Sullivan's work (1977) on the processing of juvenile offenders. This, however, would suggest that it has considerable validity. Its strength lies in the way in which it sensitises us to the possibility that our institutional mechanisms for dealing with crime may perpetuate rather than prevent it.

Responses to crime

Having discussed the causes it is now necessary to examine the responses of society to crime. These can be divided into three — policing, prison and social policy.

Where policing is concerned, the standard argument is that the solution to crime is more police, wider police powers and better technology. Yet research would suggest that these changes do not contribute notably to reducing crime. The Garda force has increased from 6,612 in 1961 to 10,869 in 1983. Over this time the crime rate has also increased, though Gardai would argue that the increase in manpower here has not been sufficient to make a major impact on crime. In other countries, however, larger increases in the size of the police force have not constituted an obstacle to the rise in the level of crime (see McCullagh 1983 for a review of the research on all the points about policing). If size is not important, neither are changes in how the police are deployed. Research on changes in the patrolling strategies of the police, most notably from motorised to beat patrols, suggests that the deterrence effect is minimal. Similarly, increases in the level of 'visible' police presence on the streets seems simply to displace crime, in that aspiring criminals move to more congenial work situations.

The case for wider powers has been argued for very strongly by the Gardai and partially conceded to them in the Criminal Justice Act 1984. Again, research from other countries suggests that such powers do not influence the crime rate. Take, for example, the power to detain on reasonable suspicion. The use of a similar power in England was largely unproductive as the charges which resulted were generally of a trivial nature, and indeed, most arose out of the citizen's resistance to the police's use of the power (McConville 1983). Moreover, such powers seem to be counter-productive for the police in that they alienate sections of the public, particularly young people, from them. These powers appear to erode the level of public confidence on which effective policing must be based. Finally, increasing the amount of technology available to the police does not appear to make a notable contribution to crime reduction. For example, sophisticated communication systems can increase the speed with which the police respond to calls for assistance, but they do not affect the detection rate, because victims and witnesses of crime delay for anything from twenty minutes to one hour before they call the police.

If policing is not particularly successful as a response to crime, neither is the prison system. Here, too, the numbers involved have grown, though not dramatically, from 3,396 people in prison in 1971 to 3,611 in 1983. Three features of the Irish prison system have been identified in various studies (e.g. Council on Social Welfare 1983). The first is that the numbers who end up in prison are a relatively small proportion of the total number convicted in the courts; in 1981, 10,819 were proceeded against in court yet only about a quarter of these were sentenced to prison. The second is the length of sentence served by most prisoners. In 1981 76 per cent of adults in prison were serving sentences of less than one year (Annual Report on Prisons, 1981). It should be noted, however, that the average sentence has been increasing over the past few years. When this is combined with limited space in prison the current over-crowding is the result. The third feature is the high rate of recidivism. In 1981, two-thirds of male prisoners had a record of previous imprisonment and about 40 per cent had four or more previous periods in prison.

This feature would suggest that the experience of prison is limited as a deterrent to further crime. It could be argued that short sentences are the cause of limited deterrence. However, research (Brody 1976) from Britain and the United States suggests that longer sentences are no more effective than short ones. Other aspects of prison have been identified as the sources of recidivism. One is the low level of resources devoted to forms of education and counselling which might alter the offender's self-image and reduce his criminal motivation. Most of the resources of the Irish prison system are directed at keeping prisoners in rather than doing anything with them while they are there. However, even if resources were directed to this area its effectiveness is by no means guaranteed. Studies of prisoners have shown that they build up a defence system, a sub-culture, to protect themselves against the deprivations of the prison system. This sub-culture discourages and enforces sanctions against excessive co-operation and responsiveness to prison authorities.

The other major factor which accounts for the failure of prison in Ireland is that prisoners are released to the same crime-producing conditions that encouraged their criminal involvement in the first place. They are no better equipped, for example, with marketable skills, to survive this environment. The skills they leave prison with are the same criminal skills that they entered it with. Indeed, the extent of these skills may have been increased by contact in prison with more experienced criminals.

This leads to the third kind of response to crime — social policies designed to eradicate crime-producing conditions. A document by the Association of Garda Sergeants and Inspectors (AGSI 1982, p. 10) suggests that 'crime can only be prevented by a determined attack on the type of social, environmental and recreational conditions that encourage the development of criminal tendencies in the first place'. Such a determined attack has not emerged in the Republic. The distributive effects of most state policies favour the middle-class. Education is a good example. It is the major allocator of social position, a major factor in the mobility chances of individuals and a key influence on chances of obtaining employment. Yet the growth in the education system in the 1960s and 1970s is one from which the middle-class have been the main beneficiaries, allowing them to reproduce their range of advantages across generations (see Clancy, Chapter 6).

We should not be surprised at the failure to deal with crime-producing conditions. Redistributing resources to eradicate such conditions means taking from some other groups in the society. Redistribution is in this sense a zero-sum game. In Ireland we do not, as yet, understand why it is that the same side always seems to win. It may be that they are able to prevent changes in policy which would work out to their disadvantage. To understand the persistence of crime-producing conditions we must move beyond the conventional boundaries of crime to include the political sociology of the welfare state.

The necessity of crime

We are concerned about crime primarily because we see it as a threat to the social fabric, and as destructive of order in society. However, there is an argument in sociology which suggests that rather than being dysfunctional to society, crime in fact plays an integral part in social stability. This argument suggests that the failure of penal institutions like prison is not accidental. The dominant groups in society, it is argued, require the presence of a criminal population. Criminals perform the role of scapegoats. They are a resource which can be used to displace public concern from other issues and problems in the society. In other words crime is a useful ideological tool to arouse generalised public fear and mobilise support for the kind of society that is under threat. Is it accidental that the emergence of the fear of crime, and the political concern about it in Ireland, have coincided with the increased strains and tensions in a society that does not appear to have solutions to the many problems which it has generated? In that sense is the concern about crime a symptom of the social disintegration of a particular kind of society or a form of defence against it?

Notes

1   We also will not discuss political crime i.e. criminal acts committed by people who would claim political motivation. An adequate treatment would require a separate chapter.
2   The masculine pronoun is used consciously in this section, as most people convicted of crimes are male.

References

ASSOCIATION OF GARDA SERGEANTS AND INSPECTORS (AGSI) 1982. *A Discussion Paper containing Proposals for a System of Community Policing*, Dublin, AGSI.

BECKER, H. 1963. *Outsiders*, Glencoe, Free Press.

BILTON, T. *et. al.* 1981. *Introductory Sociology*, London, Macmillan.

BOX, S. 1971. *Deviance, Reality and Society*, London, Holt, Rinehart and Winston.

BRODY, S.R. 1976. *The Effectiveness of Sentencing*, London, HMSO.

BREEN, R. and ROTTMAN, D. 1985. *Crime Victimisation in the Republic of Ireland*, Dublin, Economic and Social Research Institute, Paper No. 121.

CLINARD, M. (ed.). 1964. *Anomie and Deviant Behaviour*, Glencoe, Free Press.

COHEN, A. 1966. *Deviance and Social Control*, Englewood Cliffs, NJ, Prentice Hall.

COUNCIL FOR SOCIAL WELFARE, 1983. *The Prison System*, Dublin.

DEPARTMENT OF JUSTICE, Various Years. *Annual Report on Prisons*, Dublin, Stationery Office.

MATZA, D. 1969. *Becoming Deviant*, Englewood Cliffs, NJ, Prentice Hall.

McCONVILLE, M. 1983. 'Search of Persons and Premises: New Data from London', *Criminal Law Review*, September, pp. 605-614.

McCULLAGH, C. 1983. 'The Limits of Policing', *Social Studies*, Vol. 7, No. 4, pp. 237-247.

MERTON, R. 1938. 'Social Structure and Anomie', *American Sociological Review*, Vol. 3. pp. 672-82.

O'SULLIVAN, D. 1977. 'The Administrative Processing of Children in Care: some Sociological findings', *Administration*, Vol. 25. pp. 413-434.

ROTTMAN, D. 1980. *Crime in the Republic of Ireland: Statistical Trends and their Interpretation*, Dublin, Economic and Social Research Institute, paper no. 102.

ROTTMAN, D. 1984. *The Criminal Justice System: Policy & Performance*, Dublin, National Economic and Social Council.

ROTTMAN, D. and P. O'CONNELL, 1983. 'The Changing Social Structure of Ireland', *Administration*, Vol. 30, Nos. 2 and 3, pp. 63-88.

TAYLOR, I., WALTON, P. and YOUNG, J. 1973. *The New Criminology*, London, Routledge and Kegan Paul.

WARR, M. 1980. 'The Accuracy of Public Beliefs about Crime', *Social Forces*, Vol. 59, No. 2, pp. 456-470.

YOUNG, J. 1975. 'Working-Class Criminology', in I. Taylor (ed) *Critical Criminology*, London, Routledge and Kegan Paul, pp. 63-91.

18
Urbanisation in the Republic of Ireland: A Conflict Approach

KIERAN McKEOWN

Urban sociology has been concerned traditionally in both the nineteenth and twentieth centuries with the effect upon cultural values and life styles of living in an urban environment. Concern with this issue has now diminished considerably, however, given that cultural values and life styles have been shown to vary quite independently of their rural or urban context. Urban sociology has also been concerned traditionally with the patterns of residential segregation of social groups in urban areas. This concern, which was initiated in the 1920s and continued until the 1960s, has also been waning in recent years and has been replaced by an emphasis on the processes and conflicts through which residential segregation is produced. Since the 1970s, therefore, urban sociology has changed its perspective considerably and has become more interested in the conflicts of interest which take place in the urban environment (see, for example, Pickvance 1976; Cox and Johnston 1982). It is this perspective which is adopted and applied here.

The conflict model of society, which ultimately originates in the writings of Karl Marx and Max Weber, views society as consisting of a number of actors (individuals, groups, organisations, classes, etc.) who pursue their perceived self-interest. In doing so, each actor, according to this model, is frequently constrained by other actors equally in pursuit of their perceived self-interest. Potential and actual conflicts, therefore, are a feature of much social interaction. This approach is used here to clarify some of the more important aspects of urbanisation in the Republic of Ireland.

Main characteristics of urbanisation in the Republic of Ireland

The earliest traces of urbanisation in Ireland (apart from the monastic settlements of Armagh, Downpatrick, Kells and Cashel) date from the ninth century when the Vikings established settlements at various coastal locations in what are now Dublin, Cork, Limerick, Waterford and Wexford. The process of urbanisation thus initiated was greatly increased after the arrival of the Normans in 1170. As well as revitalising the Viking towns, they established a widespread network of urban centres throughout the East (for example, Dundalk, Drogheda, Navan); the South East (for example, Carlow, Kilkenny, New Ross, Youghal, Clonmel, Cashel, Thurles); and to a lesser extent in the West (Galway, Sligo, Tuam, Roscrea). Finally, the colonial plantations of the sixteenth and seventeenth centuries laid the foundations of the urban system in the North of Ireland (Belfast, Derry, Armagh, Newry, Strabane). 'By 1700, therefore', writes Butlin (1977, pp. 97–98), 'the main elements of the urban system of Ireland had been established, and it is quite a remarkable and perhaps unique feature, in western European experience, that there has been little addition of towns to that system to the present day.'

Despite the establishment of a national network of towns by the eighteenth century, the proportion of the Irish population living in towns has remained remarkably low by comparison with other European countries. In 1981, the size of the urban population in the Republic of Ireland was 1.9 million or 55.6 per cent of the total population (see Table 1). The reason for this relatively low level of urbanisation is the continuous fall in

Table 1: **Population in towns and rural areas, 1841–1981**

Population	1841	1861	1881	1901	1926	1946	1966	1971	1981
Town population (thousands)[a]	1,100	986	932	911	959	1,161	1,419	1,556	1,915
Rural population (thousands)	5,429	3,416	2,938	2,311	2,013	1,794	1,465	1,423	1,529
Total (thousands)	6,529	4,402	3,870	3,222	2,972	2,955	2,884	2,979	3,444
Percentage of total:	%	%	%	%	%	%	%	%	%
In towns	16.8	22.4	24.1	28.3	32.3	39.3	49.2	52.1	55.6
In rural areas	83.2	77.6	75.9	71.7	67.7	60.7	50.8	47.9	44.4

Source: For 1841, *Census of Population of Ireland*, 1946, General Reports, Tables 1 and 4; for 1861, *Statistical Abstract of Ireland*, 1939, Table 9; for 1881–1946, *Statistical Abstract of Ireland*, 1964, Table 9; for 1966, *Census of Population of Ireland*, 1966, Vol. 1; for 1971, *Census of Population*, 1971, Vol. 1; for 1981, *Census of Population*, 1981, Vol. 1.

[a] The 'town' population is defined as all those persons living in towns with a population of 1,500 or more.

population between 1841 and 1961. Unlike many other western countries in this period, the urban population in the Republic of Ireland declined until 1926 when the recorded urban population was less than that in 1841. Since 1926 the urban population has increased slowly and continuously and since 1960 it has increased at a more accelerated rate.

Urban areas in the Republic of Ireland are small by comparison with other urbanised societies. Only two urban areas (Dublin/Dun Laoghaire and Cork) exceed 100,000 in population (see Table 2 below). Moreover the spatial distribution of the urban population is quite uneven. Half of the entire urban population resided in the Dublin/Dun Laoghaire area in 1981, while 80 per cent of the urban population resided in the five largest urban centres. (See Table 2).

The Dublin area holds a dominant position in the Irish urban system. In 1981 it was six times larger than the next largest city, Cork. Dublin has always had a dominant position in Irish society: it was the centre of British administration in Ireland and, at least between 1750 and 1850, it was 'the second city in the Empire'. This dominance was reinforced by the transportation network of roads and canals which were completed in the eighteenth century and by the railways network which was completed in the nineteenth century. The dominance of Dublin in the Republic of Ireland continues to this day because it remains the administrative centre of government, industry, finance, the media, the arts, the trade unions, specialised research and educational institutions and many voluntary agencies.

One of the consequences of the dominance of Dublin and of the East region generally is that, as Table 3 reveals, a large proportion of higher level professional, administrative and managerial jobs are available only in that area. As a consequence, the hierarchy of urban areas, based upon their size, acquires a marked class dimension in the sense that access to power, influence and well-paid jobs is crucially related to the size of the urban area in which one lives. In terms of the built environment, it has resulted in a continuing boom in office development in Dublin city since the early 1960s (see Jones, Lang, Wooton, 1980).

Table 2: **Rank size distribution 1951, 1961, 1971, 1981 — twenty largest centres**

Urban centre	Rank in 1951	1951	*Population size (including suburbs/environs)*		
			1961	1971[a]	1981
Dublin/Dun Laoghaire	1	634,472	663,389	801,298	915,115
Cork	2	112,009	115,689	135,456	149,792
Limerick	3	50,820	51,732	63,436	75,520
Waterford	4	28,691	28,216	34,837	41,861
Galway	5	21,316	23,700	29,767	39,636
Dundalk	6	19,678	21,228	23,963	29,135
Drogheda	7	16,779	17,085	20,450	23,615
Sligo	8	13,529	13,145	15,895	23,358
Bray	9	12,062	12,615	14,583	18,002
Wexford	10	11,979	12,247	13,474	17,035
Tralee	11	11,045	12,081	13,420	16,886
Kilkenny	12	10,572	11,423	13,355	15,364
Clonmel	13	10,471	11,087	12,506	14,808
Athlone	14	9,015	10,727	11,822	14,640
Carlow	15	7,667	8,920	11,203	14,426
Killarney	16	6,298	8,410	10,429	13,164
Thurles	17	6,276	Mullingar 7,442	9,360 Lucan	11,763
Ballina	18	6,220[b]	6,825	7,635[b]	11,703
Tullamore	19	6,165[b]	Tullamore 6,642[b]	7,506[b] Swords	11,138
Ennis	20	6,097	Enniscorthy 6,251[b]	Cobh 7,141[b]	Navan 11,136

Notes:

[a] Population as revised in *Census of Population of Ireland*, Vol. 1, Table 13.

[b] Indicates towns which were relegated from Top 20 in subsequent Census.

Source: *Census of Population of Ireland* 1951, 1961 and 1981 (Vol. 1), Dublin, Stationery Office; from: Bannon, 1983, p. 270.

Table 3: **Miscellaneous measures of concentration in the east region**

Organisations	Total Number in state	Percentage in east region
Headquarters offices of:		
Central Government Departments	17	100
Embassies accredited to Ireland	22	100
State-sponsored bodies	87	86
Commercial state bodies	20	90
Trade, professional and other organisations	503	93
Trade unions	65	93
Largest public quoted companies	50	90
Banking institutions	41	95
Hire purchase firms	41	71
Insurance companies	31	100
Publishing companies	47	89
Advertising agencies	36	97
Full-time university students 1974/75	19,709	64
General service grades in civil service of principal officer level or above, 1976	341	100
Office employees 1971	170,000	59

Source: Bannon 1984, p. 251.

Urbanisation in the Republic of Ireland, despite its unique features, shares two important characteristics with many other urbanised societies. Firstly there has been a continuous decline, over a number of decades, in the size of the population residing in the inner parts of the five largest cities. The population of the inner city of Dublin, that is, the area bounded by the Royal Canal to the north and the Grand Canal to the south, has declined continuously from 1926 to the present. Similarly the inner areas of Cork, Limerick, Waterford and Galway continue to lose population (see Bannon, Eustace and O'Neill, 1981, p. 46ff). Moreover many of those who continue to reside in the inner cities are among the poorest in Irish society; they live mostly in rented dwellings, many of which are in a deteriorated condition and they are more likely to be unemployed.

The second characteristic is the major expansion of suburban development in areas contiguous to these cities. These suburban developments take the form of 'housing estates' and 'one-off houses'. In 1981, 48 per cent of all private new houses in the Republic of Ireland were built in housing estates while 32 per cent were one-off houses; the remaining 20 per cent were built by local authorities (*Department of the Environment* 1983, p. 20; 1984, p. 1a). This rapid suburban development has itself contributed to the decline of inner city residential areas because, until the mid-1970s, the bulk of all private and state investment, not only in housing, but also in retailing (see Parker 1979, 1982) was in the suburban areas. Even in the 1980s there is virtually no private investment in housing in the inner parts of the major cities of the Republic of Ireland.

With this background, it is possible to examine in greater detail the process by which urbanisation is physically expressed in the production of buildings and infrastructure.

The production of urban areas

The process by which the urban environment is produced is called property development. This process takes place through interaction between various and sometimes competing actors, each actor representing an identifiably different interest. The main actors are: developers (both private and state), landowners, the planning authority, and environmental groups. In the Republic of Ireland, the state is involved in property development through financing the production of infrastructural facilities such as roads, railways, water, sewage, electricity as well as schools, hospitals, public housing and landscaped open spaces, all of which accounted for about 75 per cent of total construction output in 1982 (see *Department of the Environment* 1983, p. 57). Private developers, by contrast, produce mostly buildings — offices, factories, houses, shops, etc. — and this accounted for about 25 per cent of total construction output in 1982 (*ibid*).

All planning and development in the Republic of Ireland takes place within the legal framework established by the Local Government (Planning and Development) Acts, 1963 to 1983. Under this law, the eighty-seven local authorities in the Republic are obliged to make a development plan indicating the location and type of developments which they will permit within their jurisdiction. This plan is put into effect by the investment decisions of the local authority itself, as well as by private developers who must receive planning permission from the local authority before they can undertake any development.

This apparently straightforward process contains numerous strains and conflicts for the various actors involved. By way of illustration, the present analysis will focus upon the constraints facing private developers, landowners and the local authority, as each attempts to pursue its interest in the development process.

The private developer, whose interest is in making a profit, is constrained by, and hence is in conflict with, the local planning authority because of the costs of making a planning application (for example, the cost of ascertaining the requirements likely to prove acceptable); the delay in obtaining a decision; and, in the event of permission being granted, the conditions which may be attached to it. Indeed the developer may be refused planning permission, as occurred in 15 per cent of all planning applications in the Republic of Ireland in 1981 (see *Department of Environment* 1982, p. 78). The net effect of these constraints is to increase the costs incurred by the developer.

The private developer may also be constrained by landowners, that is, those who own vacant land as well as those who own land occupied by a house, a shop, a factory, etc. Conflict between developers and landowners can occur in two ways. On the one hand it can occur if landowners refuse to sell their land except at an extortionate price, i.e., above the price set in a competitive market. This possibility arises if the developer is in the process of assembling a number of different sites, each of which is essential to a development project, but is hindered by one landowner who demands a price which reflects the redeveloped rather than the existing value of the site. This is known as 'price gouging' (Davis and Whinston 1961, p. 11) and is more likely to occur in an older part of the city which is undergoing a change of use (for example, from residential to office use). On the other hand, developers can be constrained if the landowners in an area (for example, owner-occupier residents living near to a proposed site for office or factory development) organise to oppose a development. This may cause a delay or even a cancellation of the proposed development and hence a thwarting of the developer's interests.

Finally the developer may be constrained by environmental groups, such as An Taisce, whose actions may cause the developer's planning application to be delayed or even refused. In addition they may cause the developer, through the planning authority, to incur extra costs in preserving or improving the amenities affected by their development (see Grist 1983, p. 42).

Landowners, too, may be in conflict with other actors in the development process. They may be in conflict, for example, with private or state property developers if a proposed development would reduce the value of their land or property. An example of this would be the development of a factory, an airport, a motorway or a dump close to a residential area. Conversely a development may increase land values in its vicinity, in which case the interest of the landowner would be advanced simultaneously with that of the developer.

Landowners may also be constrained by the local planning authority through 'planning blight'. This can occur when a planning authority has long-term plans for an area (for example, road proposals) which cause land and property values in an area to fall as soon as the plans become public knowledge. Moreover they may continue to fall even if the plans are subsequently withdrawn, as long as any suspicion remains that the plans may ultimately be implemented. This phenomenon of 'planning blight' is, for example, one of the main reasons for the deteriorated condition of many of the buildings on both sides of the river Liffey in central Dublin.

Despite these constraints landowners, particularly those who own tracts of open agricultural land near expanding urban areas, are a particularly privileged group in the Republic of Ireland. Their land appreciates greatly in value as a result of the combined effects of proximity to urban development and infra-structural investment by the state. In 1980, for example, the price of an acre of land for private residential development in the Dublin area, at £49,000, was roughly 33 times greater than the price of an acre of agricultural land, at £1,500, (see Convery and Schmid 1983, Tables 7 and 9, pp. 144–146). In the Republic of Ireland such windfall gains are liable for tax under capital gains tax (in the case of individuals) or corporation tax (in the case of companies). However, the actual amount of tax which is payable is very small in relation to the windfall gains which are made (*ibid.* pp. 141–150 and pp. 179–195). This fact may help explain why local politicians whose constituencies are located at the periphery of large and expanding urban areas are frequently under considerable pressure to rezone land from agricultural to residential use (see Komito 1983). Thus, although landowners are not systematically organised as a class, their interests are strongly protected in law and ultimately in the constitution (see Lyall 1983). Moreover, various policy recommendations, such as those contained in the 'Kenny Report' (Committee on the Price of Building Land 1973), which proposed to restrict the in-terests of landowners, have never been implemented.

Finally, the local authority itself is frequently constrained from pursuing its interest in the development process. In par-ticular it is constrained by a combination of lack of finance (owing to the abolition of domestic property taxes — 'rates' — in 1977) and the rights of landowners to receive compensation. For example, landowners are entitled to compensation if they are re-fused permission to change the use of their land (for example, from agricultural to residential) although they are not entitled to compensation if they are refused permission to change the use of their buildings (for example, from residential to office). (See Walsh 1979, Ch. 12; see also Jennings and Grist 1983). The consequence of this is that local authorities are sometimes severely constrained in their attempts to maintain amenity areas, open spaces and agricultural land in the vicinity of urban areas. The result is that planning is frequently constrained into conformity with the laws of the market and the quality of the urban environment is thereby frequently impaired.

In addition, the local authority may be constrained internally because of its own organisational structure. This is because the local authority is made up of a number of different departments with officers from different professions (architects, planners, engineers, etc.); politicians from different levels of government (local councillors and the Minister for the Environment); as well as an independently appointed appeals board (An Bord Pleanála). The interests of these various groups may be quite different and may lead to contradictory land-use decisions. This has occurred in a number of cases in the Republic of Ireland where local councillors (possibly owing to representations from landowners in their constituency) have used their statutory powers to effect land-use decisions which are entirely at variance with the decisions of the officers in the planning authority (see Komito 1983). Similarly, An Bord Pleanála sometimes reverses the decisions of the manager of the local authority on legal grounds (for example, where the manager's decision was based upon an invalid reason so as to avoid a compensation claim) but also on substantive grounds (for example, where the Bord allows a land-use which is contrary to the local authority's development plan). In 1980, An Bord Pleanála reversed 30 per cent of the decisions of the local authority, varied 17 per cent of them and confirmed 53 per cent of them (An Bord Pleanála 1981, p. 4).

The process of urban development in the Republic of Ireland, as the above analysis reveals, is thus replete with conflicts of interest between the various actors involved. These conflicts,

Table 4: **The constraints and conflicts of the development process in the Republic of Ireland**

		Constraints imposed by actors in the development process		
	Private Developer	Landowners	Local Planning Authority	Environmental Groups
Private developer		(1) Price gouging (2) Collective action to thwart a development	(1) Costs of making an application (2) Delays (3) Costly conditions (4) Possible refusal of permission	(1) Cause delay or refusal of planning permission (2) Cause amenities to be preserved or improved
Landowners	(1) A development may reduce the value of adjacent land and property		(1) Possible refusal of planning permission (2) 'Planning blight'	
The local planning authority		(1) Landowners may be entitled to compensation	(1) The interests of the different sections involved in planning may diverge.	

which are briefly summarised in matrix form in Table 4, are not unique to the Republic of Ireland: they are in fact typical of any society where there are competing and conflicting interests in relation to the built environment.

Consumption of urban areas

It is necessary finally to consider some of the issues and problems which arise from the consumption of urban areas in the Republic of Ireland. Urban areas — viewed as a spatial concentration of property — are consumed because they are used to produce goods and services (for example, factories, offices and shops) and because they are used for final consumption (for example, houses, parks, churches, theatres, pubs and art galleries). In most urban areas housing constitutes the single largest user of land and thus represents one of the most important ways in which the urban area is consumed. Housing, therefore, will be the main focus of analysis in this part of the chapter, although a fuller treatment would require a similar analysis of the conflicts associated with the consumption of other types of property, notably commercial and industrial.

In the Republic of Ireland there are approximately one million dwellings — 90 per cent of which are houses and 10 per cent of which are flats — with an average household size of 3.66 persons (*Department of the Environment* 1983, p. 29). Of these one million dwellings, 77 per cent are owner occupied, 12 per cent are rented from the local authority and 11 per cent are rented privately (*ibid.* p. 30). This tenure structure is distinctive in that the percentage of owner dwellings in the Republic of Ireland is higher than in any other European country or the United States.

Urban sociologists usually refer to these tenure groups as 'housing classes' because each has a different material interest in relation to their dwelling (see Rex and Moore 1967; Saunders 1980, ch. 2). In the Republic of Ireland, for example, each class receives different subventions from the state: owner occupiers receive a cash grant and a mortgage subsidy (in the case of first time buyers) as well as tax exemption on mortgage interest, while local authority tenants receive direct subventions in the form of subsidised rents. Tenants in the private rented sector, by contrast, receive no state subventions (see, for example, Baker and O'Brien 1979).[1] The material interests of these housing classes is also different because each is affected differently by changing property values: rising property values increase rent levels in the private rented sector, other things being equal, while they provide a tax-free capital gain for owner occupiers. Moreover, every tenant is primarily concerned with rent levels while owner occupiers with mortgages are more concerned with interest rates. In addition, as Table 5 below shows, there is considerable variation between housing classes in the percentage of household expenditure devoted to housing expenses.

These differences in material interest have led, in the case of local authority tenants, to class-based action through the National Association of Tenants' Organisations (NATO) which has campaigned effectively against rent increases in the past. Private sector tenants, by contrast, are largely disorganised as a housing class, possibly because of the high rate of turnover within this class. Owner occupiers, too, are not formally organised as a class although some of them were organised in a fragmentary way to campaign for the abolition of ground rents. The main reason why owner occupiers are not formally organ-

Table 5: **Percentage distribution of household expenditure on housing by tenure group (urban areas)**

Household tenure	1977	1978	1979	1980
Owned outright	7.3	2.9	3.3	2.6
Owned with mortgage	11.0	9.8	9.5	10.5
Rented from local authority	5.4	4.7	5.1	5.5
Rented from private owner	11.8	10.3	12.3	12.6
Rent-free	0.5	0.2	2.2	0.8

From: *Department of the Environment* 1983, p. 33.

ised as a class is that their interests are already enshrined and protected in the policies of all the major political parties. The size of the owner occupier class, coupled with the widespread commitment to the idea and the reality of private property in Irish society, has ensured that their interests have never been seriously threatened, despite repeated recommendations by policy advisers (see, for example, Blackwell 1977).

The importance of consuming housing derives not only from the fact that it is the place in which many other activities occur (eating, sleeping, recreation, procreation, etc.) but also because its location determines one's distance from work, schools, landscaped open spaces, clean air, public transport, shops, nurseries and play areas, as well as from air pollution, crime, noise, traffic hazards, dumps, etc. In other words, the location of one's home determines access to the many elements of consumption, both positive and negative, which are located within the city.

With the exception of local authority housing, access to housing, and hence to a particular neighbourhood, is through the market; the house and neighbourhood in which people live, therefore, reflects what they can afford rather than what they necessarily prefer. It is in this sense that the variation between neighbourhoods in cities visibly and systematically reflects the class hierarchy of that city. As a consequence, one's address becomes an indicator of one's class position and can operate to one's advantage or disadvantage. In the case of Dublin, numerous studies have shown that there are systematic variations between neighbourhoods and in the quality of their environment (see Brady and Parker 1975; Hourican 1978; Bannon, Eustace and O'Neill 1981).

The existence of separate neighbourhoods, inhabited by residents of similar income and tenure, and visually demarcated from each other by roads, railway lines, walls, trees or open spaces, provides the context for understanding some of the conflicts which typically arise in urban areas in the Republic of Ireland. Conflicts may occur when the residents perceive that their neighbourhood is threatened in some way, for example, by crime, pollution, stigma, noise, planning blight, dereliction, traffic congestion, poor street-lighting, etc. Faced with this situation, residents have a choice to stay or leave; to protest or remain silent. The full range of options, based upon a modification of Hirschman's model (1970), can be outlined as follows:

Table 6: **The options facing residents when confronted with a threat to their neighbourhood**

	Silence	*Protest*
Stay	(1) Acceptance of fate	(3) Protest in the area
Leave	(2) Leave quietly	(4) Protest in exile

Leaving aside option 4 (which is more appropriate to cases such as political refugees), residents may do nothing at all (option 1), leave the area (option 2), or engage in protest (option 3). In the Republic of Ireland in recent years there have been numerous examples of protests in urban areas where residents' associations and vigilante groups have taken action to protect their area from road proposals, travellers, industrial dumps, drug pushers, traffic hazards, etc. These actions, based upon what residents perceive as the protection of their material interests, frequently have a political dimension, since the local authority plays a central role in determining the location of various land uses and users. Moreover, since land uses and users are so spatially contiguous and interdependent in the urban context, it is inevitable that conflicts like this will arise over the consumption of the built environment.

Conclusion

This chapter has highlighted some of the salient features of urbanisation in the Republic of Ireland as well as some of the typical conflicts which arise in the production and consumption of its urban areas. The approach which was adopted is different from that which has prevailed until recently in urban sociology, because it has focussed upon the conflicts of interest which typically occur in the built environment in capitalist societies. In the future, urban conflicts in the Republic of Ireland seem likely to persist and, with population growth continuing throughout the 1980s, they may even intensify as the pressure for new urban development and the competition for desirable homes and neighbourhoods increases.

Notes

1   According to the Finance Act of 1985 persons over 55 years of age living in private rented accommodation are entitled to tax relief on the following terms: married couples receive tax relief on rent up to a maximum of £1,500 per annum, while a single person gets tax relief, up to a maximum of £750 per annum.

References

AN BORD PLEANÁLA 1981. *Annual Report and Accounts 1980*, Dublin, An Bord Pleanála.

BAKER, T. J. and L. M. O'BRIEN 1979. *The Irish Housing System: A Critical Overview*, Dublin, Economic and Social Research Institute.

BANNON, M. J. 1983. 'Urbanisation in Ireland: Growth and Regulation' in J. Blackwell and F. Convery (eds.) *Promise and Performance: Irish Environmental Policies Analysed*, Dublin, Resource and Environmental Policy Centre, University College, Dublin, pp. 261–285.

BANNON, M. J. 1984. 'The Irish National Settlement System' in L. S. Bourne, R. Sinclair, K. Dziewonski (eds.), *Urbanisation and Settlement Systems: International Perspectives*, Oxford, Oxford University Press, pp. 239–260.

BANNON, J. J., J. G. EUSTACE, M. O'NEILL 1981. *Urbanisation:*

Problems of Growth and Decay in Dublin, National Economic and Social Council, Report No. 55, Dublin, Stationery Office.

BLACKWELL, J. 1977. *Report on Housing Subsidies*, National Economic and Social Council, Report No. 23, Dublin, Stationery Office.

BRADY, J. and A. J. PARKER 1975. 'The Factorial Ecology of Dublin: A Preliminary Investigation', *Economic and Social Review*, Vol. 7, No. 1, pp. 35–53.

BUTLIN, R. A. 1977. 'Irish Towns in the Sixteenth and Seventeenth Centuries' in R. A. Butlin (ed.), *The Development of the Irish Town*, London, Croom Helm, pp. 61–100.

COMMITTEE ON THE PRICE OF BUILDING LAND 1973. *Report to the Minister for Local Government*, Dublin, Stationery Office.

CONVERY, F. J. and A. A. SCHMID 1983. *Policy Aspects of*

Land-Use Planning in Ireland, Dublin, Economic and Social Research Institute, Broadsheet No. 22.

COX, K. R. and R. J. JOHNSTON (eds.) 1982. *Conflict, Politics and the Urban Scene*, London, Longman.

DAVIS, O. A. and A. B. WHINSTON 1961. 'The Economics of Urban Renewal', *Law and Contemporary Problems*, Vol. 26, Winter, pp. 105–117.

DEPARTMENT OF THE ENVIRONMENT 1982. *Development Control: Advice and Guidelines*, Dublin, Department of the Environment.

DEPARTMENT OF THE ENVIRONMENT 1983. *The Human Settlements Situation and Related Trends and Policies: Ireland 1983*, Dublin, Department of the Environment.

DEPARTMENT OF THE ENVIRONMENT 1984. *Annual Bulletin of Housing Statistics, Incorporating the Quarterly Bulletin for Quarter Ended 31st December 1983*, Dublin, Department of the Environment.

GRIST, B. 1983. *Twenty Years of Planning: A Review of the System since 1963*, Dublin, An Foras Forbartha.

HIRSCHMAN, A. O. 1970. *Exit, Voice and Loyalty: Responses to Decline in Firms, Organisations and States*, Cambridge, Harvard University Press.

HOURICAN, K. 1978. 'Social Areas in Dublin', *Economic and Social Review*, Vol. 9, No. 4, pp. 301–318.

JENNINGS, R. and B. GRIST 1983. 'The Problem with Building Land', *Administration*, Vol. 31, No. 3, pp. 257–283.

JONES, LANG, WOOTON 1980. *Report on Dublin Office Property*, Dublin.

KOMITO, L. 1983. 'Development Plan Rezonings: The Political Pressures' in J. Blackwell and F. Convery (eds.), *Promise and Performance: Irish Environmental Policies Analysed*, Dublin, Resource and Environmental Policy Centre, University College, pp. 293–301.

LYALL, A. 1983. 'The Public Welfare and Rights to Private Property', in J. Blackwell and F. Convery (eds.), *Promise and Performance: Irish Environmental Policies Analysed*, Dublin, Resource and Environmental Policy Centre, University College Dublin, pp. 287–292.

PARKER, A. 1979. 'Retail Planning in Ireland' in R. L. Davies (ed.), *Retail Planning in the European Community*, London, Saxon House, pp. 177–202.

PARKER, 1982. 'The Development of Planned Shopping Centres in the Republic of Ireland', *Retail and Distribution Management*, Vol. 10, No. 2, pp. 25–29.

PICKVANCE, C. G. (ed.) 1976. *Urban Sociology: Critical Essays*, London, Tavistock Publications.

REX, J. and R. MOORE 1967. *Race, Community and Conflict: A Study of Sparkbrook*, Oxford, Oxford University Press.

SAUNDERS, P. 1980. *Urban Politics: A Sociological Interpretation*, Middlesex, Penguin Books.

WALSH, E. M. 1979. *Planning and Development Law*, Dublin, Incorporated Law Society of Ireland.

19
'You get on better with your own': Social Continuity and Change in Rural Northern Ireland

HASTINGS DONNAN and GRAHAM McFARLANE

Like all folk truisms, the comment 'you get on better with your own' is deceptive as well as suggestive: while it suggests a starting point for analysis, when uttered it can only hint at the identity of 'your own'. It will become apparent that 'your own' is a highly contextual notion, which refers to different sets of social relationships and identities. Were one to view Northern Ireland too casually, one would assume that people's 'own' are their co-religionists: fellow Catholics or fellow Protestants. However, less casual research would indicate that while these identities are indeed very important in ordering social life, they coexist with other identities (other versions of 'your own') which accompany and which, at different times and in different contexts, may qualify the importance of attachment to the Catholic or Protestant blocs. Moreover, the saying 'you get on better with your own' cannot say anything about change and continuity; about how the importance attached to different sets of relationships can vary over time in response to general processes of economic and political change in rural Northern Ireland.

To deal with these issues we will attempt to establish what the category 'your own' represents in a variety of contexts in the day to day life of the countryside. We will show that 'your own' may refer to a number of overlapping groups. At the same time we will indicate how the cultural significance of these groups has changed in response to broader social, economic and political forces impinging on rural life over the last thirty years. The time scale of thirty years has been chosen simply because it is the period over which detailed social anthropological work in the countryside has been undertaken.

The following analysis derives essentially from work carried out over this period. For convenience we have set out the time and location of different pieces of research in an Appendix, and have also indicated there the writers associated with each community. The time-honoured anthropological tradition of maintaining at least a semblance of secrecy about the precise location of research sites precludes using a map, and necessitates retaining the pseudonyms which anthropologists have created for the villages and farming townlands in which they have worked.

So, who are 'your own'? 'Your own' refers to the domains of kinship, politico-religious affiliation, locality and class.

'Your own' as family and kin

It is quite clear that kinship orders large areas of social life in the countryside. 'Your own' are your family and your relations, a network of kinship relationships which radiates outwards from oneself. Such ties are traced out on both the father's side and the mother's side and for many the importance attached to each side of the network is about equal. However, in areas where the economic infrastructure is in local hands, it seems that greater importance is attached to those people who share the same name (i.e. patrinominal kin) and this is especially the case among the owners of small businesses and farm owners — people who are most concerned with inheritance (see Leyton 1970, 1975). In other areas, where kinship is more separated from the economic infrastructure, it seems that 'name' is not as important as frequency of contact for defining the most important part of the kinship network. Here, there is a marked emphasis on kinship links traced on the mother's side, through her sisters and her mother.

Either way, one can make generalisations about the overall importance attached to close kinship: among one's close kin and family one should ideally find harmony, trust, confidentiality and support. 'You get on better with them', at least in principle. Of course, everyone knows that kinship ties are as likely to be strained as any other kind of relationship, but it is presumed that there is an intrinsic positive value attached to such relationships which is not built into other relationships. This intrinsic value is supported by everyday practices. Usually disputes among kin tend to remain on an individual level, and to be settled fairly easily (see Leyton 1966). Generally, people do not gossip about their relatives with, say neighbours, nor betray family secrets (since one's own reputation will rise and fall with theirs). While neighbours and even friends, are a potential drain on reputations, kinsfolk safeguard reputation. Also among kin the exchange of such 'items' as information, practical aid and gifts does not have to be strictly balanced.

Of course, other non-kinship relationships may share some of these positive elements, although not perhaps in such a clear-cut way. Leyton (1974b, 1975) reports that in Aughnaboy there are two distinct sets of ideas about such relationships: there is an anti-kinship/pro-friendship ideology and a pro-kinship/anti-friendship ideology. The first is sustained by the middle-class élite and the young in general, while the second is supported by the adult 'masses'. However, unless Aughnaboy is unique in rural Northern Ireland, Leyton has distinguished too sharply between kinsfolk and non-kin friends. For other researchers the relative stress on different kinds of relationship is a matter of degree; other things being equal, kinship relations will be simply stressed above, rather than against, other kinds of relationships.

Close kin and family members appear in the literature as important for many sorts of practical aid. When kin are available it is they who are regarded as the most important reservoir of aid for such things as baby-sitting and home decorating (see Blacking *et al.* 1978). This type of help is most important for village women. Even in the non-domestic economy, kin ties of all sorts provide an informal source of information about jobs, whether in the formal or the hidden economy (the importance of the latter seems to be increasing as the unemployed increase in numbers in rural areas as well as in urban areas). Moreover, despite the widely held belief that kinship and business do not mix (see Bell 1978), kin ties are often important in establishing new businesses (Leyton 1975) and new ventures in farm purchases and amalgamation (see Bufwack 1982, ch. 5). Even if the welfare state has assumed some of the supportive functions of kinship relations, it seems that in practical affairs for many people it is still kinsmen who figure most prominently, all things being equal.

Of course, all things are rarely equal, and ties of kinship might not invariably be sources of economic benefit. As general levels of cooperation in agricultural work have declined, the sharing of machinery has increasingly taken its place. Here, neighbours are more likely than kin to be involved in sharing arrangements. Further, Leyton makes the valid point that where ties of kinship cross a class divide, then there are barriers to sharing. In Aughnaboy the local business élite find it expedient to distance themselves from their economically less successful kinsfolk to prevent them making demands for jobs. They justify this by the maxim that kinship and business do not mix and by appealing to the superior claims of friendship (see above). Admittedly, this distancing of kin seems to have been applicable only to more distant kin (cousins, etc.) and does not seem to have included family members, but the case does alert us to the importance of class or status considerations in the realm of kinship. In rural Northern Ireland, as elsewhere in Europe, the socially mobile do not really have a great deal of time for their poorer cousins (sometimes they do not even have time for their poorer siblings). As Bufwack puts it, rather starkly, 'kinship bonds appear subordinate to class distinctions when the two come into conflict' (1982, p. 117).

However, it would be a distortion to discuss the importance of

kinship solely in relation to economic rationality or practical-
ities. Kinship relations are also vital in relation to life outside
work in its broadest sense. In one's time away from work at home
or outside home, kinship links are important. This seems to hold
true irrespective of time and place and seems to be the case not
only for the 'big' occasions in people's lives — life cycle occasions
such as baptisms, marriages and funerals — but for everyday
sociability as well. Certainly the life cycle events are principally
the concern of kin even though certain sorts of non-kin may also
be expected to attend. This pattern seems to have changed little
since Harris carried out her study of Ballybeg thirty years ago
and indeed a similar pattern has been reported for the four
communities studied by Blacking *et al.* in the seventies (1978, p.
28–31). A similar continuity in the importance of kinship
connections is apparent in day to day activities as well. Harris
tells us that in Ballybeg kinship played an important part in who
could and who could not be visited informally (1972, p. 144),
and this has been emphasised by almost every writer since (see
Blacking *et al.* 1978, p. 25–26; Leyton 1974b, 1975, ch. 4 and 5;
McFarlane 1978, p. 199). Even as increased geographical
distance between close kin prevents easy, direct contact, for
virtually all sections of the rural population it is regarded as
being vital to visit or somehow maintain contact at least with
'close' kin. Each Sunday, rural Northern Ireland is criss-crossed
by car loads and bus loads of people visiting kin.

  The other sense in which all things may not be equal is when
kinship relations cross the 'religious' divide. The only serious research done in this area was carried out by Blacking *et al.* in four
communities in the seventies. From the limited evidence, it
seems that in both the realm of economic cooperation and
socialising, difference in religious affiliation, Catholic or Protestant, does have a subtle constraining force on relationships.
Nevertheless, it must be stressed that religious difference does
not preclude cooperation and visiting among kin. It simply adds
to the possible sources of distance among kin. Kin who are not
co-religionists are problematic because kin should be of the
'same sort'; 'your own' kin should be 'your own' in politico-

religious terms, and prohibitions against mixed marriage are meant to support this idea (see Harris 1972, McFarlane 1979). This brings us to the Catholic and Protestant division.

'Your own' as a politico-religious category

It would hardly be surprising to be told that 'getting on better with your own' refers as much to religious and political as to kinship networks in rural Northern Ireland, as in Northern Ireland as a whole. A huge amount of social science literature has sought to account for the emergence and the reproduction of the Catholic/Nationalist, Protestant/Unionist dichotomy over time. Rural studies have carved a specific niche here, looking in detail at the domains of life where 'your own' defined in politico-religious terms is important, and investigating the various features of day to day life which serve not only to maintain this importance, but also to counteract its negative charge. Such studies have seemed to suggest that in general the degree of everyday separation of Catholic and Protestant is not as pronounced in the small towns and villages of the countryside as it is in working-class urban areas. They have also seemed to suggest that being a Catholic or a Protestant is not as important a consideration for certain activities like visiting or attending marriages and funerals, as it is for events which take place in more public arenas. Elsewhere we have warned that such generalisations can be deceptive and we have pointed out that the picture is complicated by a number of factors; there are almost always obvious exceptions to any generalisation about Northern Ireland; there exists considerable variation in the features of communities not only over space but also through time; and there are even contradictory findings in the literature (see Donnan and McFarlane 1983). Yet despite such complexity, it is possible to provide a broad outline of the culture of sectarianism in rural Northern Ireland and to indicate briefly the areas in which one 'gets on better' with one's co-religionists.

While it would be clearly important to unravel the ideas which people have about the political and religious components in the division between Catholics and Protestants (and doubtless we would find a wide range of opinions in rural Northern Ireland), unfortunately we do not have much detailed information on how groupings are conceptualised as units. Nevertheless, we do have more detail about the nature of the stereotyping which is, in the countryside especially, remarkably resilient. The list of characteristics attributed to the 'other sort' in Tyrone in the fifties (see Harris 1972, ch. 8) are virtually identical to those recorded by Blacking *et al.* (1978) in four different parts of the province in the 1970s. Protestants contrast their industriousness, cleanliness, loyalty to the state and freedom of religious expression with Catholic laziness, scruffiness, treachery, clannishness and priest domination. Catholics contrast Protestant bigotry, narrow-mindedness, discrimination and money-centredness with their own tolerance, openness, and interest in 'culture'.

So, many of the images seem to have remained unchanged, despite all attempts to show them up as distortions. It is obviously not only in the realm of attitudes that the dichotomy between Catholics and Protestants lies; in various domains of life the division lives in practice. In rural Northern Ireland, as elsewhere in the province, political aspirations can eventually be reduced to the basic question of support for the Union, and the boundaries between Nationalist or Republican and Loyalist or Unionist coincide with the religious boundary between Catholic and Protestant. Support for local businesses can follow these lines with each side patronising their own shops, agricultural suppliers and other service industries, although here there is considerable complexity, with price differentials, variation in the local availability of goods and lack of local choice entering into the equation.

In the private domain of people's lives there are barriers to communication and integration. In the field of recreation, the importance of Church-based activities, especially for women, remains little changed from the time of the earliest rural studies, and this fact alone militates against easy 'mixing' of Catholic and Protestant (see Harris 1972, Mogey 1947, p. 202). The different kinds of Church halls (and village halls) have become 'no go' areas for those of the other 'sort'. Public houses tend to have attachments to one side or another, although here it is much less easy to generalise and the differential class composition of the clientele of different bars is likely to be as sharply drawn as that based on religion.

It is marriage which links the private affairs of rural people most directly to the political domain. Though for some Protestants 'mixed' marriages as a category includes inter-denominational marriages, the idea of 'mixed' marriages is most meaningfully discussed in the context of the Catholic/Protestant divide. These marriages are both private and political (see McFarlane 1979) and the social rule which prohibits them has been fundamental for a long time and remains so today (for a somewhat controversial exception to this statement, see Buckley 1982, p. 64). For many writers, this lack of marriage across the divide and the lack of kinship ties which follow are two of the key factors which perpetuate the notion of there being two distinct sets of people labelled as 'your own'.

The more secular voluntary associations, even those designed to cross the sectarian divide, find it difficult to compete with the forces of sectarianism, especially because they represent mainly the more middle-class and élite members of communities. Meanwhile, the occasional close relationships across the divide are insufficient in number to counter-balance completely the importance of 'your own' defined in politico-religious terms. Nevertheless, most areas in rural Northern Ireland have managed to maintain a kind of *modus vivendi* which encourages people to play down the division in day to day interactions.

In all but the closest Protestant-Catholic interactions, the highly formalised process of saying nothing about the division of interest still lives on. The boundary between Catholic and Protestant is defined as much by silence as by argument. Meanwhile, interaction with strangers still depends on a process of 'telling' (i.e. identifying) the attachments of the other. One could argue that there has been a subtle shift into another code here over the last fifteen years or so. As the 'troubles' have de-

veloped again, so the norm which constrains people to say nothing about the situation has been supplemented by other, conflicting, norms. In the seventies, a norm emerged which asserted
that when confronted with violent deeds one should comment
upon them. In many small interactions, the politics of outrage
played out in the media were also present: if one's 'own' had
carried out the act, and one is talking to someone who is not of
one's 'own', then one should be volubly outraged. If one of the
'other sort' carried out the deed, then one is not only outraged,
but also expects outrage from their fellows.

So 'telling', silence and voluble outrage all serve to evidence
the dichotomy between 'your own' and the 'other sort'. Not only
that, these processes serve to reinforce the dichotomy. However,
a debate does open up here. Does the 'telling', the silence and
the voluble outrage indicate a desire to maintain reasonable relationships, or are they a consequence of fear (the former point of
view is taken by Harris (1972), the latter by Larsen (1982))? In
other words, are they an indicator of a deep-seated integration
between Catholic and Protestant, or are they a superficial
veneer of good relations? The social anthropological image of
rural Northern Ireland tends to crystallise towards the former
point of view: every community is presented as having a degree
of integration in spite of division. For some, the integrative
forces are in some kind of precarious balance (see Harris,
Larsen, Leyton); for others the positive, integrative forces seem
to outweigh the negative forces (see especially Buckley and
Bufwack). That some writers have emphasised integration more
than others may be partly due to wishful thinking, or alternatively to the choice of fieldwork locations (few anthropologists
are likely to wish to research in areas with high levels of violence). It may even be due to differences in the amount of
communal violence — differences which may be influenced in
turn by the date of the study, the demographic balance between
Catholic and Protestant and the local history of communal
division.

However the 'integration' image was concocted, and no
matter how much of it measures up to empirical reality and how

much of it reflects ideological concerns, the image does correspond with the imagery presented by most of the people interviewed in rural communities. While people do refer to a 'community' of Catholics and a 'community' of Protestants in the context of Northern Ireland society as a whole, at the local level there need not be separate communities, except in areas where one side may be overwhelmingly in the majority (there are Catholic and Protestant villages and neighbourhoods, in the folk view). Much more general is the idea that each locality is a single community which is divided — the house with two sides (see Larsen and Leyton). The image is of communities of both Catholics and Protestants (a point most explicitly set out in Bufwack 1982, ch. 8, and throughout Glassie, 1982). As a consequence, locality provides a sense of identity; it is a referent for 'your own'.

'Your own' as fellow community members

Like the inhabitants of most of rural Europe, people in rural Northern Ireland are parochial in a positive sense: there is a sense of belonging to distinct communities. Almost all commentators on rural Northern Ireland society have remarked on the strong feelings of local identity which they have encountered. There is therefore some sense in which we can talk about an Aughnaboy identity, a Ballybeg identity or a Kilbroney identity. Although each of these areas might be internally divided along any one of a number of social, economic or sectarian lines, they nevertheless see themselves as one body when viewed against the larger context of Northern Ireland society in general. This feeling has expressed itself in the form of all members of the community taking an interest in affairs and events which affect the reputation of the area as a whole; thus, for example, everyone in Ballybeg took an interest in the results of sporting events which, though actively supported and organised on sectarian lines, were of concern to all (Harris 1972, p. 135). Over the last twenty years this notion of community identity seems to have persisted, and for the four communities which they have studied, Blacking *et al.* report a similar interest in sporting events organised on an inter-village basis (1978, p. 37). Each community also seems to share a common repository of knowledge: knowledge of individual reputations, local nicknames or local history (see Glassie 1982; McFarlane 1978).

Of course there are *degrees* of belonging to particular communities. As in most communities, in these islands at least, there is usually a category of native inhabitants who were born and brought up in each community, conceptually surrounded by strangers of various kinds. Some strangers are more strangers than others: in-marrying spouses can often make it through the boundary (although their pedigrees remain with them, for use in gossip if necessary), as can people who can trace any kind of kinship link to a community. Further, even people who have managed to establish reasonable neighbourly relations can be accepted into the fold, though here membership is constantly open to public negotiation. We will return to these issues in a moment.

It must be stressed that the idea of community identity does not carry with it any implication of community harmony for anyone except a small minority of the rural population. That 'you get on better with your own' in this context does not mean that there are no conflicts. If anything, most people have an idea of local history similar to that which seems to have preoccupied community researchers throughout Britain in the 1980s: the community has taken a turn for the worse, it has lost the great sense of community feeling characteristic of the past. The existence of community spirit is seen to reflect more the dreams or wishes of local politicians or voluntary associations according to many people. Of course, we would have to assess these folk histories of the decline of community with care, since most people are looking back with nostalgia to a time when they were young, a time very different from the more responsible years of adulthood. The past may have been no more balmy than the present.

There are indeed conflicts to be found in all communities,

ranging from disputes about control over people to disputes about important things like land, both between individual neighbours and even between Catholic and Protestant (see Leyton 1966 for a general overview of disputes). The competition over land purchase has been reported for the entire period under review (Harris 1972, p. 168; Bufwack 1982, p. 78).

Nevertheless, despite the conflicts going on within communities, and regardless of whether or not we agree that they have increased, it is quite clear that vis-à-vis the outside (especially vis-à-vis Belfast) people do sustain a sense of collective identity. On the other hand, commonsense tells us that this sense of belonging has problems when it is confronted by acts of political violence; when what are perhaps only superficial good relations are disrupted. More precisely, a sense of belonging will have problems when violence takes place in a more mixed community (Unionist/Nationalist, Catholic/Protestant). In more homogeneous communities, political violence with outsiders may actually reaffirm boundaries and a sense of belonging. In mixed communities, political violence can obviously have the opposite effect; it will act against such ideas of belonging (see Harris 1979 for an elaboration of this point).

It would be difficult, however, to pin-point the amount of political violence which would be necessary to tip the balance away from an image of 'two yet one' towards an image of two distinct groupings based on Catholic and Protestant affiliation. For much of the time, social communities in Northern Ireland seem to operate mechanisms whereby this image of 'two yet one' is maintained. Community members blame outsiders for violence, or local hot-heads who have let the bonds of community slip because of drink or worse (drugs were often blamed in the seventies for violence). A large part of the folk theorising has connections with the politics of outrage played out in the media, in the sense that people in rural communities may have adopted the general media perspective that rational people do not get involved in violence to achieve their political goals, but even this received wisdom is rarely challenged in day to day life. It is plain, nevertheless, that in the border areas of Northern

Ireland many people do not hold the 'two but one' image any longer. Many Protestants especially have the true 'siege mentality' in that area, a view which can only intensify as Protestant farm families leave.

While political violence may have effects on the sense of belonging in different areas, other processes seem to be working to reaffirm community boundaries and membership in areas nearer to major urban centres. In villages and farming townlands in areas which planners describe as the accessible countryside, there have been population movements of various kinds from the urban areas to the countryside. Some of this geographical movement has been in the public housing sector, while other parts of this urban to rural counterstream have involved middle-class professionals, or retired professionals, competing to purchase properties coming on the private housing market. In the seventies, these middle-class immigrants were attracted by what was then the relative cheapness of rural properties; by the general idea that living in the countryside is a move up the status hierarchy and/or by romantic, or at least partially romantic, ideas about the pleasures of life in rural areas. Competition over housing and house sites between the local population and the non-local population (labelled by such terms as 'interlopers' and 'runners') has done much to solidify the boundaries between them.

However, this process, which might be called suburbanisation, does not necessarily create a boundary around *all* locals and the immigrants. In fact there is evidence to suggest that there can be an accommodation between the middle-class immigrant and the more wealthy business and farming interests in the countryside. For large farmers, the immigrants are after all soaking up a lot of the vacant cottages on farming land (deriving from the decreased demand for agricultural labour) and paying good prices for these and indeed for house sites. Local business people see these middle-class immigrants as their equals. So the boundary is between only some of the locals and the middle-class immigrants. The division is most exaggerated between the non-élite and the middle-class immigrants because of perceived differences in lifestyles based on class ideas, coinciding with differences based on length of residence. It is for this reason that the concept of 'local' tends to connote not only a sense of belonging, but also a sense of being one of the ordinary folk, a member of the non-élite. Class concepts are clearly present here.

'Your own' as the same class

Although perhaps not quite so marked as in other western societies, class ideas are clearly part of the culture of Northern Ireland people. It is true that in rural Northern Ireland there is a general norm that one should play down class distinctions in everyday life in pursuit of the polite fiction of equality and in deference to a general value placed on modesty or non-assertiveness. The widespread characteristic of denying what are presumed to be non-merited claims for superiority by the subtle put-down, or by gossip, existed in the fifties and still exists (see Harris 1972; Leyton 1975; McFarlane 1978). Ideas about class are seemingly accompanied by other ideas about social ranking. Some of the latter are reputational, and rank people along such scales as religiosity, industriousness, friendliness and so on; some are based on educational and occupational achievement. We can refer to these other scales as scales pertaining to individual 'standing' in the community, and they seem to differ from class ideas. Class ideas refer not to individuals as such, but to layers of society based on such criteria as access to, or possession of, power, wealth, education (again), occupation (again) and styles of life (see McFarlane 1978, ch. 1, for a brief discussion of class models).

There is some disagreement about how these two ranking schemes fit together. For Leyton, class defined locally in terms of occupation is given priority in Aughnaboy, placing people in a given stratum of local society. The other criteria (which we refer to as defining 'standing') seem to operate to place people *within* different strata (see Leyton 1975, ch. 3). For people in Ballycuan, McFarlane argues that the two schemas do not really 'fit' together at all. Some of the criteria for assessing class may be the same as those used to assess standing (occupation, education), but the two schemes are nevertheless separate in local eyes. The problem for many self-assessed ordinary people is that some people do confuse the two and seem to be assuming that class position in itself merits some kind of deference or distinction in day to day life.

Despite these apparent differences in how people gauge the various ranking schemes, it remains quite clear that class ideas do structure many aspects of social life in the countryside. Usually only two or three classes are regarded as relevant in people's eyes. In many rural areas the 'gentry' are now so distant from the practical affairs of the community that they are in a sense set aside from consideration (see Shanks 1982) and middle-class groupings are juxtaposed to the working-class, or the 'ordinary folk', depending upon one's point of view. Social networks tend to fall within class strata, or at least the effective networks so cluster (see Bufwack 1982, ch. 7; Harris 1972, ch. 5; Leyton 1975, ch. 3). Class, as we have seen, provides for social distance among kin as well as among co-religionists and neighbours. Class ideas also seem to structure marriage choices, though perhaps not so forcefully as religion.

Leadership roles in rural communities have been almost monopolised by the middle-class, as the gentry have generally stepped aside since the war. The minister, the priest, the doctor, the teacher, as well as other professionals, occupied these roles in the fifties and still do so (see Blacking et al. 1978; Harris 1961). However, there may have been subtle changes. With the emergence of new-style voluntary associations coinciding with the centralisation of governmental organisation in the seventies, it seems that the monopoly of quiet leadership in community affairs held by the minister, priest and doctor has been challenged by other community activists, not least by members of political parties.

The division between the classes is rarely made overt: generally it finds expression in more subtle ways. Class tends to provide for barriers to informal communication in the community, as gossip channels tend to circulate within classes (although there is obviously some slippage between different networks). Different kinds of avoidance behaviour can be practised too: moving around only by car, drinking in separate bars in public houses and so on (cars have done away with the necessity for stopping to have a chat on the road, one can now signal one's social concern with the subtle wag of the finger at the steering wheel). Nevertheless, antagonism does get expressed. Among Protestants, causes of rancour between the middle-class and the 'ordinary folk' are the overt non-sectarianism of the middle-class Protestants (from the point of view of the working-class Protestants), and the bitterness of the working-class Protestants (from the point of view of the middle-class Protestants). Harris recorded this in the fifties in Ballybeg and Blacking *et al.* recorded it in four different communities in the province, at the time in the seventies when the inter-class political links among Protestants were at their most strained.

Admittedly it is the so-called 'ordinary folk' in individual communities who are much more likely to talk about 'your own' in terms of ideas about class, but day to day practice indicates that the notion is there even in the middle-class cultural repertoire.

Conclusion

We have now identified the various categories of people to whom the term 'your own' can be attached and we have shown how relationships in these categories structure day to day life in rural communities. People's social life would have considerable solidity and fixity if 'your own' constituted a permanent and unchanging group. But in rural areas especially, though not exclusively, the different sets of relationships cross-cut each other. This leads to a constant state of flux in everyday interaction and a need to negotiate continuously between different identities and relationships. It is this which makes it difficult to say that one identity has more weight or is more important than another in any absolute sense. If people are continually switching from one identity to another from situation to situation, it becomes

problematic to assign primacy to any single identity. Nevertheless, at particular times, in particular places or with particular
people, some identities may be consistently more highly
weighted than others. Thus some writers have suggested that the
ability to identify the religion of the people one meets has always
been, and continues to be, an important feature of almost every
social encounter in Northern Ireland society (Burton 1979).
Certainly it is not difficult to imagine that in periods of heightened sectarian tension, for example, politico-religious identity
may be most significant, while the weight attributed to this may
well diminish in times of relative calm, when an identity like
shared community membership may emerge as being more
important.

   Throughout this chapter we have generalised from various
local studies and from personal experience, to rural Northern
Ireland as a whole. It may be argued that this material is far
from equal in quality and depth, and that the generalisations
which we have made must therefore be treated with caution.
That we freely admit. However, it must also be admitted that
there have been few attempts at making any comparisons
between different communities in Northern Ireland. This, of
course, is surprising since social anthropology is supposed to
pursue the 'comparative method' not only between societies but
also between different areas in the same society. Social anthropologists working in Northern Ireland have looked around the
world for similar kinds of society (Leyton 1974a refers to primitive dualistic societies, for instance) and have even compared
communities in two different parts of Ireland (see Harris 1979).
However, the only comparisons made among communities
within Northern Ireland tend to be very much 'in passing', even
when they do exist. For the most part, communities have been
presented as if they exist in a kind of vacuum, and the pursuit of
similarities and differences has hardly even begun.

Appendix

Date and location of social anthropological fieldwork in rural Northern Ireland, 1950–1984

LOCATION

	Armagh	Antrim	Down	Fermanagh	Derry	Tyrone
1950						Ballybeg (S)
1960			Aughnaboy (S) Blackrock (S)			
1970		Glentarf (N)	Kilbroney (S) Naghera (S) Ballycuan (N) Drumness (S) Kilbeg (C)	Ballymenone (S) Glenleven (S)		Ballybeg (S)
1980		Listymore (N) The Route (N)	Ballycuan (N)			

N=North,   C=Central,   E=East,   S=South,   W=West

Researchers and locations

Researcher(s)	Location
Blacking *et al*	Ballycuan, Drumness, Glenleven, Glentarf
Buckley	Kilbeg, Listymore
Bufwack	Naghera
Glassie	Ballymenone
Harris	Ballybeg
Larsen	Kilbroney
Leyton	Blackrock, Aughnaboy
McFarlane	Ballycuan
Shanks	The Route

Acknowledgements: We would like to thank the editor of *Studies* for his permission to make use of some material published here in another form.

References

BELL, J. 1978. 'Relations of Mutual Aid between Ulster Farmers', *Ulster Folklife*, Vol. 24, pp. 48–58.

BLACKING, J. *et al.* 1978. *Situational Determinants of Recruitment in Four Northern Irish Communities.* SSRC, British Library.

BUCKLEY, A. D. 1982. *A Gentle People: A Study of a Peaceful Community in Ulster*, Cultra, Ulster Folk and Transport Museum.

BUCKLEY, A. D. 1983. 'Playful Rebellion: Social Control and the Framing of Experience in an Ulster Community', *Man* (n.s.), Vol. 18, pp. 383–393.

BUFWACK, M. S. 1982. *Village without Violence: an Examination of a Northern Irish Community*, Cambridge, Mass, Schenkman.

BURTON, F. 1979. 'Ideological

Social Relations in Northern Ireland', *British Journal of Sociology*, Vol. 30, pp. 61–80.

DONNAN, H. and G. McFAR-LANE 1983. 'Informal Social Organisation', in Darby, J. (ed.), *Northern Ireland: The Background to the Conflict*, Belfast, Appletree, pp. 110–135.

GLASSIE, H. 1982. *Passing the Time: Folklore and History of an Ulster Community*, Dublin, O'Brien Press.

HARRIS, R. 1961. 'The Selection of Leaders in Ballybeg, Northern Ireland', *Man* (n.s.), Vol. 8, pp. 137–149.

HARRIS, R. 1972. *Prejudice and Tolerance in Ulster: A Study of Neighbours and 'Strangers' in a Border Community*, Manchester, Manchester University Press.

HARRIS, R. 1979. 'Community Relationships in Northern and Southern Ireland: A Comparison and a Paradox', *Sociological Review*, Vol. 27, pp. 41–53.

LARSEN, S. S. 1982. 'The Two Sides of the House: Identity and Social Organisation in Kilbroney, Northern Ireland', in Cohen, A. P. (ed.), *Belonging: Identity and Social Organisation in British Rural Cultures*, Manchester, Manchester University Press, pp. 131–164.

LEYTON, E. 1966. 'Conscious Models and Dispute Regulation in an Ulster Village', *Man* (n.s.), Vol. 1, pp. 534–542.

LEYTON, E. 1970. 'Spheres of Inheritance in Aughnaboy', *American Anthropologist*, Vol. 72, pp. 1378–1388.

LEYTON, E. 1974a. 'Opposition and Integration in Ulster', *Man* (n.s.), Vol. 9, pp. 185–198.

LEYTON, E. 1974b. 'Irish Friends and "Friends": the Nexus of Friendship, Kinship and Class in Aughnaboy', in Leyton, E. (ed.), *The Compact: Selected Dimensions of Friendship*, St John's, Memorial University, pp. 93–104.

LEYTON, E. 1975. *The One Blood: Kinship and Class in an Irish Village*, St John's, Memorial University.

McFARLANE, W. G. 1978. 'Gossip and Social Relations in a Northern Irish Village', Unpublished PhD thesis, Queen's University, Belfast.

McFARLANE, W. G. 1979. '"Mixed" Marriages in Ballycuan, Northern Ireland', *Journal of Comparative Family Studies*, Vol. 10, pp. 191–205.

MOGEY, J. McF. 1947. *Rural Life in Northern Ireland: Five Regional Studies made for the Northern Ireland Council for Social Services*, London, Oxford University Press.

SHANKS, A. N. 1982. 'Families and Places: Social Relations among Northern Irish Gentry', Unpublished PhD thesis, Queen's University, Belfast.

20
Power, Control and Media Coverage of the Northern Ireland Conflict

MARY KELLY

The images which the media offers are many and diverse: images of 'terrorism' from Northern Ireland; of 'Superman' from science fiction; of passive and consumerised female sexuality; of a highly futuristic and technocratic society; of the staid news reader; of the politician; of the aftermath of a bomb. Who selects these images? Who owns and controls the media? What is the relationship between those who own the media — frequently large corporations or in the case of broadcasting, the state — and the media professions: the journalists, the producers, the song and script writers, the editors? Why are certain images and representations consistently chosen, highlighted and repeated rather than others? How influential are these images and symbols? How are they communicated to, and understood by, large and diverse audiences? Given that audiences draw on many other sources of meaning, in particular from the primary socio-cultural contexts of the family, work, school and friends, how do they interpret media messages?

These are typically some of the questions raised and investigated by sociologists in attempting to understand the role of the media in contemporary society. Three issues have been of particular concern to sociologists: what are the effects of the media? Who owns and controls the media? What are the meanings of media messages? I shall look at each of these in turn, before going on to present a short case study of the media coverage of the conflict in Northern Ireland, which exemplifies some of the ways in which sociologists investigate and analyse the media in our society.

What are the effects of the media on the individual?

Since the 1920s media researchers have been interested in systematically investigating the influence of the media on the attitudes and behaviour of audience members. In the early days, researchers were mainly interested in the influence of films, later moving on to radio and subsequently to television. Some researchers, particularly in the USA, have investigated the effects of violent TV programmes on children and adolescents. A general conclusion of this research is that some children *may* be encouraged in their aggressive behaviour by viewing *some* types of violent TV programmes. This tends to occur, however, only under certain conditions.

One such important condition is an existing predisposition in the child to be aggressive. A second concerns the attitudes towards aggression of those in the child's immediate social environment. In general, these attitudes must be accepting of aggressive behaviour — or even encourage aggression — if the child is to act aggressively. A third condition is the particular form of violence seen by the child. (Research in this area is very extensive. Examples, sometimes from different perspectives and drawing different conclusions, can be found in Brown 1976, Noble 1975, Comstock *et al.* 1975, Howitt 1982, ch. 5, Lowery *et al.* 1983.)

These two findings — firstly, that TV does not generally *create* attitudes or behavioural responses in the viewer but may *confirm* existing predispositions; and secondly, that the attitudes of significant others in the immediate social environment of the viewer are the primary sources influencing attitudes and behaviour — are typical of a wide range of research findings on media effects. These findings hold true whether the research has examined the influence of media violence on children or the influence of election television on voters.

The importance of understanding the attitudinal and behavioural predispositions of the audience has led to a change in many media researchers' view of the audience. Previously, media researchers frequently viewed the audience as passive, and asked: what does the media do to people? Since the 1970s, however, they have more frequently seen the audience as active, and asked: what do people do with the media? This is often entitled a 'uses and gratifications' approach. It focusses on how individuals actively use media content to obtain gratification; to fulfil their own pre-existing needs and interests. (See Blumer *et al.* 1974; McQuail *et al.* 1972).

Who owns and controls the media?

A second major issue for media researchers is who owns and controls the media. Media researchers in both Britain and the USA have investigated those groups who own and control such media industries as newspapers and magazines, films and commercial TV, the record industry and commercial radio. They have investigated the extent to which a small elite group may control extensive media interests. In particular, they have analysed the extent and power of multinational media corporations (see, for example, Murdock *et al.* 1977, 1978; Curran *et al.* 1981).

Many smaller countries, including Ireland, are heavily dependent on imported products from multinational media corporations. For example, over four-fifths of all the records bought in the Republic of Ireland originate abroad, produced in the main by such multinational media conglomerates as CBS, EMI, Polygram and WEA. In relation to television, two-thirds of the population in the Republic of Ireland can now receive all the British channels, and two-thirds of the content on RTE itself is imported (McLoone *et al.* 1984). As in many other small countries this level of dependence evidences strong Anglo-American imperialism (see, for example, Tunstall 1977, MacBride *et al.* 1980).

In investigating who owns and controls the media it is also important to assess the role of the state, in particular its influence over such public service organisations as RTE and the BBC. In the Republic of Ireland, the powers of the Minister for Communications include the appointment of members of the RTE Authority, regulating the hours of broadcasting, and decisions as to the financial basis of RTE, including the level of the licence fee. The minister is also responsible for introducing broadcasting legislation and for invoking censorship laws, as will be discussed in greater detail below (see Broadcasting Authority (Amendment) Bill, 1975).

Of course media researchers recognise that ownership of media industries, whether by private interests or by the state, does not necessarily mean that owners exert direct editorial control. Media professionals frequently seek to carve out an area of relative independence and discretion in their work. Thus the relationships between owners and media professionals — such as editors and journalists — need detailed examination, especially in terms of the extent to which each attempts to influence or control media content (see Gans 1980; Evans 1984).

The meanings of media messages

The third major question raised by media researchers is how can we understand and analyse the meaning of media messages. This is sometimes entitled a 'cultural studies' approach to the media.

This approach assumes that the media forms but one part of a much broader cultural scene, a scene which includes many diverse cultures. These cultures include, for example, different class, regional, generational, gender and linguistic cultures. The media tend to articulate and amplify *some* of these cultures while ignoring others. Thus the news tends to focus on the activities and views of political and economic élites, who also tend to be male, while ignoring to a large degree the lives of women and the working class. News also tends to focus on the other extreme of the social spectrum — on those who are seen as a social problem or as a threat to society. Thus, such groups as travellers, drug addicts, criminals, members of the working class when on strike, and in the political sphere, terrorists, tend to receive heavy news coverage. Furthermore, these 'problem' groups frequently tend to be presented in a negative light (see, for example, Cohen *et al.* 1981; Kelly 1983).

The recognition of the highly selective nature of media content has led to research into its 'agenda setting' powers. By this is meant its power, through consistently highlighting particular issues, to ensure that these issues are placed on the public agenda for discussion, debate and perhaps action. While it is difficult to gain conclusive evidence of the media's agenda setting powers, it does appear that when individuals are heavily dependent on the media for knowledge about particular issues and have few alternative sources of information, the media may indeed have the power to both focus attention on this issue and to define the terms in which it is discussed (Patterson 1980; Weaver *et al.* 1981).

In attempting to analyse how meanings are selected by media producers and how they are communicated to the audience, researchers have become increasingly sensitive to the importance of understanding different media forms or genres. Thus the media researcher who is interested in understanding how violence is portrayed on television needs to analyse the very different ways in which violence is represented in, for example, TV news, in a thriller, in a current affairs programme on battered women, in a cartoon or in a boxing match. It is in terms of these forms or genres that media producers portray violence, and it is in terms of these forms that viewers interpret what is being portrayed (see McLoone *et al.* 1984; Fiske *et al.* 1978).

Thus, in the analysis of media content, many communications researchers have moved beyond a simple quantitative approach which counted, for example, the number of violent acts which occur in an evening's television viewing or the number of times women are presented in passive roles. Rather, many are now interested in a more qualitative analysis of how these topics are treated within different media forms. The judgment that the latter is a more appropriate type of content analysis has been reinforced by audience research, which indicates the importance of genre and the context within which a topic is treated for viewer reaction (see Gunter *et al.* 1984).

Lastly, the cultural studies approach has investigated how different audiences respond to and interpret media content. It emphasises how groups in different social positions and with different cultural values — such as middle-class as opposed to working-class groups, or men as opposed to women, or different generations — tend to select very different media forms and content to which to attend. Furthermore, when groups with different cultural values are exposed to the same media content, for example shown the same TV programme, they have been found to interpret its content in very different ways. Each group draws on its own cultural knowledge and values when responding to, enjoying and evaluating the programme. The audience is hence no longer seen as an undifferentiated 'mass' audience. On the contrary, the audience is seen as highly differentiated, each group with its own culture, values and interests, which materially influence how members respond to the media message (see Morley 1980).

An analysis will be offered below of some aspects of the news coverage of the conflict in Northern Ireland — especially how the security forces on the one hand and 'terrorists' on the other have been portrayed. This analysis draws in the main on a cultural studies perspective, in an attempt to describe and understand the highly selective nature of this media portrayal. The first section examines some of the constraints on journalists attempting to report on Northern Ireland. The second offers a brief résumé of research findings regarding how the news media reported the Northern conflict in the 1970s, while in the third section a brief analysis is undertaken of how the escape of thirty-eight Republican prisoners from the Maze Prison in 1983 was reported by newspapers in Britain, Northern Ireland and the Republic of Ireland. One of the focal points of interest in this analysis is to investigate if patterns of reporting have changed in the 1980s.

Constraints on news reporting

The selectivity of the news media in what it chooses to cover regarding the conflict and violence in Northern Ireland, and in how it chooses to cover it, is influenced by the way in which political élites define the situation. It is also influenced by the policies of news organisations, by the sources of news on which journalists depend, and by the extent to which the state attempts to control news reporting through state censorship. It is to an examination of these we now turn.

Many media researchers have noted that political and other élites are frequently the 'primary definers' of news stories (see Hall *et al.* 1981). This can clearly be seen when the content of British and Irish news coverage of Northern Ireland is compared. In Britain, political élites define the conflict as a vicious attack by an unrepresentative minority on legitimate organs of the state. This attack must be defeated. The role of the media is to help in containing and eliminating this evil, to mobilise the community to this end by defining the perpetrators of violence as totally unacceptable, inhuman and outside the terrain of 'reasonable' human beings. Thus, the 'story' of Northern Ireland in the British media tends to be a story of a continual procession of unique, inexplicable and violent events. Such reporting firmly excludes the Northern Ireland conflict from the category of colonial or anti-imperialist struggles (see Elliott 1977; Curtis 1984).

In the Republic of Ireland, political élites define the political struggle of the minority community as a legitimate cause, most adequately represented by the constitutional activity of the SDLP. The media are hence less preoccupied with the single story of violence and more concerned about political developments and the political future of the province. However, the attempt to gain political ends by violent means is decried by the Republic's élites, as it is by British élites. Coverage of violent incidents in Northern Ireland by the Republic's media has been found to be low key and 'cut to the bare bones of what had happened, where, and who was involved simply in terms of age and sex' (Elliott 1977, p. 362). Violence for which the British security forces may have been responsible is more explicitly reported in the Republic's media, but again in a restrained manner.

The tendency of journalists, especially those from the British media, to rely on information from the press offices of the security forces for news reports regarding violent incidents, has been well recognised and turned to their own advantage by the security forces in Northern Ireland. Richard Clutterbuck (ex Major General) has described the development of the Army's 'Information Policy' in Northern Ireland in the 1970s. The job of the Army PR office was '... not merely to react to the media — or to events — but to take a positive initiative in presenting the news to the best possible advantage for the security forces' (Clutterbuck 1981, p. 96). He notes how, if journalists showed a 'hostile bias' in their reports, or refused to play according to the army's rules, they could be refused information, especially 'off-the-record' briefings and discussions, and could thus be cut off from sources necessary to their work. The security forces are consequently ideally placed to manipulate journalists' dependence on their good offices (*ibid.* p. 106). The tendency of some journalists to accept the security forces line uncritically, however, is not only due to their dependence on them and their need to keep open their access to the army's PR operation, but also to the attitude of their editors to the Northern Ireland conflict. This can perhaps be most clearly seen in the case of broadcasting.

In the early seventies both the BBC and IBA rapidly and effectively centralised editorial control over coverage of Northern Ireland, moving it upwards in the administrative hierarchy. They established strict controls surrounding interviews with groups banned under the Prevention of Terrorism Act (e.g. the IRA, INLA and the UVF). The BBC guidelines on such interviews require any decision to interview a member of a banned organisation to be referred up the management chain, through the editors of news and current affairs, the controller of programmes in Northern Ireland to the Director General. Furthermore, permission has to be sought before such an interview is even undertaken, and the interview is vetted before transmission (see Francis 1977).

It has also been noted that senior executives and editorial staff in both BBC Northern Ireland and in UTV are almost exclusively Protestant, with the consequence that 'the final choice and interpretation of events for viewers and listeners comes through only one filter: the Ulster Protestant one' (Lennon 1983, p. 8; see also Schlesinger 1978; and on the interrelationship between BBC Northern Ireland and Unionism, see Cathcart 1984).

Besides the security forces' PR activities and the editorial policy of broadcasters, state control of broadcasting also contributes to the reporting of violence in Northern Ireland 'as a stream of irrational and incomprehensible events'. Successive British ministers have clearly stated their policies and attitudes regarding the representation of 'terrorists' in broadcasts. Statements by the British Minister of Posts and Telecommunications in 1971 epitomise their views. The normal broadcasting rules of balanced coverage, he claimed, did not apply to 'terrorists'. It was not required to strike an even balance between the IRA and the Ulster government, or between the army and the terrorists (Schlesinger 1978, p. 211). The BBC Board of Governors has acquiesced in this state definition regarding who is 'the enemy' and who is the 'terrorist', and has acknowledged that 'as between the British Army and the gunman, the BBC is not and cannot be impartial' (*ibid.* p. 212).

In the Republic of Ireland, state censorship of the broadcasting coverage of the conflict in Northern Ireland has been more direct and explicit. In the early 1970s there was considerable conflict between RTE and the government over the latter's strictures regarding transmitting interviews, or journalists' reports of interviews, with those who advocated the obtaining of their objectives through violent means (for details see Elliott *et al.* 1979, pp. 59–64; MacConghail 1984).

In October 1976 the Minister for Posts and Telegraphs, Conor Cruise O'Brien, formalised state censorship by invoking

Section 31 of the Broadcasting Act and directing RTE, in writing, to refrain from broadcasting interviews, or reports of interviews, with spokesmen of prohibited organisations. Since then successive Ministers of Posts and Telegraphs have annually renewed this ban with hardly a murmur from the Oireachtas, or indeed from the public. The ban includes the IRA, Provisional Sinn Fein, the INLA, the UDA and any proscribed organisation in Northern Ireland e.g. the UVF.

Cruise O'Brien has elaborated in some detail his reasons for introducing censorship of 'illegal organisations'. Victory in the struggle between the state's security forces and 'anti-democratic terrorism' he argues, 'depends on the degree to which the society at large sees the terrorist as the enemy ...' (O'Brien 1978, p. 79). To ensure this 'the best way for a democracy to deal with what is called political violence is to set aside its supposedly political character and concentrate on its criminal aspect as an armed conspiracy' (*ibid.* p. 80). Such conspiracies in Ireland, he states, seek legitimation in emotional appeals, especially by drawing on the legitimating cloak of Republicanism. The emotional appeal of Republicanism, he argues, makes it difficult, if not impossible, to refute 'by rational argument alone'. Television in particular, he suggests, has the power to generate emotion, and this makes its use particularly attractive to terrorist groups, who are interested in promoting and justifying violence.

The assumption — so central to any censorship policy — is that audience members are incapable of formulating rational judgments and thus must be protected from themselves. Cruise O'Brien argues that given a potentially highly charged and emotional audience, balanced reporting in which both sides of the story are told does not give sufficient protection to the state. The public interest must be protected, not only from the rare case of the reporter actively sympathetic to the IRA, but more especially from a 'kind of neutral professionalism, indifferent to social consequences' (*ibid.* p. 126).

The definitions of political élites, and their power to enforce their definitions where broadcasting is concerned, have contributed to the highly selective nature of news reporting about

Northern Ireland. So also have the values and practices of news organisations and journalists — especially the dependence of some British journalists on the reports and definitions of the security forces.

The inadequacy of news coverage is compounded by the lack of current affairs programmes on Northern Ireland. In current affairs on all channels there has been very little analysis of the causes of the violence, little in-depth investigation of the motivation and organisation of any of the major participants, whether Catholic or Protestant or the security forces, and little if any examination of the roles played by the British and Irish states in the conflict. As Peter Taylor, a journalist with BBC's *Panorama* and a consistent critic of the coverage of Northern Ireland on BBC and ITV, has stated: 'Reporting political violence in Northern Ireland is no problem ... Explaining it is. In attempting to analyse its causes one inevitably calls into question many of the assumptions on which popular conceptions of the conflict are based — assumptions which the government is anxious to perpetuate' (quoted in Lennon 1983, p. 11). In RTE the ban on interviews with the IRA, the INLA and with Provisional Sinn Fein, despite the electoral gains of the latter in Northern Ireland and indeed its local authority representation in the Republic, is undoubtedly one of the major reasons for this lack of analysis. One of the consequences is a public lack of understanding not only of the situation in Northern Ireland, but of the contribution of Republicanism to this country, a contribution which cannot be understood if it is simply dismissed as emotional and irrational.

Reporting the conflict in Northern Ireland

Philip Elliott (1977) undertook a detailed study of how Northern Ireland was reported in the daily newspapers, and on radio and television news in Britain and Northern Ireland over two three-week periods in 1974 and 1975. He found that there was a very heavy concentration on stories about violent incidents and law enforcement, especially in the British media, to the exclusion of reports about the political — or any other — situation. This reporting, Elliott suggests, tended to concentrate on so-called 'factual' and 'objective' reporting of the who, what, when and where of a continuous procession of violent incidents. It was preoccupied with the 'what' rather than the 'why' of violence.

This form of reporting, Elliott argues, poses as 'value free' and objective while it is in fact heavily value laden, emphasising those facts which make the violence less rather than more explicable. It thereby implies that the violence is senseless and irresponsible. Little attempt was made to explain the motives and policies of the so-called 'terrorists'. Instead, descriptive labels rather than explanations were offered: they were the actions of the 'gunman', 'bomber' and 'terrorist'. Elliott also notes that this form of reporting often tended to highlight the personal characteristics of 'innocent victims' of the latest violence. This emphasis on human interest stories, he argues, with its highlighting of women, young children, and indeed animals as victims of violence, tends to exaggerate the terror quality of the action (see also Elliott 1976, 1980; Curtis 1984).

In the face of these irrational 'terrorist acts', the army was presented as responding rather than initiating action. It was seen as playing a 'peace keeping' role, as somehow above and outside a conflict characterised by two warring factions. This view of Olympian detachment, Elliott notes, was shared and supported by the British government. In their representation of the British army, the news media drew heavily on popular cultural myths: the well-trained and disciplined army unit of World War II fame, the 'our lads' myth, their boy scout image as they held the peace line between the irrational and warring Irish (see also Fiske et al. 1978, pp. 41–44).

The Northern Ireland papers in their coverage of 'the troubles' also tended towards the reporting of a procession of violent incidents, especially in the *Belfast Telegraph*, the highest circulation Northern paper. In the two other main Northern Ireland papers, the *Irish News* (which circulates mainly among Catholics) and the *News Letter* (which circulates mainly among

Protestants) there was a tendency for the *News Letter* to play down loyalist paramilitary violence, while the *Irish News* tended to play it up, as well as give greater coverage to Catholic victims of violence, and to stories reporting violence attributed to the security forces.

Elliott compared this reporting to that in the Republic's daily papers and to RTE's radio news at 1.30. He found a somewhat less exclusive emphasis on violence than in the British press and a greater tendency to report political initiatives and actions in Northern Ireland, as well as a more frequent tendency to question the 'official' British army interpretation of an event. The Republic's media presented a longer historical dimension and in particular reported the activities of those whom they saw as the legitimate political representatives of 'the minority community' — the SDLP. Elliott notes that the concept of 'the minority community', and the activities of what the British tended to refer to as the 'mainly Catholic SDLP', were almost totally ignored by the British media.

Analysis of the newspaper coverage of the Maze escape

It is of interest to analyse if, after fourteen years of violence, media coverage has changed. Has the length of the conflict led to a greater felt need to understand the causes of the violence? Has it led to an analysis of the subcultural support for violence, or of the political motives for violence? Or is reporting still dominated by symbols of the well-armed security forces defending the community as a whole; the secure containment of the convicted 'gunman'; the irrational violent acts of the terrorist?

To examine these questions I undertook a short case study of the newspaper coverage of the escape of thirty eight Republican prisoners from the high security Maze Prison outside Belfast which occurred on Sunday, 25 September 1983. I examined three sets of papers: three daily papers published in Dublin, the *Irish Press*, the *Irish Times* and the *Irish Independent*; three daily papers published in Belfast, the *News Letter*, the *Belfast Telegraph* and the *Irish News*; and three dailies published in Manchester and London, *The Times*, the *Express* and the *Mirror*.

Newspaper coverage of the escape of thirty-eight prisoners from the Maze Prison drew on many of the images and symbols previously noted by researchers as typifying the representation of the conflict in Northern Ireland by the British media: the image of the security forces as alert, disciplined and armed, mobilised to defend the community as a whole— the surveillance of the circling helicopter potently symbolising this. 'Winning the fight against the gunman' is their proclaimed duty; to apprehend and provide public 'proof' of criminality; to ensure secure containment in such prisons as the H-Blocks at the Maze Prison, described thus by the *Irish Independent*:

> Full of electronic equipment the blocks cost £1m each to build and the 133 acres prison ... took £15m to complete. So intense is the flood-lighting airline pilots can see the glow, soon after leaving Liverpool. The prison has 30ft high walls and fences.

On the other hand, the image of the 'gunman' is frequently that of a violent, irrational and evil force, against whose violence the community as a whole must mobilise. Philip Elliott (1976) has suggested that such reporting has the social function of symbolically 'cauterising' or casting out what is defined as a major threat to the community or state. Cauterisation asks no questions as to why the violence occurs; why the security forces must be so heavily armed against citizens of their own state; why Northern Ireland has a higher proportion of its citizens in jail than any other country in Europe; why high security prisons such as the Maze are needed. On the contrary, it emphasises those symbols which highlight the mobilisation of the army on behalf of the community as a whole; the solidarity of the community and its leaders; the expulsion and rejection from the community of the perceived evil.

The security forces were presented in all the papers as rapidly and efficiently instigating 'a huge manhunt':

> The mass escape from the top security prison started a huge manhunt in the North, and at dusk the entire area for miles around the jail was a ring of steel, with massive reinforcements of RUC and British soldiers aided by fleets of helicopters with searchlights and tracker dogs, engaged in an intensive comb-out of the entire countryside. (*Irish Press*)

Mobilising and directing the security forces were the political leaders. Their activities were being 'directly overseen' by the Secretary of State Mr Prior, who 'took charge of the operation' and vowed that there would be 'no hiding place North or South for jail breakers.'

These messages were repeated for at least three days on the front pages of all papers, with some rather questionable news angles being developed. The *Express* on Tuesday announced: SECRET ARMY ON TERROR TRAIL: SAS HUNTS MASS ESCAPE KILLERS, and continued:

> A secret SAS operation was under way last night to track down the 21 terrorist prisoners — nine of them ruthless killers — still on the run in Ulster. More than 100 men from the world's top anti-terrorist squad are involved in the hunt, and others are standing by.

The papers continuously reemphasised the high degree of organisation, the skill and the weaponry of the army and police. They carried out 'carefully planned operations', coordinated 'from police headquarters in Belfast through divisional commanders'. News photos showed them searching cars 'cradling' automatic rifles.

It wasn't only the security forces in the North which were seen to mobilise:

> Security forces in the Republic were put on a full scale alert last night as the size of the Maze Prison breakout became clear ... Extra units of the Special Task Force were sent to the border from Dublin, all units in the border counties were mobilised and those on leave recalled. (*Irish Press*)

On Tuesday the *Irish Press* headlined: ELITE SQUAD SPEAR-
HEADS BORDER HUNT. All papers nodded approvingly:
the *Irish News* noted that the 'members of the Garda Special
Task Force — the Republic's élite anti-terrorist squad — were
in the front line along the South Armagh border.' Southern
politicians were seen to be fully behind the man hunt, *The Times*
(London) stating 'Dr. Garret Fitzgerald, the Irish Prime
Minister promised full co-operation in the hunt.'

The papers, especially those in Northern Ireland urged co-
operation with the security forces and reproduced and amplified
their messages: STAY AWAY FROM THESE DES-
PERADOS headlined the *Belfast Telegraph*, echoing the words
of a senior police officer. The *News Letter*'s editorial stated that
'The security forces must be allowed to undertake vigorous and
extensive search operations. It is in the interests of all reasonable
people in Northern Ireland that these dangerous men are recaptured — and as soon as possible.'

There was thus widespread agreement among the newspapers
in the Irish Republic, Northern Ireland and Britain regarding
the representation of the security forces. Indeed, they appeared
almost as a mirror image — one with its SAS, the other with its
Special Task Force, each with its own political élite seen as
directing and mobilising the security forces in a man hunt on the
community's behalf.

In the representation of the IRA, however, there was much
less unanimity. The IRA were reported in terms of four images
or frames, each of these tending to shade into the next. These
included:

1. Republicans: drawing at least some support from working
    class Republican areas in Northern Ireland and supported
    by Sinn Fein.
2. Men of violence: disciplined, dedicated members of the
    Provisional IRA.
3. Terrorists: trained, ruthless, vicious killers.
4. Animals, scum.

In the first of these frames the escape was represented as undertaken by 'Republican prisoners', who had a history and tradi-

tion of escape attempts, and whose escape was celebrated by Sinn Fein and in Republican areas of Northern Ireland.

This was a frame which was included — along with others — in the *Irish News*, and to a somewhat lesser extent by the papers in the Republic of Ireland, especially the *Irish Press*. In a somewhat contradictory way it was a frame which was also preached against in all three of the Republic's papers. It was a frame recognised and rejected in the *News Letter*, and a frame highly critically covered by the British media.

Although the *Irish News* covered 'the hunt' for the escapees as vigorously as any of the other papers and used it as its main story, it also consistently referred to the escapees as 'Republican' or 'IRA' prisoners. It ran a story on previous escapes entitled: WHEN THE IRA PLANNED OTHER SPECTACULARS and another entitled: OVER, UNDER AND ROUND — THE CONSTANT STRUGGLE, which included a photo of the seven escapees from the Maidstone prison ship in 1972, captioned: 'The Magnificent Seven'. It reported sporadic bonfires (presumably in celebration of the Maze escape) on Sunday night in Unity Flats and Ballymurphy, and reproduced photos of two large wall graffiti from the Falls Road which again celebrated the jail break. It also reported Gerry Adams's (Sinn Fein MP for West Belfast) statement that 'When British P.O.Ws escaped from Nazi prisons like Colditz, they were hailed as heroes, and Irish nationalists view the H-Block escapees in the same light.'

The Republic's press also called the escapees 'Republicans', and ran stories of previous escapes (except for the *Irish Independent*). They noted, however, that some escapees were 'later recaptured in the South and brought before the Special Criminal Court' (*Irish Press*). The Republic's newspapers also tended more towards an image of the escapees as criminal — they, along with all the other papers, except for the *Irish News*, carried 'mug-shots' of the escapees, each with its tally of name, age, address and conviction. Such police mug-shots tend to imply criminality and it is of interest to note that the *Irish News* tended to use photos which gave not only a close-up of the head, but also the shoulders and top of the chest and thus the individual clothing of each of the escapees could be seen. The Republic's papers tended to carry Sinn Fein statements defining the escapees as heroes and that the escape 'had brought a feeling of jubilation in Nationalist and Republican areas' (*Irish Times*). These statements, however, tended to be reported on the inside pages and often as the last paragraph. Suspecting support in the Republic of Ireland for these republican sentiments, the *Irish Times* and the *Independent* published cautionary editorials, instructing their readers in the correct interpretation of the escape:

> The mass escape of prisoners from the Maze may become something of a folk-legend over the years. It should not. Many of the men who escaped were in prison because of murders, shooting and vicious violence. Some of them were high ranking leaders in the Provisionals and INLA, and if they stay free they will try to repair some of the damage caused by 'supergrasses' to their respective organisations. And if they succeed, we can expect more murders, more bombings and more violence. (*Irish Independent*).

The British press used what they called the 'boasts' of the IRA to highlight further their inhumanity and cruelty, contrasting it with the sorrow of the relatives of the prison officer who died during the break-out. The *Mirror* headlined: PROVOS BRAG OF JAIL ESCAPE AS THE MAN THEY MURDERED IS BURIED. It continued that the *Republican News* (the Sinn Fein newspaper) 'boasts that the mass escape has damaged the Government's pride and morale ... The paper gloats that during the break-out, in which a prison officer died, one officer had a gun stuck in his mouth.' *The Times* noted that the mourning at the prison officer's funeral was 'in stark contrast to the jubilation over the escape in the *Republican News*'.

The second news frame was that the IRA was a highly disciplined organisation, committed to using violence to further its aims. This frame typified the coverage in the *Irish Independent*, and as this frame veered towards the third and 'terrorist' frame, typified some aspects of the coverage in the *News Letter*. In terms of this frame the escape had been an organised and planned event, the *Irish Independent* claiming that 'The mass escape was solely organised to free 15 top IRA men needed to reorganise the command structure of the Provisionals following the crippling damage caused by supergrasses.' The *News Letter*, drawing on the evocative 'Godfather' image, claimed that the escape was planned to release 'some of the dedicated terrorists that the Provisionals' Godfathers wanted back in action to toughen the murder campaign.' It then went on to claim that the plan had gone wrong — nineteen of the escapees having been recaptured.

The third and fourth news frames were the least equivocating. The IRA were ruthless terrorists, trained to terror and hardened by it. They emphasised Secretary of State James Prior's explanation for the escape — it was due to the ruthless, committed and violent nature of the IRA: 'Where you have a vast number of life prisoners, all very desperate men, a lot of rotten eggs in one basket, there is always a great difficulty in controlling them' (*Belfast Telegraph*). He was also reported in most papers as noting that 250 of the 850 prisoners in the Maze were carrying life sentences: 'We are dealing with a group of utterly determined and ruthless men who are out to cause as much trouble as they can ... No other prison, anywhere, has to cope with such an embittered and committed group, with little to lose by attempting to escape' (*Irish News*).

The third frame shaded into the fourth which placed the actions of these ruthless terrorists completely outside the bounds of rational and understandable human action — they were animals, scum. None of the papers drawing on these frames (*News Letter, Belfast Telegraph, The Times, Mirror* and *Express*) called the escapees 'Republican prisoners'. They were 'terrorist killers', trained, vicious and ruthless members of the IRA. The *Mirror*'s front page, carrying twenty-one mug-shots of the escapees, ran a huge headline: FACES OF TERROR. It described the IRA in an editorial as a 'fanatical band of killers transformed by the Irish love of romance and legend into brave, patriotic boys, even when that patriotism is the killing of innocent women and teenagers.'

The *Mirror* and the *Express* were the most likely to use animal imagery to represent the hunt for the escapees, although this was also occasionally used by the *Belfast Telegraph* and *The Times*. The 'murderous scum' as the *Sunday Express* editorial called them, would be 'flushed out', 'hunted down', 'rounded up' and 'put back behind bars'. The *Mirror* quoted a 'senior police officer': 'We are up against armed terrorists who have nothing to lose. It is like trying to tackle a pack of cornered wolves.'

Two conclusions may be drawn from this analysis of the newspaper coverage of the escape from the Maze Prison. The first is the high degree of similarity in the coverage of the security forces: in each of the three sets of papers examined, they, with their guns, helicopters and surveillance equipment, are represented in terms of approbation, with the highest degree of approval being conferred on the 'élite anti-terrorist squads' the SAS and the Special Task Force. The security forces, backed by their respective governments, were seen to efficiently mobilize on the community's and state's behalf in the face of this 'terrorist' threat.

This case study would thus indicate that there has been little change over the past fourteen years in how the media in Britain and Northern Ireland report the activities of their security forces. With regard to the Republic of Ireland, it would appear that when the Dublin government sees itself as threatened by the 'men of violence' coming 'South', or when it wishes to placate the British government regarding the 'harbouring' of terrorists, it then mobilises its own security forces. The activities of these forces are subsequently reported in tones of idealisation and approval similar to those of their counterparts in Britain.

The dependence of journalists on the security forces' PR operation for information about the escape, the search and the recaptures, is evident in the similarity of the reports and photographs across all the papers. The most extreme instance of this was the releasing of a video made by the RUC of the recapture of two of the escapees. This was shown to all journalists who did not witness the recapture itself.

However, while the security forces of both states were reported in a very similar manner, major differences occurred in the way in which the IRA were portrayed, as newspapers reflected not only the definitions of political élites but also some of the attitudes and values of their readers. This is perhaps particularly true of the more Republican oriented papers.

Four frames were used which can be summarised briefly, if rather grossly, as follows: a republican frame, highlighted in some of the representations of the IRA in the *Irish News* and to a lesser extent in the *Irish Press*. This overlapped with the committed 'men of violence' frame highlighted in some of the *Irish Times* coverage, but particularly in that of the *Irish Independent*. This frame again veered towards the 'terrorist' frame, central in the *News Letter*, the *Belfast Telegraph* and *The Times* (London) which overlapped with the 'animals/scum' frame which characterised some of the reports in the *Mirror* and *Express*.

Conclusion

Media sociologists, especially those who work within a cultural studies framework, attempt to analyse the media as one part of a particular society and culture. They see the media as interacting with and being influenced by that society. In particular they see a need to examine the extent to which the media is influenced by powerful groups within that society. Media sociologists also see the media as being highly selective in the cultural meanings it consistently highlights, and they ask: whose definition of the situation does the media choose to reproduce and amplify?

In this paper the use of the Northern Ireland case study has enabled us to examine some of these questions. In particular, it has enabled us to examine the tendency of the media to amplify the definitions of political élites, and consequently to marginalise the definitions of opposition groups, especially when such groups are seen as a threat to the state itself.

In democratic states such as the Republic of Ireland and Britain, there are two sides to the maintenance of law and order: consent and coercion. As Weber (1947, p. 154) has noted, the state lays claim to the 'monopoly of the legitimate use of physical force in the enforcement of its order'. A statement by Conor Cruise O'Brien (1978, p. 33) exemplifies this claim: 'The *force* used by a democratic state against the terrorist is legitimate, while the *violence* of the terrorist is not legitimate.' In order to ensure that the state's force continues to be seen as legitimate, considerable ideological and symbolic work needs to be done. It has been argued by some sociologists that the media in democratic societies play a central role in orchestrating those images and symbols which contribute to legitimating state violence, and to delegitimating the violence of protest against the state (see, for example, Schlesinger 1981; Elliott 1983).

The dominant political ideology in both Britain and the Republic defines the IRA as 'the enemy'; an armed conspiracy against the state. As such, censorship of the broadcasting coverage of the Northern Ireland conflict is seen as an appropriate response, whether this censorship is overt as in RTE, or covert as in the BBC and Independent Television. Censorship is particularly rigid with regard to questioning the government's interpretation of the conflict or investigation of the political motives of those involved — hence interviews with the 'men of violence' are out. In the Republic of Ireland there is fear that the audience may be sympathetic to the political motivation of the IRA and Sinn Fein. In Britain, as both Elliott and Schlesinger have noted, the reporting of the Northern Ireland conflict is seen as war reporting. The state has defined the activities of terrorist organisations as irrational and evil; a threat to the security of the state. As such, these organisations should be unambiguously and categorically labelled as the enemy; the criminal outside the gates of civilised action. In such a war situation, the propaganda or PR efforts of the security forces are seen as legitimate.

It should be noted that the media do not, of themselves, create an ideology legitimating the activities of the security forces or legitimating increased state coercion. Its role is to translate the dominant political definitions of the situation into the appropriate media genre, into words and images: when an army or police bullet kills a civilian the media do not shout 'murder', rather it becomes a 'regrettable accident'. This translation process is aided and abetted by the security forces PR — especially for the British media.

Television and news-photo images can indeed play a potent role: the whirling helicopter, the soldiers with rifles, the mug-shot. Words are another weapon: 'Words represent categorizations of the world from a point of view. They exist within systems which are organized and represent ideological systems. Hence a word such as "freedom fighter" or "terrorist" does not exist in a vacuum but in the context of sets of related words' (Kress 1983, p. 124). These systems of related words are particular ways of looking at the world; particular frames; particular ideologies. Thus the labels used in reporting the Northern Ireland conflict, from 'republican' through to 'scum'; the use of the passive voice when reporting violence by the security forces; the endless litany giving the 'who, where, what and how' details of violent events; the reporting of the statements of some but not others; all these contribute to the construction and manufacture of a very particular kind of news story, elaborating a particular ideology.

Even when the extent and nature of the conflict in Northern Ireland begins to escape the boundaries of these images, words and news stories, and hence begins to question their adequacy, explanations are rarely offered in the media. Why is the Maze more like a concentration camp than a prison? Why has it a higher concentration of 'rotten eggs', and 'lifers' than any other prison? How is it that the 'terrorists' and 'men of violence' can gain electoral support?

A final question media researchers ask is 'What influence does the media's coverage of Northern Ireland have?' While no research has been carried out on this topic, certain media influences might be reasonably expected, given our knowledge from other research on media effects, agenda setting, and the responses of different groups in different cultural situations. It might thus be expected that the media's definition of the conflict and violence in Northern Ireland might be most influential when the media are the only source of information about Northern Ireland. It may thus be most influential in Britain and least influential in Northern Ireland.

The definition by the media of the violence in Northern Ireland as irrational and barbaric is likely to be least influential in communities which already hold strong Republican views and which, at least to some degree, support the violence. Here, the day-to-day experiences over a decade and a half of the hostile actions of the security forces; the sense of injustice; Republican traditions and motives learned within the family, friendship groups and the community, are all likely to be a much stronger source of values than national media definitions. Furthermore, many of these communities have their own locally controlled media which are likely to be more significant in defining and reinforcing attitudes than the national media.

In the Republic of Ireland, I would expect there to be deep ambivalence. The knowledge of the contribution of Republican violence to the establishment of the state, as well as the Republican definitions and ideology learned by many through both school and family, cannot be easily dismissed from consciousness as simply the emotional 'cult of 1916' (Cruise O'Brien, quoted in *Irish Times*, November 1983). Yet many are dependent for their knowledge of the Northern Ireland situation on the media — especially television (see Chubb 1984, p. 76), which owing to censorship is extremely narrow and limited in its coverage. This has the consequence of presenting the violence as unmotivated and irrational, a procession of inexplicable events led by a tiny minority of violent men. I would thus expect considerable confusion and lack of understanding in the Republic of Ireland of the forces which contribute to the continuance of the violence. I would further argue that, in the long term, ignorance rarely contributes to the resolution of conflict.

References

BLUMLER, JAY and KATZ ELIHU (eds.) 1974. *The Uses of Mass Communications*, Beverly Hills, CA: Sage.

BROWN, RAY (ed.) 1976. *Children and Television*, Beverly Hills, CA: Sage.

CATHCART, REX 1984. *The Most Contrary Region: The BBC in Northern Ireland 1924-1984*, Belfast, Blackstaff.

CHUBB, BASIL 1984. 'The Political Role of the Media in Contemporary Ireland', in B. Farrell (ed.), *Communications and Community in Ireland*, Dublin, Mercier.

COHEN, STANLEY and JOCK YOUNG (eds.) 1981. *The Manufacture of News: Social Problems, Deviance and the Mass Media*, London, Constable.

COMSTOCK, GEORGE et al. 1975. *Television and Human Behaviour*, New York, Columbia University Press.

CURRAN, JAMES AND JEAN SEATON 1981. *Power Without Responsibility: The Press and Broadcasting in Britain*, Glasgow, Fontana.

CURTIS, LIZ 1984. *Ireland: the Propaganda War*, London, 1984.

CLUTTERBUCK, RICHARD 1981. *The Media and Political Violence*, London, Macmillan.

ELLIOTT, PHILIP 1976. 'Misreporting Ulster: News as Field-Dressing', *New Society*, 25 November, pp. 389-401.

ELLIOTT, PHILIP 1977. 'Reporting Northern Ireland', in *Ethnicity and the Media*, Paris, UNESCO, pp. 263-376.

ELLIOTT, PHILIP 1980. 'Press Performance as Political Ritual', in H. Christian (ed.), *The Sociology of Journalism*, Keele, University of Keele, pp. 141-177.

ELLIOTT, PHILIP and PETER GOLDING 1979. *Making the News*, London, Longman.

ELLIOTT, PHILIP, GRAHAM MURDOCK and PHILIP SCHLESINGER, 1983. 'Terror and the State: A Case Study of the Discourses of Television', *Media Culture and Society*, Vol. 5, pp. 155-177.

EVANS, HAROLD 1984. *Good Times, Bad Times*, London, Weidenfeld and Nicolson.

FISKE, JOHN and JOHN HARTLEY 1978. *Reading Television*, London, Methuen.

FRANCIS, RICHARD 1977. *Broadcasting to a Community in Conflict: The Experience of Northern Ireland*, London, BBC.

GANS, HERBERT 1980. *Deciding What's News*, London, Constable.

GUNTER, BARRY and ADRIAN FURNHAM 1984. 'Perceptions of Television Violence: Effects of Programme Genre and Type of Violence on Viewers' Judgements of Violent Portrayals', *British Journal of Social Psychology*, Vol. 23, pp. 155-164.

HALL, STUART et al. 1981. 'The Social Production of News: Mugging in the Media', in S. Cohen and J. Young (eds.), *The Manufacture of News, Social Problems, Deviance and the Mass Media*, London, Constable, pp. 335-367.

HOWITT, DENNIS 1982. *Mass Media and Social Problems*, Oxford, Pergamon.

KELLY, MARY 1983. 'Media Coverage of the Deprived', in Council for Social Welfare (eds.), *Conference on Poverty*, 1981, Dublin, Council for Social Welfare.

KRESS, GUNTHER 1983. 'Linguistic and Ideological Transformations in News Reporting', in H. Davis and P. Walton (eds.), *Language, Image, Media*, Oxford, Blackwell.

LENNON, PETER 1983. 'Broadcasting Problems in Northern Ireland', in *The Listener*, 23 June, pp. 10-11; and 30 June, pp. 7-8.

LOWERY, SHARON and MELVIN de FLUER 1983. *Milestone in Mass Communication Research*, New York, Longman.

MacCONGHAIL, MUIRIS 1984. 'The Creation of RTE and the Impact of Television', in B. Farrell (ed.), *Communications and Community in Ireland*, Dublin, Mercier, pp. 64-74.

MacBRIDE, SEAN et al. 1980. *Many Voices, One World: Communication and Society Today and Tomorrow*, Paris, UNESCO.

McLOONE, MARTIN and JOHN MacMAHON (eds.) 1984. *Television and Irish Society*, Dublin, RTE/IFI.

McQUAIL, DENIS, JAY BLUMLER and RAY BROWN 1972. 'The Television Audience: A Revised Perspective', in D. McQuail (ed.), *Sociology of Mass Communication*, Harmondsworth, Penguin, pp. 135-165.

MORLEY, DAVID 1980. *The 'Nationwide' Audience*, London, British Film Institute.

MURDOCK, GRAHAM and PETER GOLDING 1978. 'Beyond Monopoly: Mass Communication in an Age of Conglomerates', in P. Beharrell and G. Philo (eds.), *Trade Unions and the Media*, London, Macmillan.

MURDOCK, GRAHAM and PETER GOLDING 1977. 'Capitalism, Communication and Class Relations', in J. Curran (ed.), *Mass Communication and Society*, London, Edward Arnold.

NOBLE, GRANT 1975. *Children in Front of the Small Screen*, London, Constable.

O'BRIEN, CONOR CRUISE 1978. *Herod, Reflections on Political Violence*, London, Hutchinson.

PATTERSON, THOMAS 1980. *The Mass Media Election: How Americans Choose their President*, New York, Praeger.

SCHLESINGER, PHILIP 1978. *Putting Reality Together*, BBC News, London, Constable.

SCHLESINGER, PHILIP 1981. '"Terrorism", the Media and the Liberal-Democratic State: A Critique of the Orthodoxy', *Social Research*, Vol. 48, No. 1, pp. 74-99.

TUNSTALL, JEREMY 1977. *The Media are American: Anglo-American Media in the World*, London, Constable.

WEAVER, DAVID et al. 1981. *Media Agenda Setting in a Presidential Election*, New York, Praeger.

WEBER, MAX 1947. *The Theory of Social and Economic Organization*, New York, Free Press.

Index

Authors' names are given in the index when there is a discussion of their work. The bibliography at the end of each chapter lists all the works relevant to each chapter.